ATTACK ON TITAN

14

HAJIME ISAYAMA

Episode 55:
Pain
5

Episode 56:
Actors
51

Episode 57:
Kenny the Ripper
97

Episode 58:
Gunshots
143

"Attack on Titan" Character Introductions

104th Corps

duated at
top of her
ining corps,
asa is a
hly talented
dier. Her
ents were
rdered
ore her
s when she
s a child,
Eren saved
life. Since
n, she has
de it her
sion to
tect him.

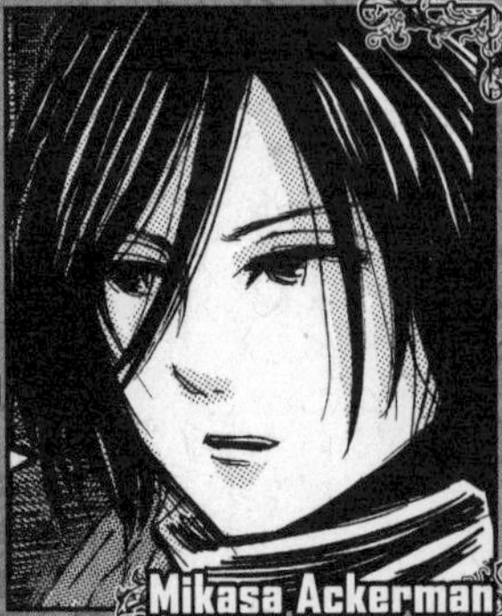

Mikasa Ackerman

Eren joined the Survey Corps out of his longing for the outside world and his hatred of the Titans. He has the power to turn himself into a Titan, but its origins are unknown.

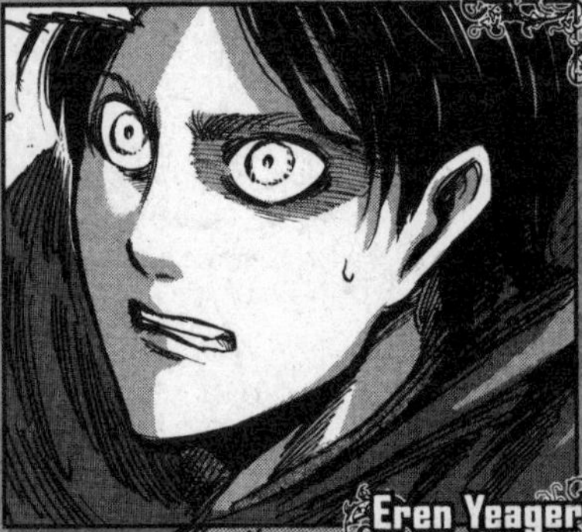

Eren Yeager

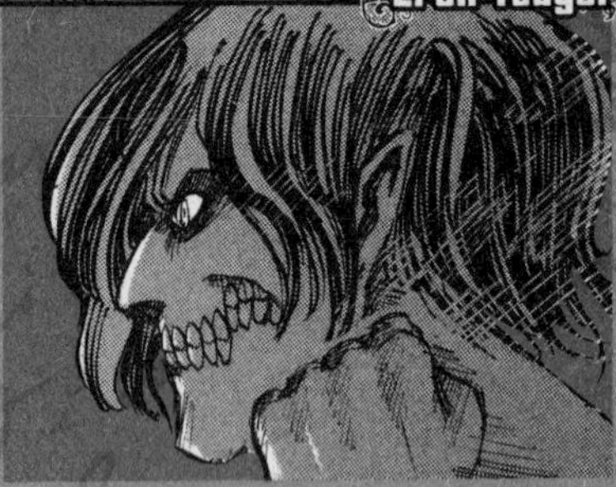

en and Mikasa's
ildhood friend.
ough Armin isn't
hletic in the least,
possesses both
arp observational
wers and keen
sight, and he
hibits an
traordinary ability
develop
rategies.

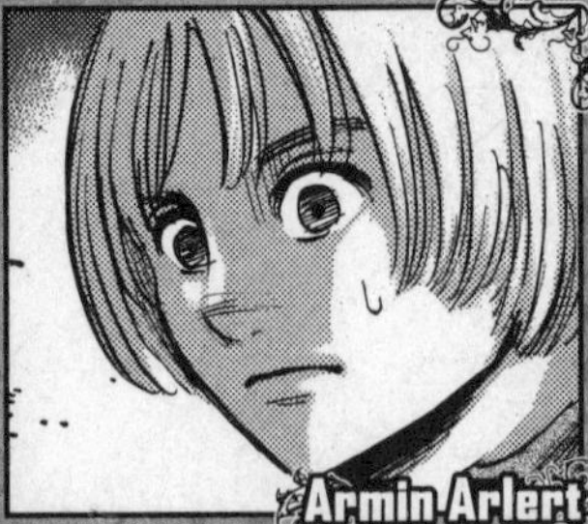

Armin Arlert

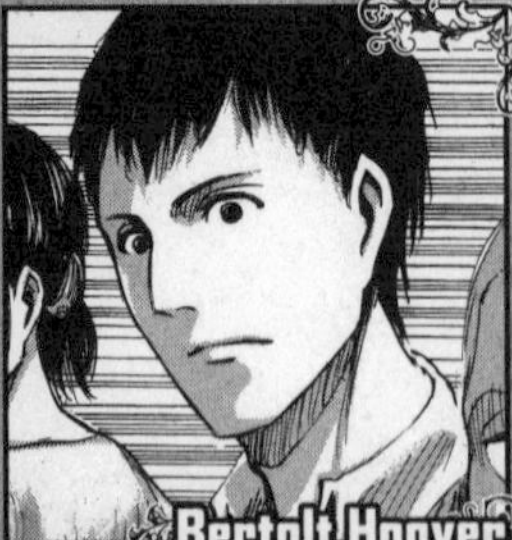

Bertolt Hoover

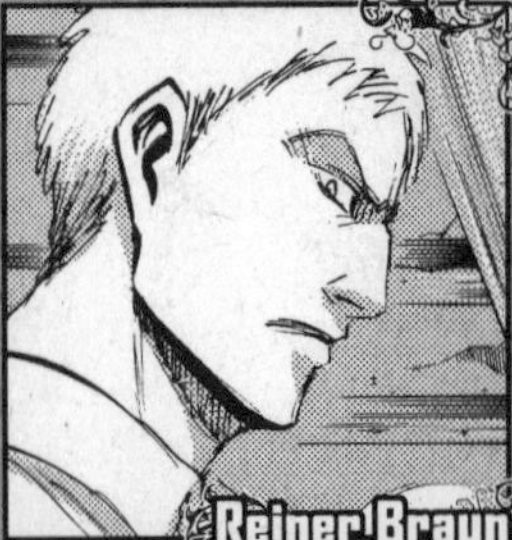

Reiner Braun

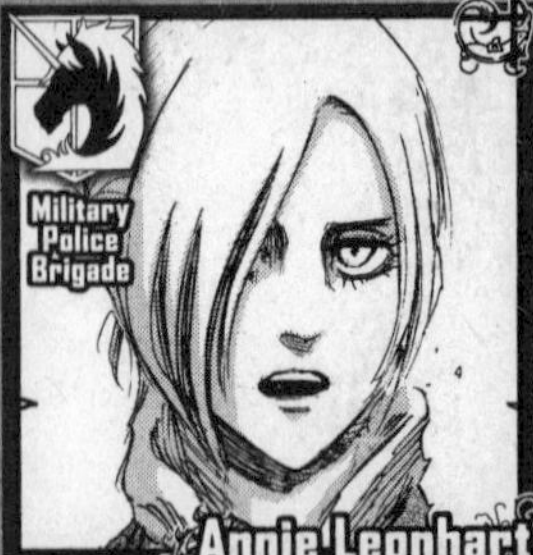
Military Police Brigade

Annie Leonhart

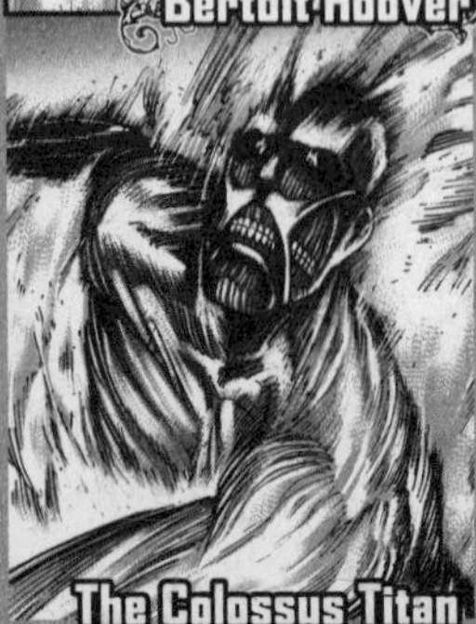

The Colossus Titan

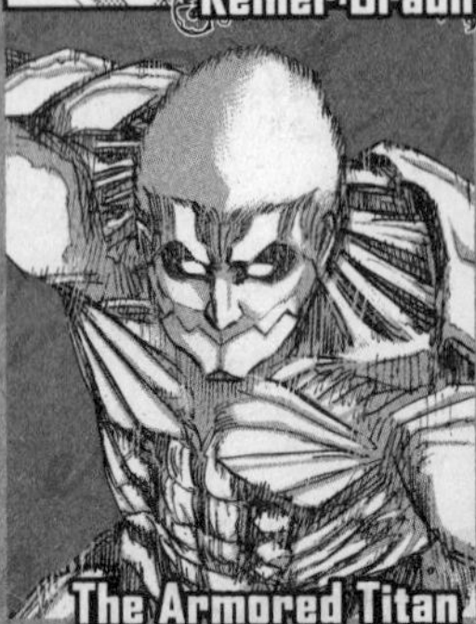

The Armored Titan

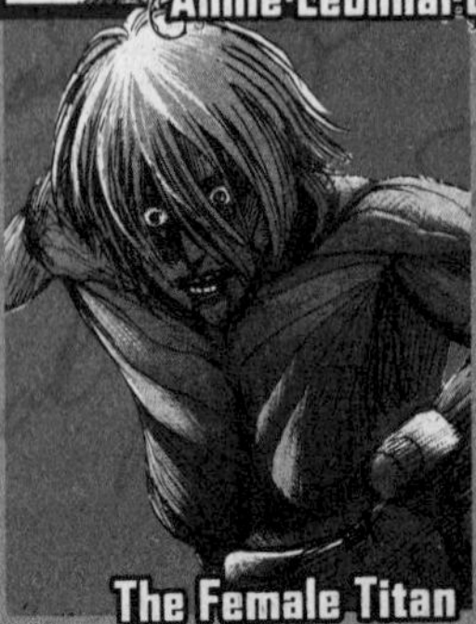

The Female Titan

The Garrison

Defenders of cities who work to reinforce the walls.

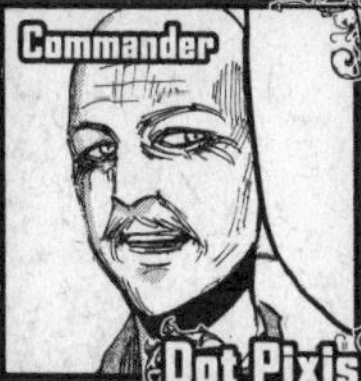
Commander
Dot Pixis

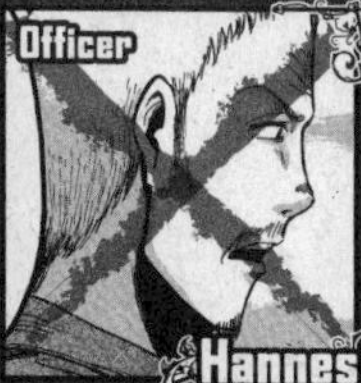
Officer
Hannes

Survey Corps

Soldiers who are prepared to sacrifice themselves as they brave the Titan territory outside the walls.

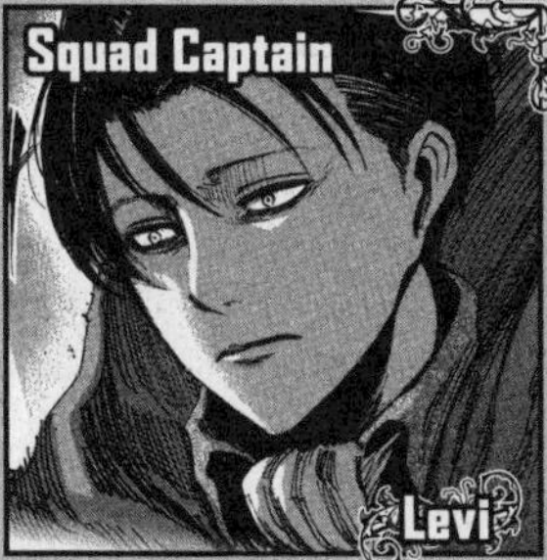
Squad Captain
Levi

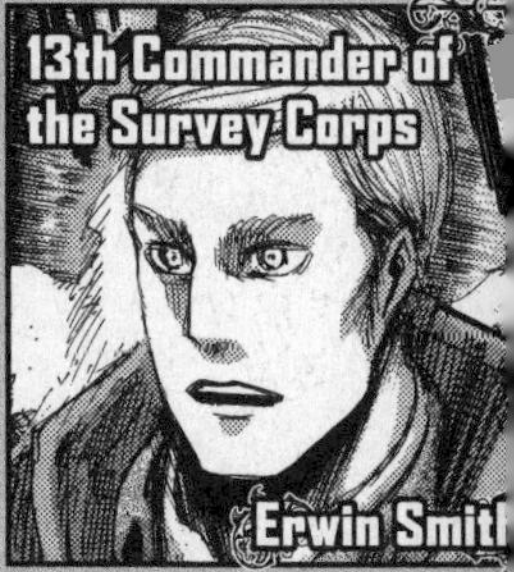
13th Commander of the Survey Corps
Erwin Smit

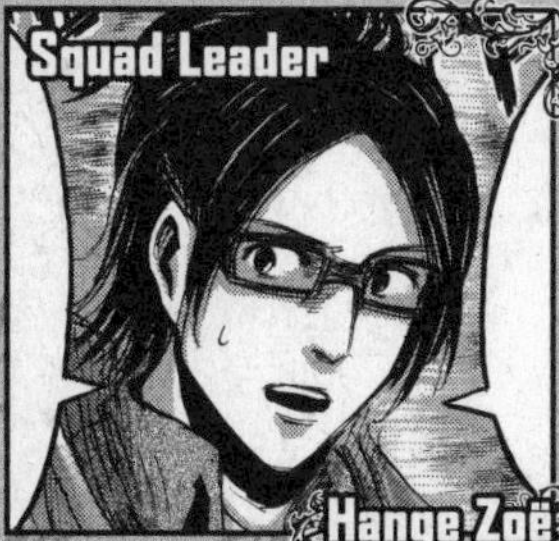
Squad Leader
Hange Zoë

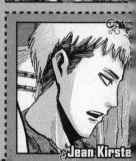

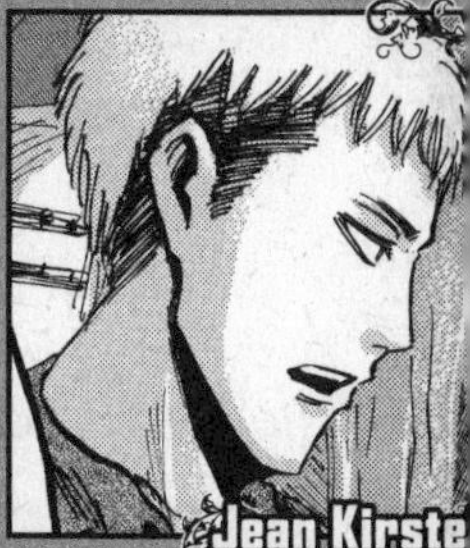
Jean Kirste

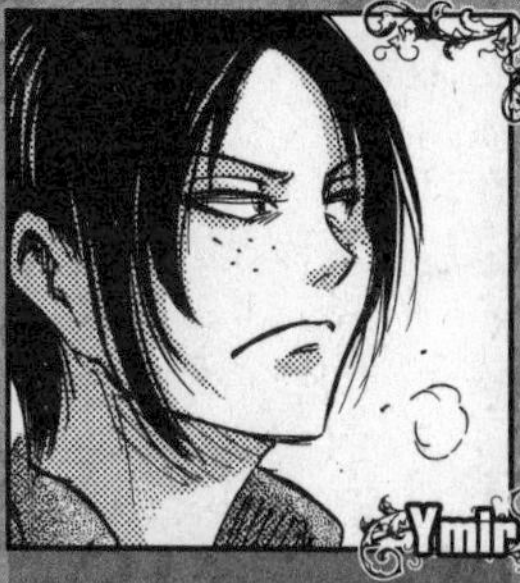
Ymir

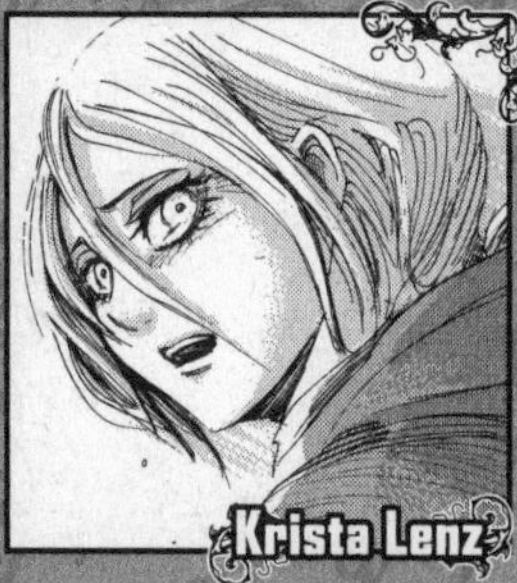
Krista Lenz

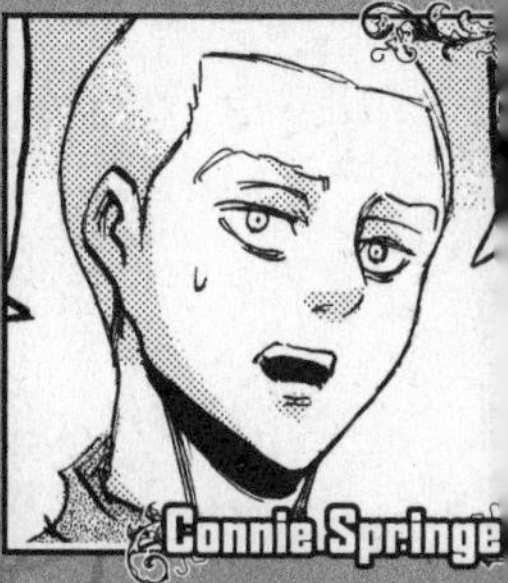
Connie Springe

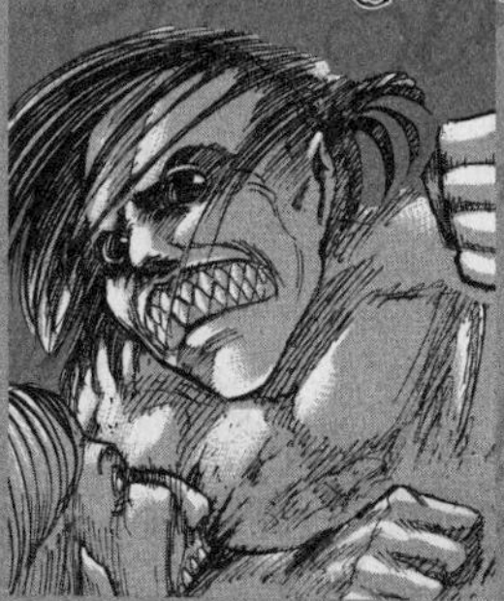

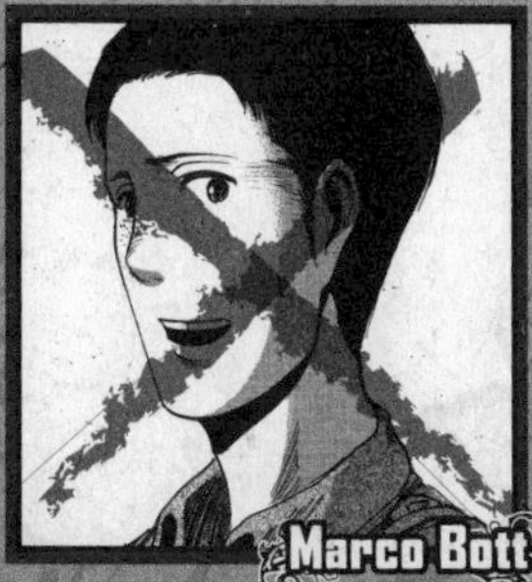
Marco Bott

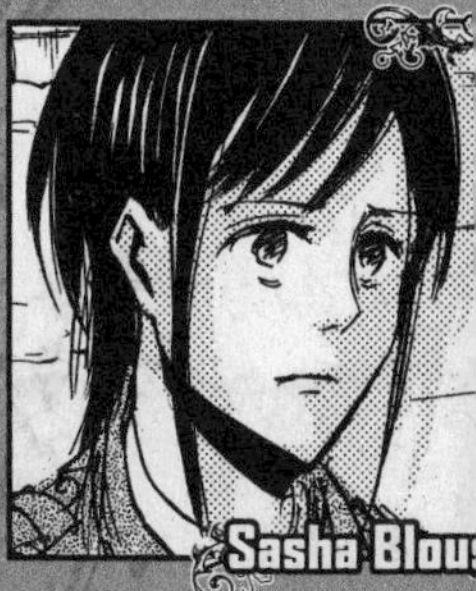
Sasha Blou

ATTACK on TITAN

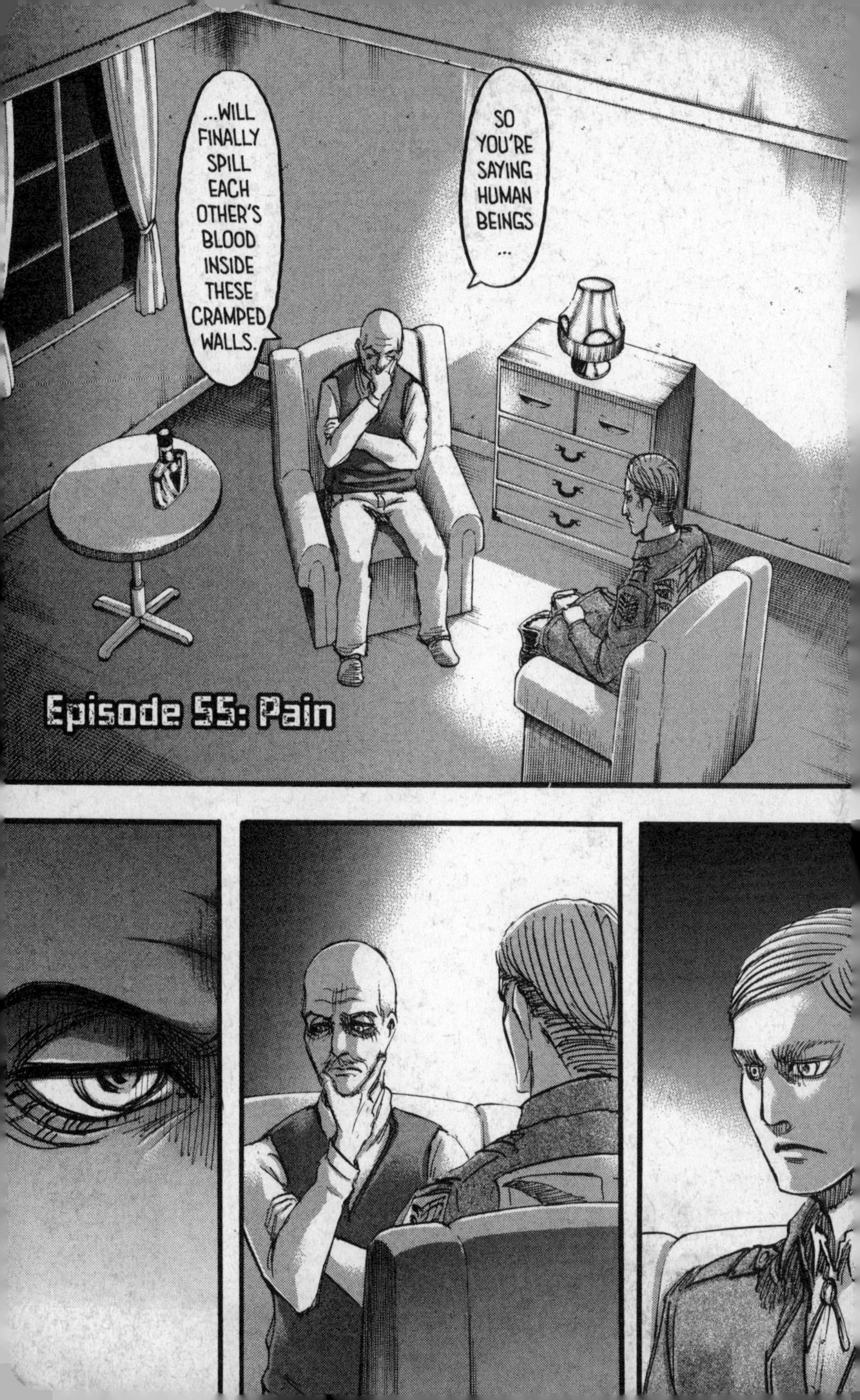
SO YOU'RE SAYING HUMAN BEINGS...
...WILL FINALLY SPILL EACH OTHER'S BLOOD INSIDE THESE CRAMPED WALLS.
Episode 55: Pain

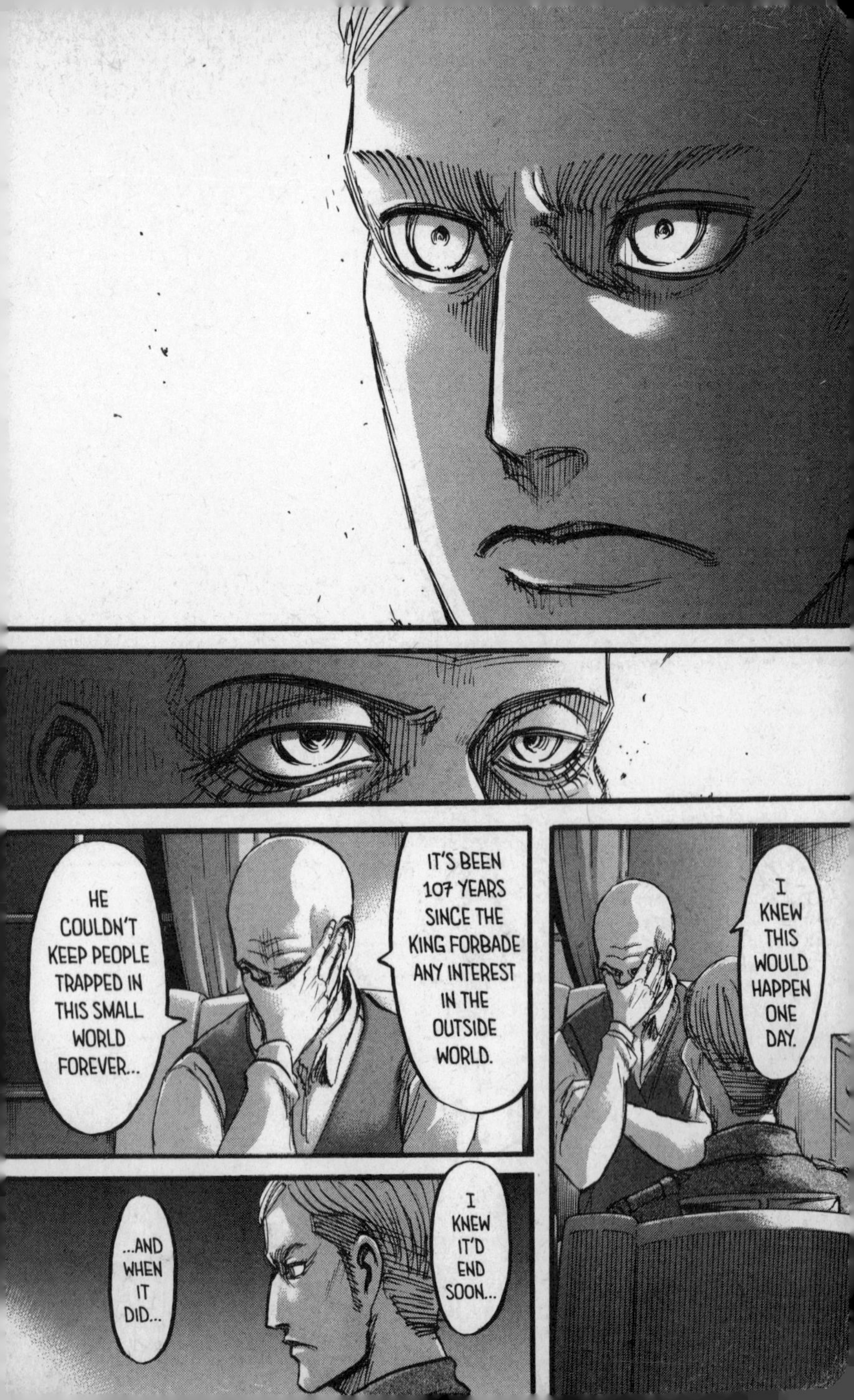
I KNEW THIS WOULD HAPPEN ONE DAY.
IT'S BEEN 107 YEARS SINCE THE KING FORBADE ANY INTEREST IN THE OUTSIDE WORLD.
HE COULDN'T KEEP PEOPLE TRAPPED IN THIS SMALL WORLD FOREVER...
I KNEW IT'D END SOON...
...AND WHEN IT DID...

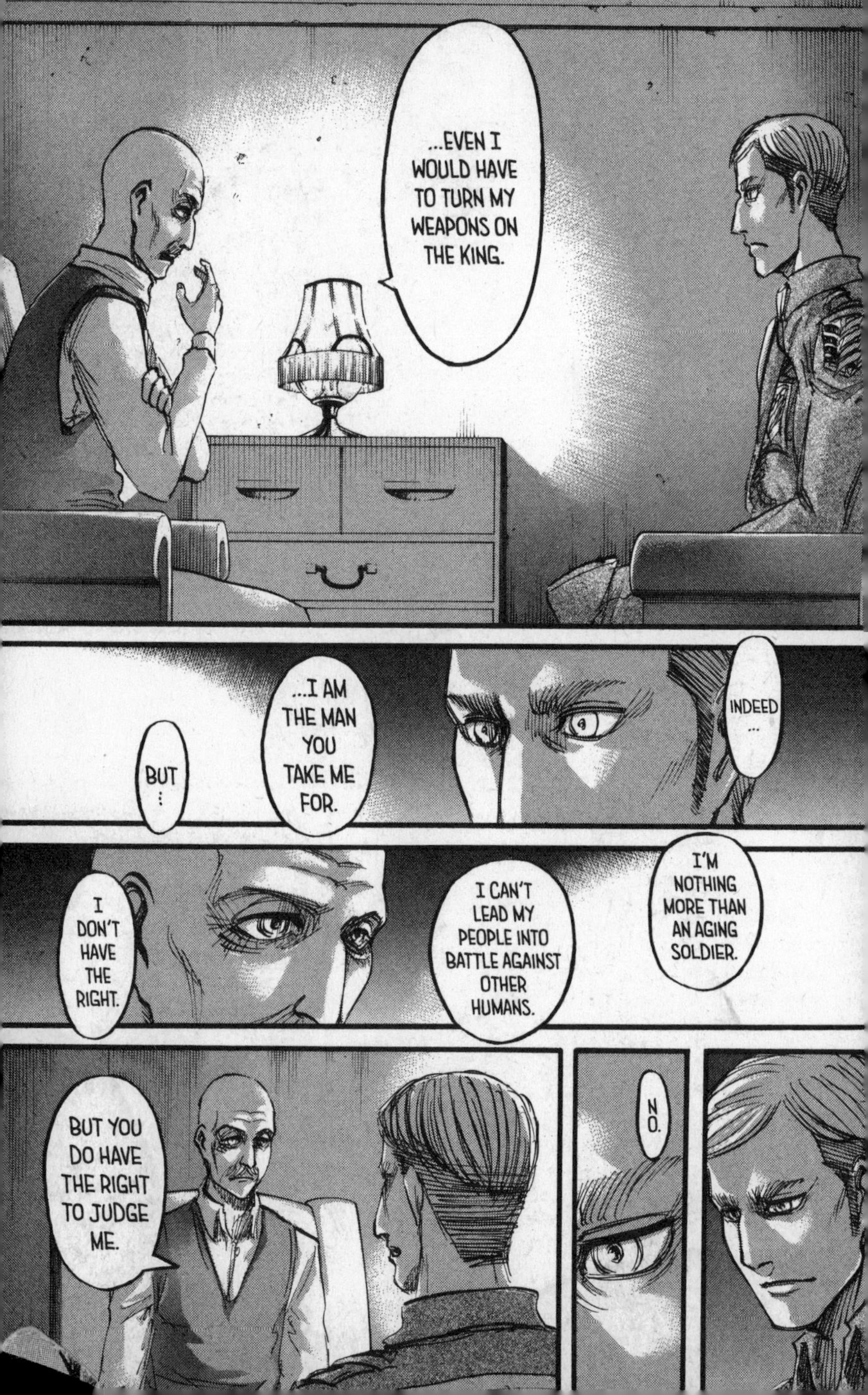
...EVEN I WOULD HAVE TO TURN MY WEAPONS ON THE KING.
INDEED...
...I AM THE MAN YOU TAKE ME FOR.
BUT...
I'M NOTHING MORE THAN AN AGING SOLDIER.
I CAN'T LEAD MY PEOPLE INTO BATTLE AGAINST OTHER HUMANS.
I DON'T HAVE THE RIGHT.
NO.
BUT YOU DO HAVE THE RIGHT TO JUDGE ME.

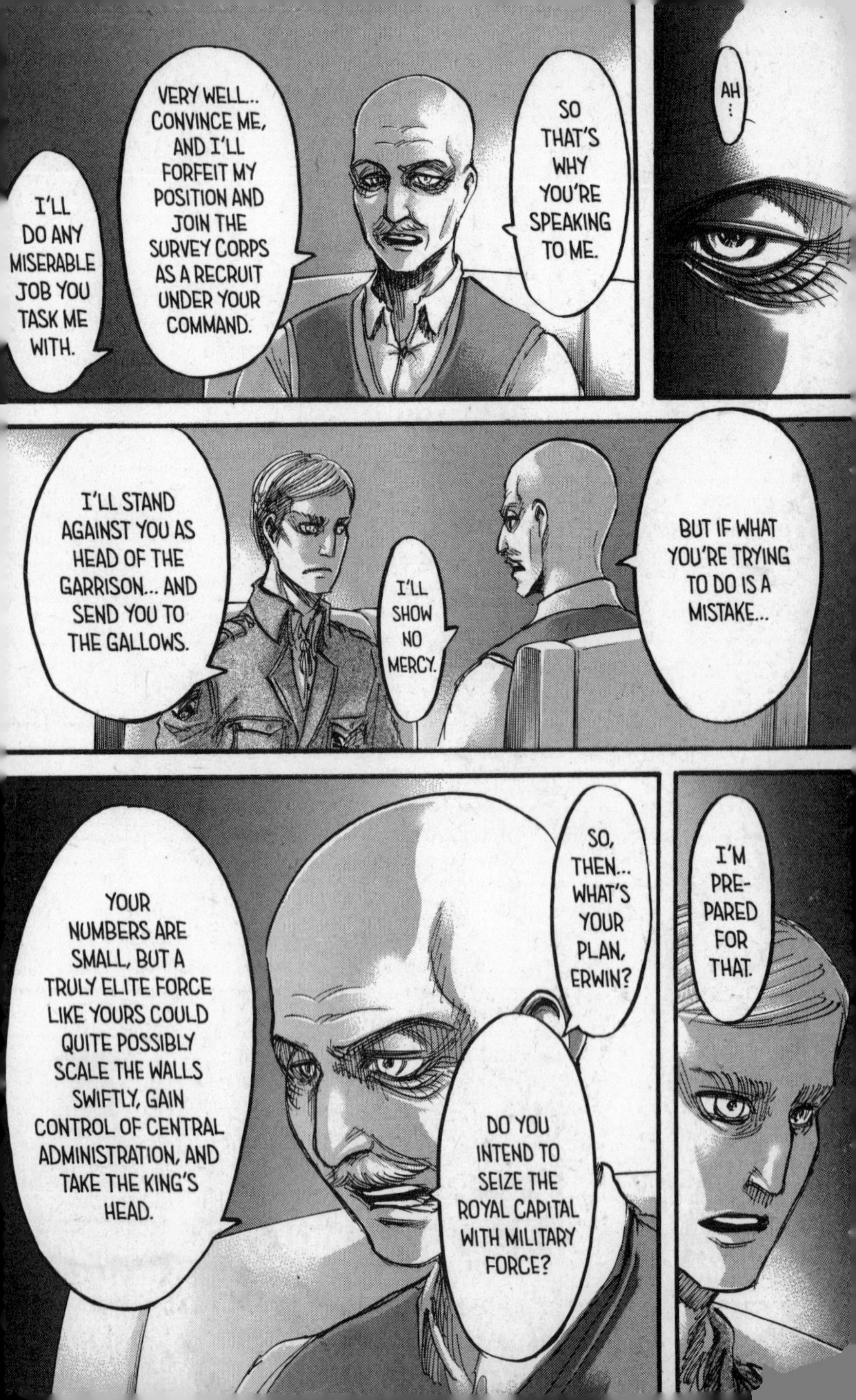
AH...
SO THAT'S WHY YOU'RE SPEAKING TO ME.
VERY WELL.. CONVINCE ME, AND I'LL FORFEIT MY POSITION AND JOIN THE SURVEY CORPS AS A RECRUIT UNDER YOUR COMMAND.
I'LL DO ANY MISERABLE JOB YOU TASK ME WITH.
BUT IF WHAT YOU'RE TRYING TO DO IS A MISTAKE...
I'LL SHOW NO MERCY.
I'LL STAND AGAINST YOU AS HEAD OF THE GARRISON... AND SEND YOU TO THE GALLOWS.
I'M PRE-PARED FOR THAT.
SO, THEN... WHAT'S YOUR PLAN, ERWIN?
DO YOU INTEND TO SEIZE THE ROYAL CAPITAL WITH MILITARY FORCE?
YOUR NUMBERS ARE SMALL, BUT A TRULY ELITE FORCE LIKE YOURS COULD QUITE POSSIBLY SCALE THE WALLS SWIFTLY, GAIN CONTROL OF CENTRAL ADMINISTRATION, AND TAKE THE KING'S HEAD.

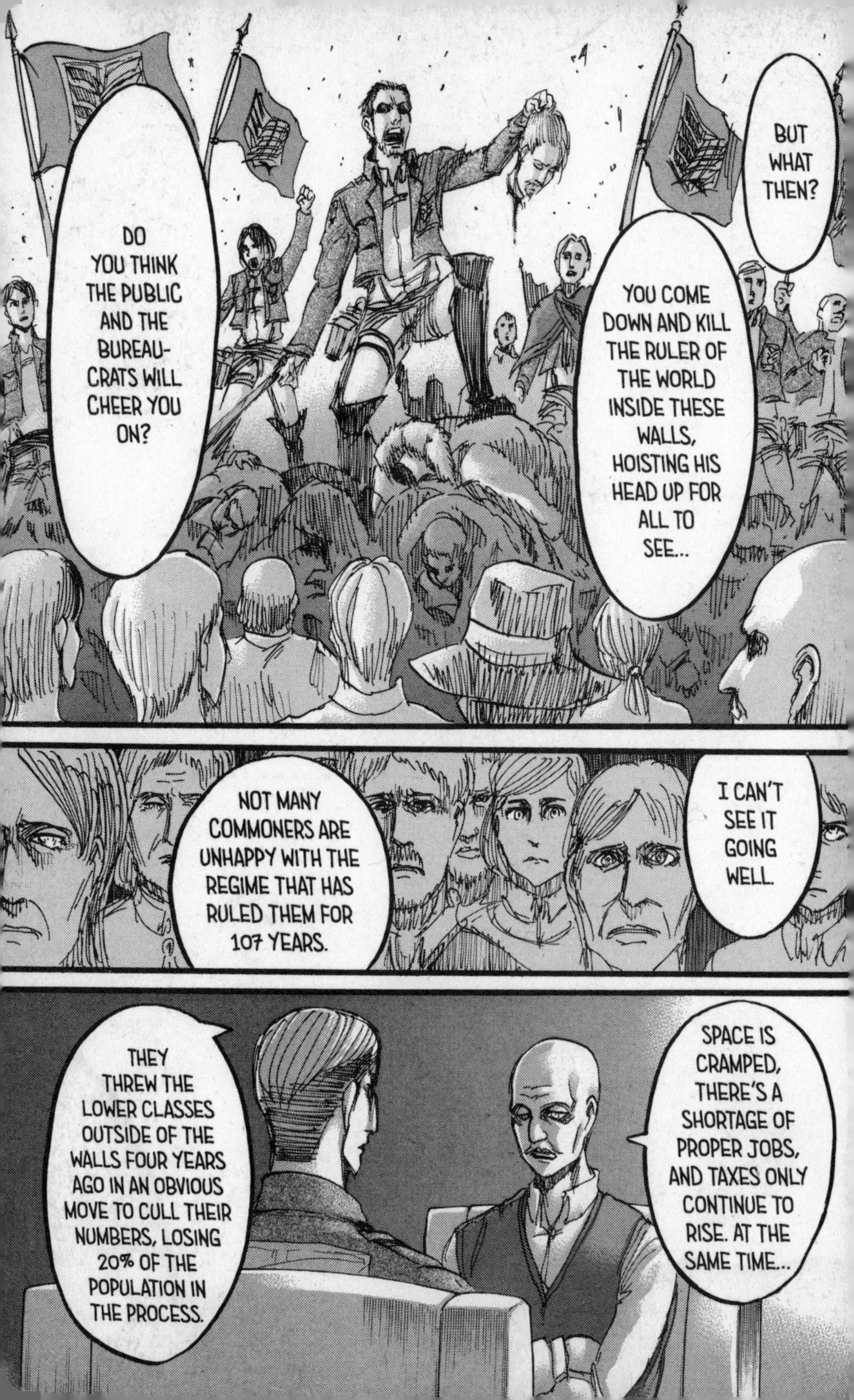
YOU COME DOWN AND KILL THE RULER OF THE WORLD INSIDE THESE WALLS, HOISTING HIS HEAD UP FOR ALL TO SEE...
BUT WHAT THEN?
DO YOU THINK THE PUBLIC AND THE BUREAU-CRATS WILL CHEER YOU ON?
I CAN'T SEE IT GOING WELL.
NOT MANY COMMONERS ARE UNHAPPY WITH THE REGIME THAT HAS RULED THEM FOR 107 YEARS.
SPACE IS CRAMPED, THERE'S A SHORTAGE OF PROPER JOBS, AND TAXES ONLY CONTINUE TO RISE. AT THE SAME TIME...
THEY THREW THE LOWER CLASSES OUTSIDE OF THE WALLS FOUR YEARS AGO IN AN OBVIOUS MOVE TO CULL THEIR NUMBERS, LOSING 20% OF THE POPULATION IN THE PROCESS.

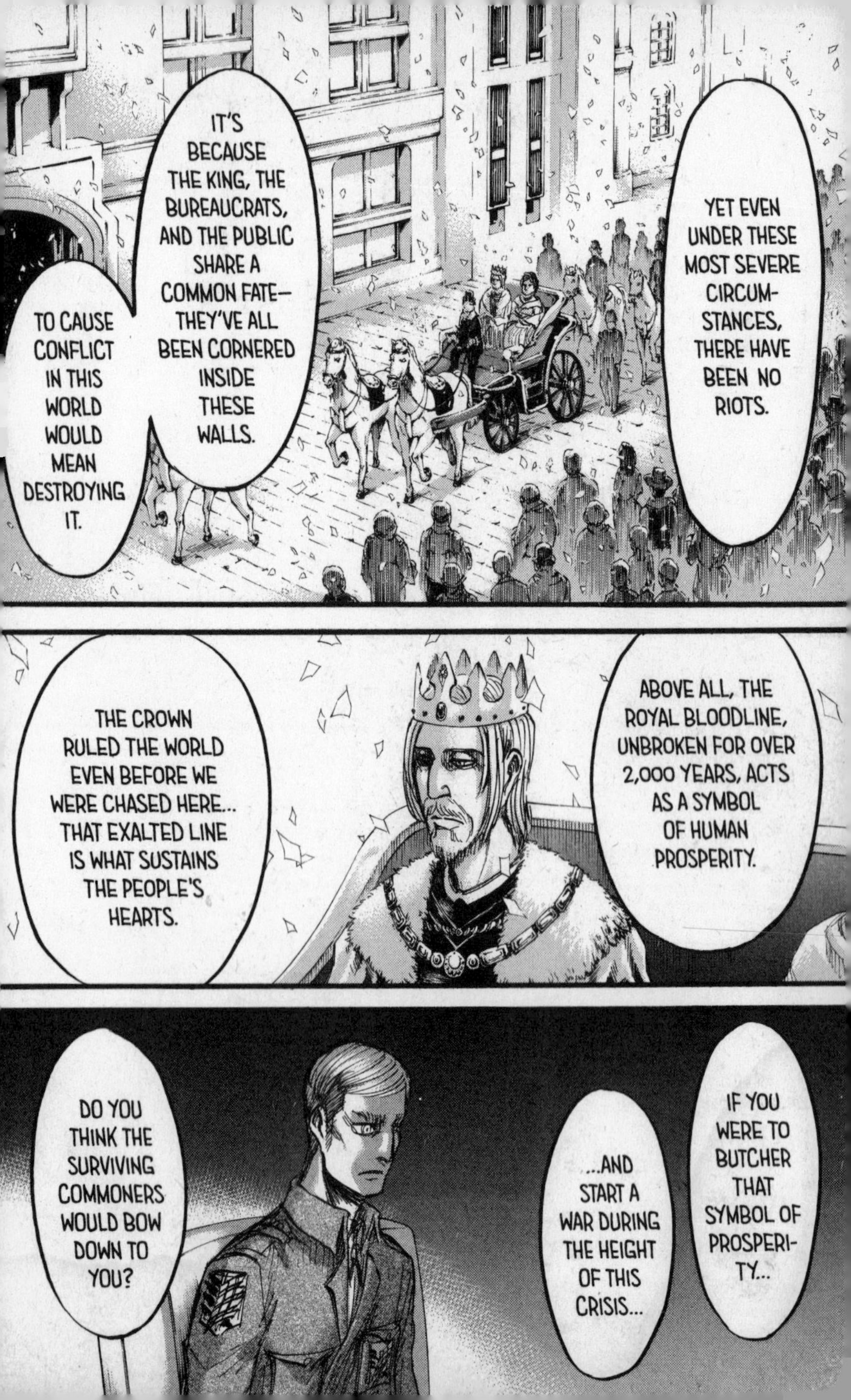
YET EVEN UNDER THESE MOST SEVERE CIRCUMSTANCES, THERE HAVE BEEN NO RIOTS.
IT'S BECAUSE THE KING, THE BUREAUCRATS, AND THE PUBLIC SHARE A COMMON FATE—THEY'VE ALL BEEN CORNERED INSIDE THESE WALLS.
TO CAUSE CONFLICT IN THIS WORLD WOULD MEAN DESTROYING IT.
ABOVE ALL, THE ROYAL BLOODLINE, UNBROKEN FOR OVER 2,000 YEARS, ACTS AS A SYMBOL OF HUMAN PROSPERITY.
THE CROWN RULED THE WORLD EVEN BEFORE WE WERE CHASED HERE... THAT EXALTED LINE IS WHAT SUSTAINS THE PEOPLE'S HEARTS.
IF YOU WERE TO BUTCHER THAT SYMBOL OF PROSPERITY...
...AND START A WAR DURING THE HEIGHT OF THIS CRISIS...
DO YOU THINK THE SURVIVING COMMONERS WOULD BOW DOWN TO YOU?

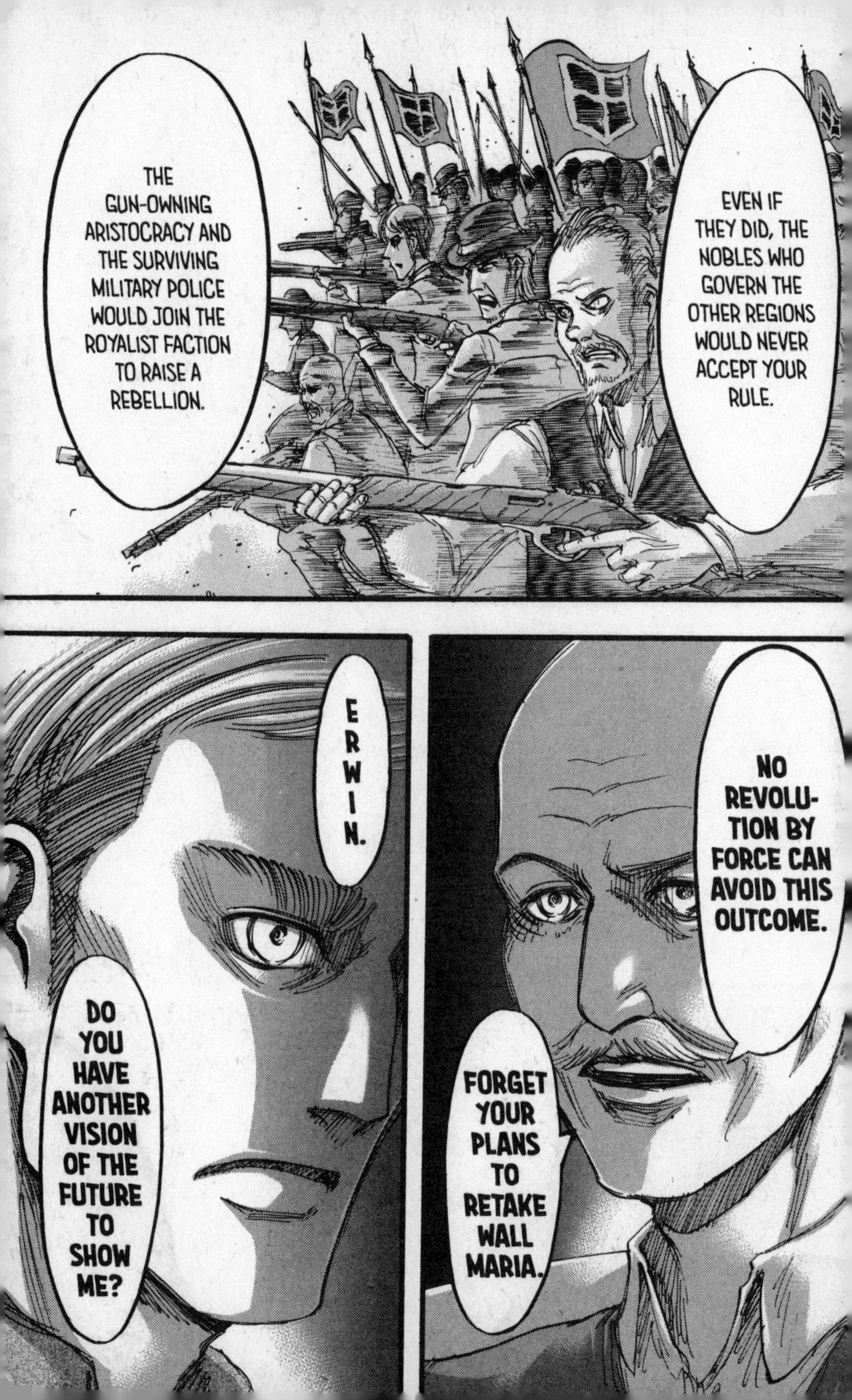
THE GUN-OWNING ARISTOCRACY AND THE SURVIVING MILITARY POLICE WOULD JOIN THE ROYALIST FACTION TO RAISE A REBELLION.
EVEN IF THEY DID, THE NOBLES WHO GOVERN THE OTHER REGIONS WOULD NEVER ACCEPT YOUR RULE.
NO REVOLUTION BY FORCE CAN AVOID THIS OUTCOME.
FORGET YOUR PLANS TO RETAKE WALL MARIA.
ERWIN.
DO YOU HAVE ANOTHER VISION OF THE FUTURE TO SHOW ME?

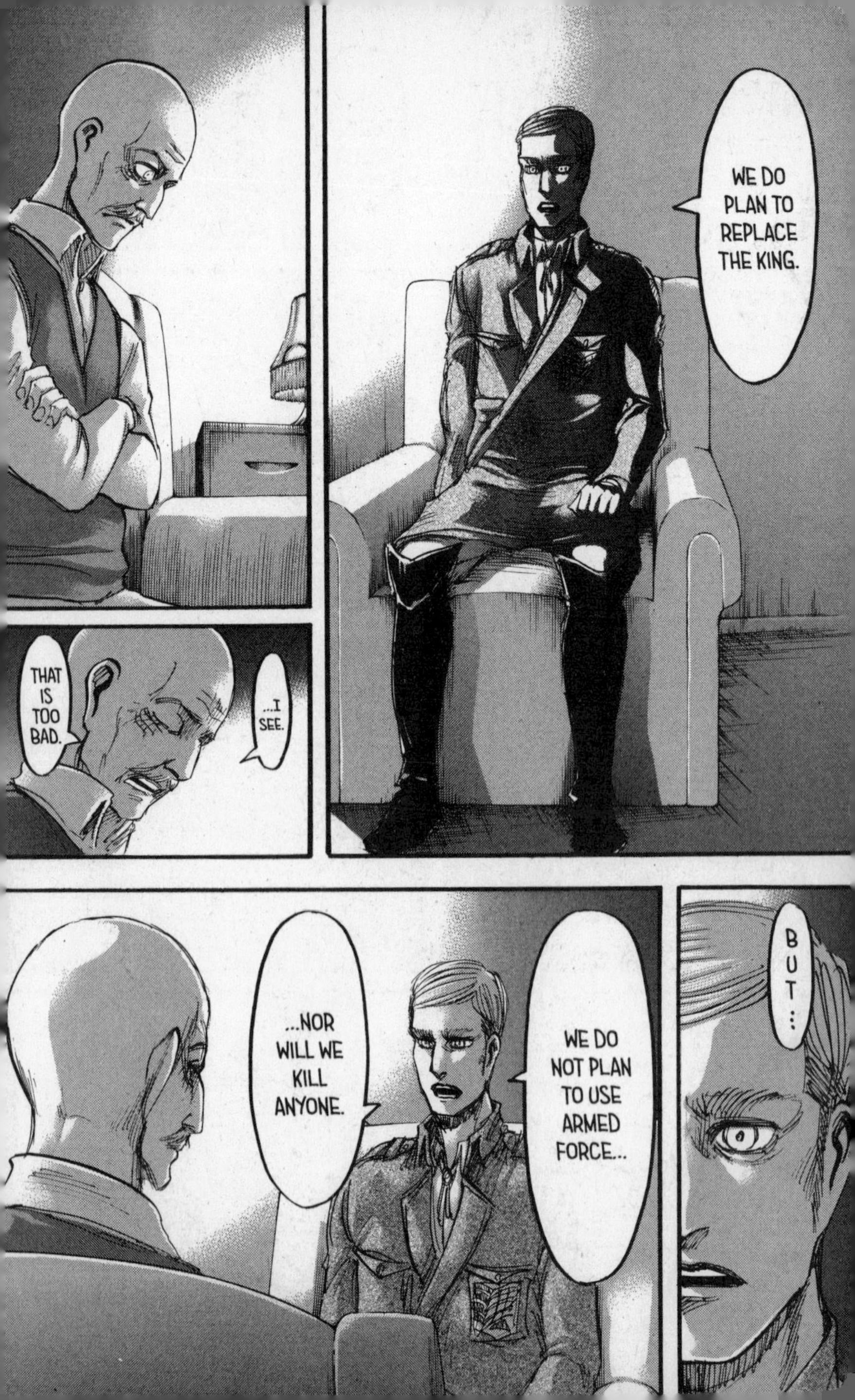
WE DO PLAN TO REPLACE THE KING.
...I SEE.
THAT IS TOO BAD.
BUT...
WE DO NOT PLAN TO USE ARMED FORCE...
...NOR WILL WE KILL ANYONE.

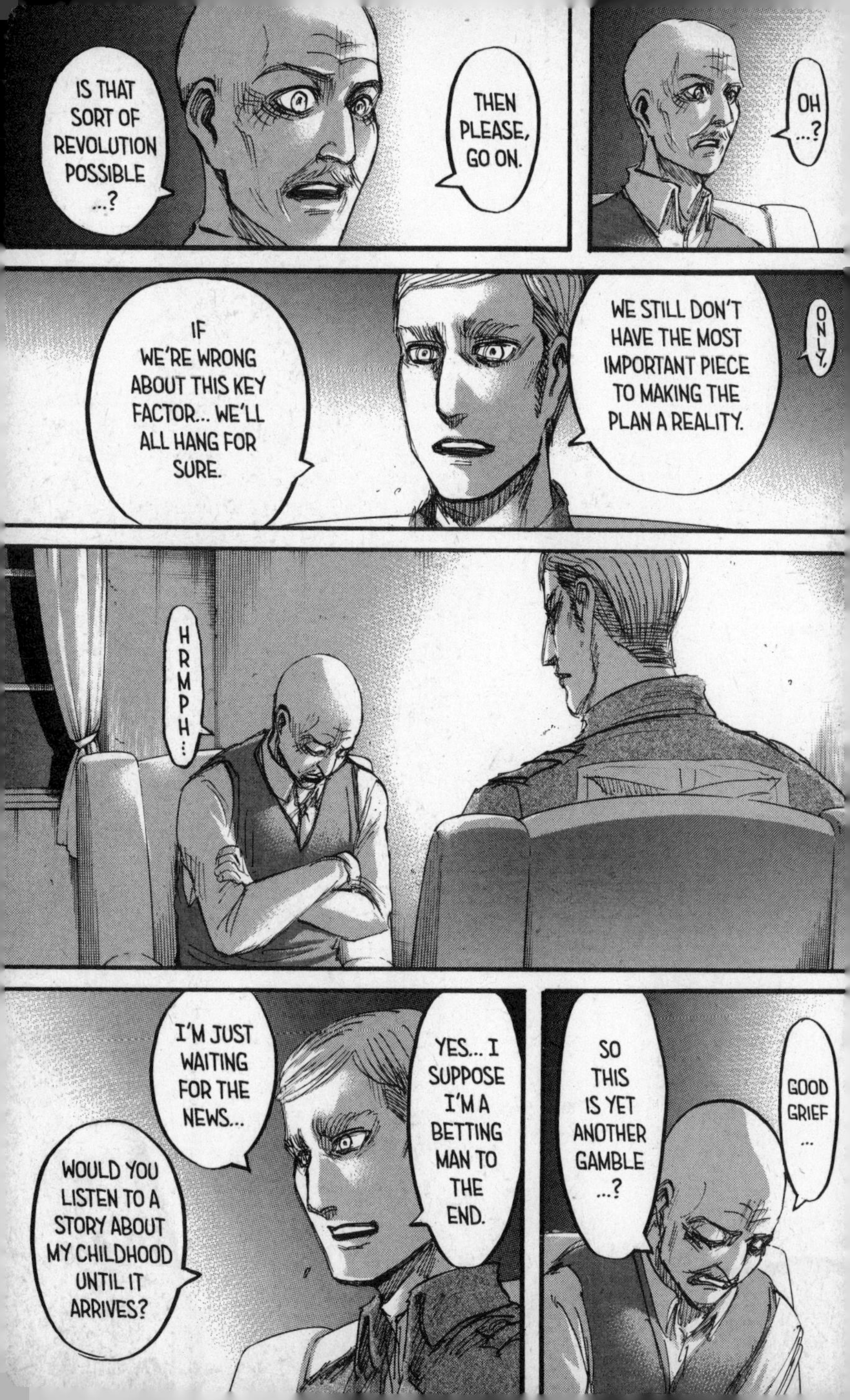

OH ...?
THEN PLEASE, GO ON.
IS THAT SORT OF REVOLUTION POSSIBLE ...?
ONLY,
WE STILL DON'T HAVE THE MOST IMPORTANT PIECE TO MAKING THE PLAN A REALITY.
IF WE'RE WRONG ABOUT THIS KEY FACTOR... WE'LL ALL HANG FOR SURE.
HRMPH...
GOOD GRIEF ...
SO THIS IS YET ANOTHER GAMBLE ...?
YES... I SUPPOSE I'M A BETTING MAN TO THE END.
I'M JUST WAITING FOR THE NEWS...
WOULD YOU LISTEN TO A STORY ABOUT MY CHILDHOOD UNTIL IT ARRIVES?

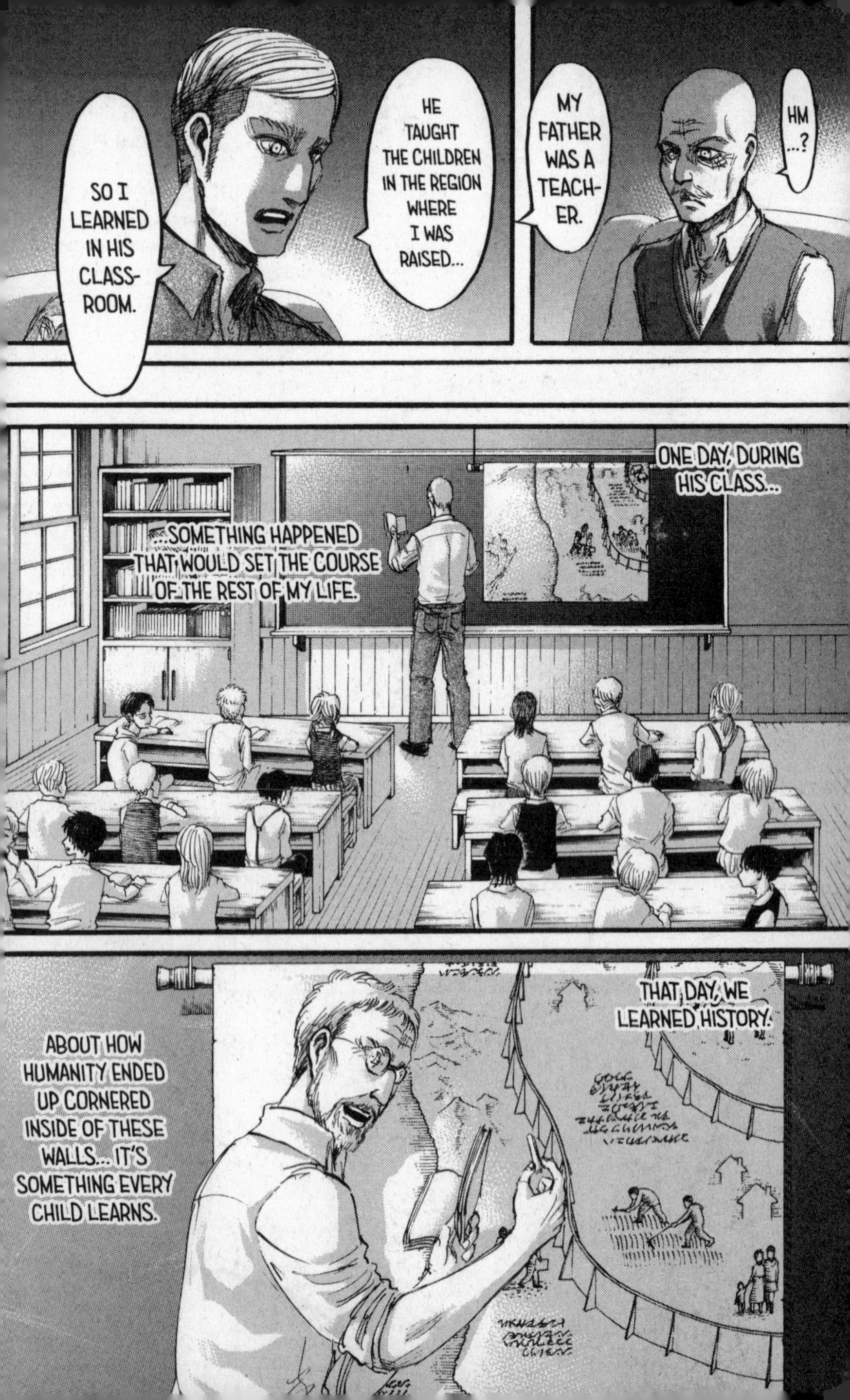
HM ...?
MY FATHER WAS A TEACH-ER.
HE TAUGHT THE CHILDREN IN THE REGION WHERE I WAS RAISED...
SO I LEARNED IN HIS CLASS-ROOM.
ONE DAY, DURING HIS CLASS...
...SOMETHING HAPPENED THAT WOULD SET THE COURSE OF THE REST OF MY LIFE.
THAT DAY, WE LEARNED HISTORY.
ABOUT HOW HUMANITY ENDED UP CORNERED INSIDE OF THESE WALLS... IT'S SOMETHING EVERY CHILD LEARNS.

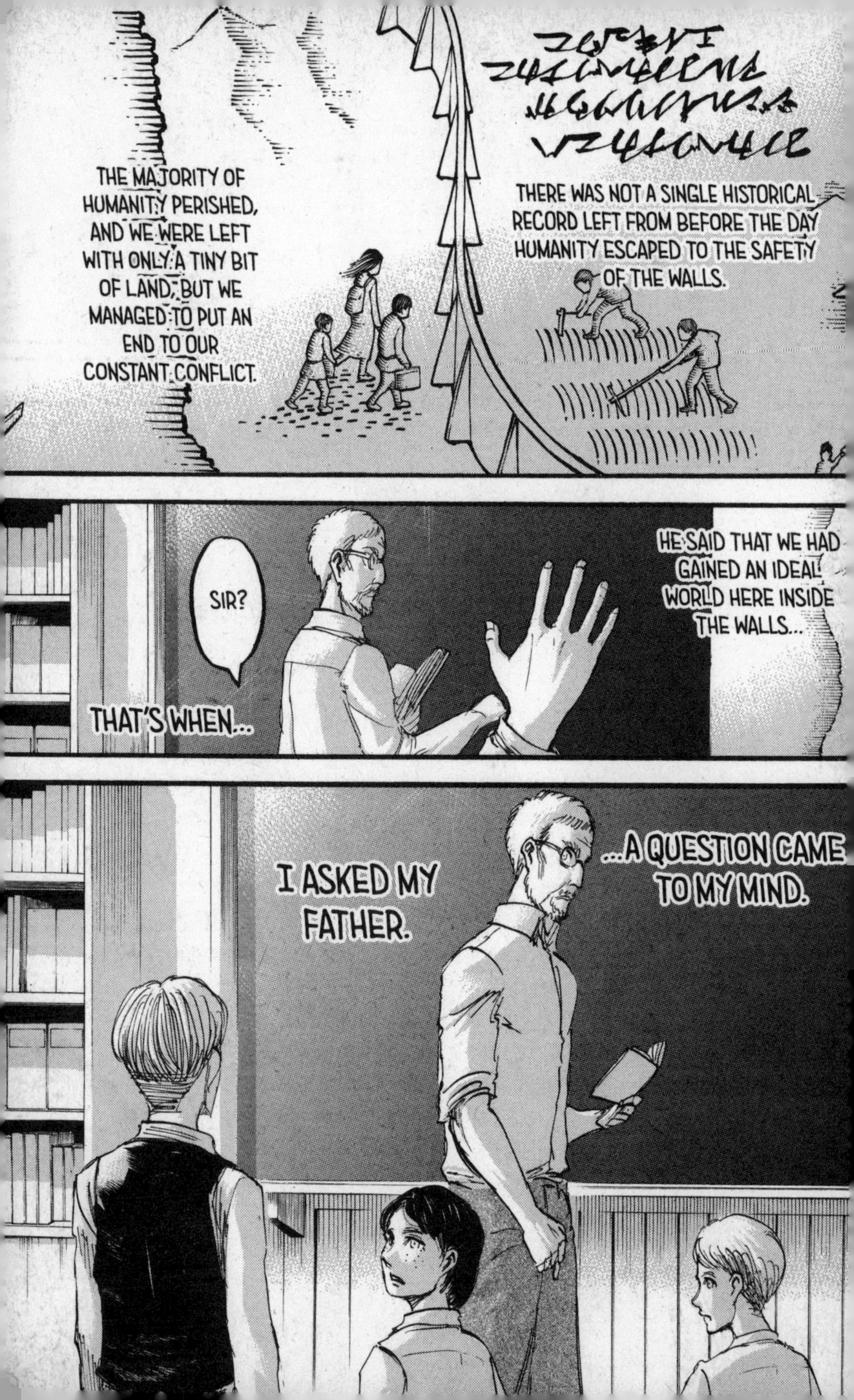
THERE WAS NOT A SINGLE HISTORICAL RECORD LEFT FROM BEFORE THE DAY HUMANITY ESCAPED TO THE SAFETY OF THE WALLS.
THE MAJORITY OF HUMANITY PERISHED, AND WE WERE LEFT WITH ONLY A TINY BIT OF LAND, BUT WE MANAGED TO PUT AN END TO OUR CONSTANT CONFLICT.
HE SAID THAT WE HAD GAINED AN IDEAL WORLD HERE INSIDE THE WALLS...
SIR?
THAT'S WHEN...
...A QUESTION CAME TO MY MIND.
I ASKED MY FATHER.

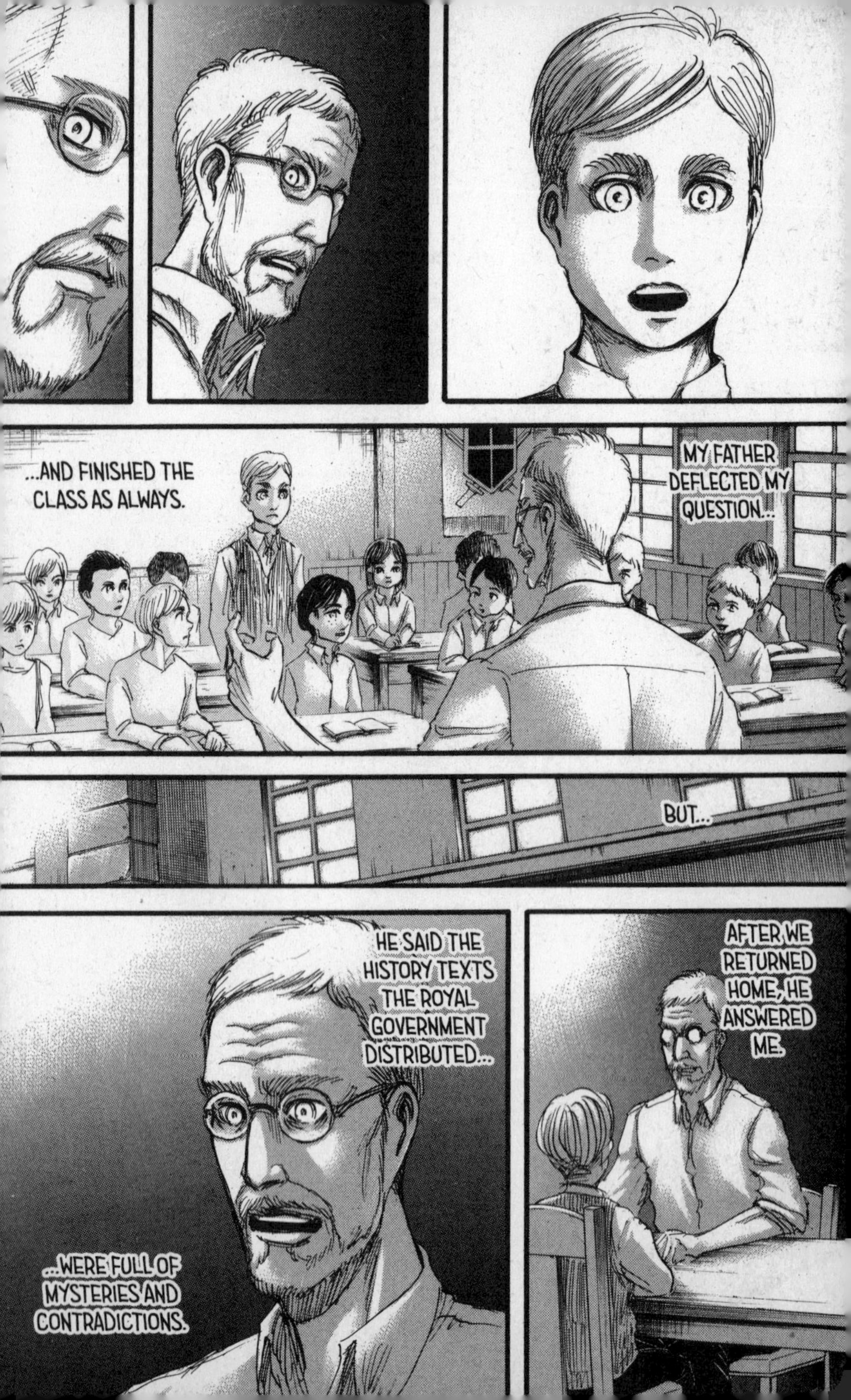
MY FATHER DEFLECTED MY QUESTION...
...AND FINISHED THE CLASS AS ALWAYS.
BUT...
AFTER WE RETURNED HOME, HE ANSWERED ME.
HE SAID THE HISTORY TEXTS THE ROYAL GOVERNMENT DISTRIBUTED...
...WERE FULL OF MYSTERIES AND CONTRADICTIONS.

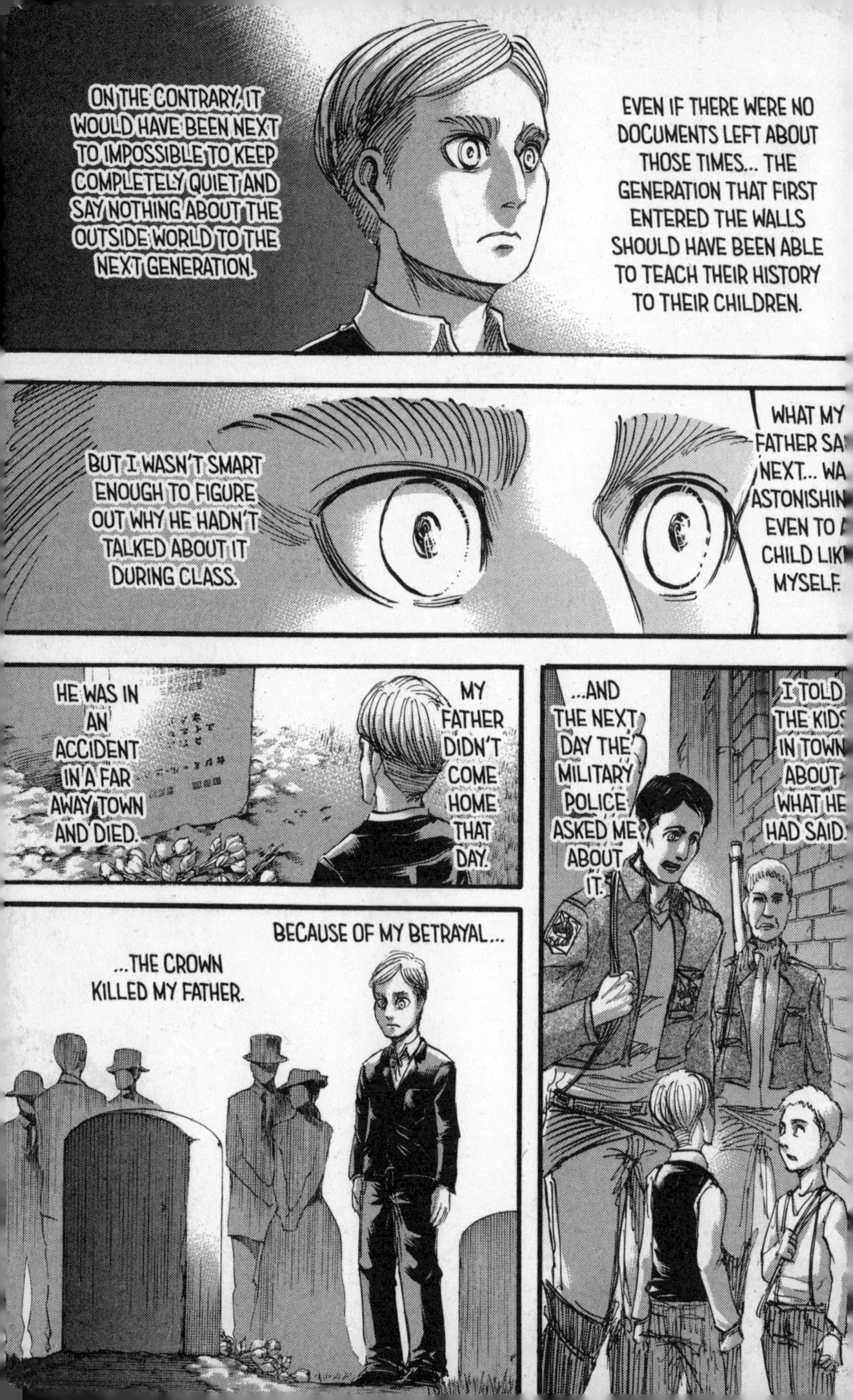
EVEN IF THERE WERE NO DOCUMENTS LEFT ABOUT THOSE TIMES... THE GENERATION THAT FIRST ENTERED THE WALLS SHOULD HAVE BEEN ABLE TO TEACH THEIR HISTORY TO THEIR CHILDREN.
ON THE CONTRARY, IT WOULD HAVE BEEN NEXT TO IMPOSSIBLE TO KEEP COMPLETELY QUIET AND SAY NOTHING ABOUT THE OUTSIDE WORLD TO THE NEXT GENERATION.
WHAT MY FATHER SA NEXT... WA ASTONISHIN EVEN TO A CHILD LIK MYSELF.
BUT I WASN'T SMART ENOUGH TO FIGURE OUT WHY HE HADN'T TALKED ABOUT IT DURING CLASS.
I TOLD THE KIDS IN TOWN ABOUT WHAT HE HAD SAID.
...AND THE NEXT DAY THE MILITARY POLICE ASKED ME ABOUT IT.
MY FATHER DIDN'T COME HOME THAT DAY.
HE WAS IN AN ACCIDENT IN A FAR AWAY TOWN AND DIED.
BECAUSE OF MY BETRAYAL...
...THE CROWN KILLED MY FATHER.

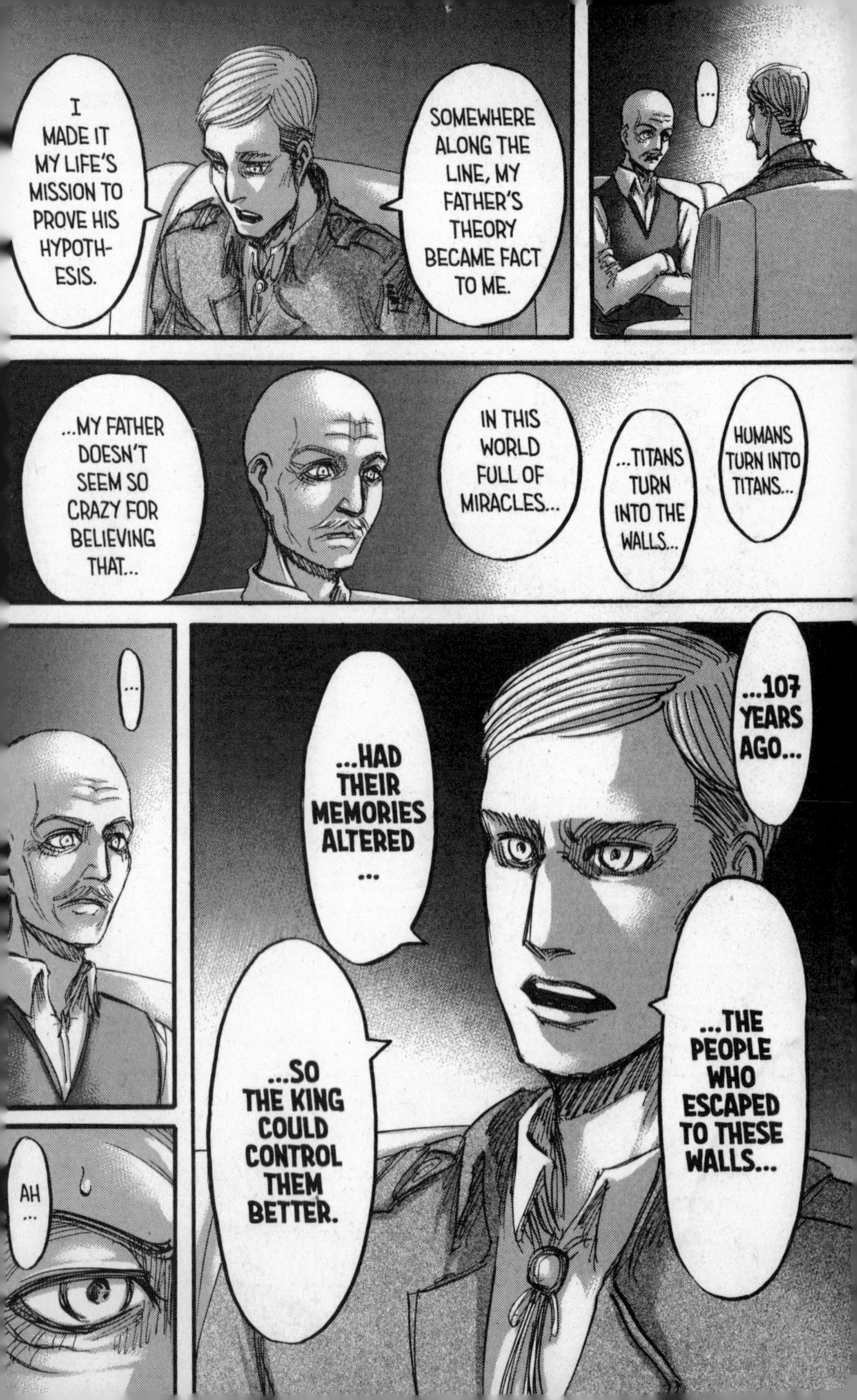
...
SOMEWHERE ALONG THE LINE, MY FATHER'S THEORY BECAME FACT TO ME.
I MADE IT MY LIFE'S MISSION TO PROVE HIS HYPOTH-ESIS.
HUMANS TURN INTO TITANS...
...TITANS TURN INTO THE WALLS...
IN THIS WORLD FULL OF MIRACLES...
...MY FATHER DOESN'T SEEM SO CRAZY FOR BELIEVING THAT...
...107 YEARS AGO...
...THE PEOPLE WHO ESCAPED TO THESE WALLS...
...HAD THEIR MEMORIES ALTERED...
...SO THE KING COULD CONTROL THEM BETTER.
...
AH ...

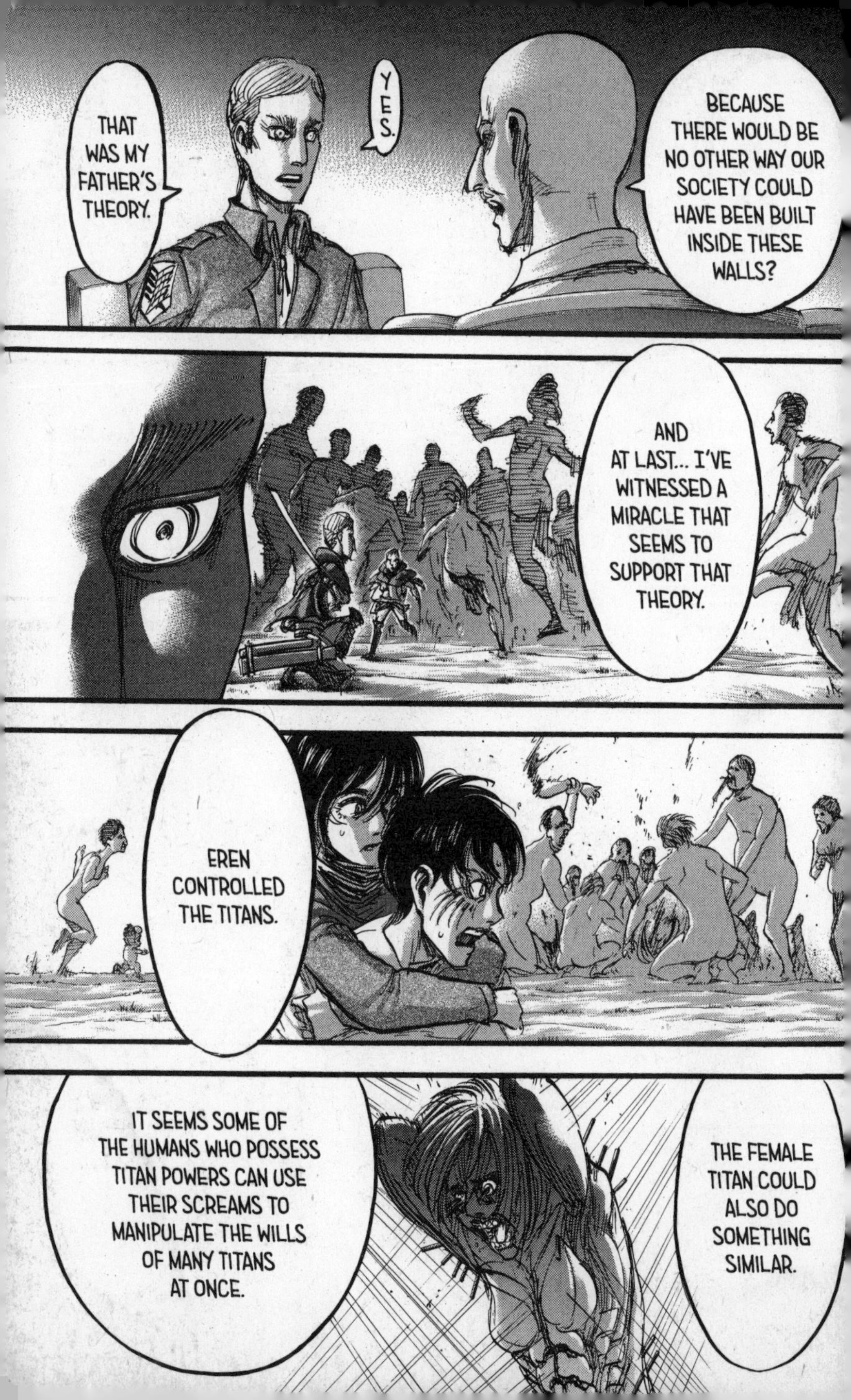
BECAUSE THERE WOULD BE NO OTHER WAY OUR SOCIETY COULD HAVE BEEN BUILT INSIDE THESE WALLS?
YES.
THAT WAS MY FATHER'S THEORY.
AND AT LAST... I'VE WITNESSED A MIRACLE THAT SEEMS TO SUPPORT THAT THEORY.
EREN CONTROLLED THE TITANS.
IT SEEMS SOME OF THE HUMANS WHO POSSESS TITAN POWERS CAN USE THEIR SCREAMS TO MANIPULATE THE WILLS OF MANY TITANS AT ONCE.
THE FEMALE TITAN COULD ALSO DO SOMETHING SIMILAR.

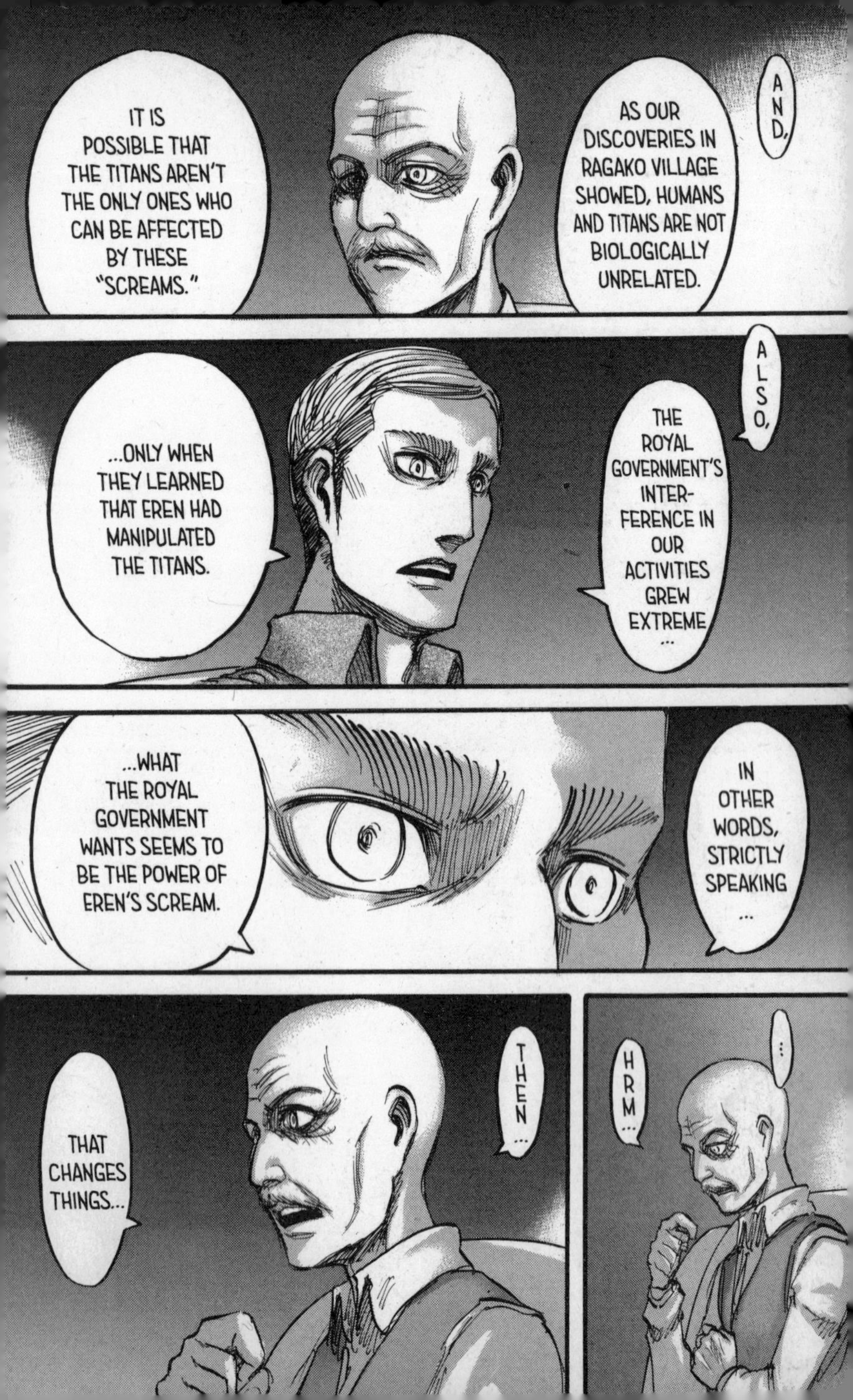
AND,
AS OUR DISCOVERIES IN RAGAKO VILLAGE SHOWED, HUMANS AND TITANS ARE NOT BIOLOGICALLY UNRELATED.
IT IS POSSIBLE THAT THE TITANS AREN'T THE ONLY ONES WHO CAN BE AFFECTED BY THESE "SCREAMS."
ALSO,
THE ROYAL GOVERNMENT'S INTER-FERENCE IN OUR ACTIVITIES GREW EXTREME...
...ONLY WHEN THEY LEARNED THAT EREN HAD MANIPULATED THE TITANS.
IN OTHER WORDS, STRICTLY SPEAKING...
...WHAT THE ROYAL GOVERNMENT WANTS SEEMS TO BE THE POWER OF EREN'S SCREAM.
...
HRM...
THEN...
THAT CHANGES THINGS...

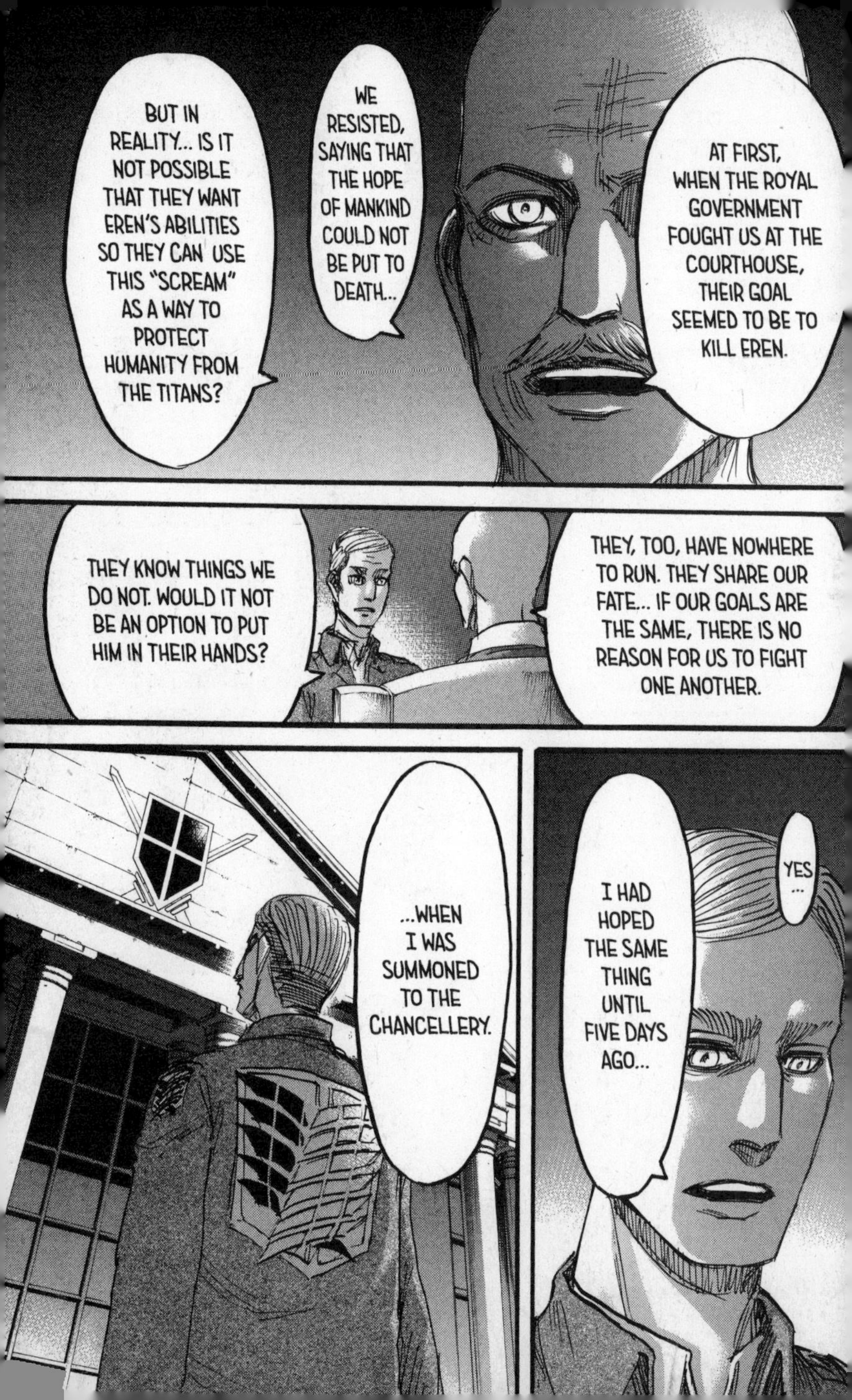
AT FIRST, WHEN THE ROYAL GOVERNMENT FOUGHT US AT THE COURTHOUSE, THEIR GOAL SEEMED TO BE TO KILL EREN.
WE RESISTED, SAYING THAT THE HOPE OF MANKIND COULD NOT BE PUT TO DEATH...
BUT IN REALITY... IS IT NOT POSSIBLE THAT THEY WANT EREN'S ABILITIES SO THEY CAN USE THIS "SCREAM" AS A WAY TO PROTECT HUMANITY FROM THE TITANS?
THEY, TOO, HAVE NOWHERE TO RUN. THEY SHARE OUR FATE... IF OUR GOALS ARE THE SAME, THERE IS NO REASON FOR US TO FIGHT ONE ANOTHER.
THEY KNOW THINGS WE DO NOT. WOULD IT NOT BE AN OPTION TO PUT HIM IN THEIR HANDS?
YES...
I HAD HOPED THE SAME THING UNTIL FIVE DAYS AGO...
...WHEN I WAS SUMMONED TO THE CHANCELLERY.

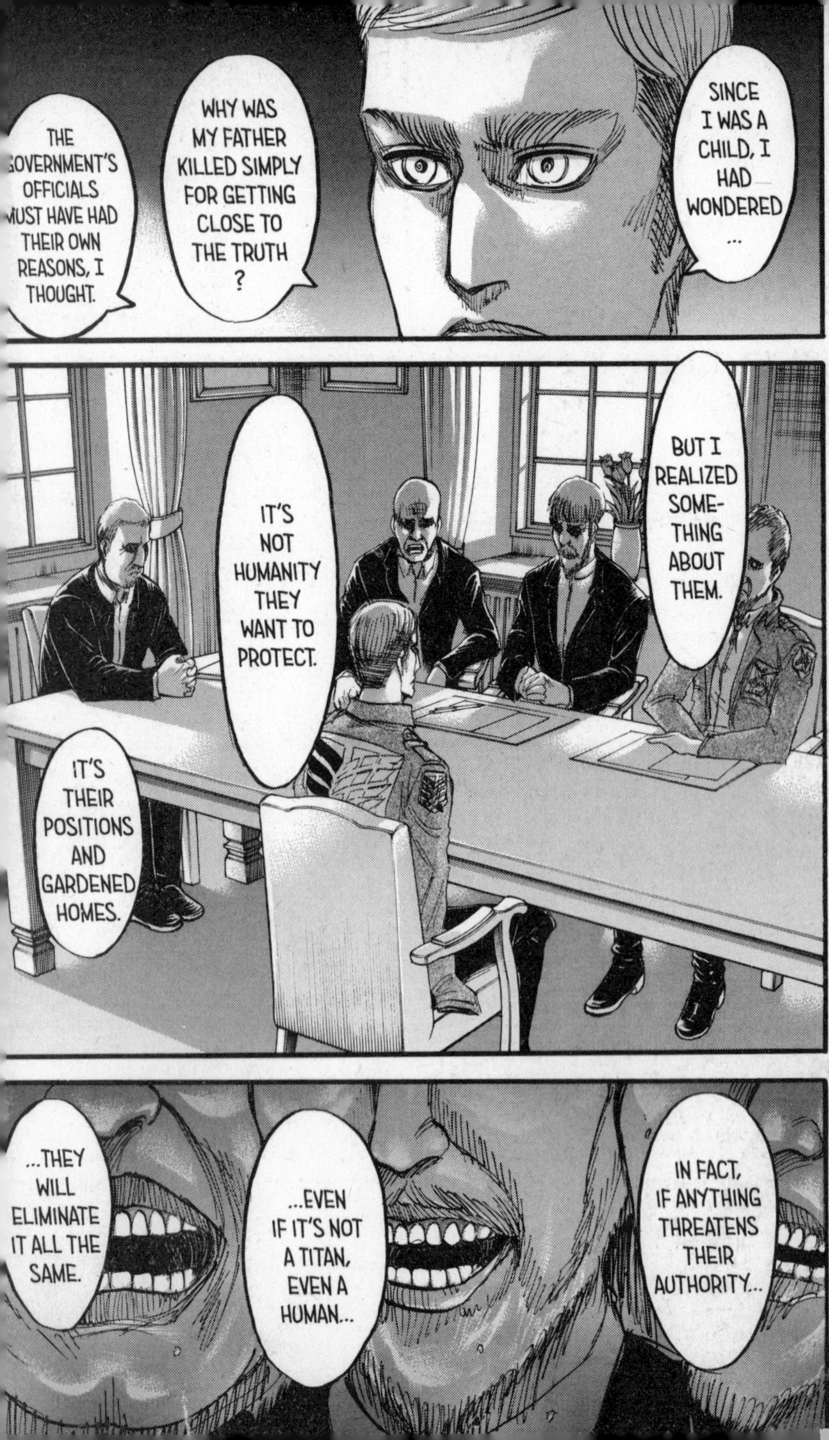
SINCE I WAS A CHILD, I HAD WONDERED ...
WHY WAS MY FATHER KILLED SIMPLY FOR GETTING CLOSE TO THE TRUTH ?
THE GOVERNMENT'S OFFICIALS MUST HAVE HAD THEIR OWN REASONS, I THOUGHT.
BUT I REALIZED SOME-THING ABOUT THEM.
IT'S NOT HUMANITY THEY WANT TO PROTECT.
IT'S THEIR POSITIONS AND GARDENED HOMES.
IN FACT, IF ANYTHING THREATENS THEIR AUTHORITY...
...EVEN IF IT'S NOT A TITAN, EVEN A HUMAN...
...THEY WILL ELIMINATE IT ALL THE SAME.

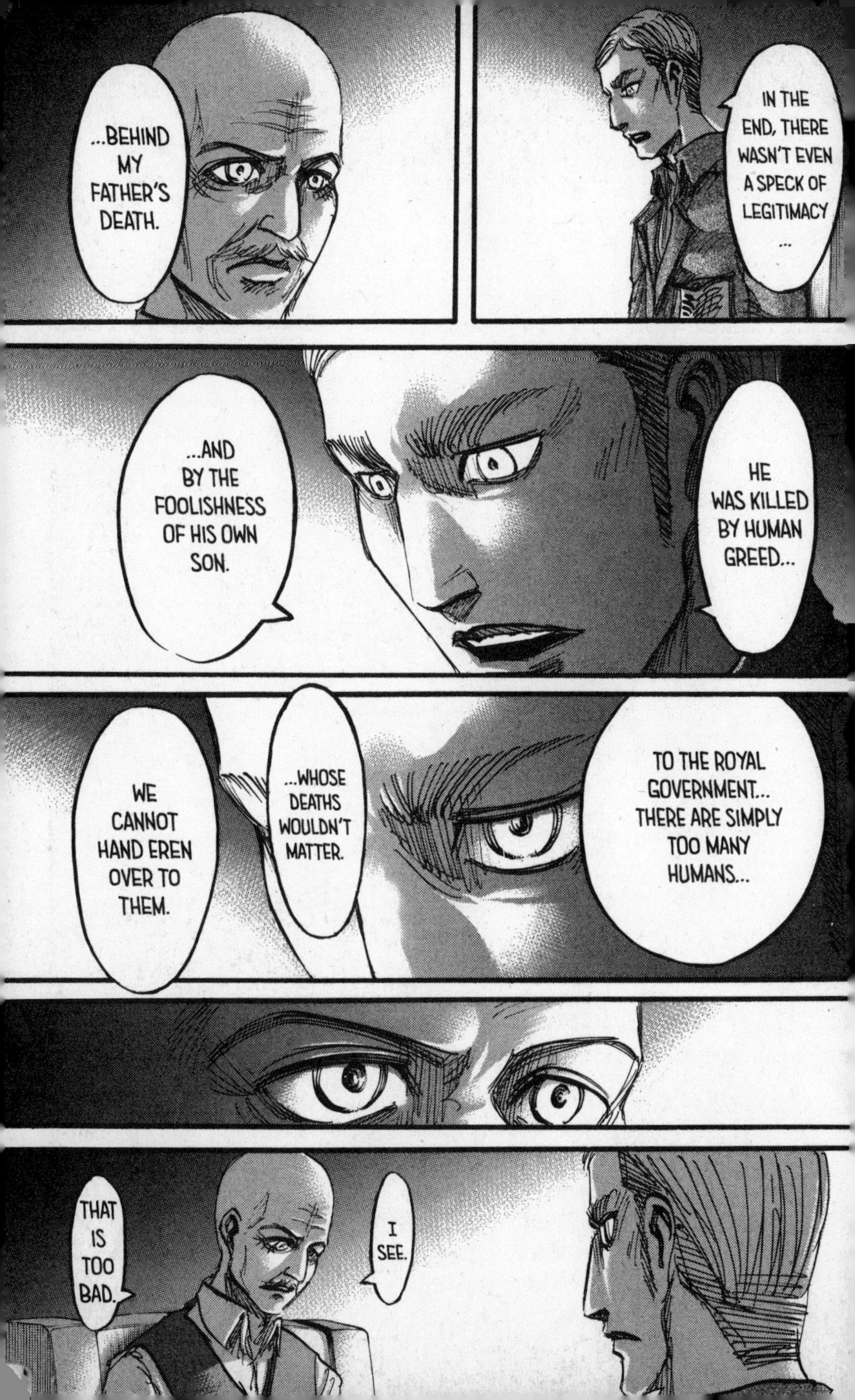
IN THE END, THERE WASN'T EVEN A SPECK OF LEGITIMACY ...
...BEHIND MY FATHER'S DEATH.
HE WAS KILLED BY HUMAN GREED...
...AND BY THE FOOLISHNESS OF HIS OWN SON.
TO THE ROYAL GOVERNMENT... THERE ARE SIMPLY TOO MANY HUMANS...
...WHOSE DEATHS WOULDN'T MATTER.
WE CANNOT HAND EREN OVER TO THEM.
I SEE.
THAT IS TOO BAD.

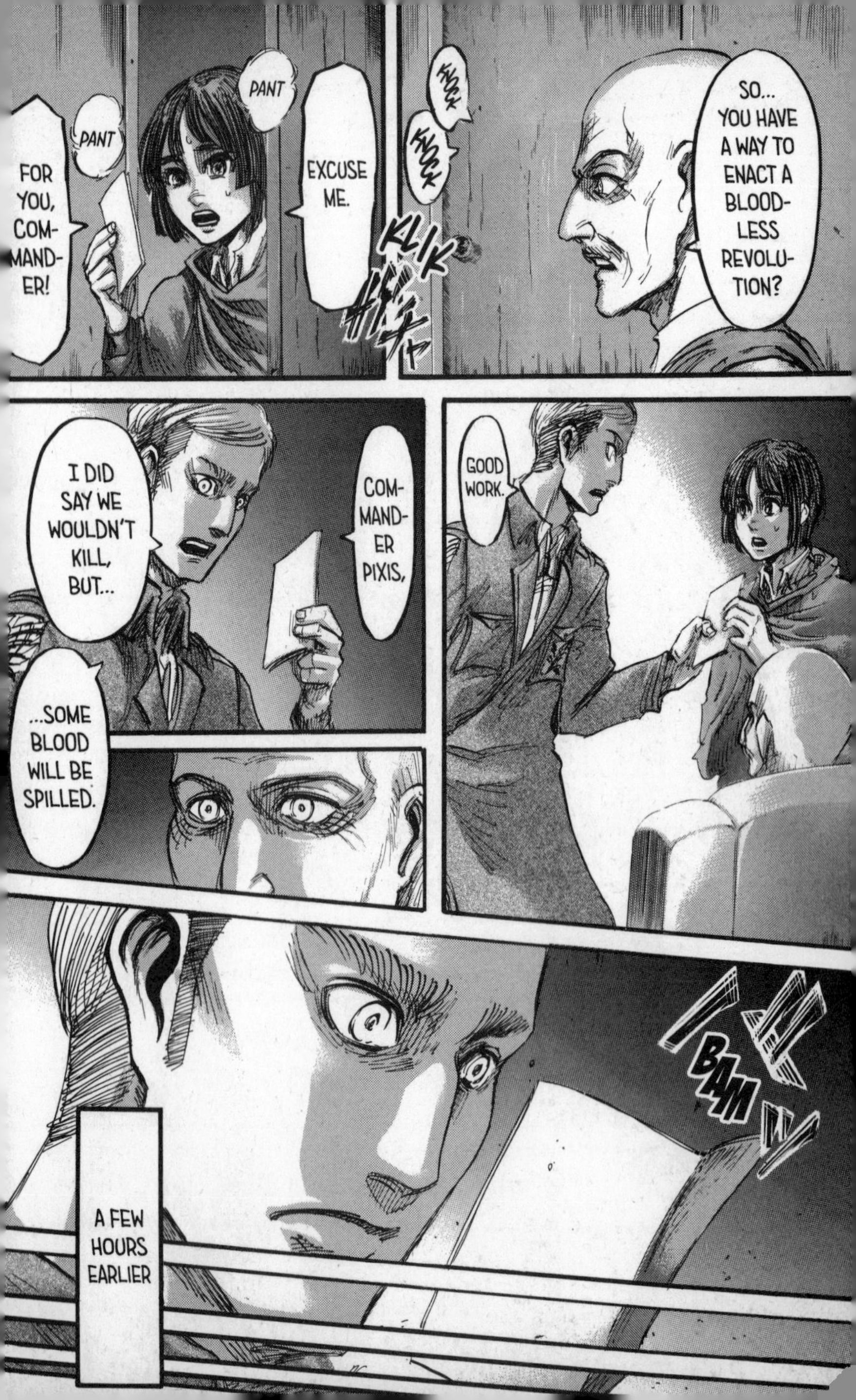
SO... YOU HAVE A WAY TO ENACT A BLOODLESS REVOLUTION?
KNOCK
KNOCK
KLIK
PANT
EXCUSE ME.
PANT
FOR YOU, COMMANDER!
GOOD WORK.
COMMANDER PIXIS,
I DID SAY WE WOULDN'T KILL, BUT...
...SOME BLOOD WILL BE SPILLED.
BAM
A FEW HOURS EARLIER

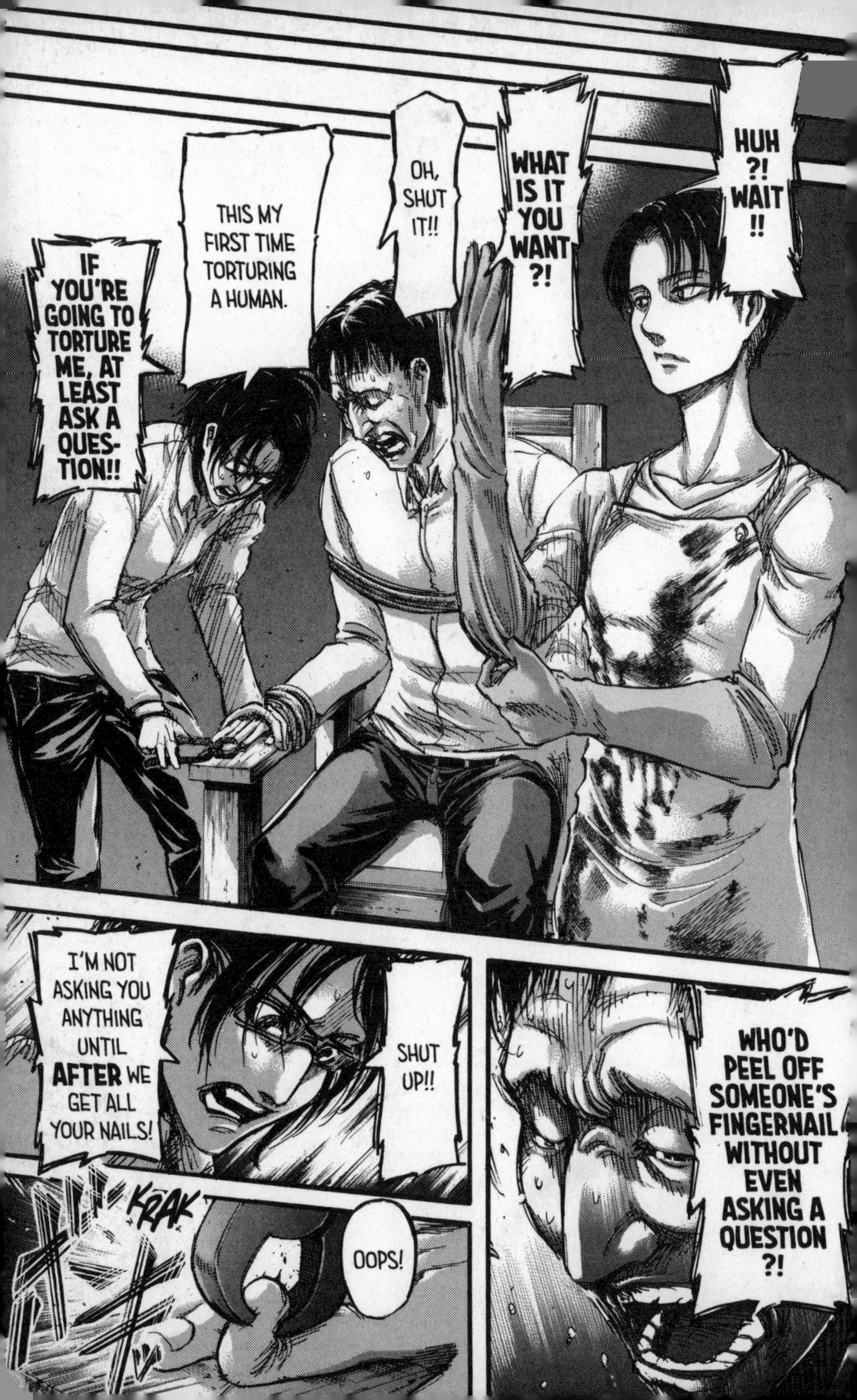
HUH ?! WAIT !!
WHAT IS IT YOU WANT ?!
OH, SHUT IT!!
THIS MY FIRST TIME TORTURING A HUMAN.
IF YOU'RE GOING TO TORTURE ME, AT LEAST ASK A QUES-TION!!
WHO'D PEEL OFF SOMEONE'S FINGERNAIL WITHOUT EVEN ASKING A QUESTION ?!
I'M NOT ASKING YOU ANYTHING UNTIL AFTER WE GET ALL YOUR NAILS!
SHUT UP!!
KRAK
OOPS!

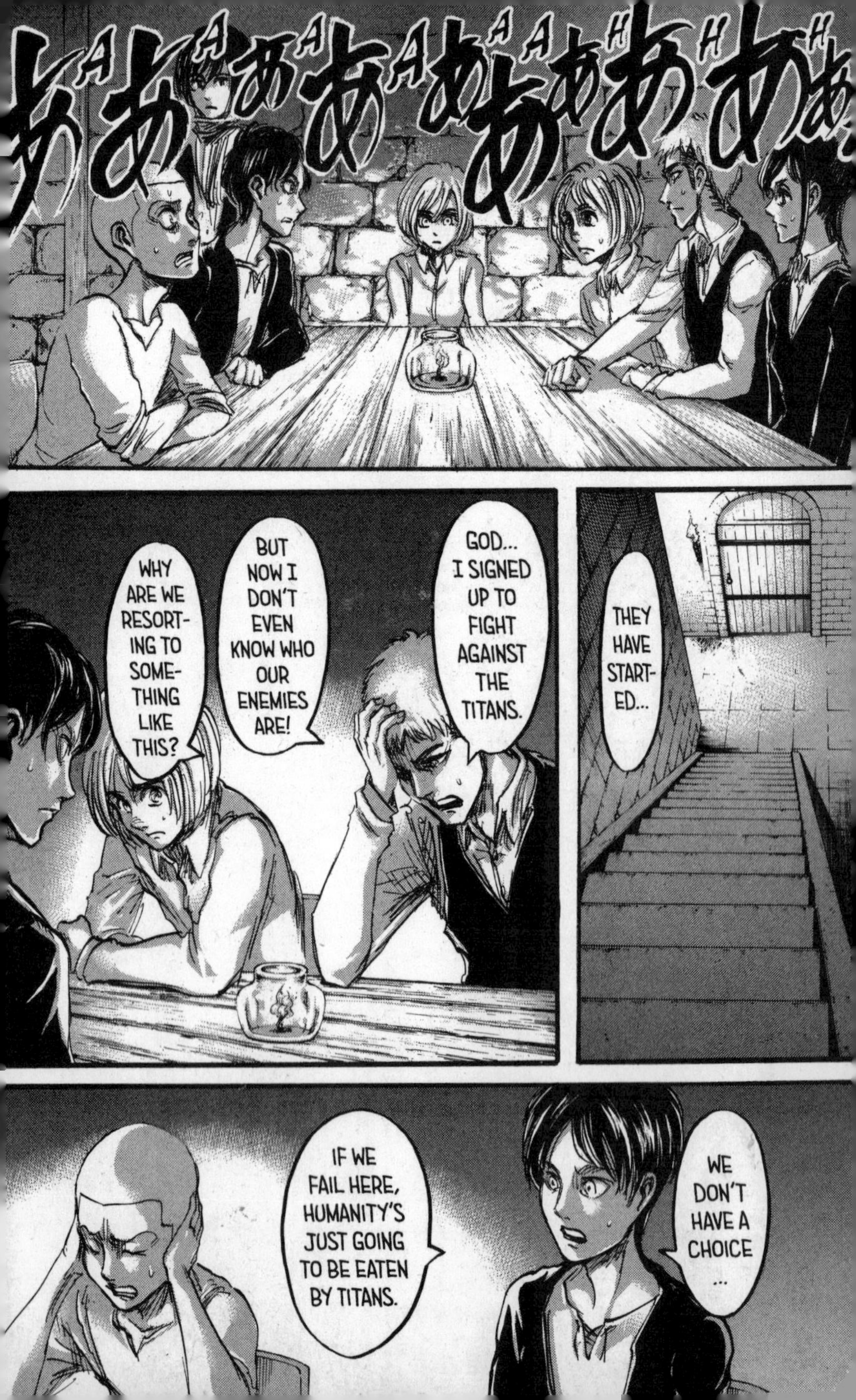
AAAAAAHHH
THEY HAVE STARTED...
GOD... I SIGNED UP TO FIGHT AGAINST THE TITANS.
BUT NOW I DON'T EVEN KNOW WHO OUR ENEMIES ARE!
WHY ARE WE RESORTING TO SOMETHING LIKE THIS?
WE DON'T HAVE A CHOICE...
IF WE FAIL HERE, HUMANITY'S JUST GOING TO BE EATEN BY TITANS.

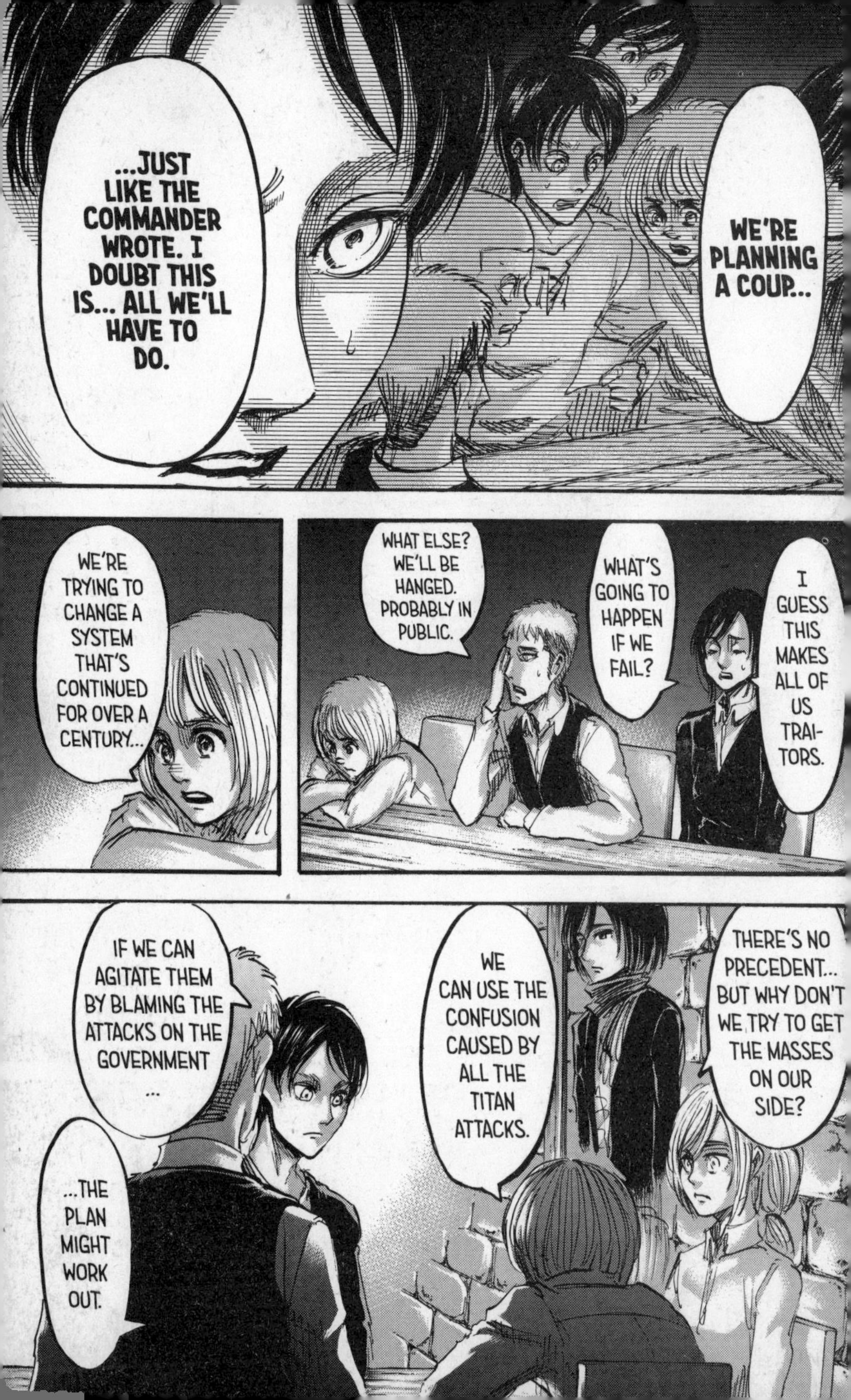
WE'RE PLANNING A COUP...
...JUST LIKE THE COMMANDER WROTE. I DOUBT THIS IS... ALL WE'LL HAVE TO DO.
I GUESS THIS MAKES ALL OF US TRAI-TORS.
WHAT'S GOING TO HAPPEN IF WE FAIL?
WHAT ELSE? WE'LL BE HANGED. PROBABLY IN PUBLIC.
WE'RE TRYING TO CHANGE A SYSTEM THAT'S CONTINUED FOR OVER A CENTURY...
THERE'S NO PRECEDENT... BUT WHY DON'T WE TRY TO GET THE MASSES ON OUR SIDE?
WE CAN USE THE CONFUSION CAUSED BY ALL THE TITAN ATTACKS.
IF WE CAN AGITATE THEM BY BLAMING THE ATTACKS ON THE GOVERNMENT ...
...THE PLAN MIGHT WORK OUT.

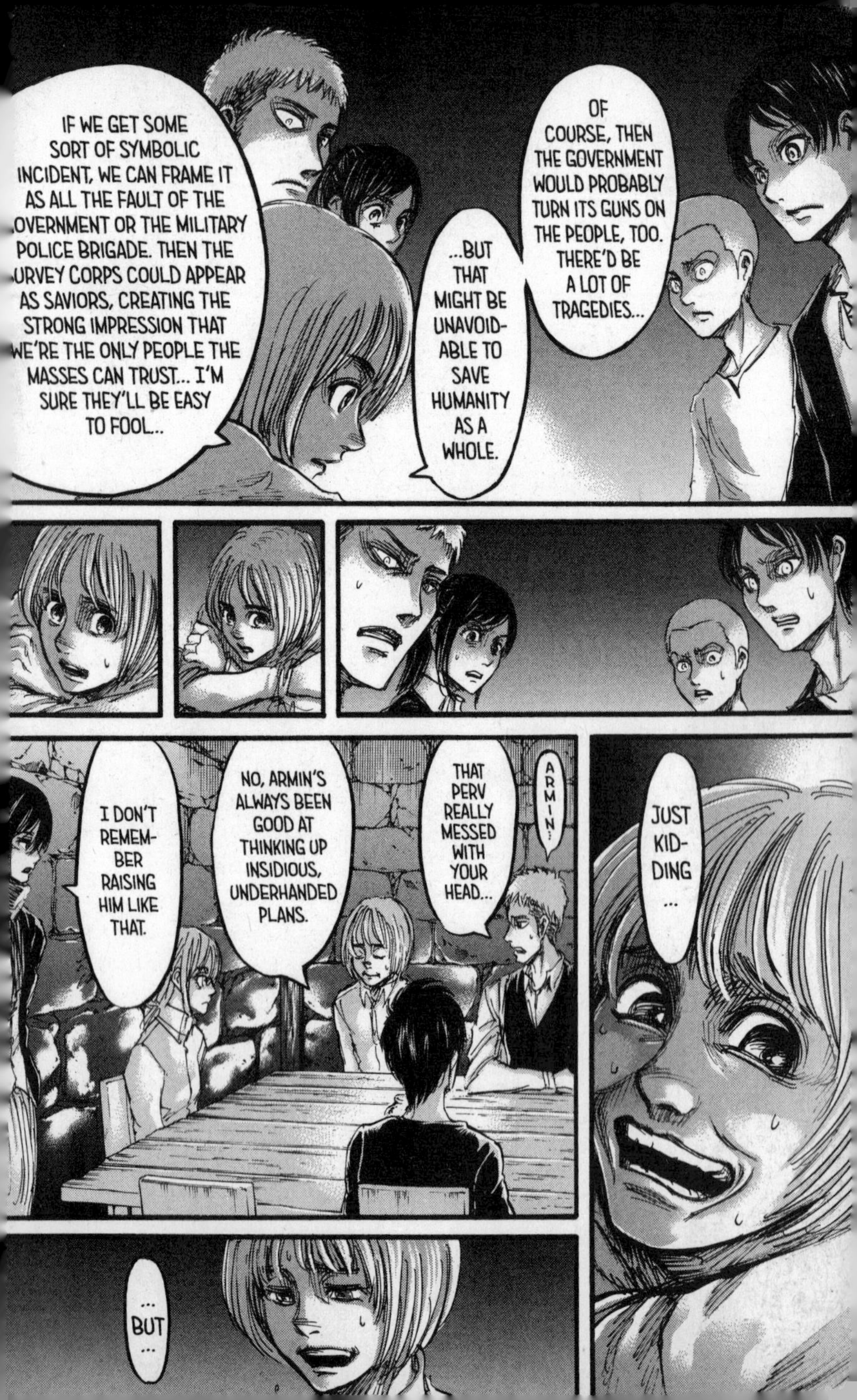
OF COURSE, THEN THE GOVERNMENT WOULD PROBABLY TURN ITS GUNS ON THE PEOPLE, TOO. THERE'D BE A LOT OF TRAGEDIES...
...BUT THAT MIGHT BE UNAVOID-ABLE TO SAVE HUMANITY AS A WHOLE.
IF WE GET SOME SORT OF SYMBOLIC INCIDENT, WE CAN FRAME IT AS ALL THE FAULT OF THE OVERNMENT OR THE MILITARY POLICE BRIGADE. THEN THE URVEY CORPS COULD APPEAR AS SAVIORS, CREATING THE STRONG IMPRESSION THAT WE'RE THE ONLY PEOPLE THE MASSES CAN TRUST... I'M SURE THEY'LL BE EASY TO FOOL...
JUST KID-DING...
ARMIN...?
THAT PERV REALLY MESSED WITH YOUR HEAD...
NO, ARMIN'S ALWAYS BEEN GOOD AT THINKING UP INSIDIOUS, UNDERHANDED PLANS.
I DON'T REMEM-BER RAISING HIM LIKE THAT.
...BUT...

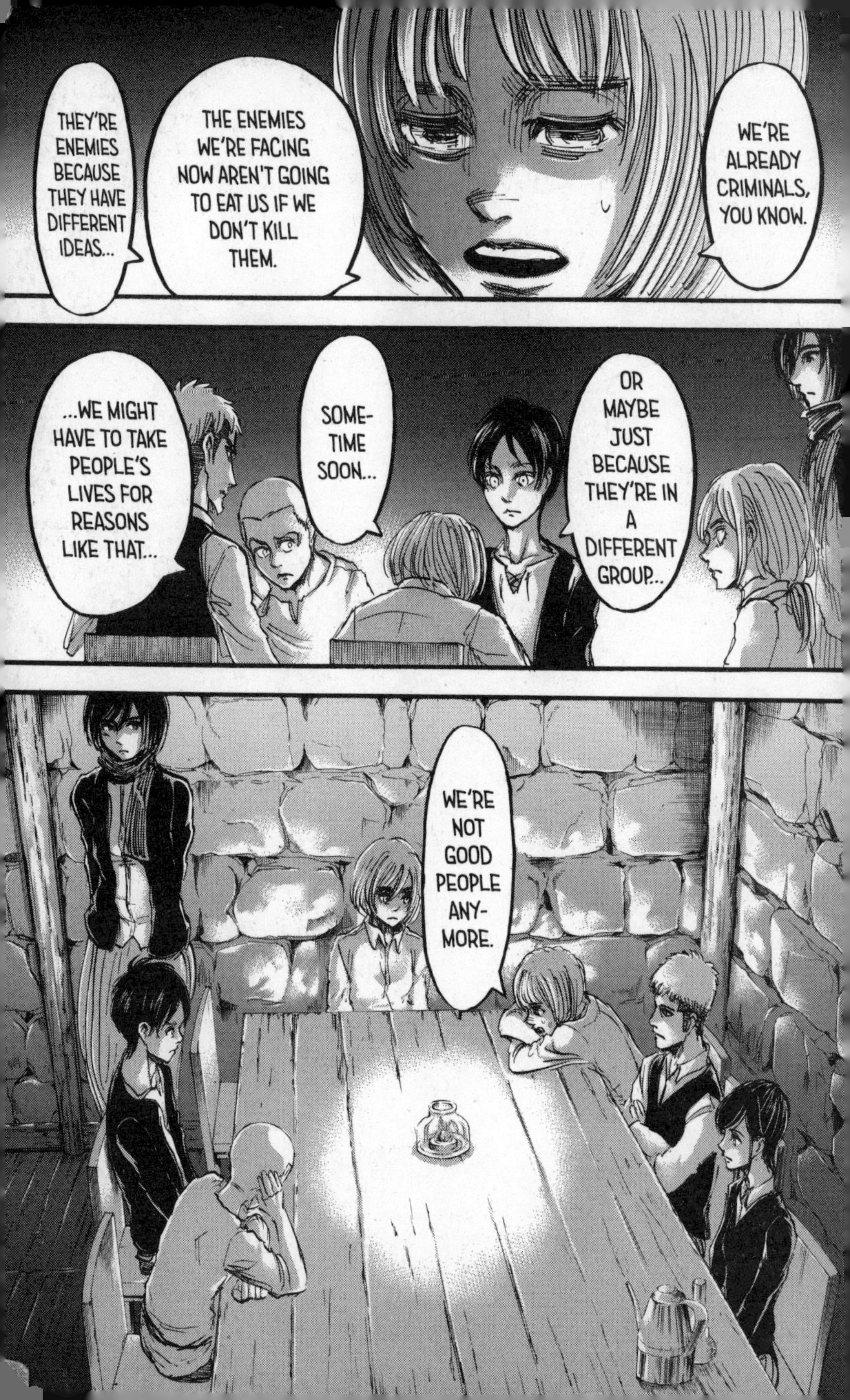
WE'RE ALREADY CRIMINALS, YOU KNOW.
THE ENEMIES WE'RE FACING NOW AREN'T GOING TO EAT US IF WE DON'T KILL THEM.
THEY'RE ENEMIES BECAUSE THEY HAVE DIFFERENT IDEAS...
OR MAYBE JUST BECAUSE THEY'RE IN A DIFFERENT GROUP...
SOME-TIME SOON...
...WE MIGHT HAVE TO TAKE PEOPLE'S LIVES FOR REASONS LIKE THAT...
WE'RE NOT GOOD PEOPLE ANY-MORE.

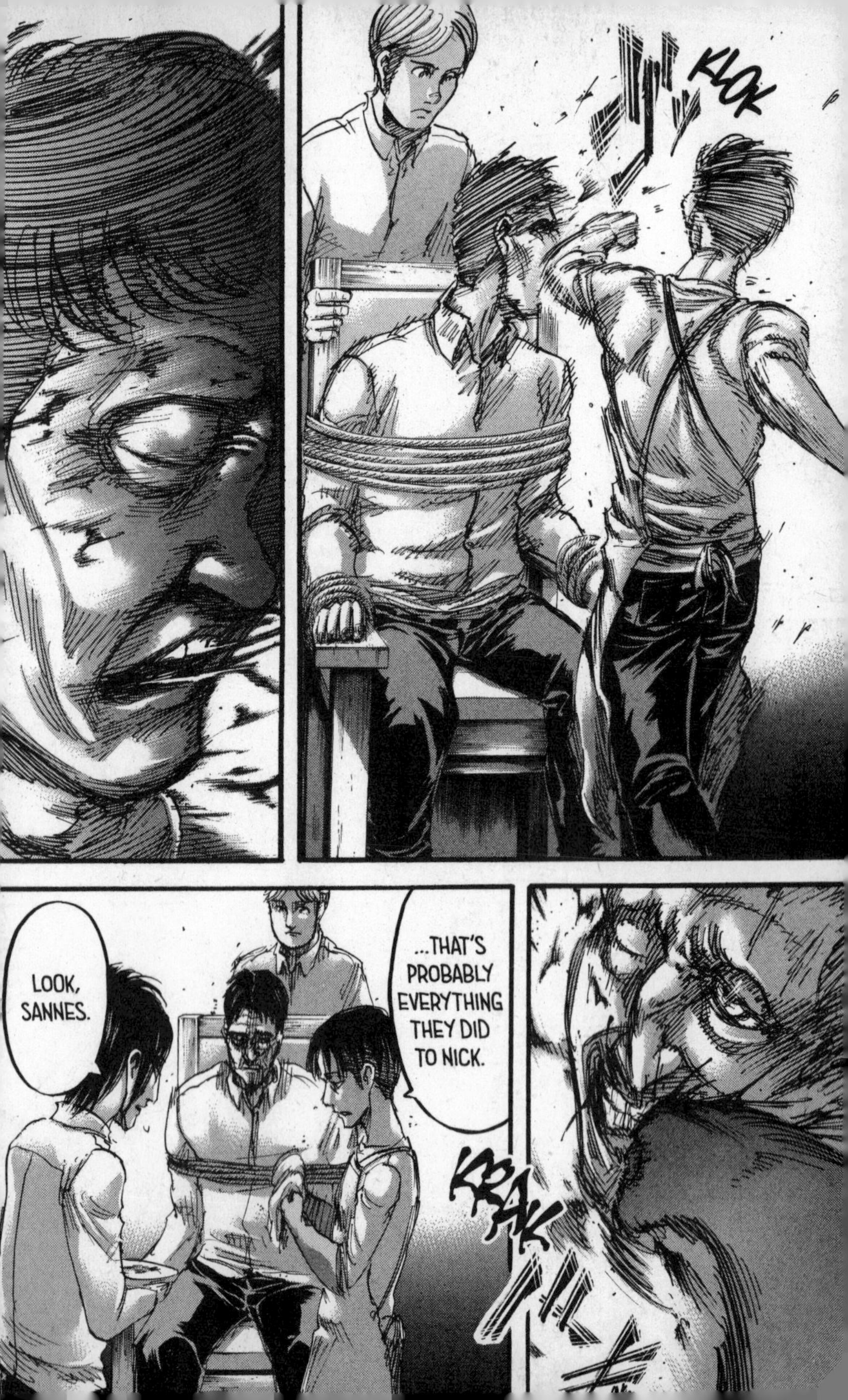
KLOK
KRAK
...THAT'S PROBABLY EVERYTHING THEY DID TO NICK.
LOOK, SANNES.

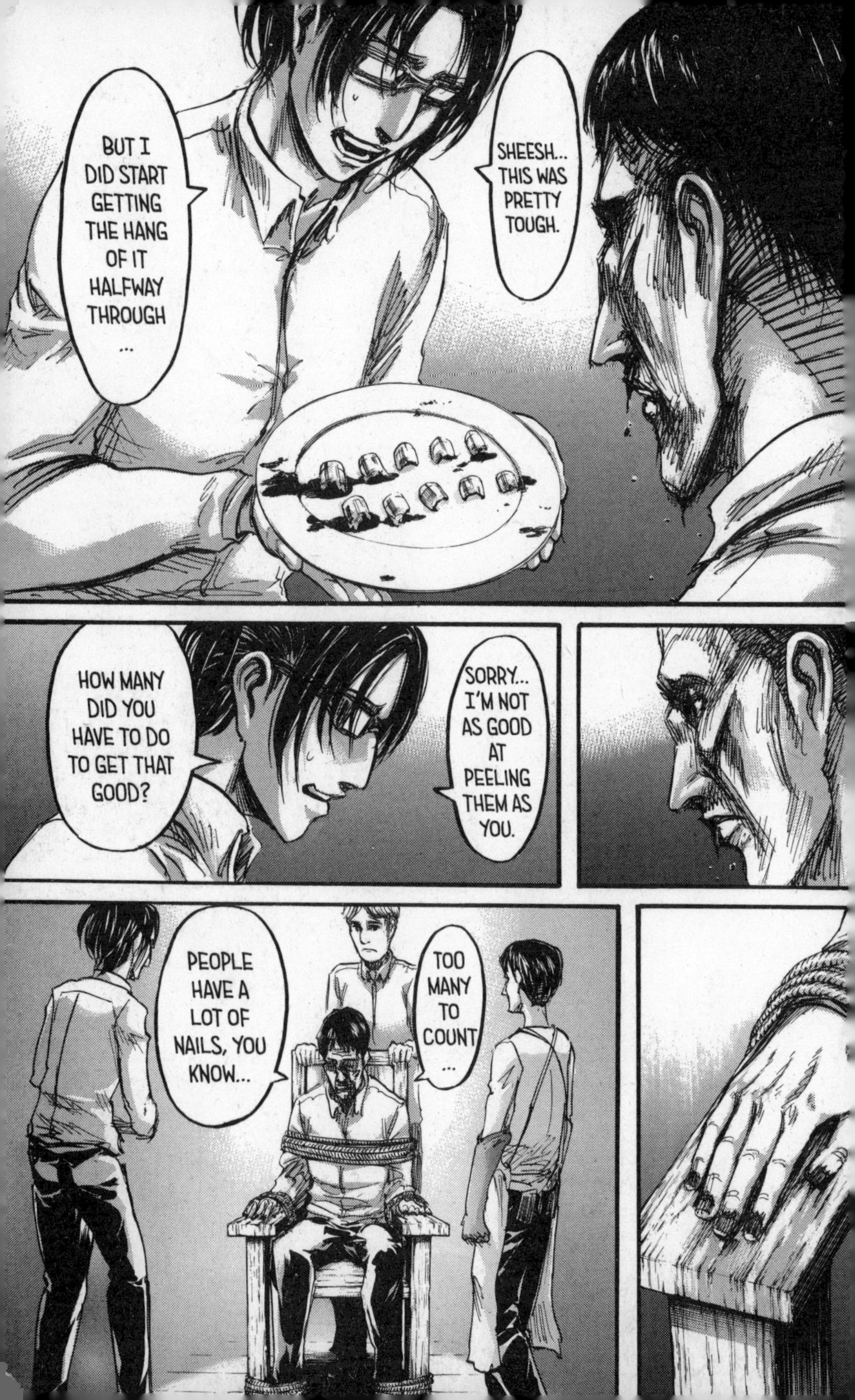
SHEESH... THIS WAS PRETTY TOUGH.
BUT I DID START GETTING THE HANG OF IT HALFWAY THROUGH ...
SORRY... I'M NOT AS GOOD AT PEELING THEM AS YOU.
HOW MANY DID YOU HAVE TO DO TO GET THAT GOOD?
TOO MANY TO COUNT ...
PEOPLE HAVE A LOT OF NAILS, YOU KNOW...

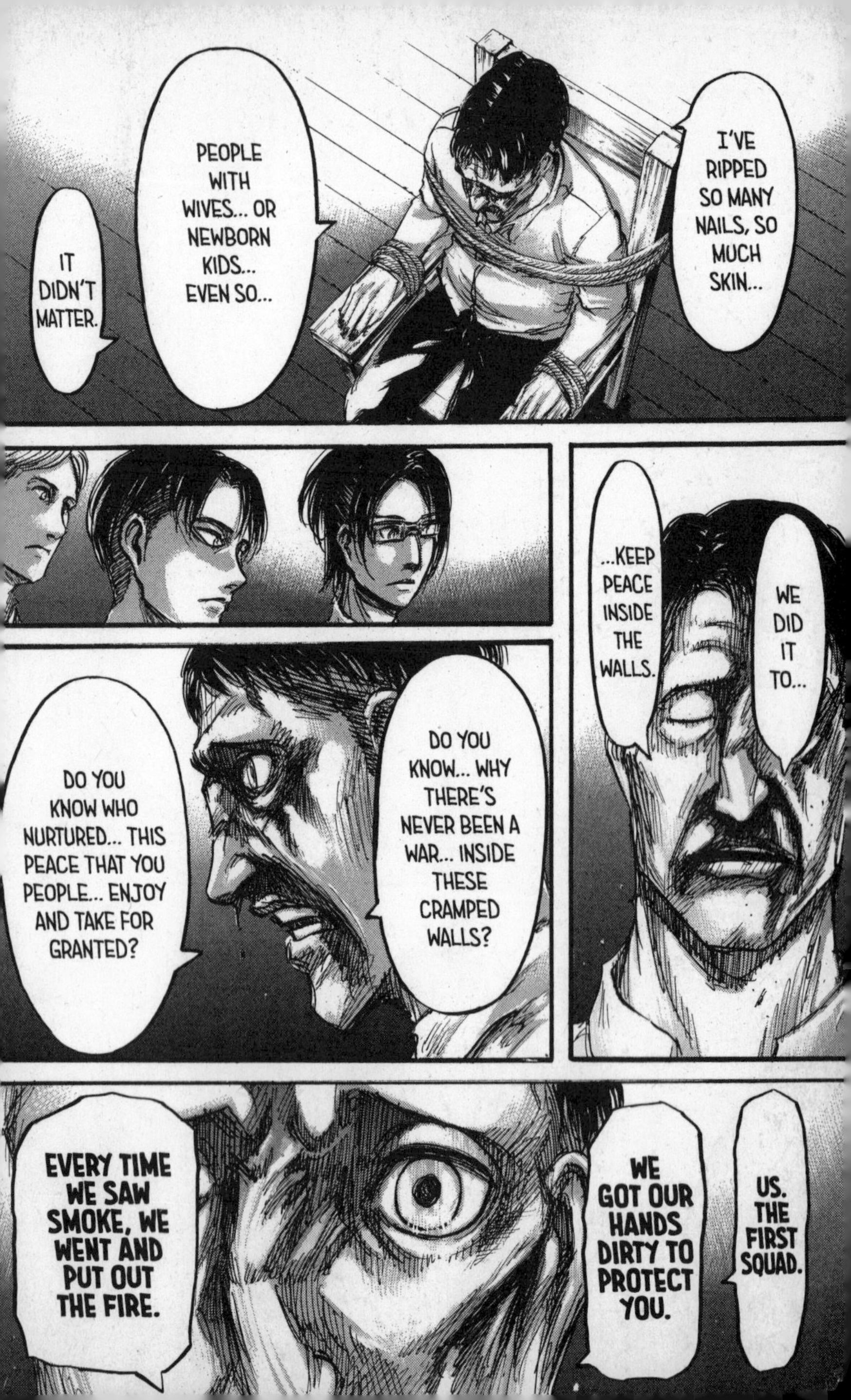
I'VE RIPPED SO MANY NAILS, SO MUCH SKIN...
PEOPLE WITH WIVES... OR NEWBORN KIDS... EVEN SO...
IT DIDN'T MATTER.
WE DID IT TO...
...KEEP PEACE INSIDE THE WALLS.
DO YOU KNOW... WHY THERE'S NEVER BEEN A WAR... INSIDE THESE CRAMPED WALLS?
DO YOU KNOW WHO NURTURED... THIS PEACE THAT YOU PEOPLE... ENJOY AND TAKE FOR GRANTED?
US. THE FIRST SQUAD.
WE GOT OUR HANDS DIRTY TO PROTECT YOU.
EVERY TIME WE SAW SMOKE, WE WENT AND PUT OUT THE FIRE.

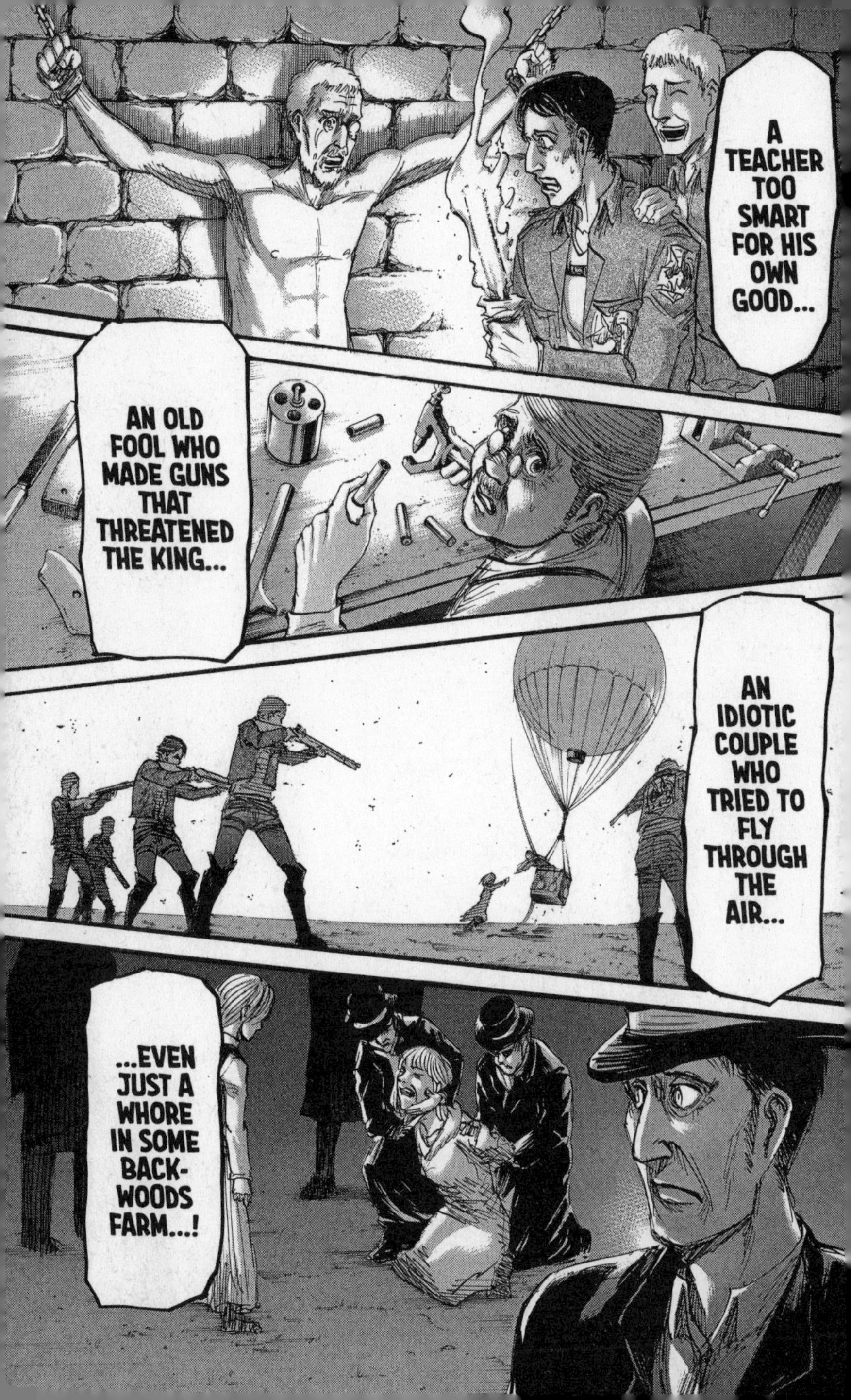
A TEACHER TOO SMART FOR HIS OWN GOOD...
AN OLD FOOL WHO MADE GUNS THAT THREATENED THE KING...
AN IDIOTIC COUPLE WHO TRIED TO FLY THROUGH THE AIR...
...EVEN JUST A WHORE IN SOME BACK-WOODS FARM...!

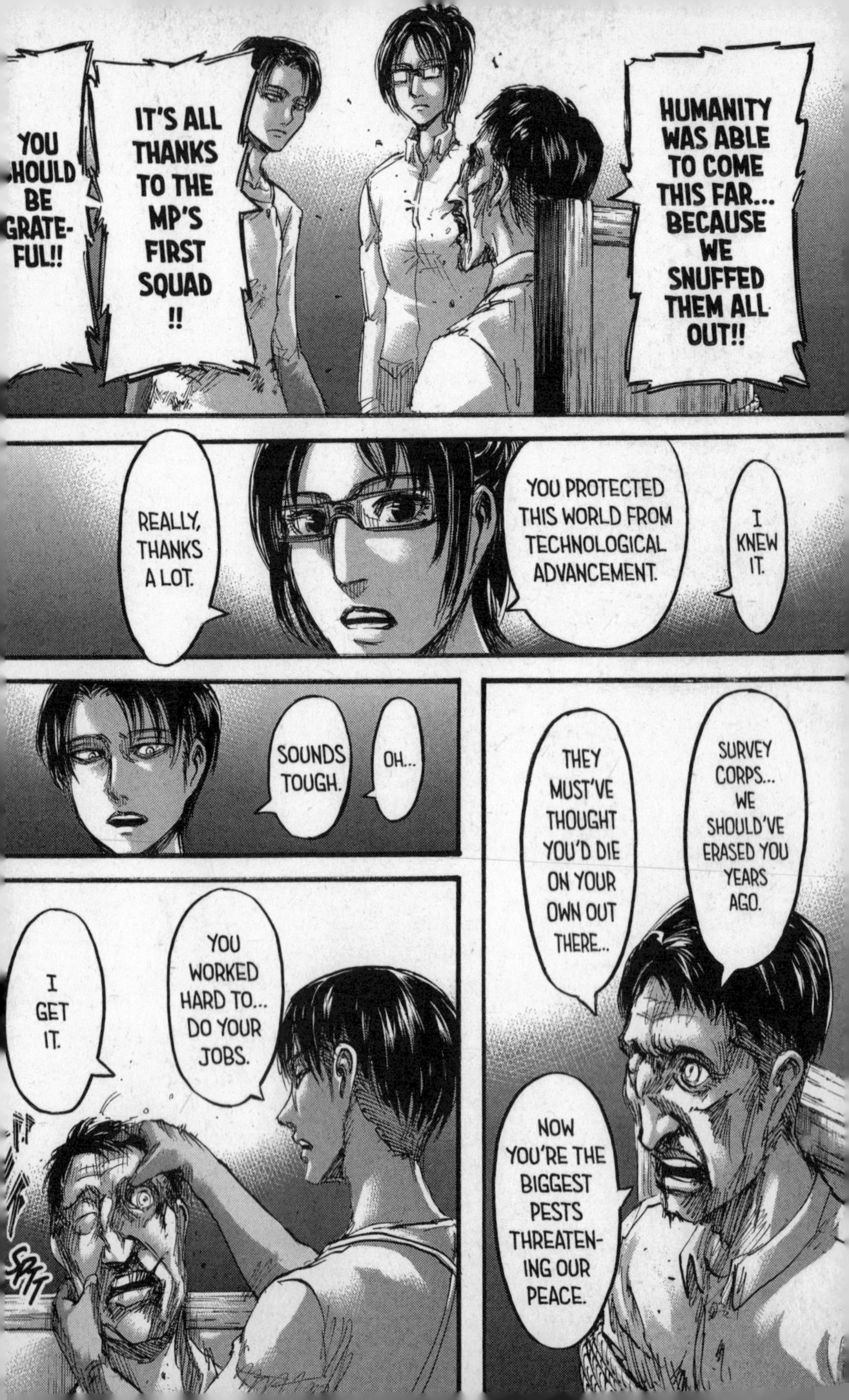
HUMANITY WAS ABLE TO COME THIS FAR... BECAUSE WE SNUFFED THEM ALL OUT!!
IT'S ALL THANKS TO THE MP'S FIRST SQUAD !!
YOU HOULD BE GRATE- FUL!!
I KNEW IT.
YOU PROTECTED THIS WORLD FROM TECHNOLOGICAL ADVANCEMENT.
REALLY, THANKS A LOT.
SURVEY CORPS... WE SHOULD'VE ERASED YOU YEARS AGO.
THEY MUST'VE THOUGHT YOU'D DIE ON YOUR OWN OUT THERE...
NOW YOU'RE THE BIGGEST PESTS THREATEN- ING OUR PEACE.
OH...
SOUNDS TOUGH.
YOU WORKED HARD TO... DO YOUR JOBS.
I GET IT.

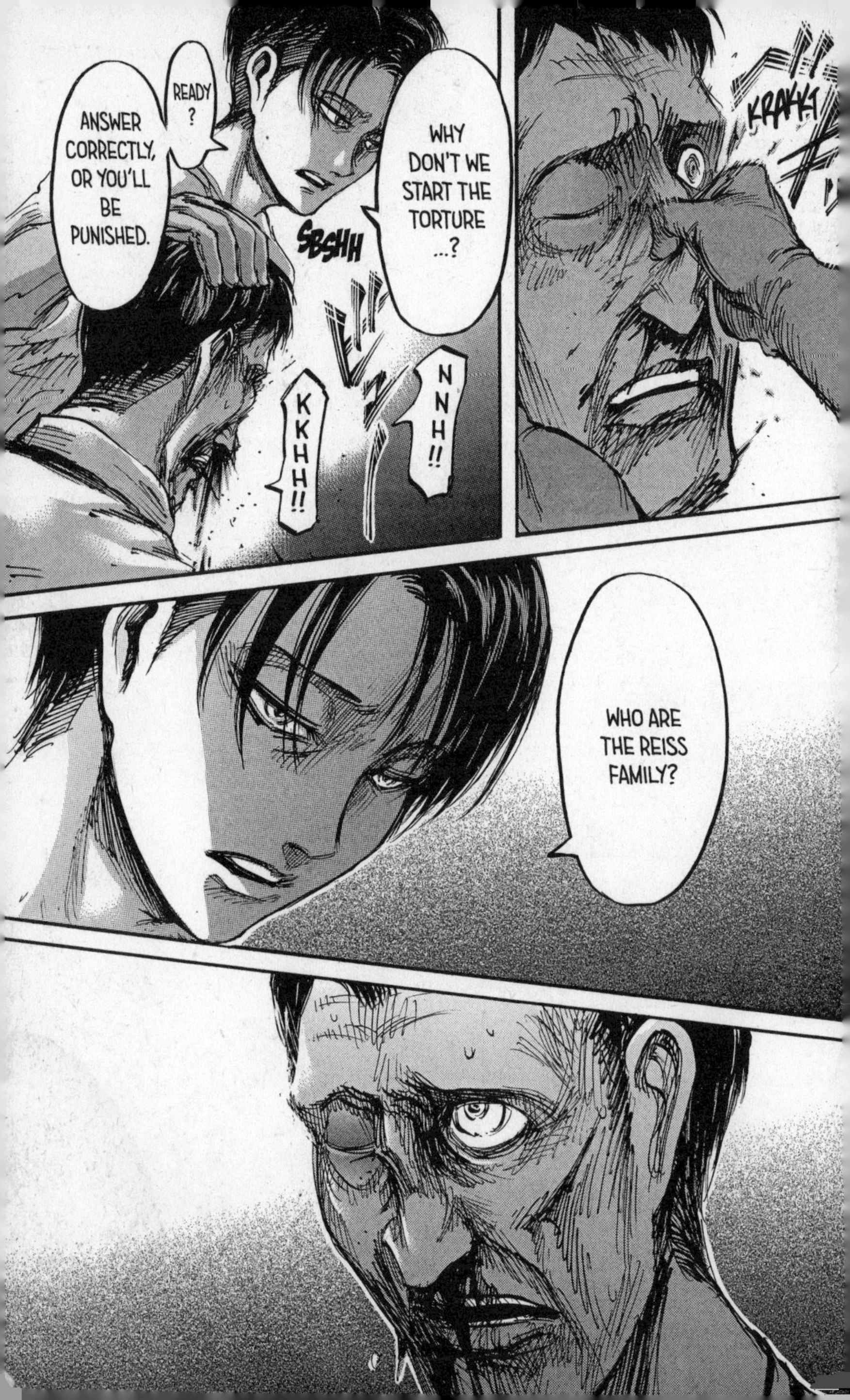
KRAKK!
WHY DON'T WE START THE TORTURE ...?
READY?
ANSWER CORRECTLY, OR YOU'LL BE PUNISHED.
SBSHH
NNH!!
KKHH!!
WHO ARE THE REISS FAMILY?

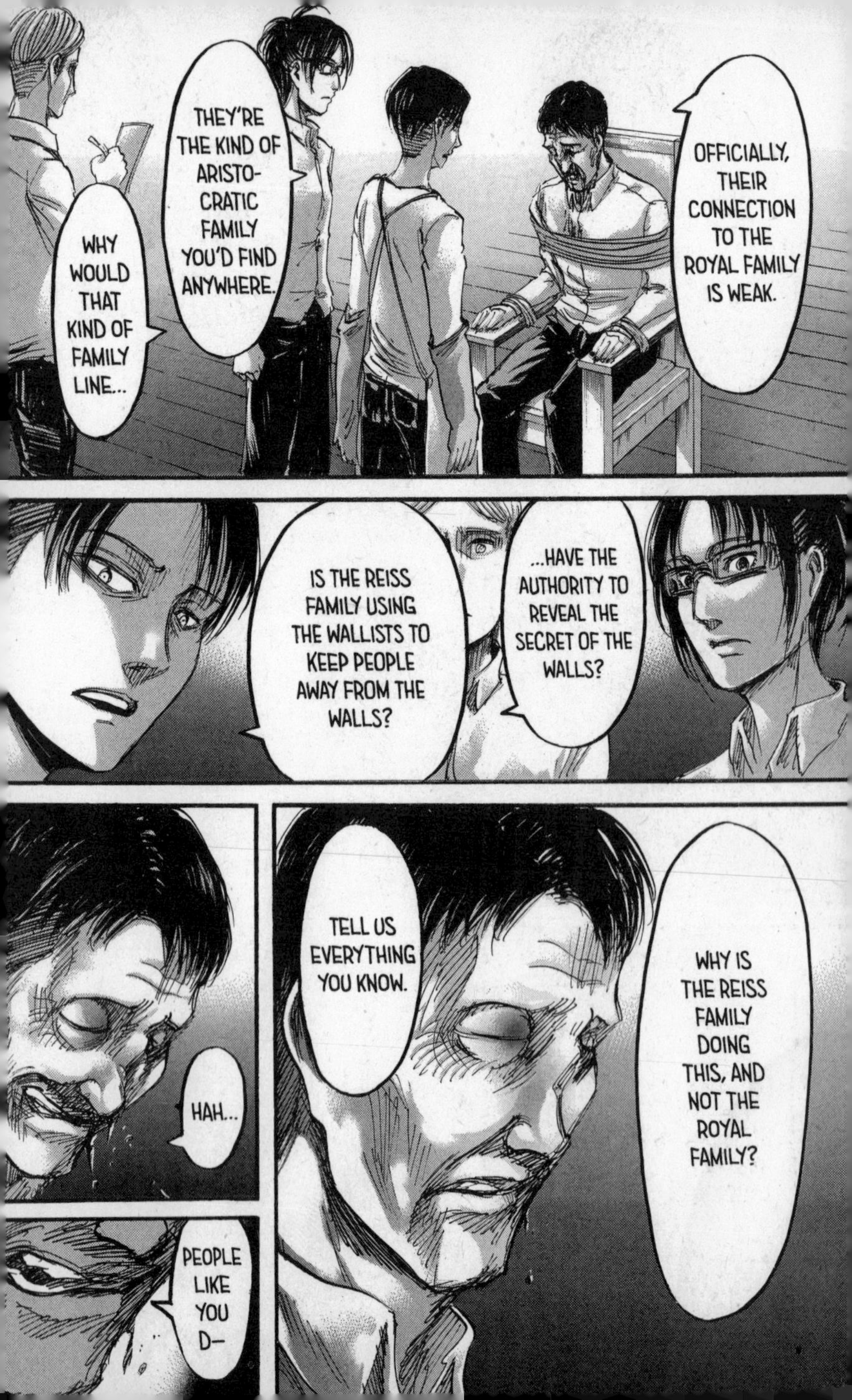
OFFICIALLY, THEIR CONNECTION TO THE ROYAL FAMILY IS WEAK.
THEY'RE THE KIND OF ARISTO-CRATIC FAMILY YOU'D FIND ANYWHERE.
WHY WOULD THAT KIND OF FAMILY LINE...
...HAVE THE AUTHORITY TO REVEAL THE SECRET OF THE WALLS?
IS THE REISS FAMILY USING THE WALLISTS TO KEEP PEOPLE AWAY FROM THE WALLS?
WHY IS THE REISS FAMILY DOING THIS, AND NOT THE ROYAL FAMILY?
TELL US EVERYTHING YOU KNOW.
HAH...
PEOPLE LIKE YOU D–

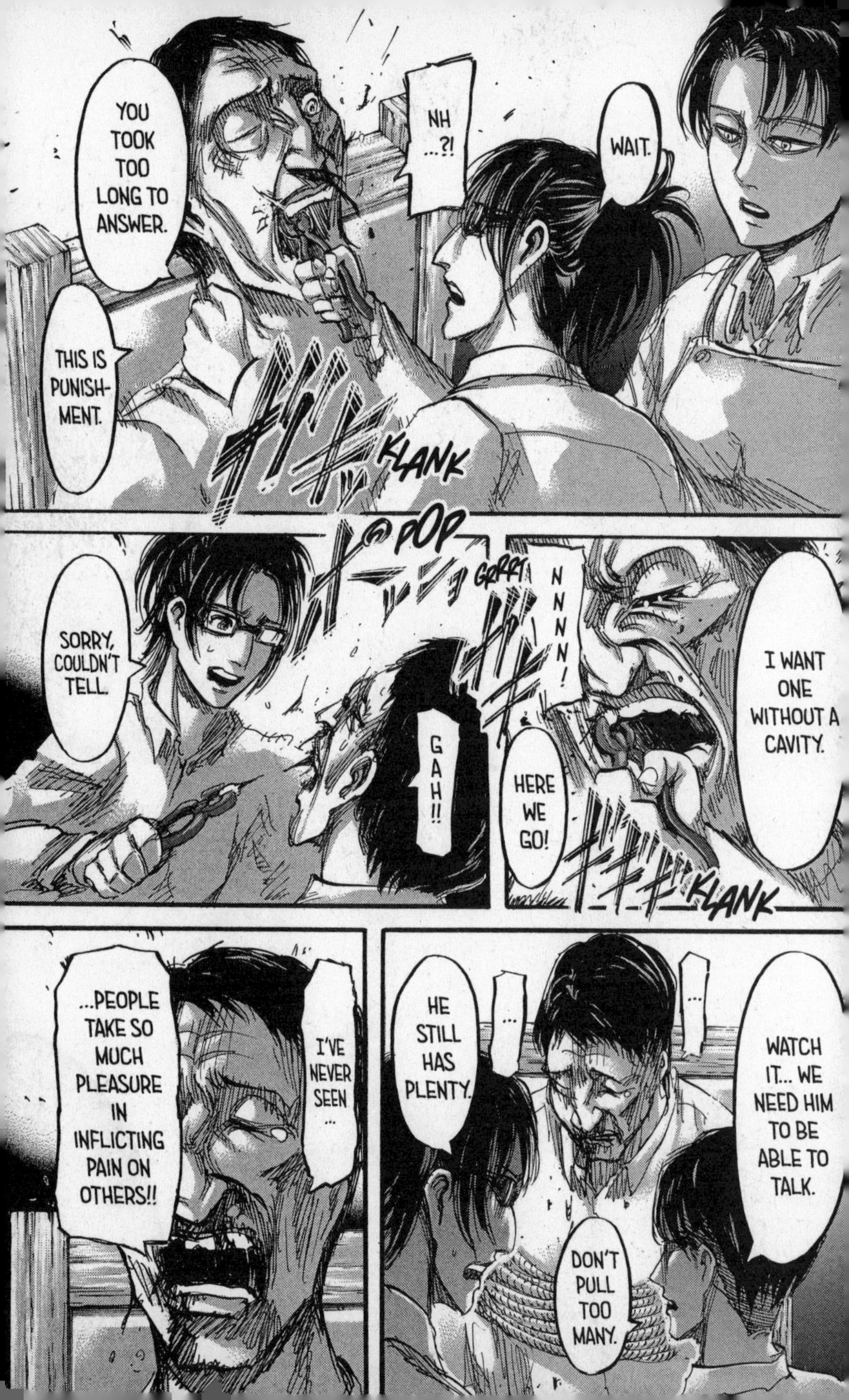
WAIT.
NH ...?!
YOU TOOK TOO LONG TO ANSWER.
THIS IS PUNISH-MENT.
KLANK
I WANT ONE WITHOUT A CAVITY.
NNNN!
GRRRT
HERE WE GO!
KLANK
POP
GAH!!
SORRY, COULDN'T TELL.
WATCH IT... WE NEED HIM TO BE ABLE TO TALK.
...
...
HE STILL HAS PLENTY.
DON'T PULL TOO MANY.
I'VE NEVER SEEN ...
...PEOPLE TAKE SO MUCH PLEASURE IN INFLICTING PAIN ON OTHERS!!

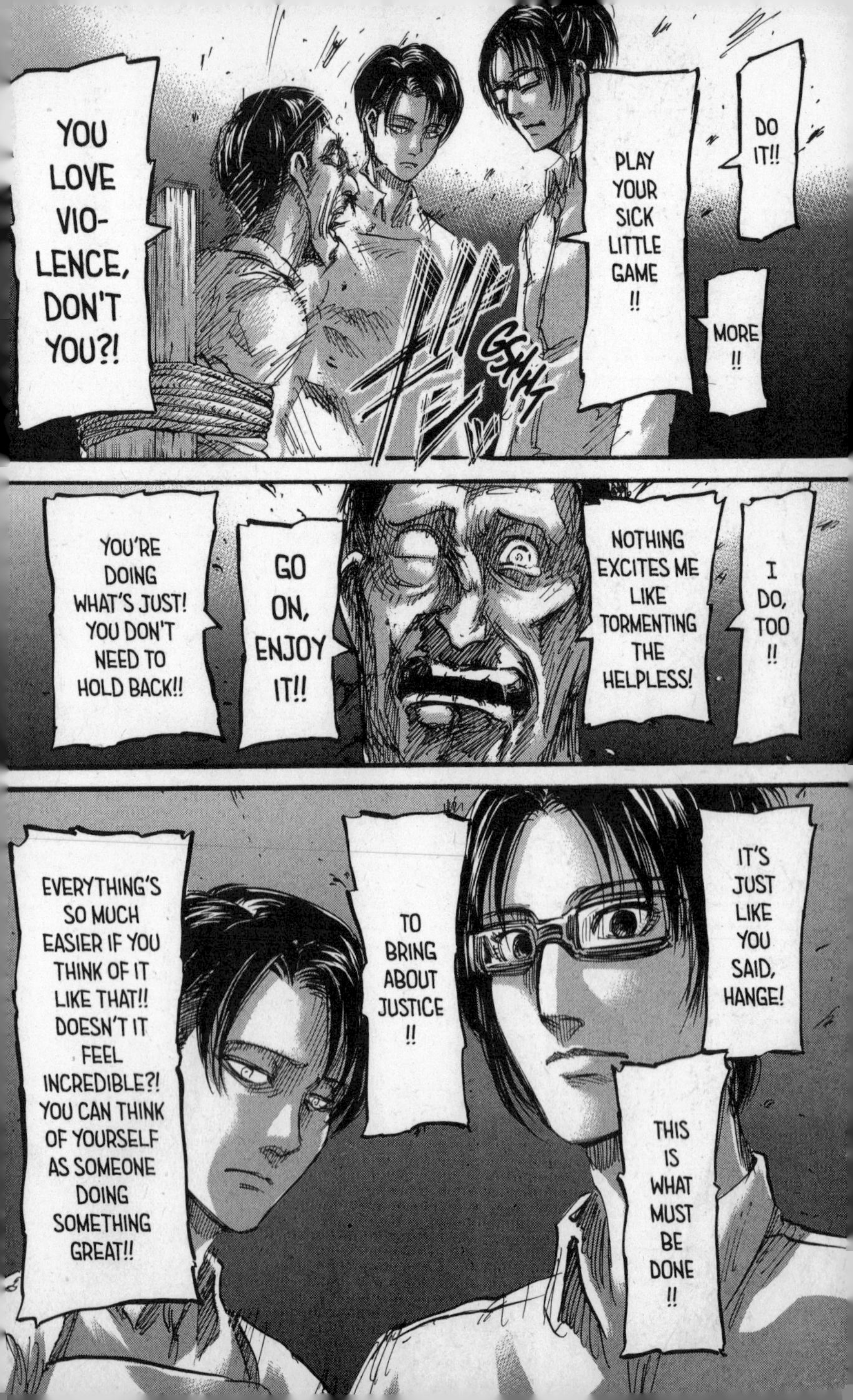
DO IT!!
MORE !!
PLAY YOUR SICK LITTLE GAME !!
YOU LOVE VIO-LENCE, DON'T YOU?!
I DO, TOO !!
NOTHING EXCITES ME LIKE TORMENTING THE HELPLESS!
GO ON, ENJOY IT!!
YOU'RE DOING WHAT'S JUST! YOU DON'T NEED TO HOLD BACK!!
IT'S JUST LIKE YOU SAID, HANGE!
THIS IS WHAT MUST BE DONE !!
TO BRING ABOUT JUSTICE !!
EVERYTHING'S SO MUCH EASIER IF YOU THINK OF IT LIKE THAT!! DOESN'T IT FEEL INCREDIBLE?! YOU CAN THINK OF YOURSELF AS SOMEONE DOING SOMETHING GREAT!!

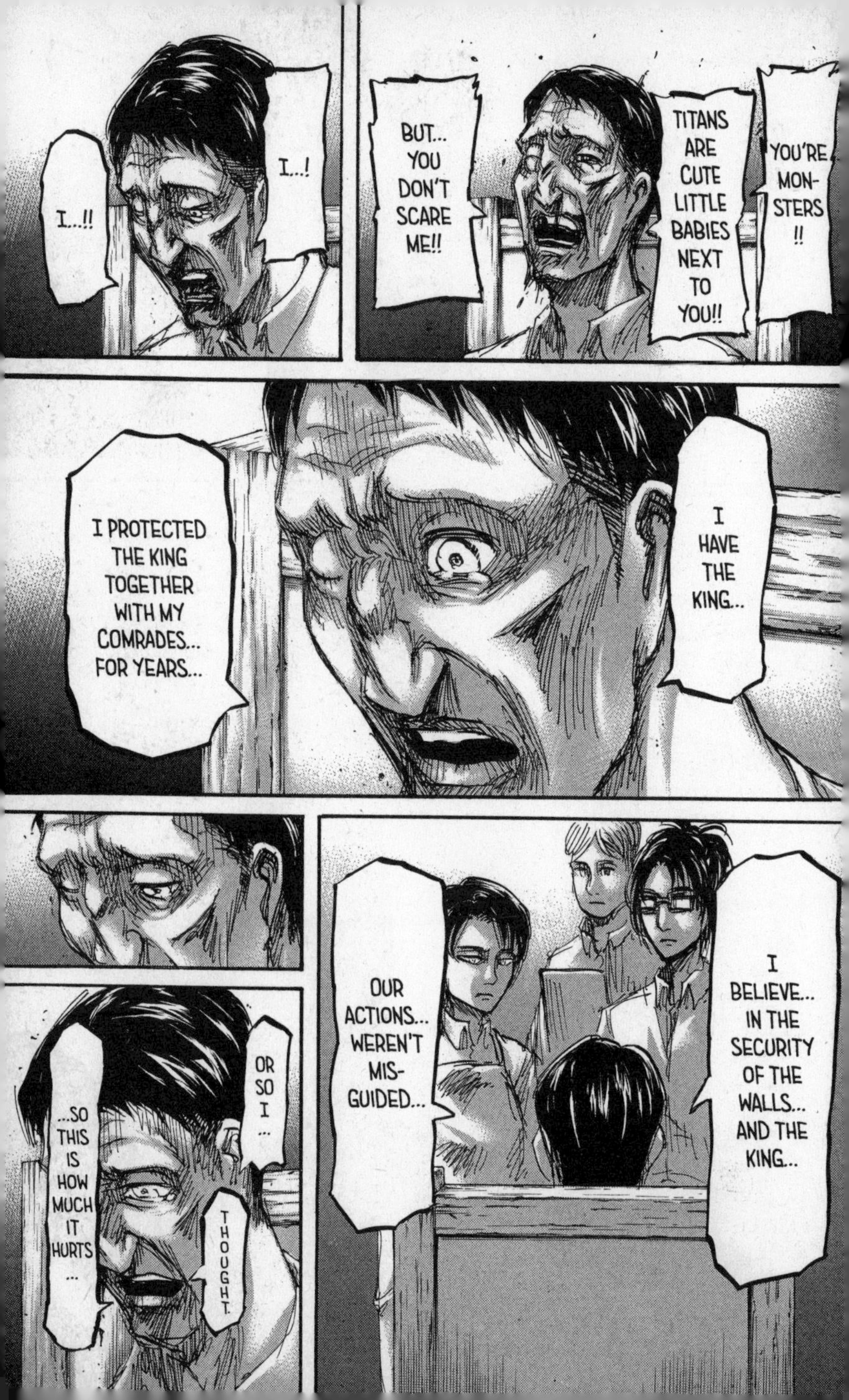
YOU'RE MONSTERS!!
TITANS ARE CUTE LITTLE BABIES NEXT TO YOU!!
BUT... YOU DON'T SCARE ME!!
I...!
I...!!
I HAVE THE KING...
I PROTECTED THE KING TOGETHER WITH MY COMRADES... FOR YEARS...
I BELIEVE... IN THE SECURITY OF THE WALLS... AND THE KING...
OUR ACTIONS... WEREN'T MIS-GUIDED...
OR SO I ...
THOUGHT.
...SO THIS IS HOW MUCH IT HURTS...

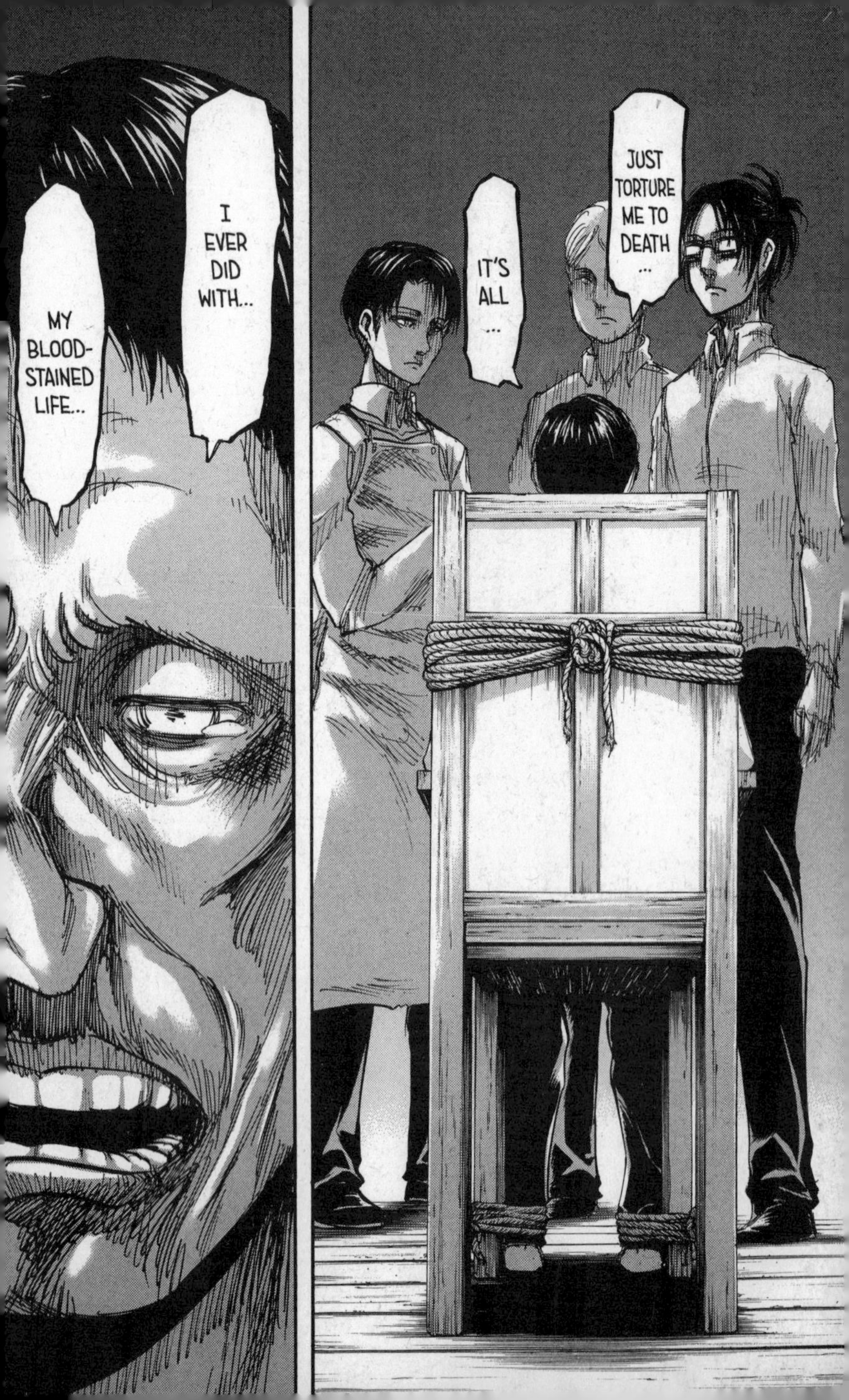
JUST TORTURE ME TO DEATH ...
IT'S ALL ...
I EVER DID WITH...
MY BLOOD-STAINED LIFE...

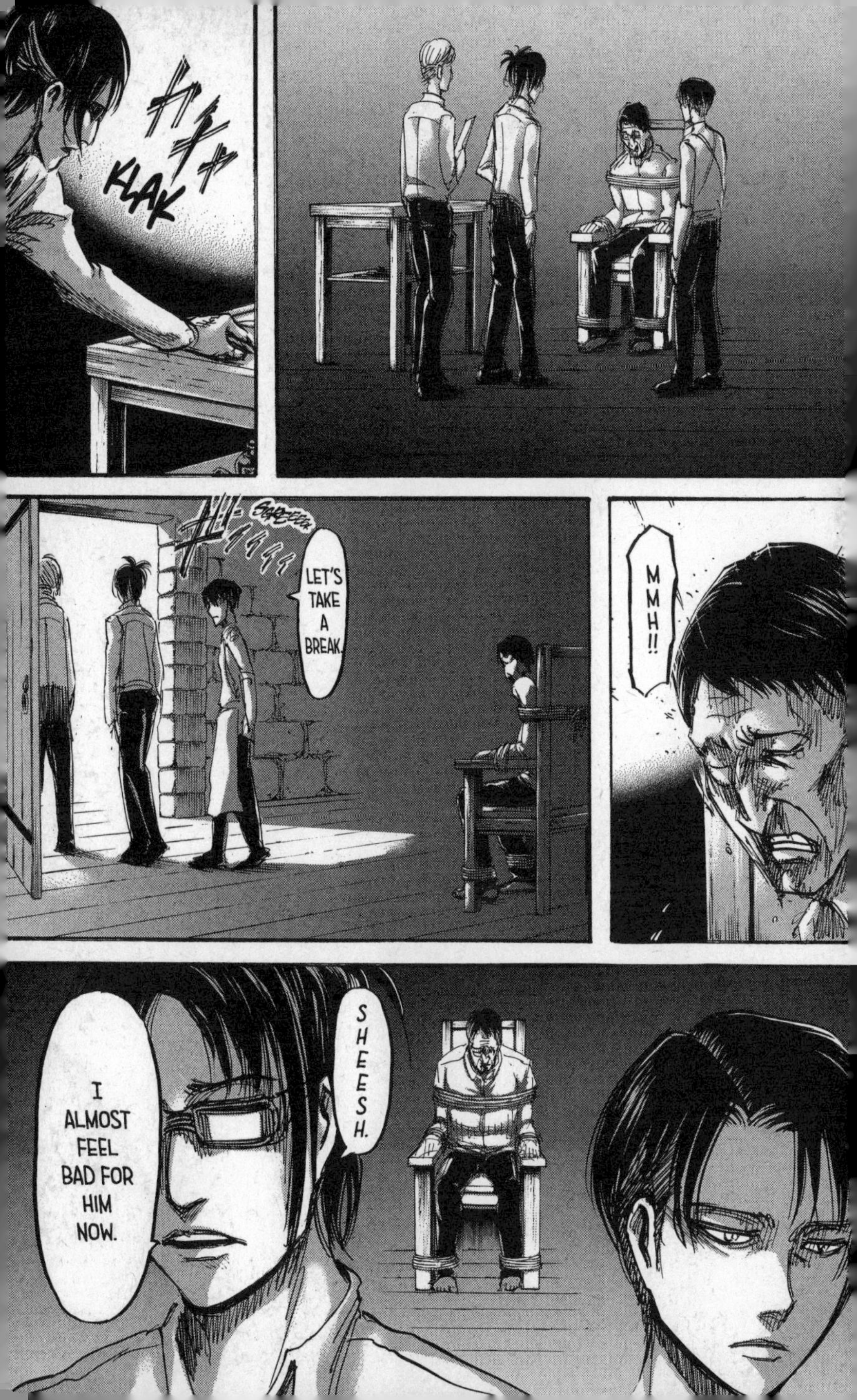
KLAK
MMH!!
LET'S TAKE A BREAK.
SHEESH.
I ALMOST FEEL BAD FOR HIM NOW.

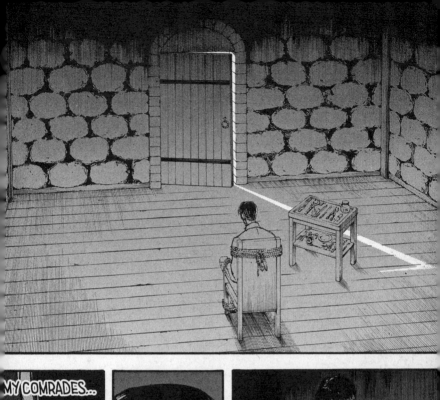

MY COMRADES...

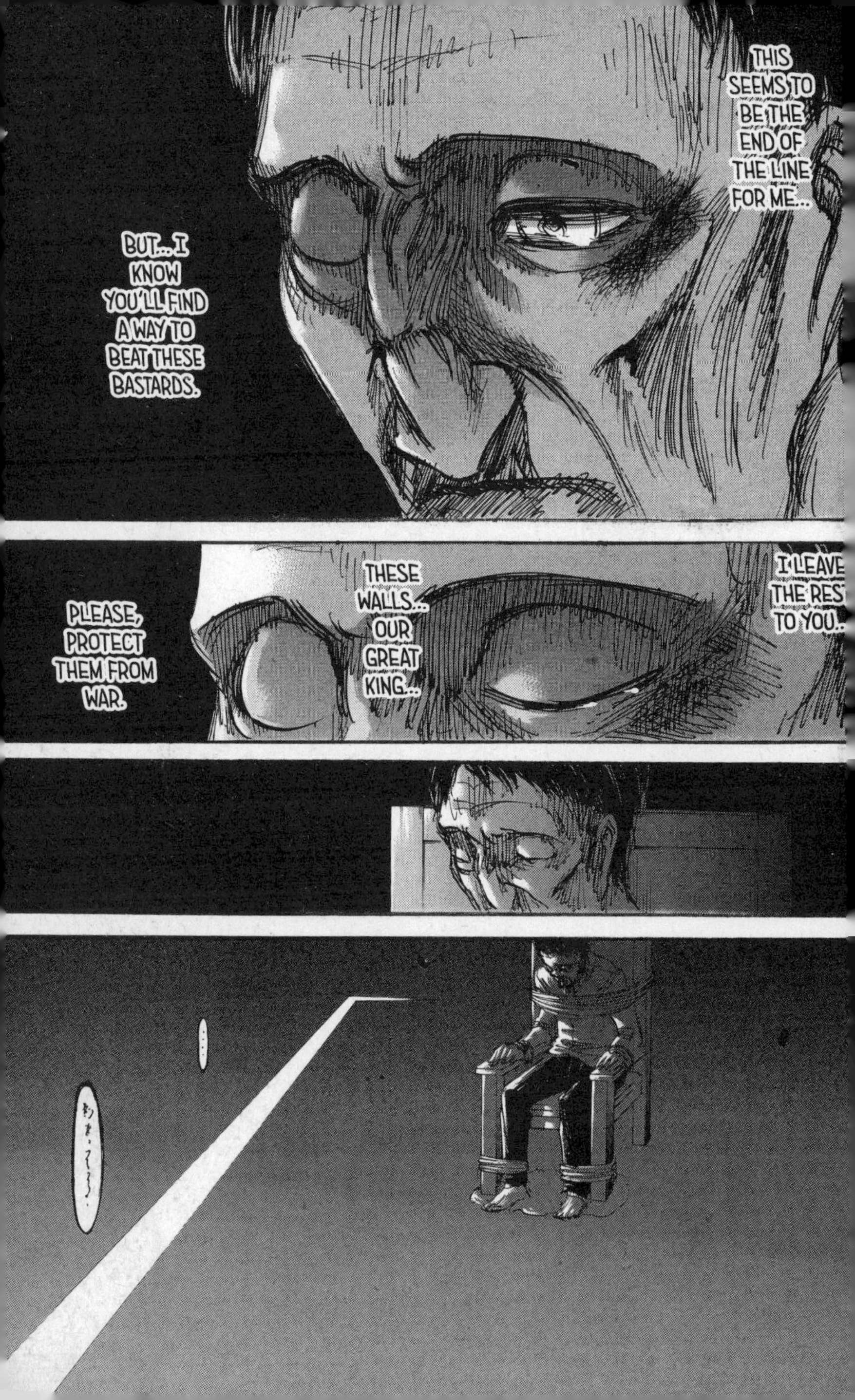
THIS SEEMS TO BE THE END OF THE LINE FOR ME...
BUT... I KNOW YOU'LL FIND A WAY TO BEAT THESE BASTARDS.
I LEAVE THE REST TO YOU...
THESE WALLS... OUR GREAT KING...
PLEASE, PROTECT THEM FROM WAR.
...

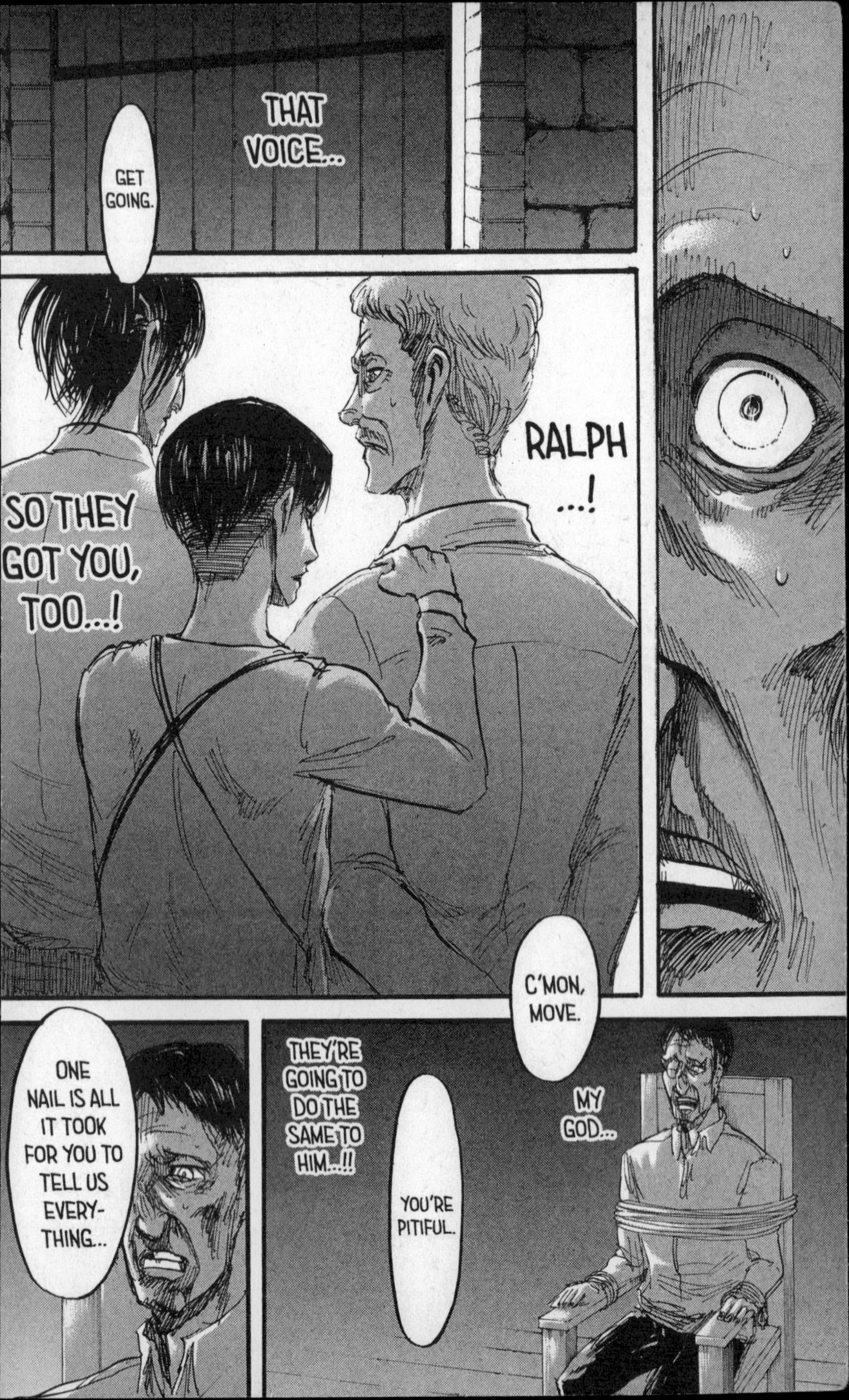
THAT VOICE...
GET GOING.
RALPH ...!
SO THEY GOT YOU, TOO...!
C'MON, MOVE.
MY GOD...
THEY'RE GOING TO DO THE SAME TO HIM...!!
YOU'RE PITIFUL.
ONE NAIL IS ALL IT TOOK FOR YOU TO TELL US EVERY-THING...

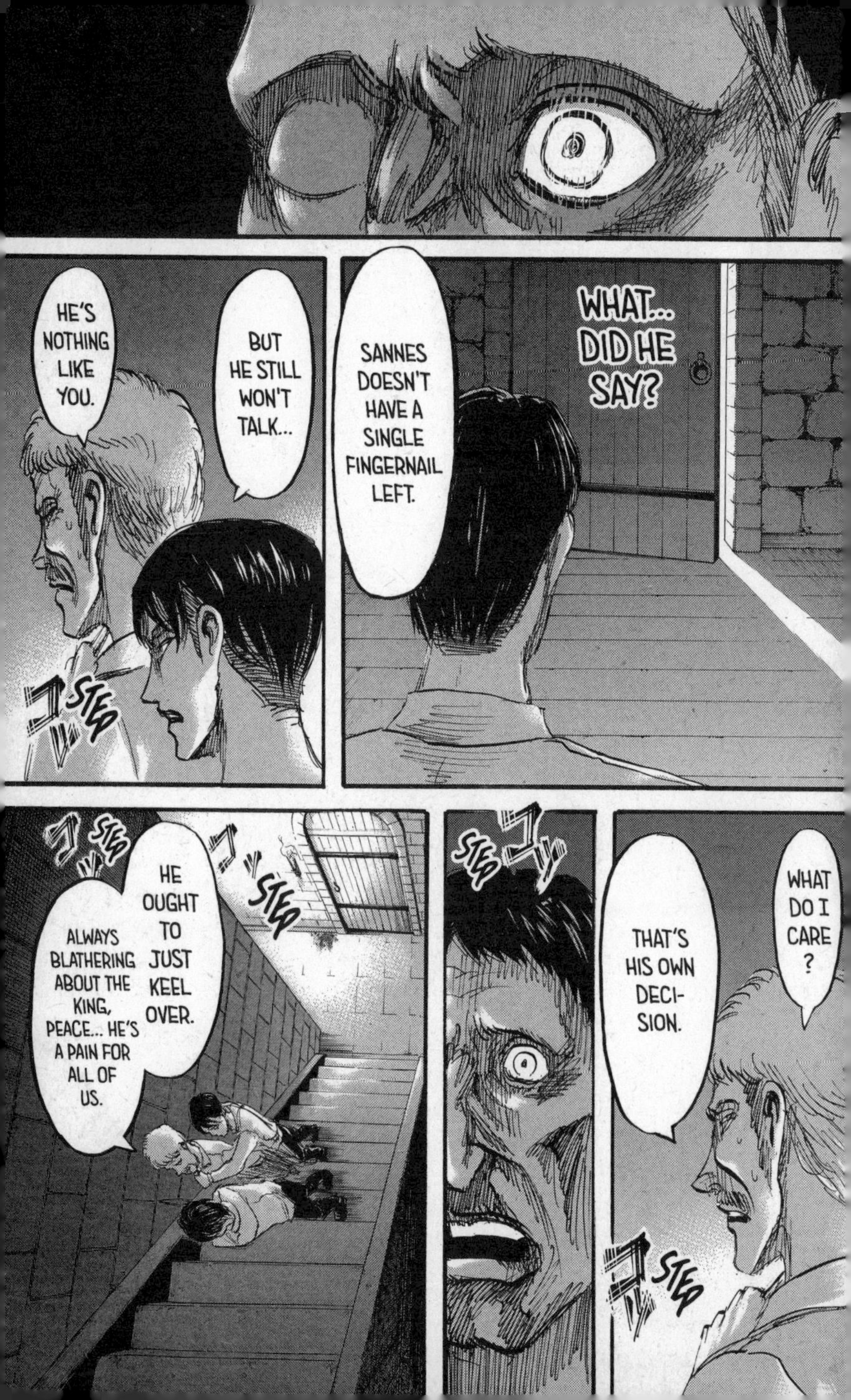
WHAT... DID HE SAY?
SANNES DOESN'T HAVE A SINGLE FINGERNAIL LEFT.
BUT HE STILL WON'T TALK...
HE'S NOTHING LIKE YOU.
STEP
WHAT DO I CARE?
THAT'S HIS OWN DECI-SION.
STEP
STEP
HE OUGHT TO JUST KEEL OVER.
ALWAYS BLATHERING ABOUT THE KING, PEACE... HE'S A PAIN FOR ALL OF US.
STEP
STEP

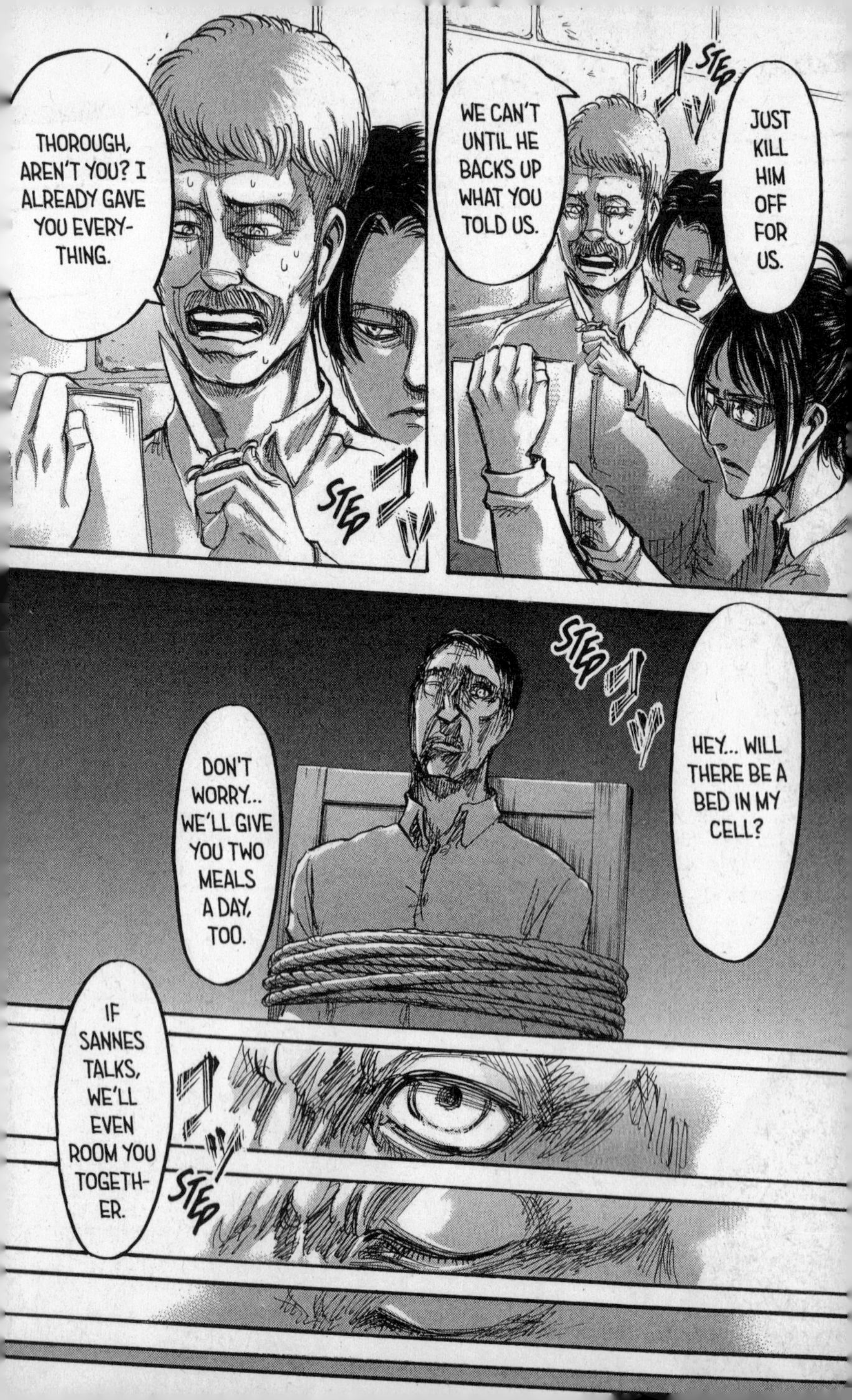
STEP
JUST KILL HIM OFF FOR US.
WE CAN'T UNTIL HE BACKS UP WHAT YOU TOLD US.
THOROUGH, AREN'T YOU? I ALREADY GAVE YOU EVERY-THING.
STEP
STEP
HEY... WILL THERE BE A BED IN MY CELL?
DON'T WORRY... WE'LL GIVE YOU TWO MEALS A DAY, TOO.
IF SANNES TALKS, WE'LL EVEN ROOM YOU TOGETH-ER.
STEP

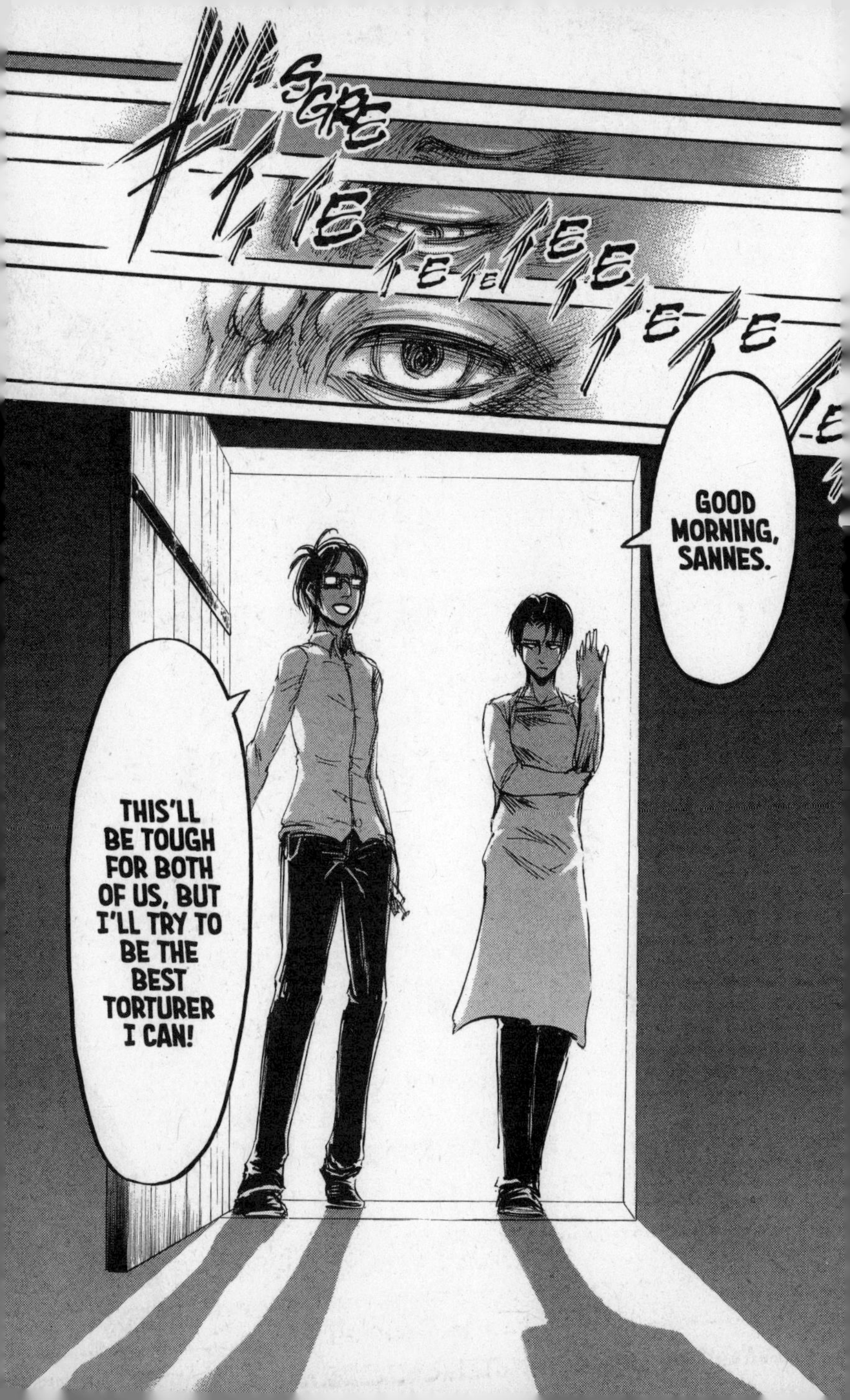
SCREEEEEEEEEEE
GOOD MORNING, SANNES.
THIS'LL BE TOUGH FOR BOTH OF US, BUT I'LL TRY TO BE THE BEST TORTURER I CAN!

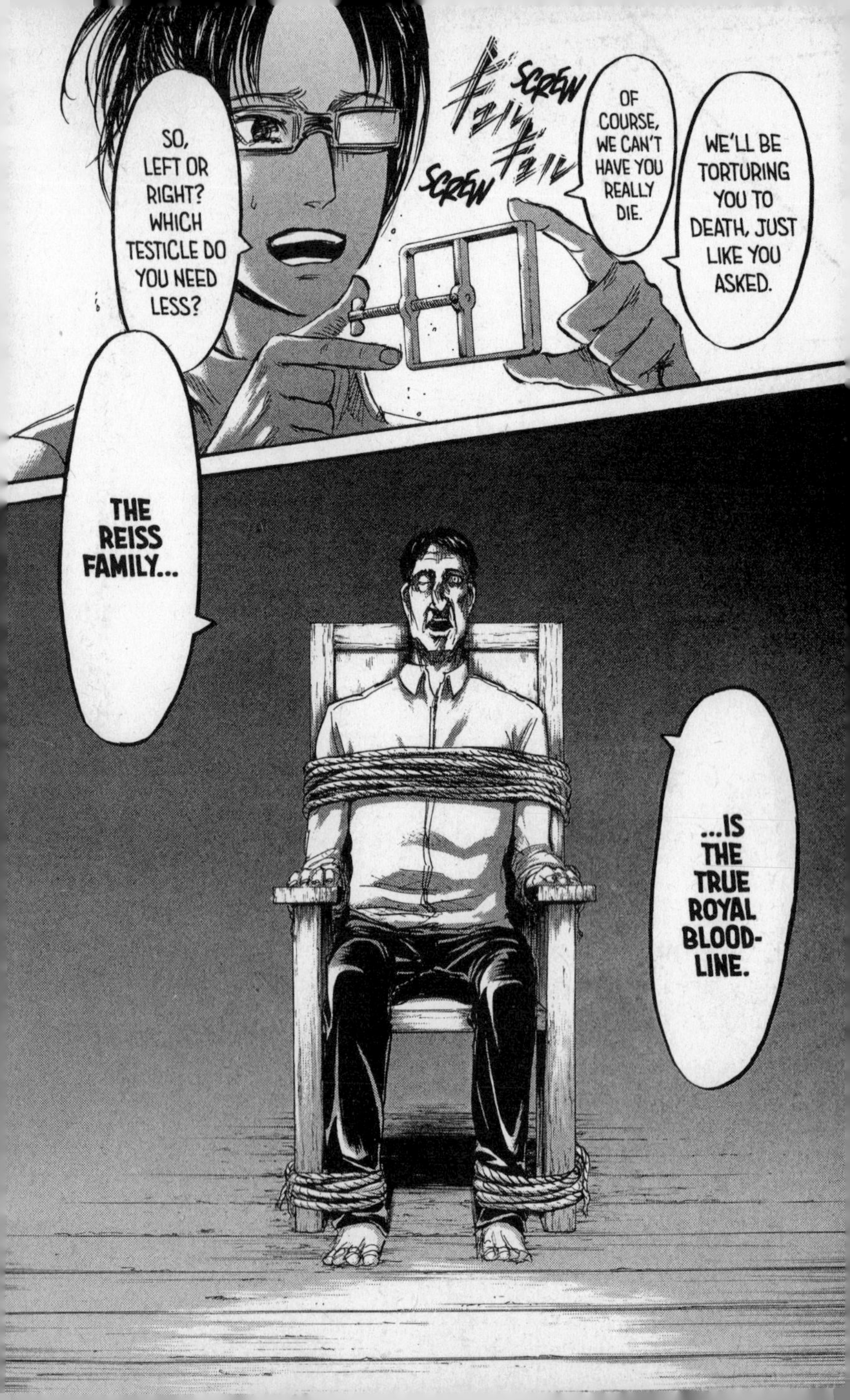
WE'LL BE TORTURING YOU TO DEATH, JUST LIKE YOU ASKED.
OF COURSE, WE CAN'T HAVE YOU REALLY DIE.
SCREW
SCREW
SO, LEFT OR RIGHT? WHICH TESTICLE DO YOU NEED LESS?
THE REISS FAMILY...
...IS THE TRUE ROYAL BLOODLINE.

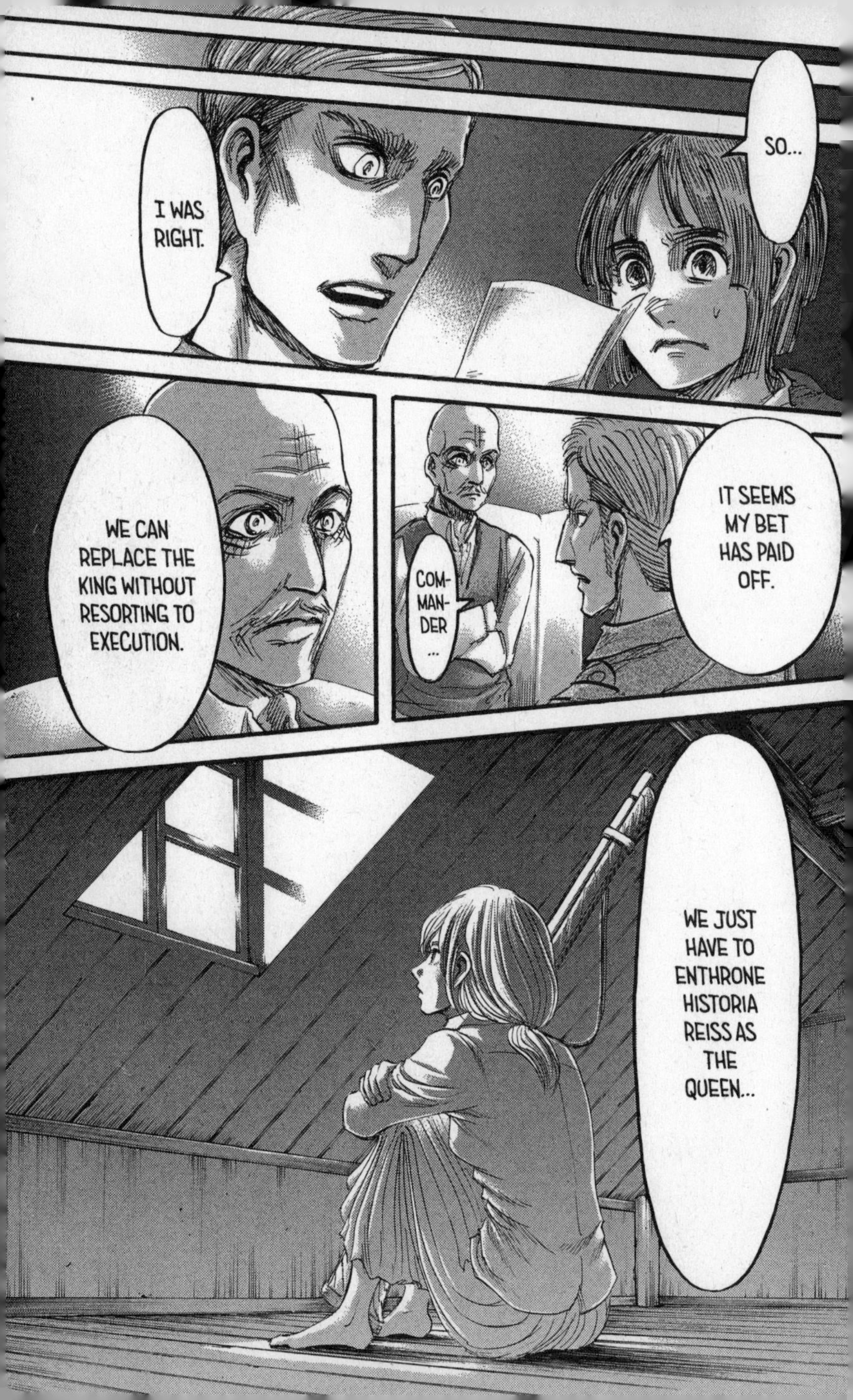

SO...
I WAS RIGHT.
IT SEEMS MY BET HAS PAID OFF.
COM-MAN-DER...
WE CAN REPLACE THE KING WITHOUT RESORTING TO EXECUTION.
WE JUST HAVE TO ENTHRONE HISTORIA REISS AS THE QUEEN...

ATTACK on TITAN

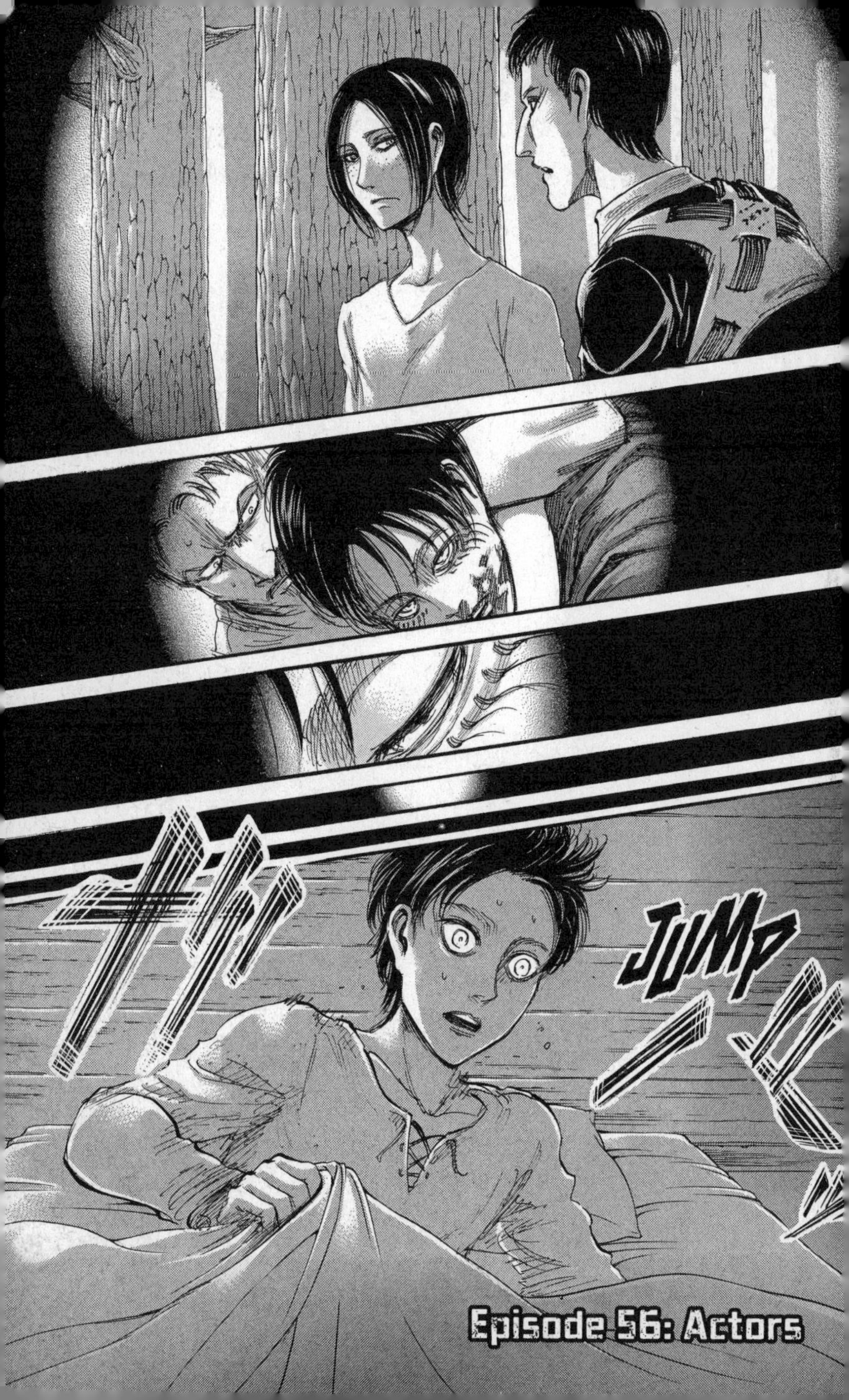
JUMP
Episode 56: Actors

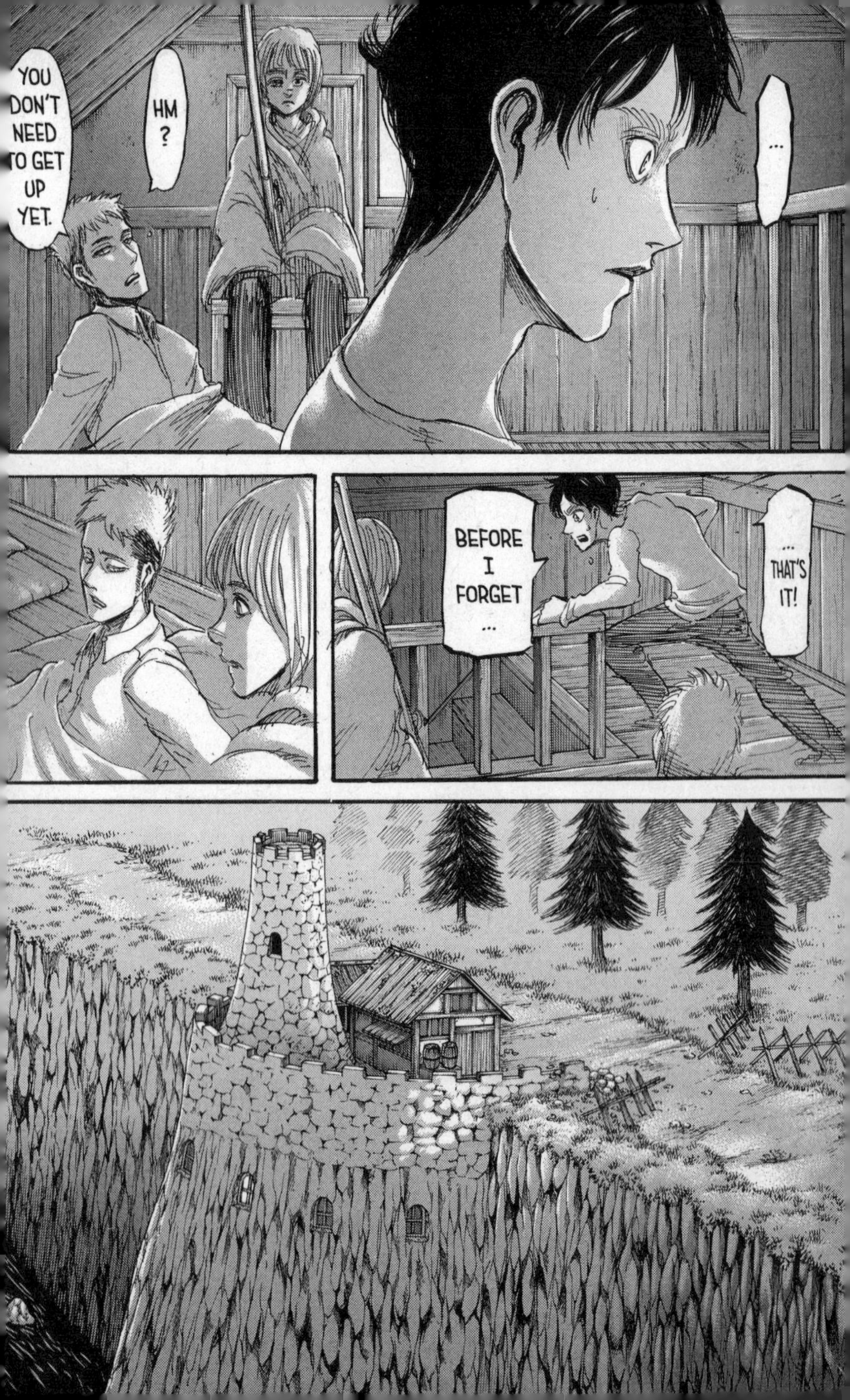
...
HM ?
YOU DON'T NEED TO GET UP YET.
... THAT'S IT!
BEFORE I FORGET ...

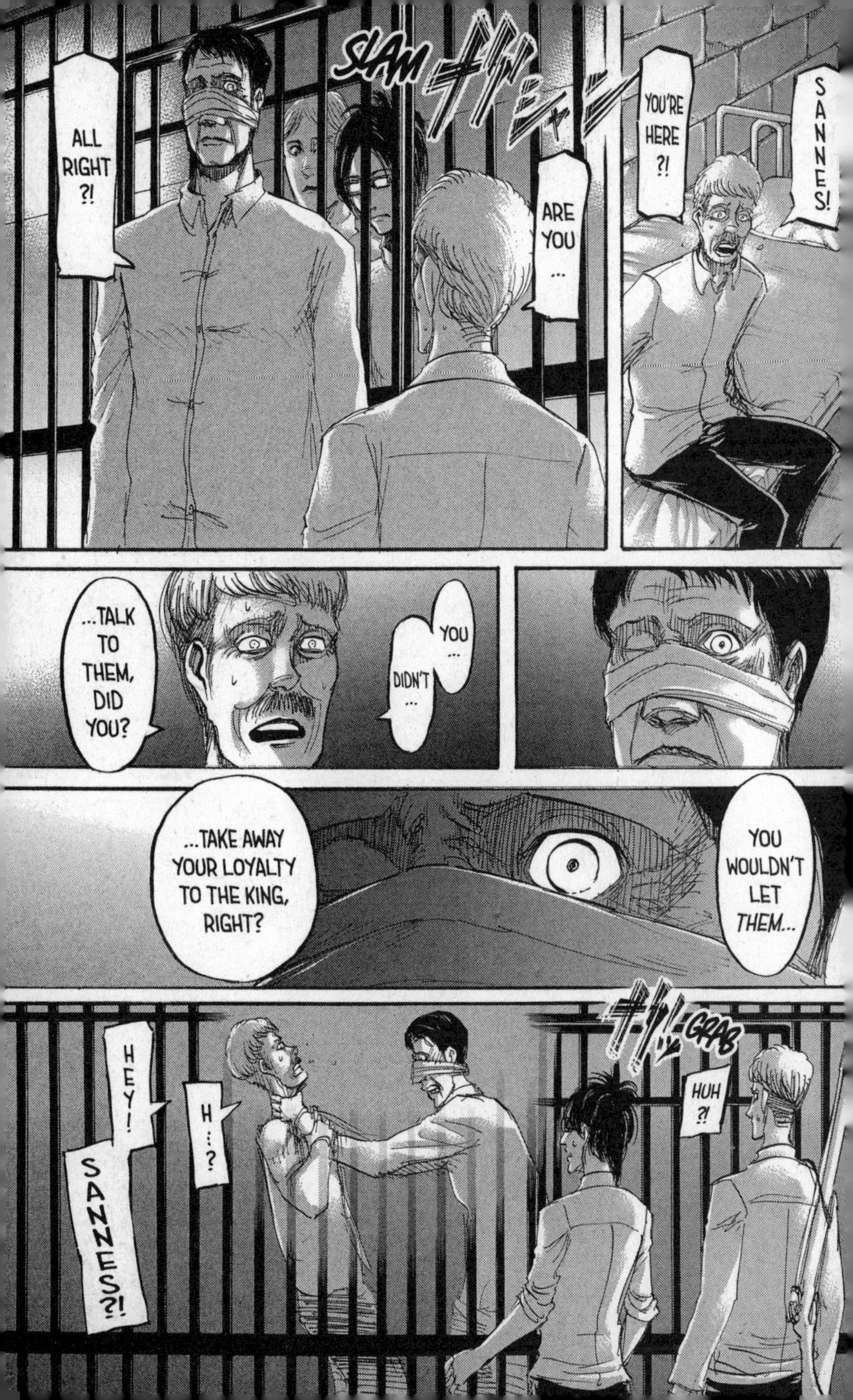
SANNES!
YOU'RE HERE ?!
SLAM
ARE YOU ...
ALL RIGHT ?!
YOU ... DIDN'T ...
...TALK TO THEM, DID YOU?
YOU WOULDN'T LET THEM...
...TAKE AWAY YOUR LOYALTY TO THE KING, RIGHT?
GRAB
HUH ?!
H...?
HEY! SANNES?!

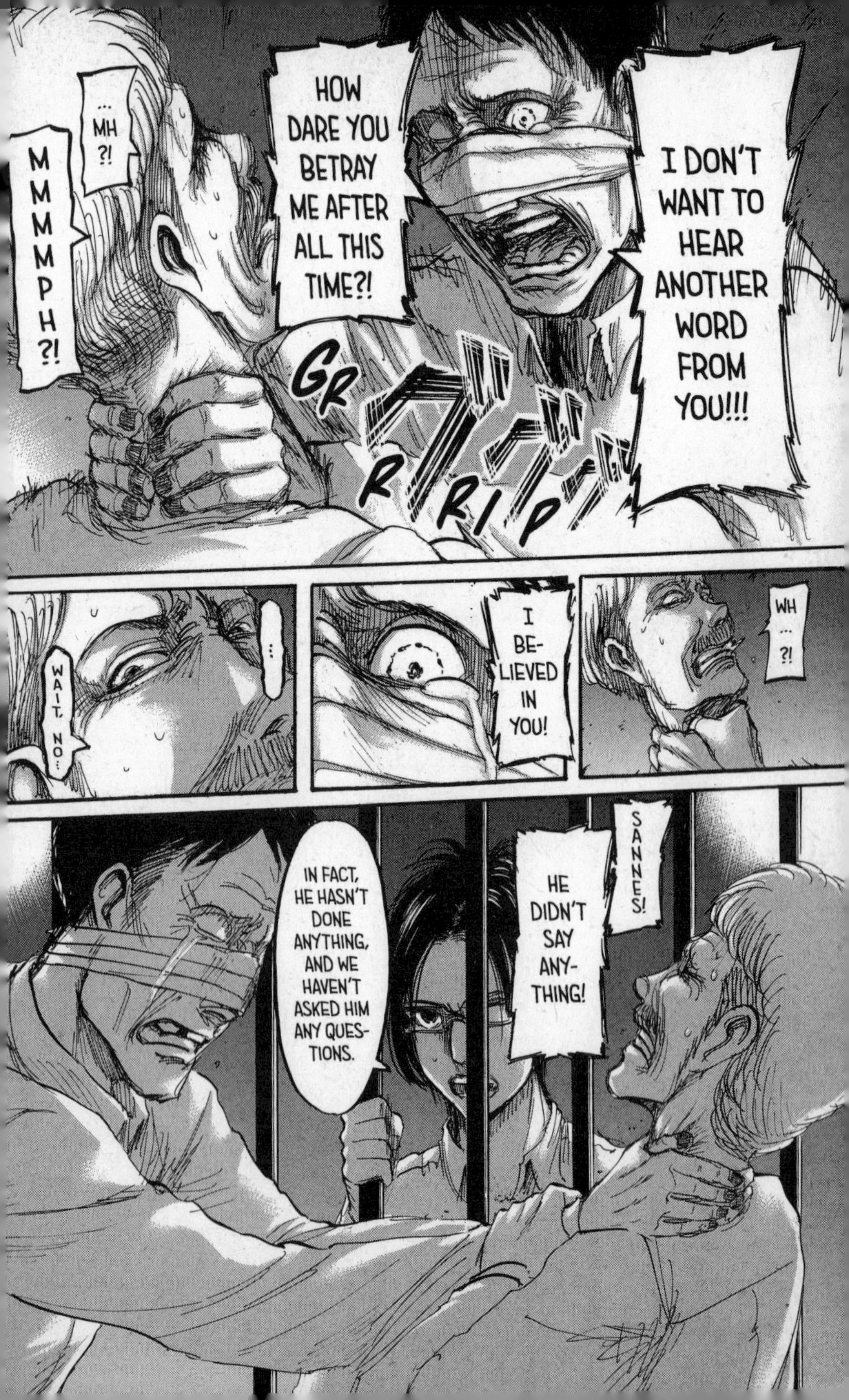
I DON'T WANT TO HEAR ANOTHER WORD FROM YOU!!!
HOW DARE YOU BETRAY ME AFTER ALL THIS TIME?!
GRRRIP
...MH ?!
MMMMPH ?!
WH... ?!
I BELIEVED IN YOU!
...
WAIT, NO...
SANNES!
HE DIDN'T SAY ANYTHING!
IN FACT, HE HASN'T DONE ANYTHING, AND WE HAVEN'T ASKED HIM ANY QUESTIONS.

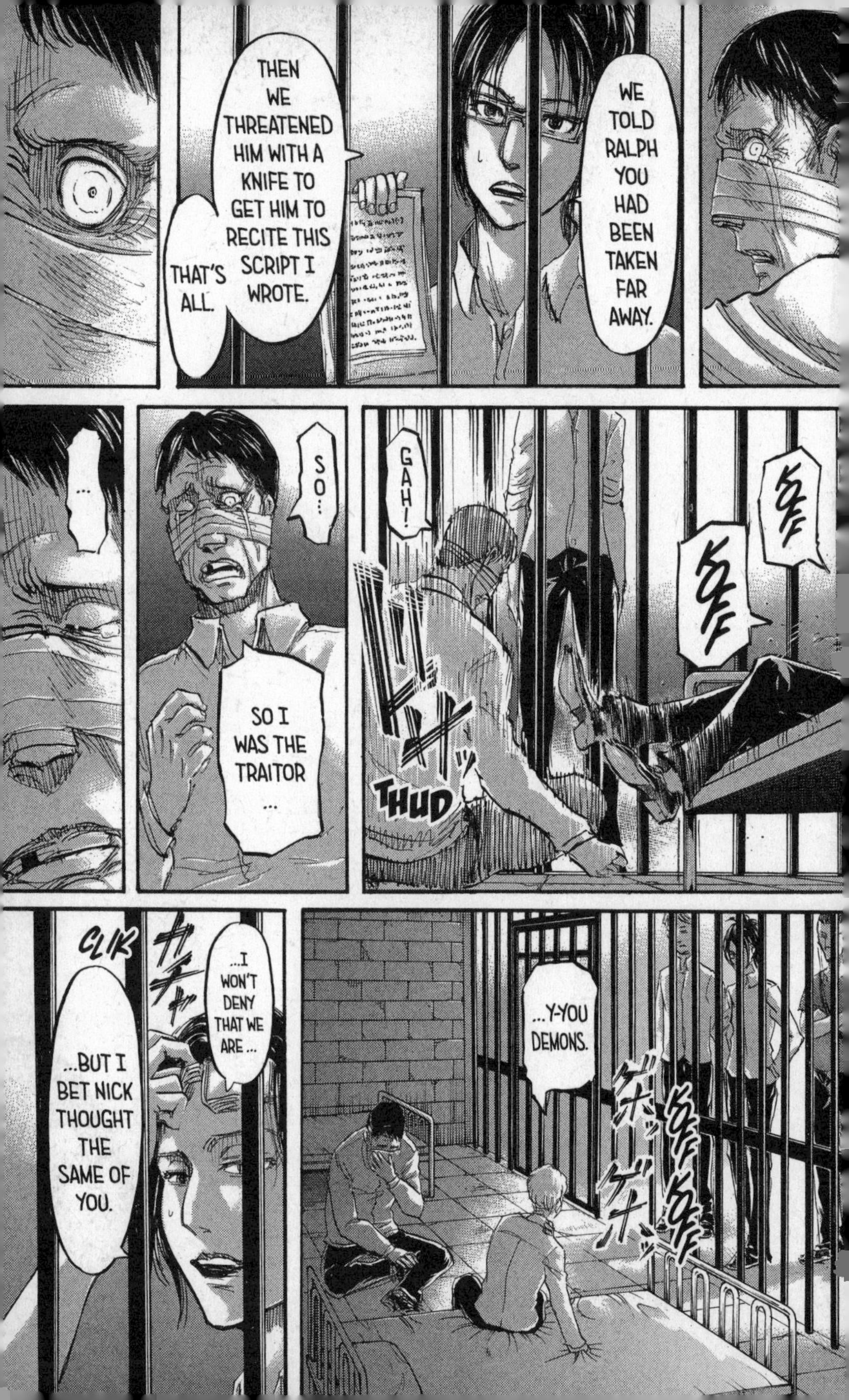
WE TOLD RALPH YOU HAD BEEN TAKEN FAR AWAY.
THEN WE THREATENED HIM WITH A KNIFE TO GET HIM TO RECITE THIS SCRIPT I WROTE.
THAT'S ALL.
KOFF
KOFF
GAH!
THUD
SO...
SO I WAS THE TRAITOR ...
...
...Y-YOU DEMONS.
KOFF KOFF
...I WON'T DENY THAT WE ARE...
CLIK
...BUT I BET NICK THOUGHT THE SAME OF YOU.

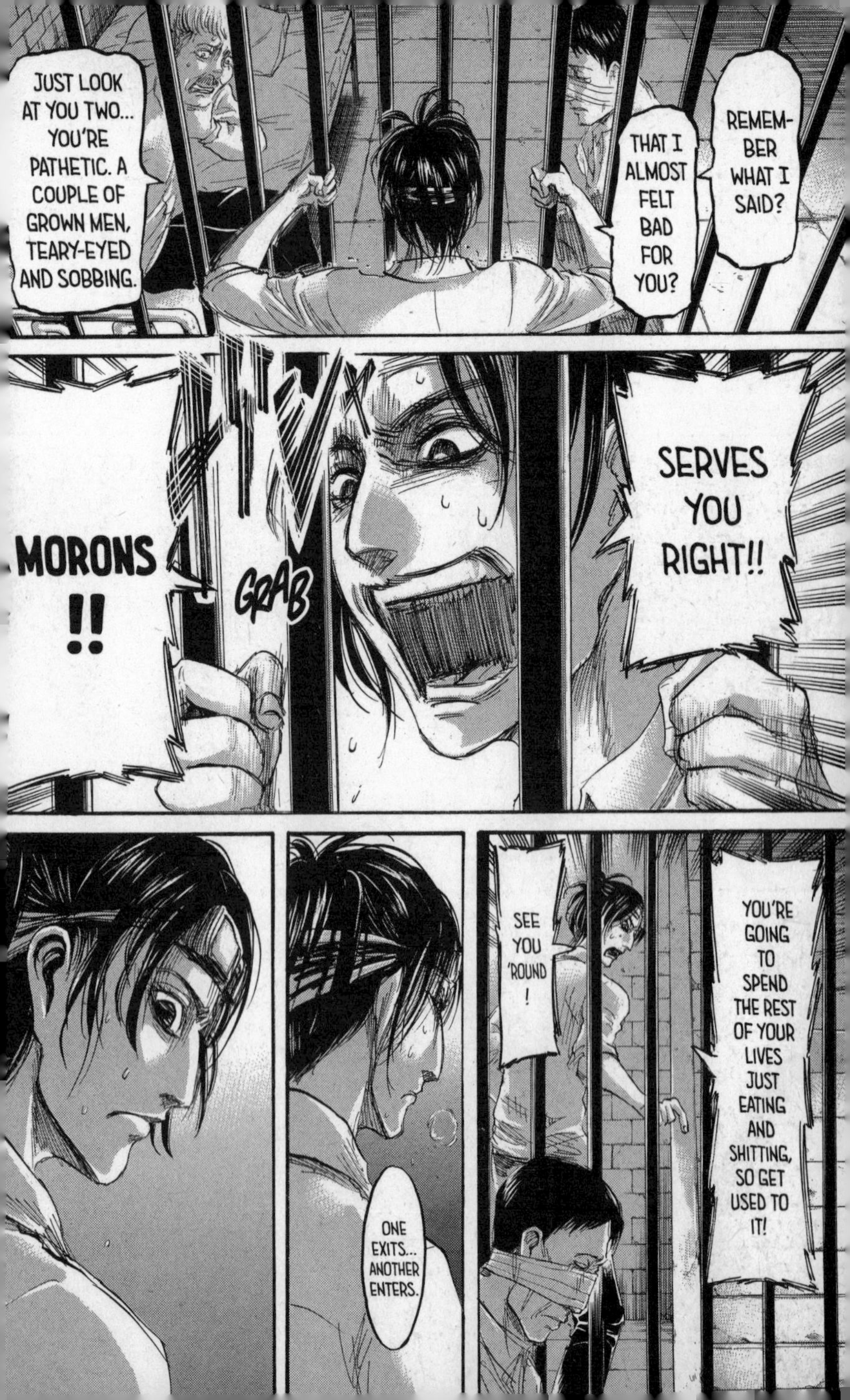
REMEMBER WHAT I SAID?
THAT I ALMOST FELT BAD FOR YOU?
JUST LOOK AT YOU TWO... YOU'RE PATHETIC. A COUPLE OF GROWN MEN, TEARY-EYED AND SOBBING.
SERVES YOU RIGHT!!
GRAB
MORONS!!
YOU'RE GOING TO SPEND THE REST OF YOUR LIVES JUST EATING AND SHITTING, SO GET USED TO IT!
SEE YOU 'ROUND!
ONE EXITS... ANOTHER ENTERS.

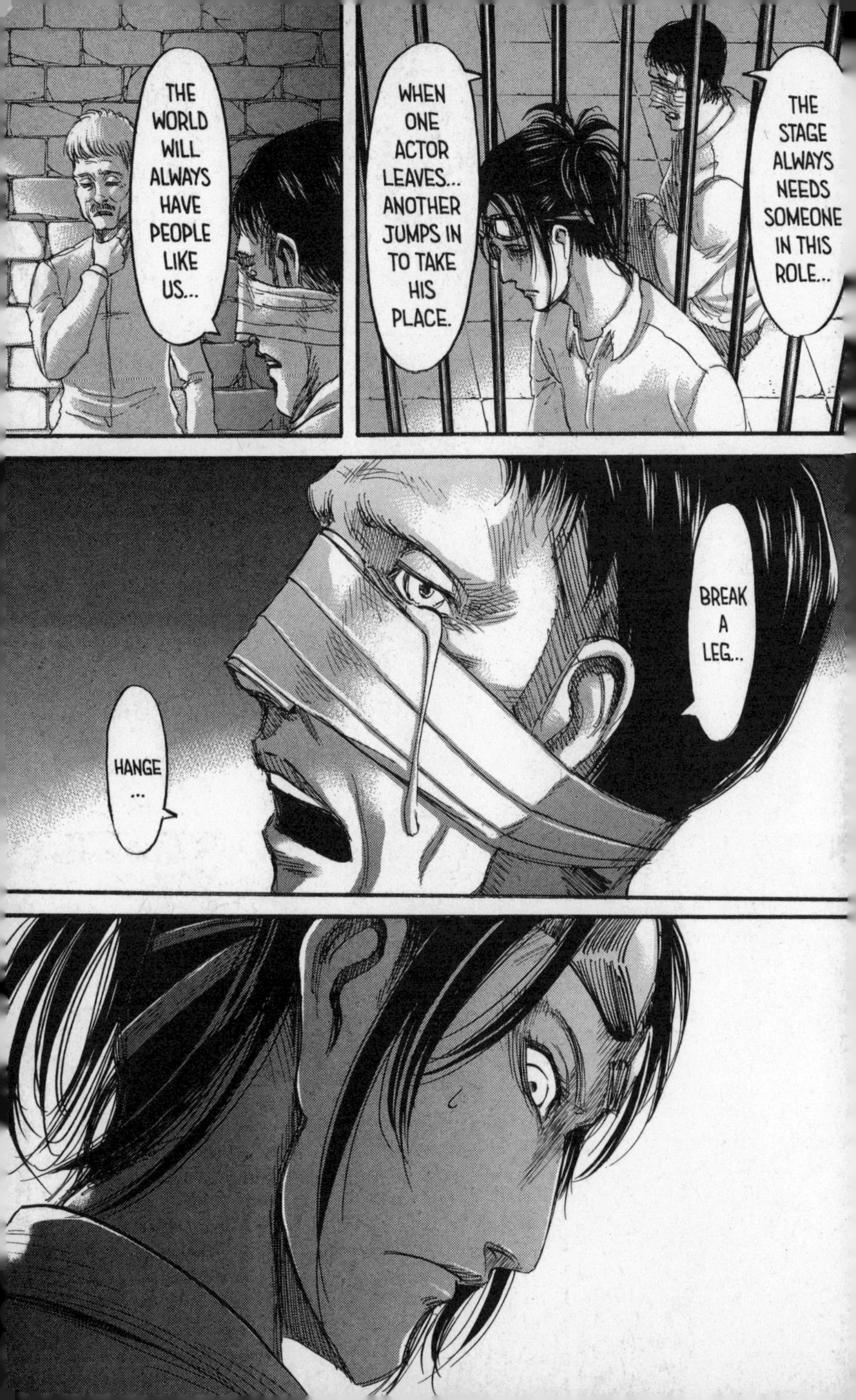
THE STAGE ALWAYS NEEDS SOMEONE IN THIS ROLE...
WHEN ONE ACTOR LEAVES... ANOTHER JUMPS IN TO TAKE HIS PLACE.
THE WORLD WILL ALWAYS HAVE PEOPLE LIKE US...
BREAK A LEG...
HANGE ...

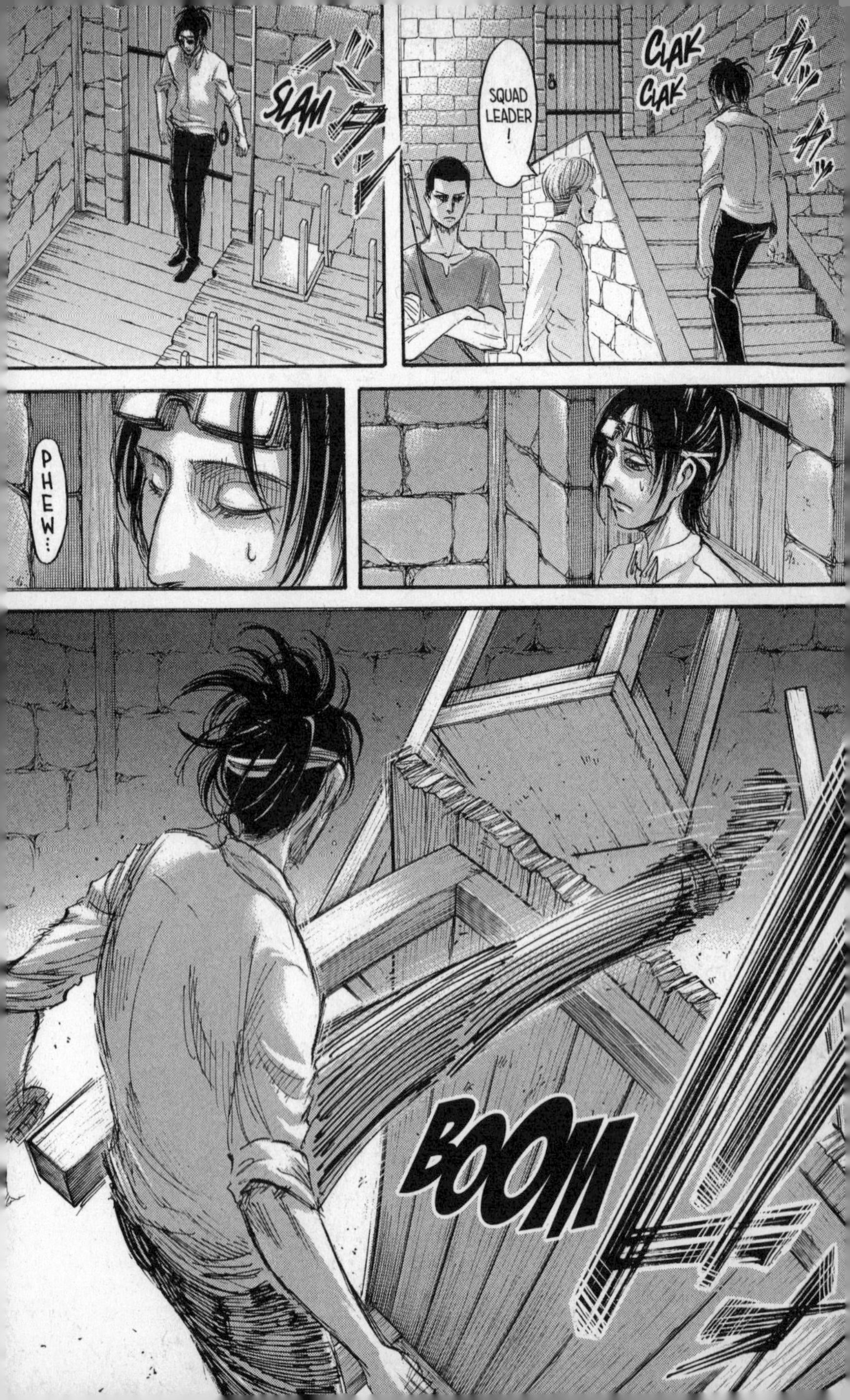
CLAK
CLAK
SQUAD LEADER!
SLAM
PHEW...
BOOM

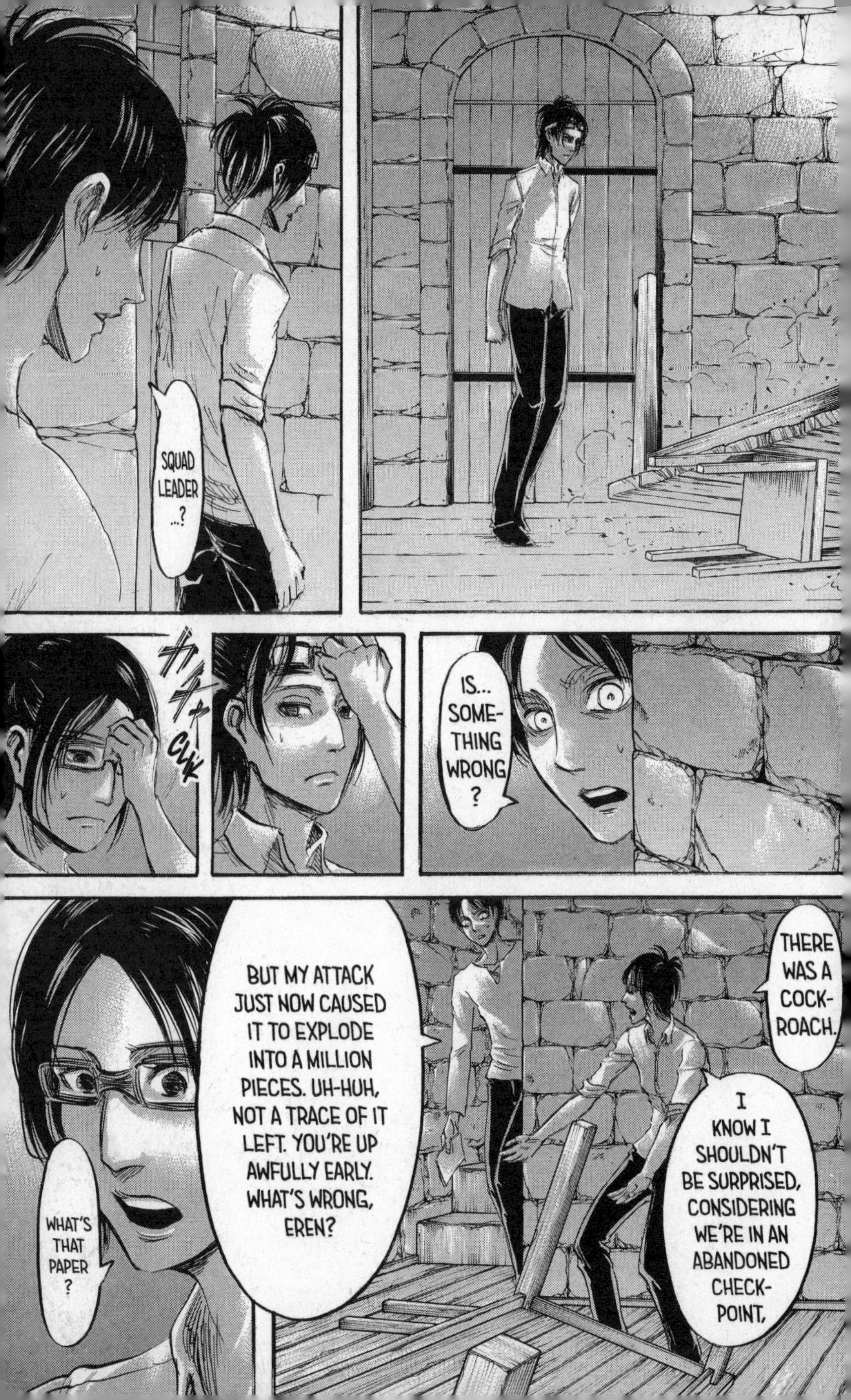
SQUAD LEADER ...?
IS... SOMETHING WRONG?
CLIK
THERE WAS A COCKROACH.
I KNOW I SHOULDN'T BE SURPRISED, CONSIDERING WE'RE IN AN ABANDONED CHECKPOINT,
BUT MY ATTACK JUST NOW CAUSED IT TO EXPLODE INTO A MILLION PIECES. UH-HUH, NOT A TRACE OF IT LEFT. YOU'RE UP AWFULLY EARLY. WHAT'S WRONG, EREN?
WHAT'S THAT PAPER?

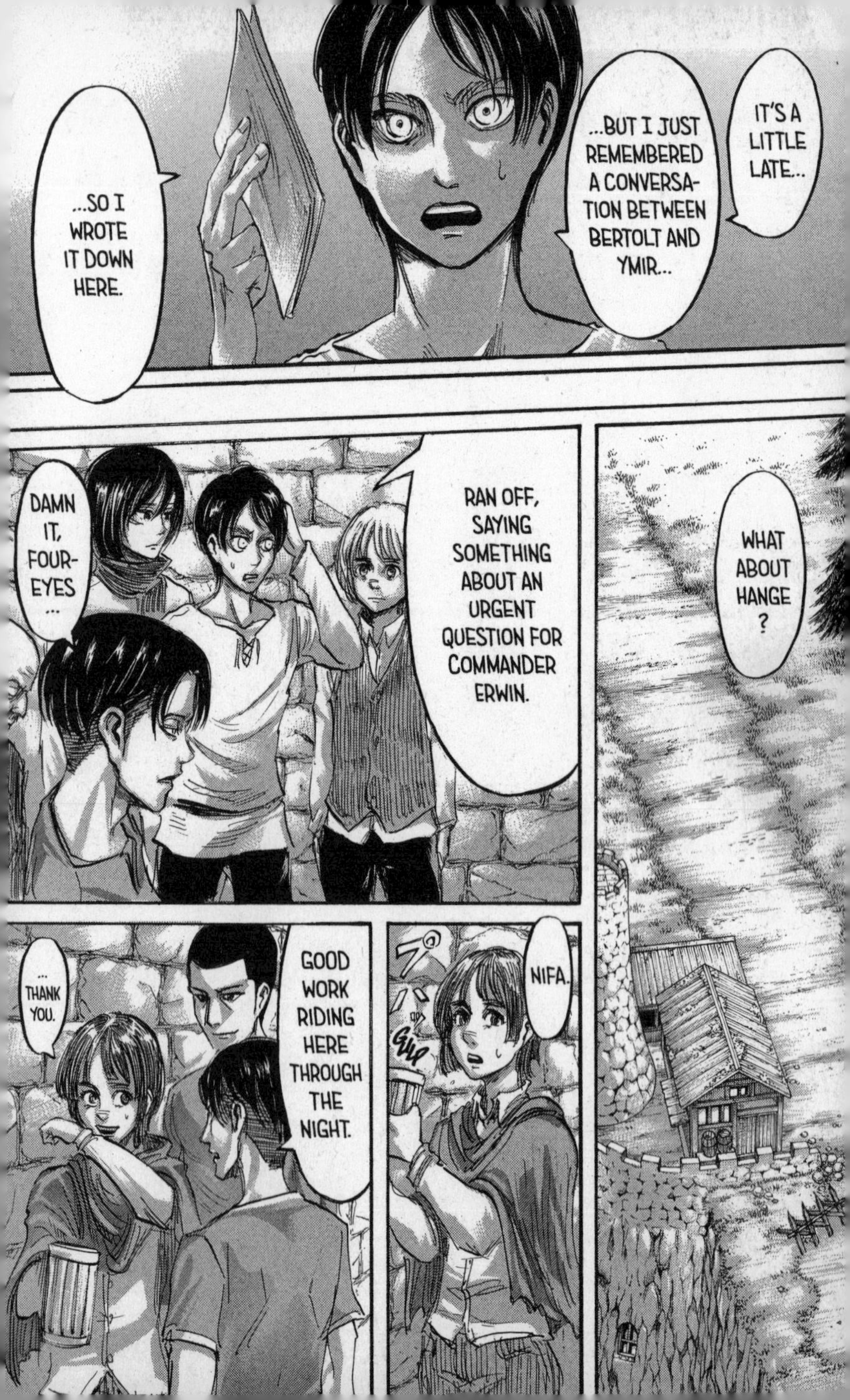

IT'S A LITTLE LATE...
...BUT I JUST REMEMBERED A CONVERSATION BETWEEN BERTOLT AND YMIR...
...SO I WROTE IT DOWN HERE.
WHAT ABOUT HANGE?
RAN OFF, SAYING SOMETHING ABOUT AN URGENT QUESTION FOR COMMANDER ERWIN.
DAMN IT, FOUR-EYES...
NIFA.
GOOD WORK RIDING HERE THROUGH THE NIGHT.
...THANK YOU.

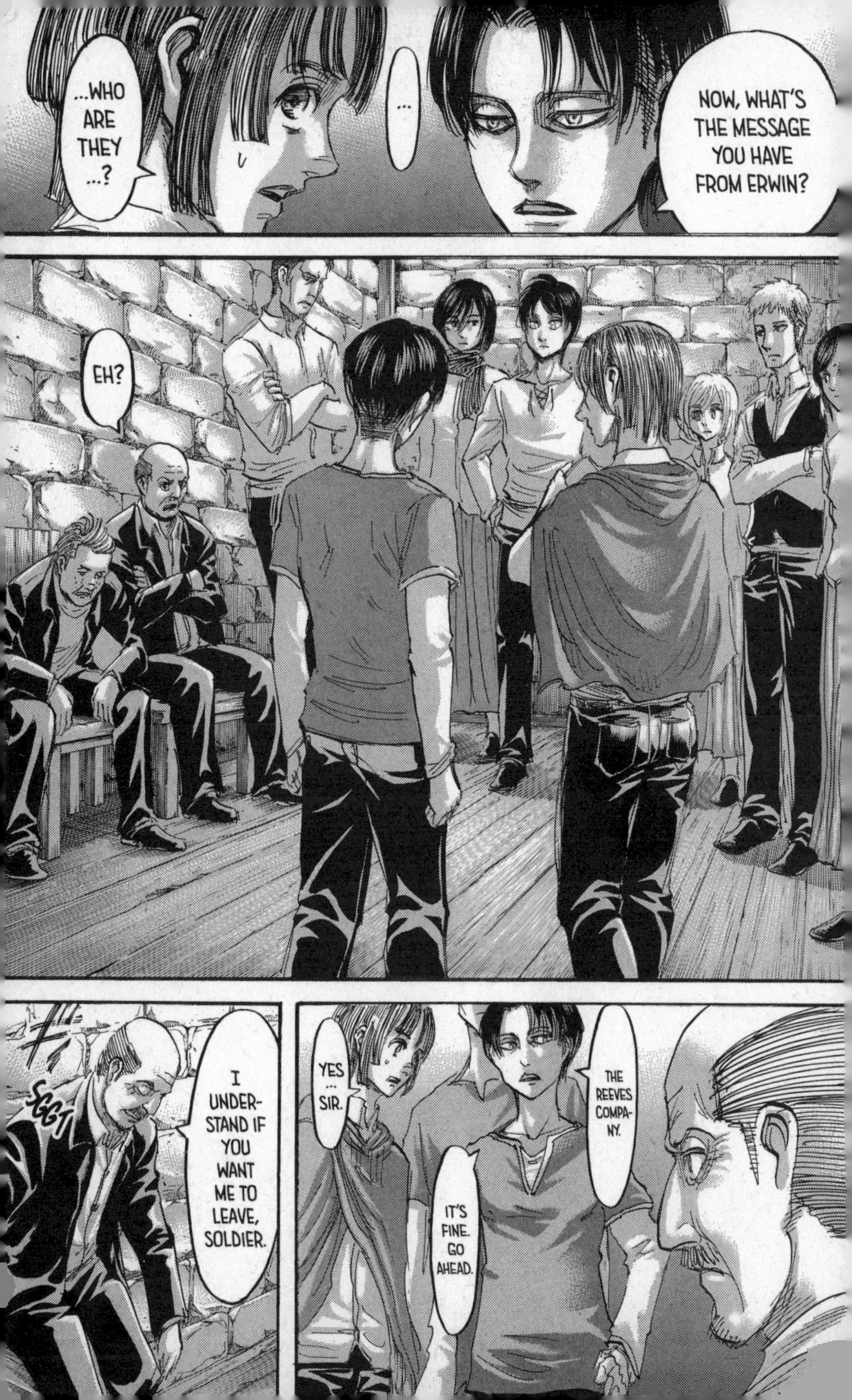
NOW, WHAT'S THE MESSAGE YOU HAVE FROM ERWIN?
...
...WHO ARE THEY ...?
EH?
THE REEVES COMPANY.
YES ... SIR.
IT'S FINE. GO AHEAD.
I UNDERSTAND IF YOU WANT ME TO LEAVE, SOLDIER.
SGGT

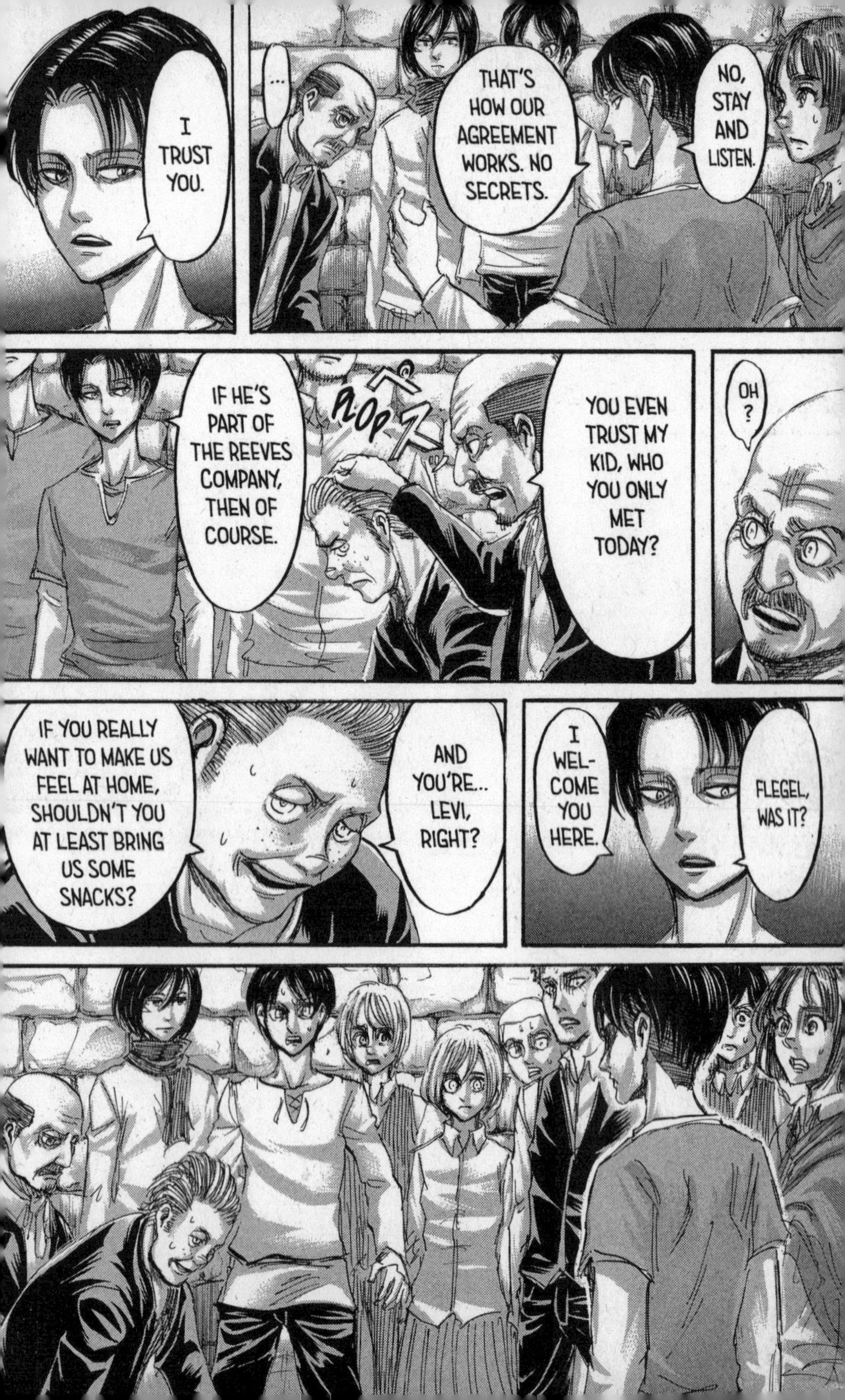
NO, STAY AND LISTEN.
THAT'S HOW OUR AGREEMENT WORKS. NO SECRETS.
...
I TRUST YOU.
OH ?
YOU EVEN TRUST MY KID, WHO YOU ONLY MET TODAY?
PLOP
IF HE'S PART OF THE REEVES COMPANY, THEN OF COURSE.
FLEGEL, WAS IT?
I WELCOME YOU HERE.
AND YOU'RE... LEVI, RIGHT?
IF YOU REALLY WANT TO MAKE US FEEL AT HOME, SHOULDN'T YOU AT LEAST BRING US SOME SNACKS?

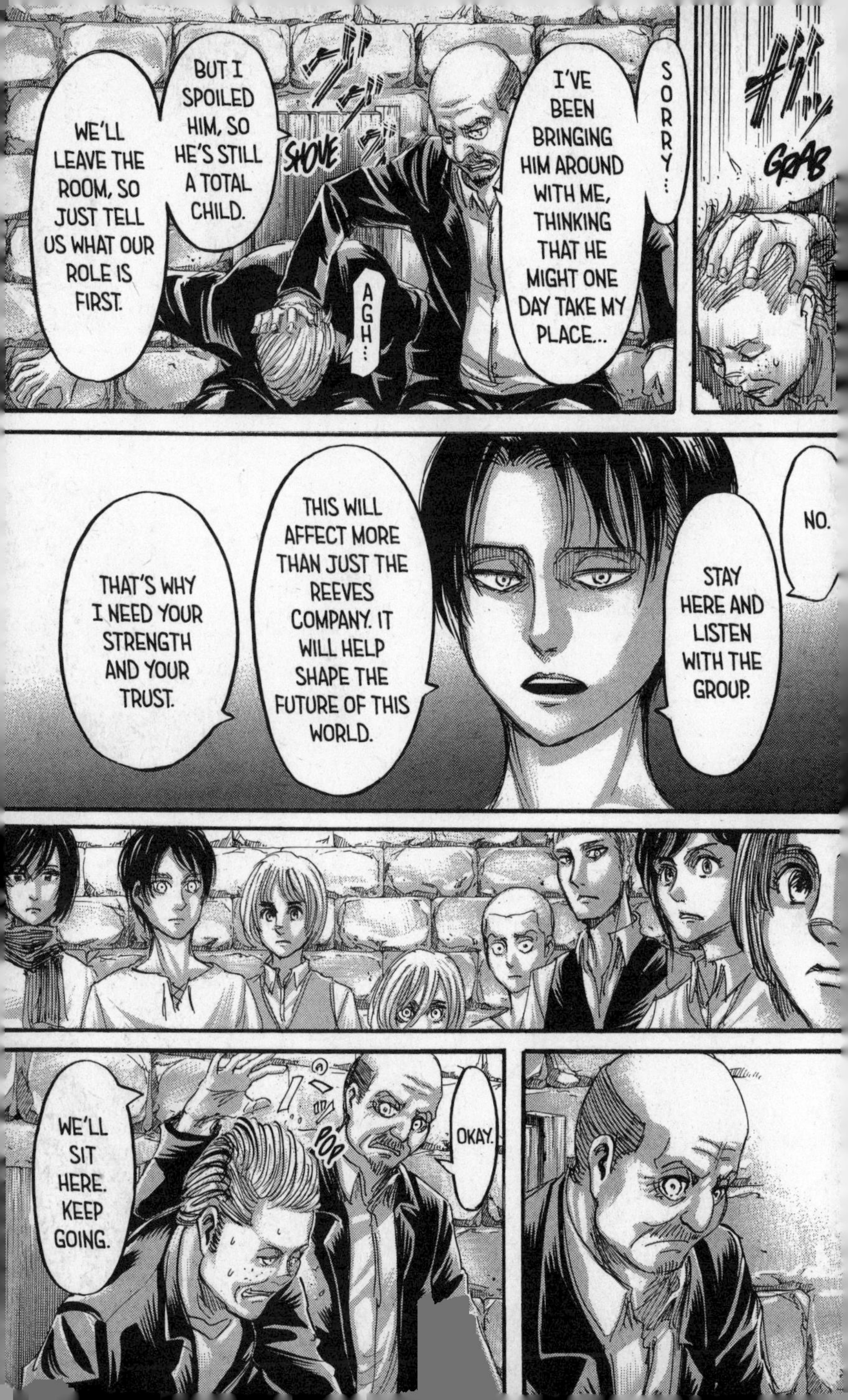
GRAB
SORRY...
I'VE BEEN BRINGING HIM AROUND WITH ME, THINKING THAT HE MIGHT ONE DAY TAKE MY PLACE...
BUT I SPOILED HIM, SO HE'S STILL A TOTAL CHILD.
SHOVE
AGH...
WE'LL LEAVE THE ROOM, SO JUST TELL US WHAT OUR ROLE IS FIRST.
NO.
STAY HERE AND LISTEN WITH THE GROUP.
THIS WILL AFFECT MORE THAN JUST THE REEVES COMPANY. IT WILL HELP SHAPE THE FUTURE OF THIS WORLD.
THAT'S WHY I NEED YOUR STRENGTH AND YOUR TRUST.
OKAY.
POP
WE'LL SIT HERE. KEEP GOING.

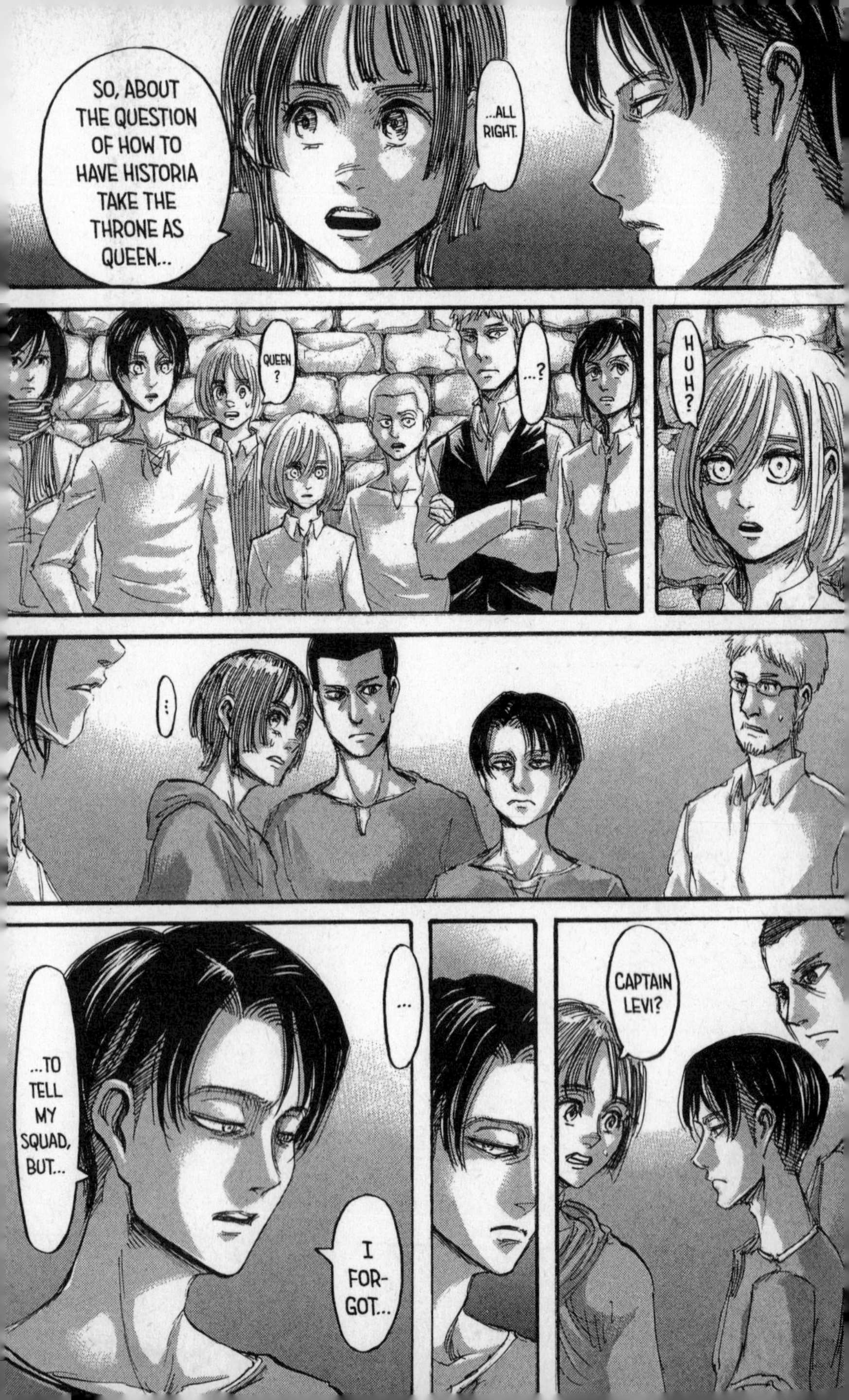
...ALL RIGHT.
SO, ABOUT THE QUESTION OF HOW TO HAVE HISTORIA TAKE THE THRONE AS QUEEN...
HUH?
...?
QUEEN?
...
CAPTAIN LEVI?
...
...TO TELL MY SQUAD, BUT...
I FOR-GOT...

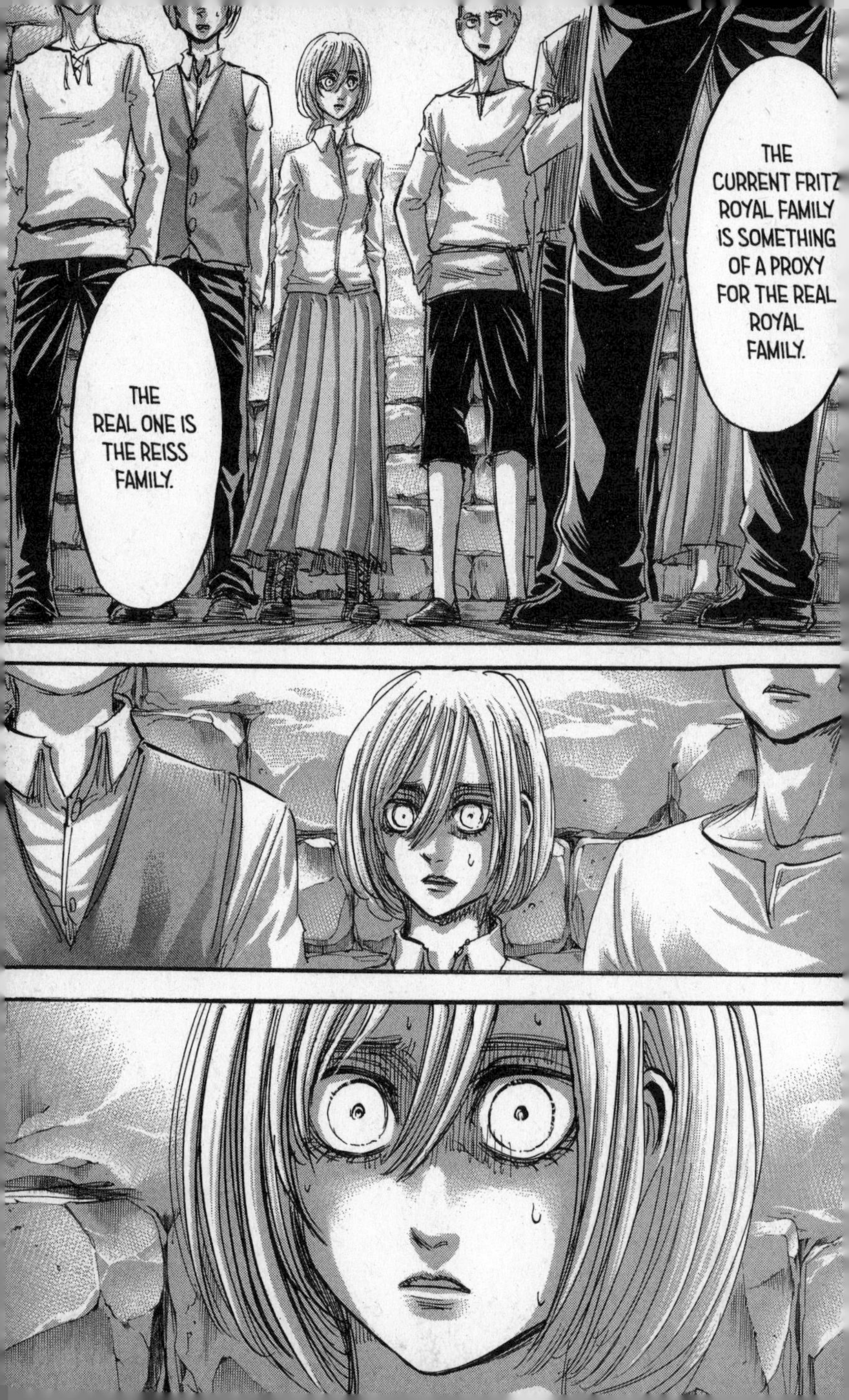
THE CURRENT FRITZ ROYAL FAMILY IS SOMETHING OF A PROXY FOR THE REAL ROYAL FAMILY.
THE REAL ONE IS THE REISS FAMILY.

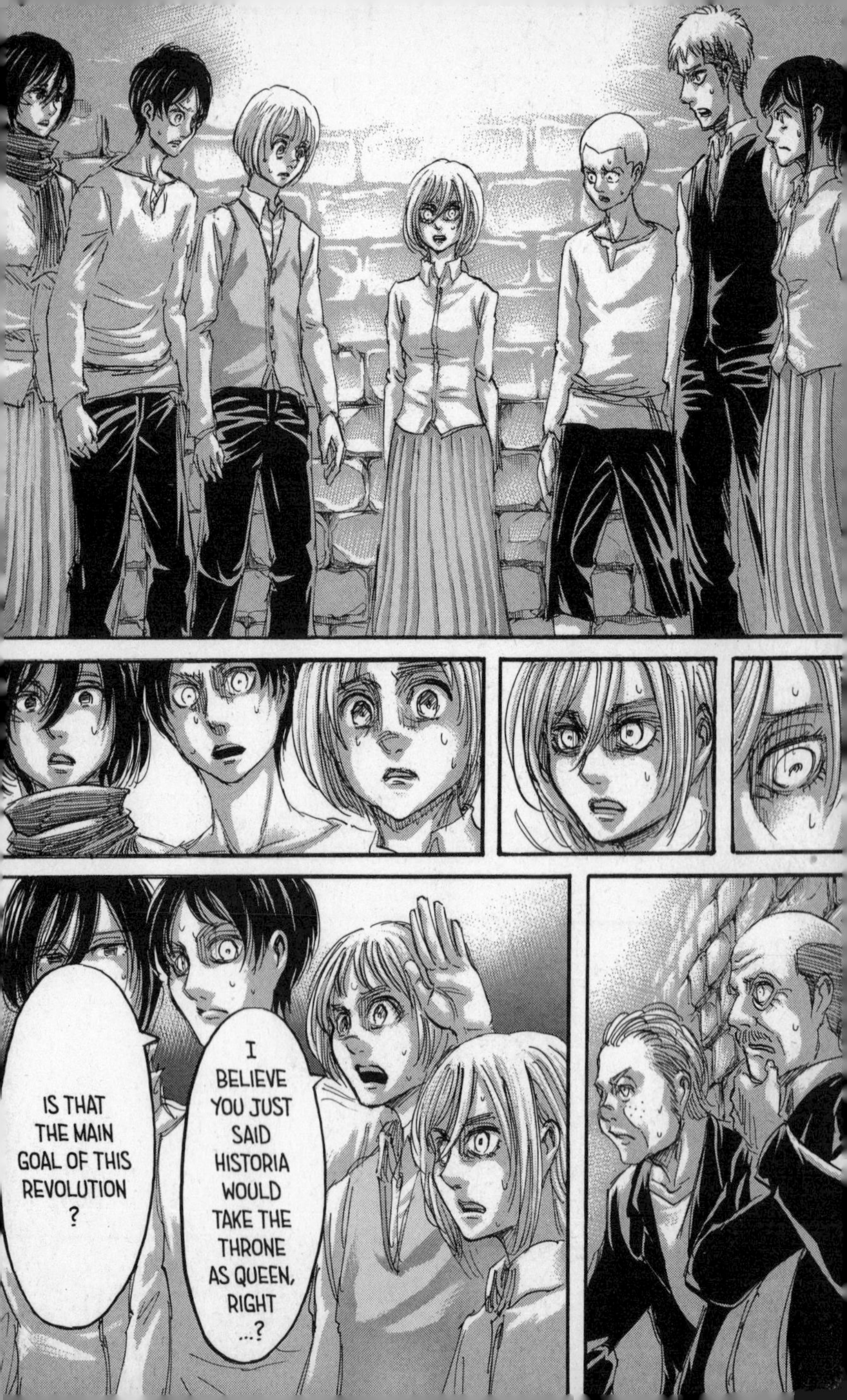
I BELIEVE YOU JUST SAID HISTORIA WOULD TAKE THE THRONE AS QUEEN, RIGHT ...?
IS THAT THE MAIN GOAL OF THIS REVOLUTION ?

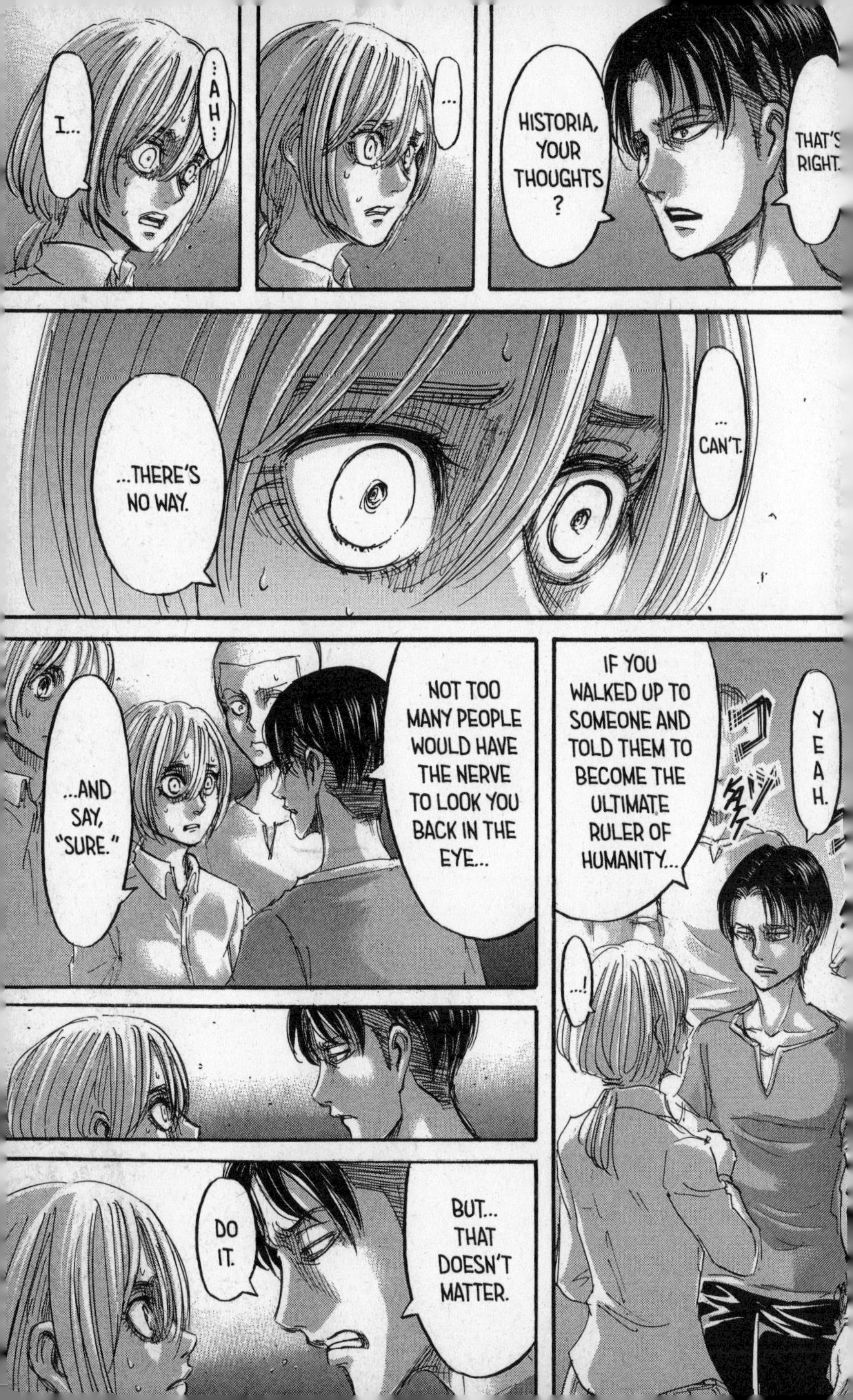
THAT'S RIGHT.
HISTORIA, YOUR THOUGHTS?
...
...AH...
I...
... CAN'T.
...THERE'S NO WAY.
YEAH.
IF YOU WALKED UP TO SOMEONE AND TOLD THEM TO BECOME THE ULTIMATE RULER OF HUMANITY...
...!
NOT TOO MANY PEOPLE WOULD HAVE THE NERVE TO LOOK YOU BACK IN THE EYE...
...AND SAY, "SURE."
BUT... THAT DOESN'T MATTER.
DO IT.

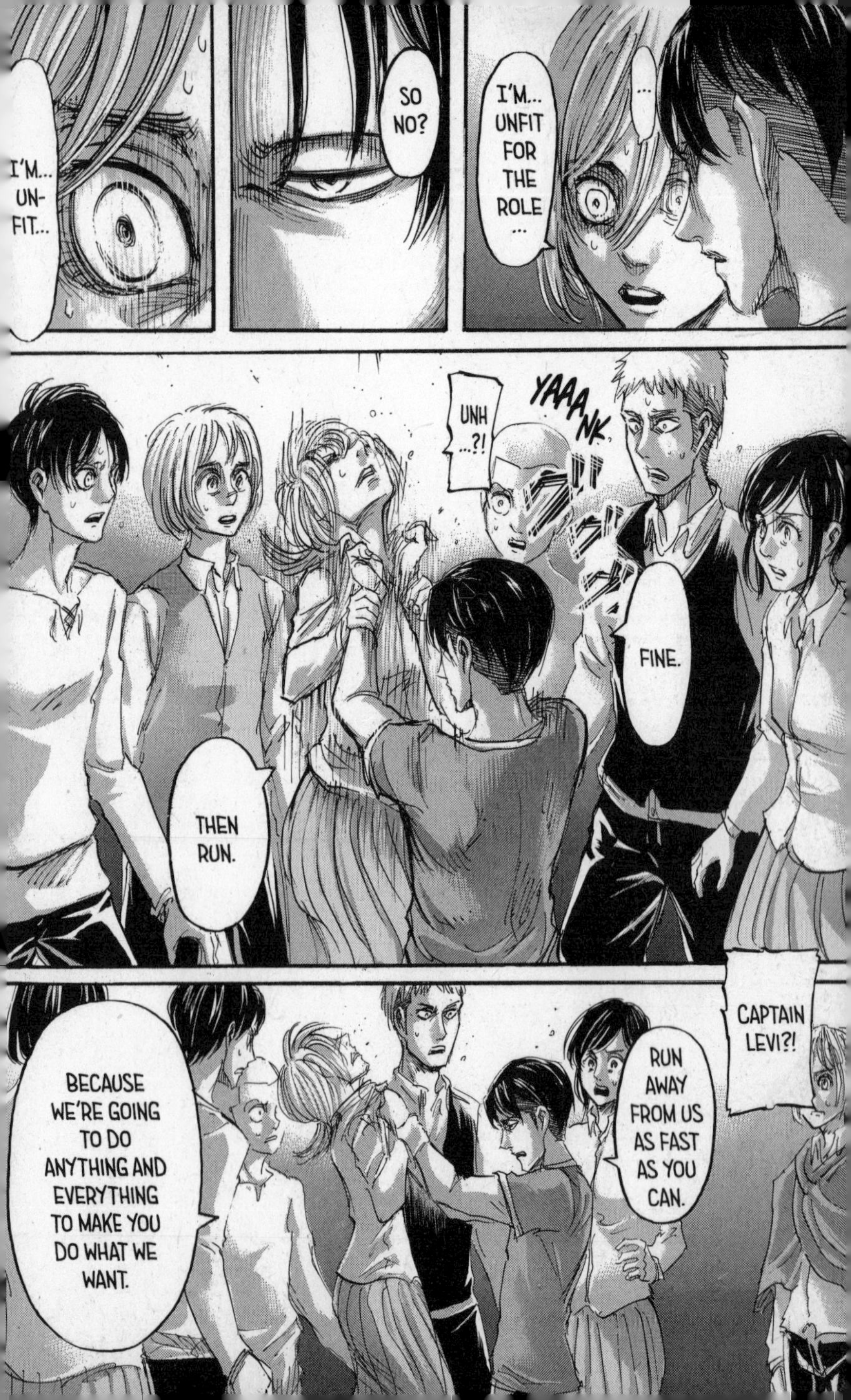
...
I'M... UNFIT FOR THE ROLE ...
SO NO?
I'M... UN-FIT...
YAAANK
UNH ...?!
FINE.
THEN RUN.
CAPTAIN LEVI?!
RUN AWAY FROM US AS FAST AS YOU CAN.
BECAUSE WE'RE GOING TO DO ANYTHING AND EVERYTHING TO MAKE YOU DO WHAT WE WANT.

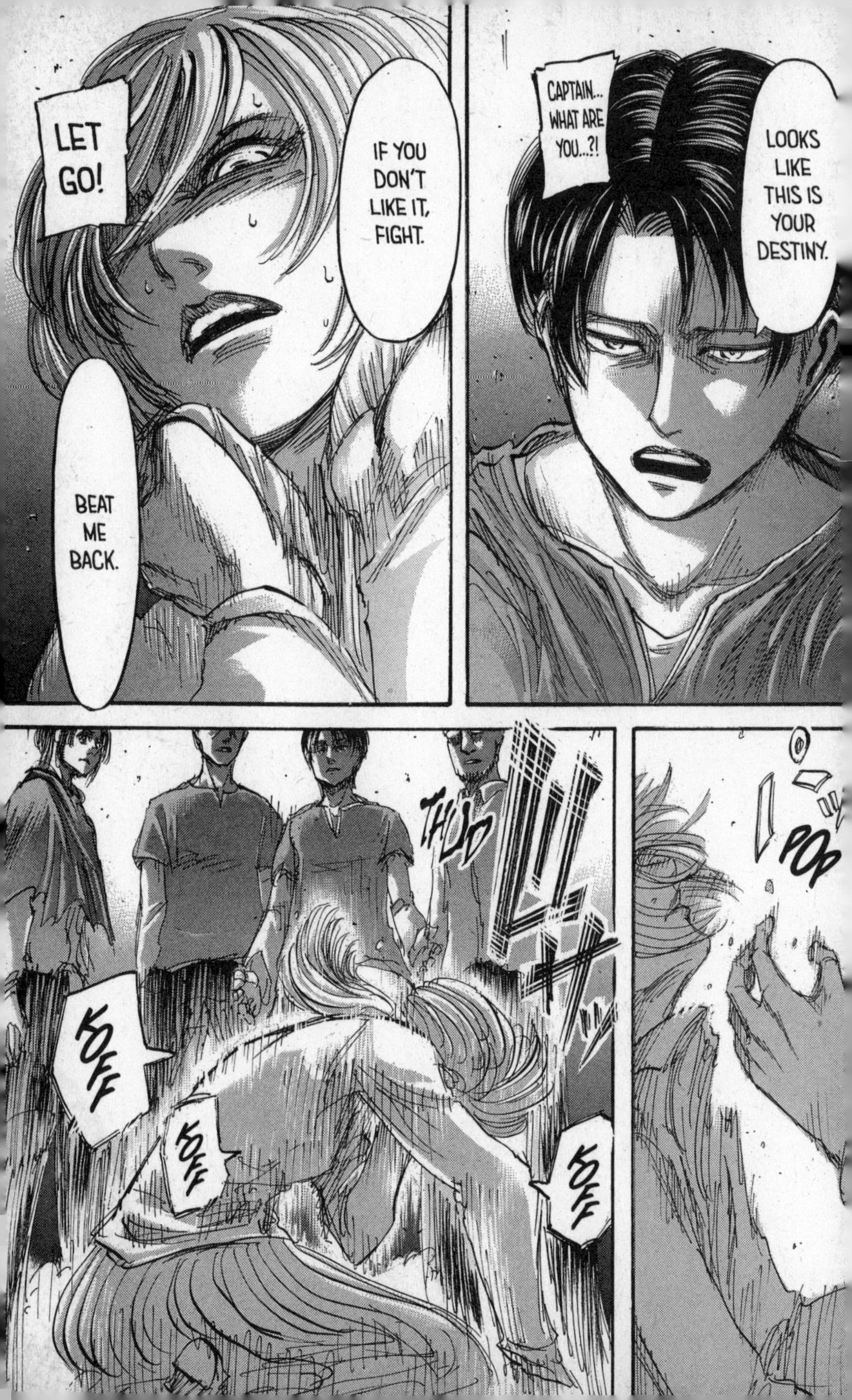
LOOKS LIKE THIS IS YOUR DESTINY.
CAPTAIN... WHAT ARE YOU...?!
IF YOU DON'T LIKE IT, FIGHT.
LET GO!
BEAT ME BACK.
POP
THUD
KOFF
KOFF
KOFF

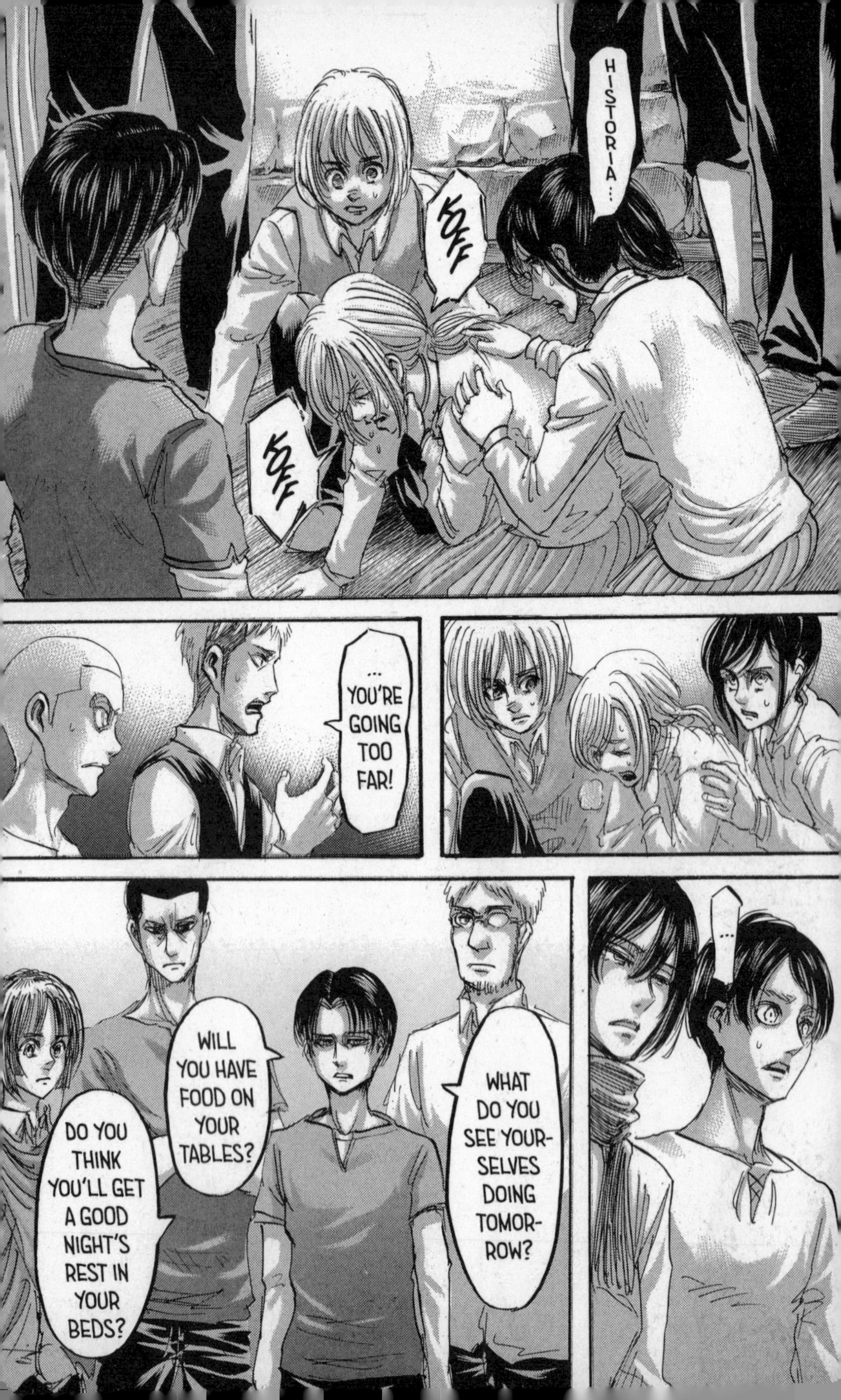
HISTORIA...
KOFF
KOFF
... YOU'RE GOING TOO FAR!
!
...
WHAT DO YOU SEE YOUR-SELVES DOING TOMOR-ROW?
WILL YOU HAVE FOOD ON YOUR TABLES?
DO YOU THINK YOU'LL GET A GOOD NIGHT'S REST IN YOUR BEDS?

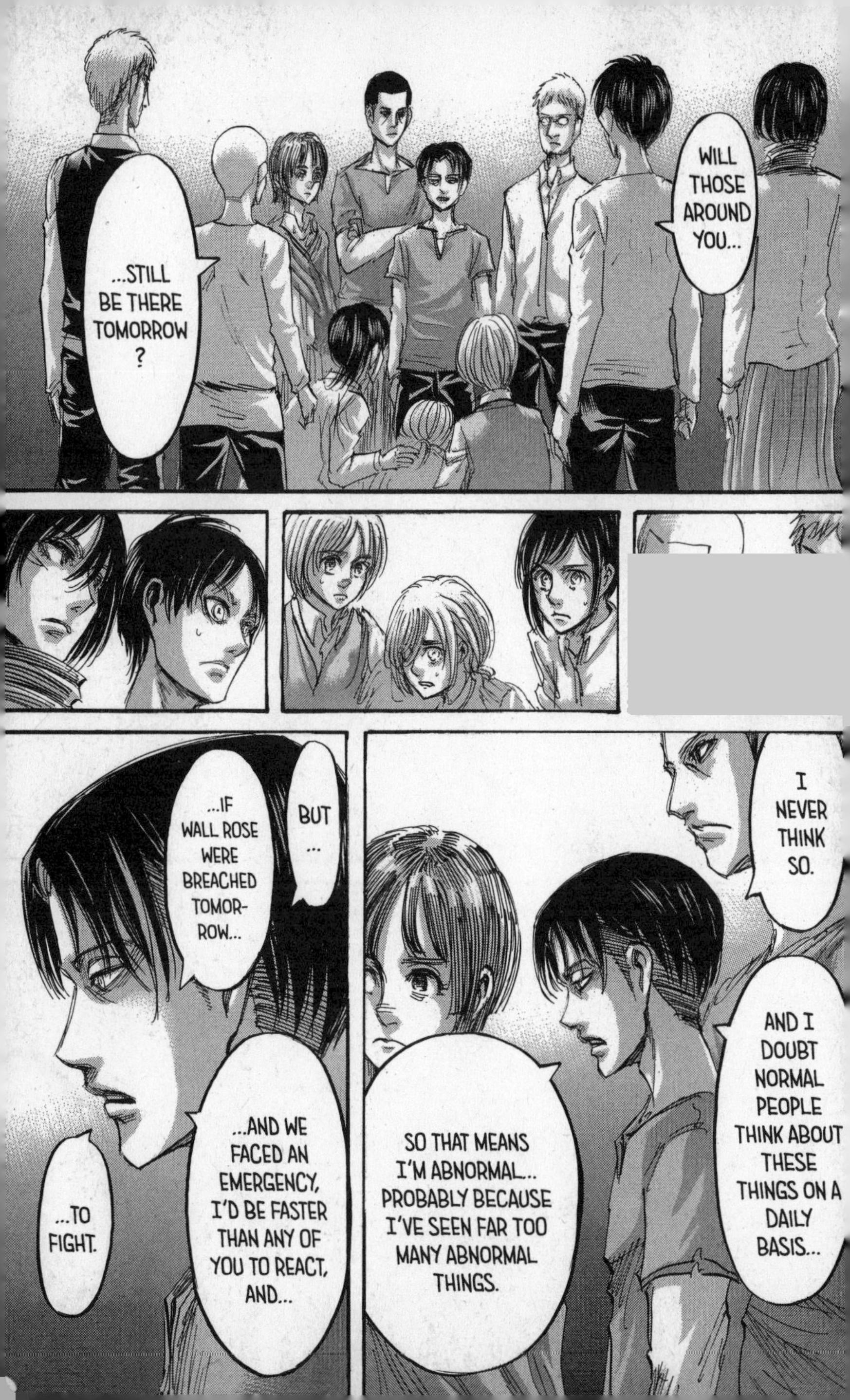
WILL THOSE AROUND YOU...
...STILL BE THERE TOMORROW?
I NEVER THINK SO.
AND I DOUBT NORMAL PEOPLE THINK ABOUT THESE THINGS ON A DAILY BASIS...
SO THAT MEANS I'M ABNORMAL... PROBABLY BECAUSE I'VE SEEN FAR TOO MANY ABNORMAL THINGS.
BUT...
...IF WALL ROSE WERE BREACHED TOMOR-ROW...
...AND WE FACED AN EMERGENCY, I'D BE FASTER THAN ANY OF YOU TO REACT, AND...
...TO FIGHT.

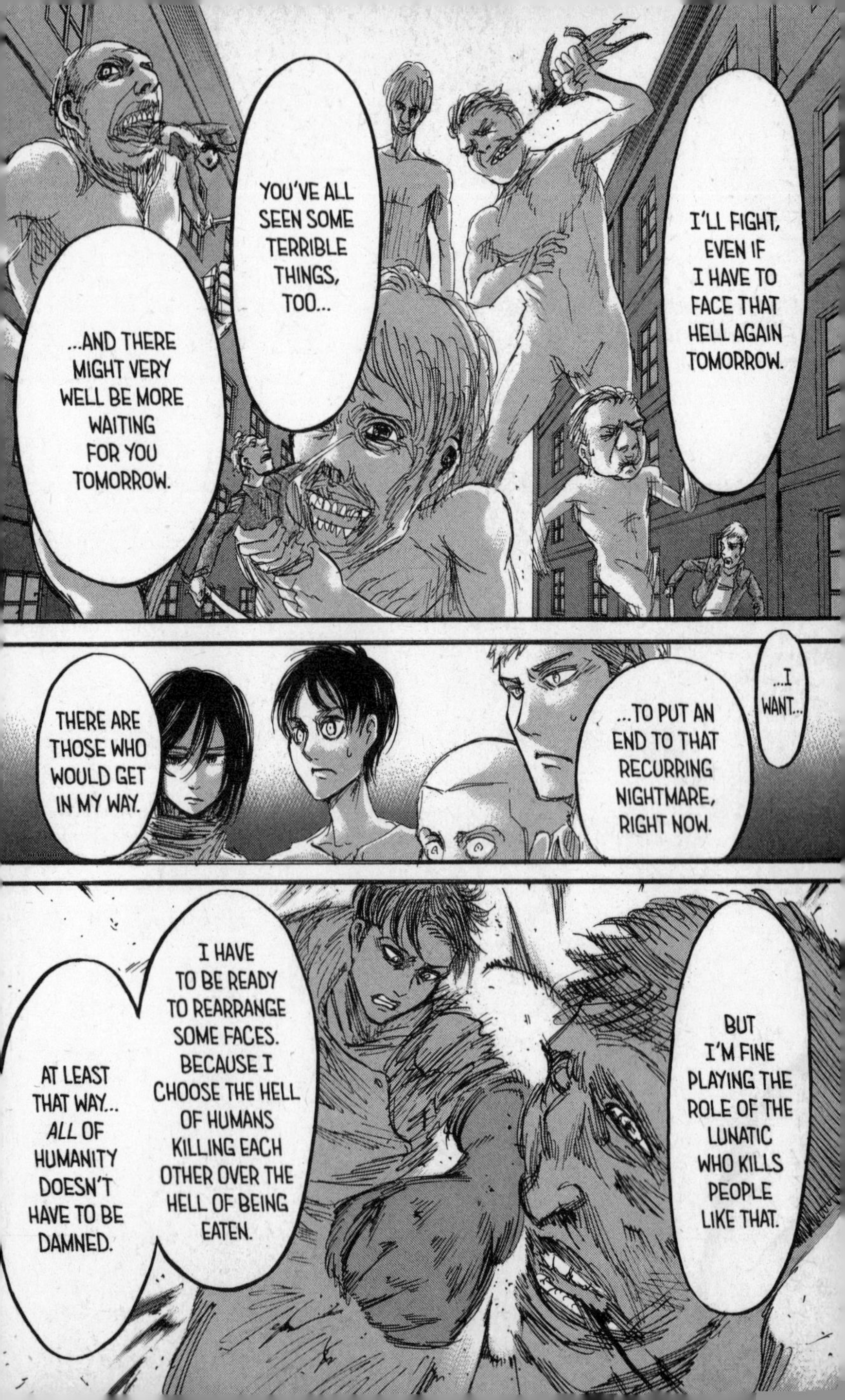
I'LL FIGHT, EVEN IF I HAVE TO FACE THAT HELL AGAIN TOMORROW.
YOU'VE ALL SEEN SOME TERRIBLE THINGS, TOO...
...AND THERE MIGHT VERY WELL BE MORE WAITING FOR YOU TOMORROW.
...I WANT...
...TO PUT AN END TO THAT RECURRING NIGHTMARE, RIGHT NOW.
THERE ARE THOSE WHO WOULD GET IN MY WAY.
BUT I'M FINE PLAYING THE ROLE OF THE LUNATIC WHO KILLS PEOPLE LIKE THAT.
I HAVE TO BE READY TO REARRANGE SOME FACES. BECAUSE I CHOOSE THE HELL OF HUMANS KILLING EACH OTHER OVER THE HELL OF BEING EATEN.
AT LEAST THAT WAY... *ALL* OF HUMANITY DOESN'T HAVE TO BE DAMNED.

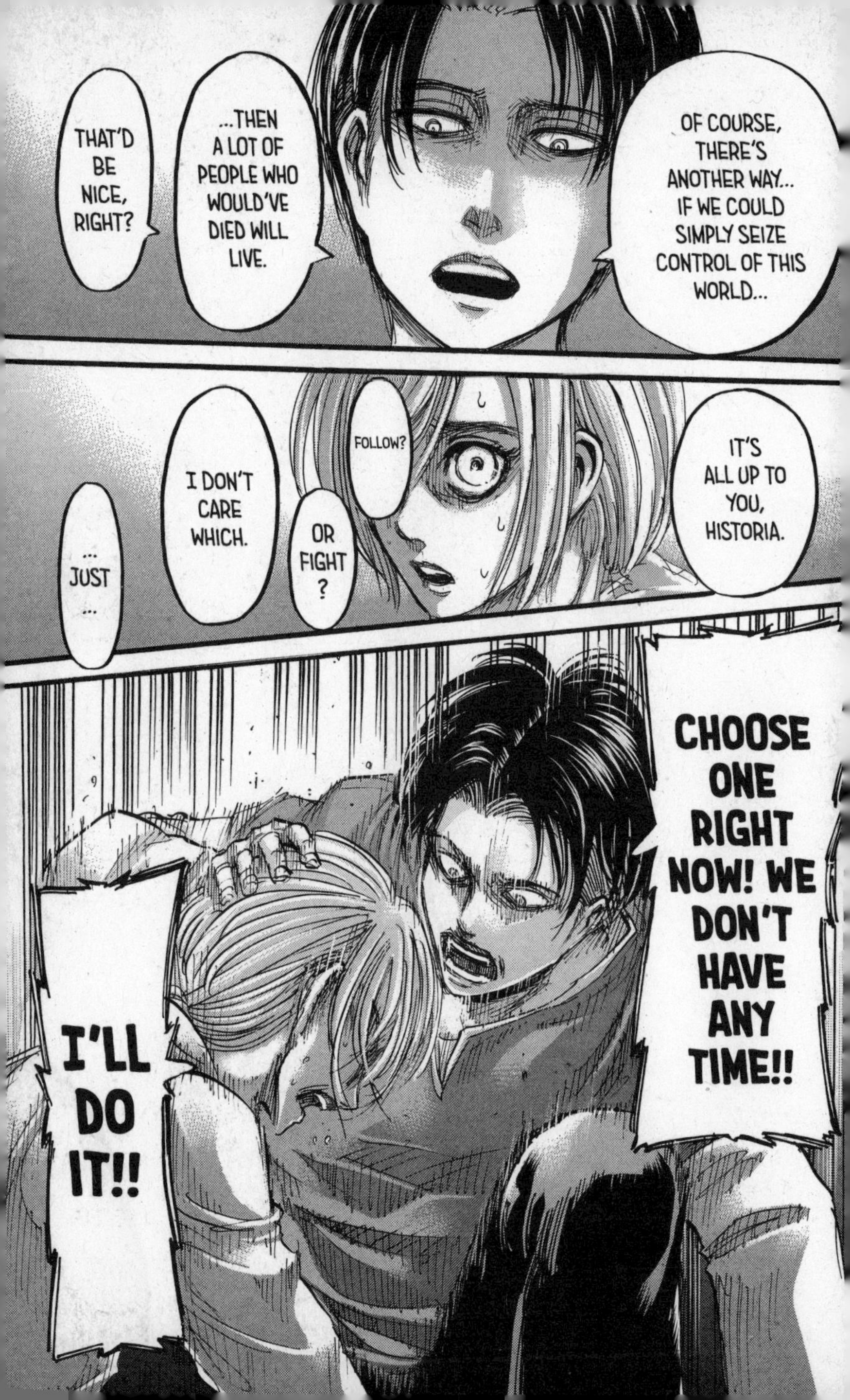
OF COURSE, THERE'S ANOTHER WAY... IF WE COULD SIMPLY SEIZE CONTROL OF THIS WORLD...
...THEN A LOT OF PEOPLE WHO WOULD'VE DIED WILL LIVE.
THAT'D BE NICE, RIGHT?
IT'S ALL UP TO YOU, HISTORIA.
FOLLOW?
OR FIGHT?
I DON'T CARE WHICH.
... JUST ...
CHOOSE ONE RIGHT NOW! WE DON'T HAVE ANY TIME!!
I'LL DO IT!!

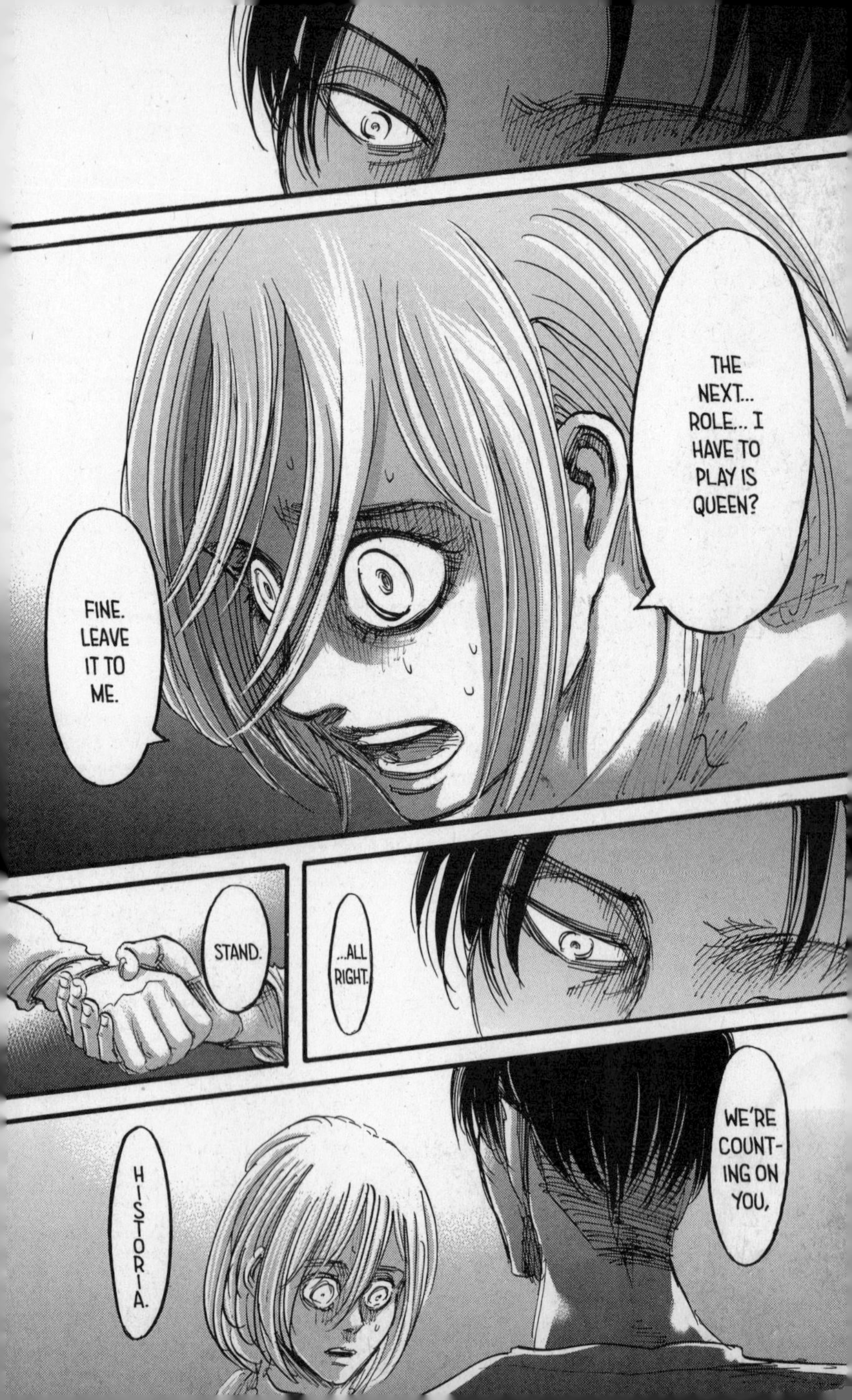
THE NEXT... ROLE... I HAVE TO PLAY IS QUEEN?
FINE. LEAVE IT TO ME.
...ALL RIGHT.
STAND.
WE'RE COUNT-ING ON YOU,
HISTORIA.

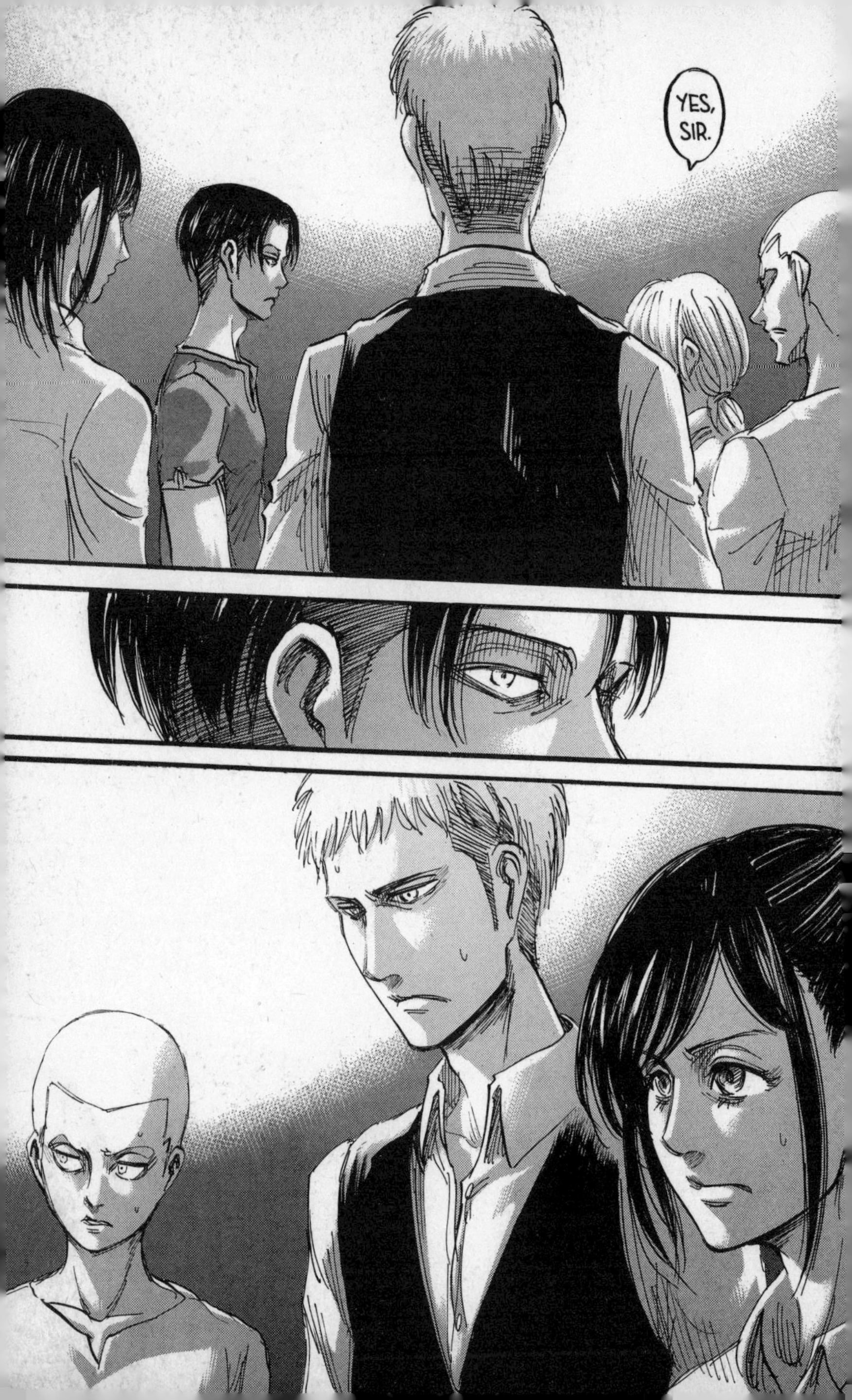
YES, SIR.

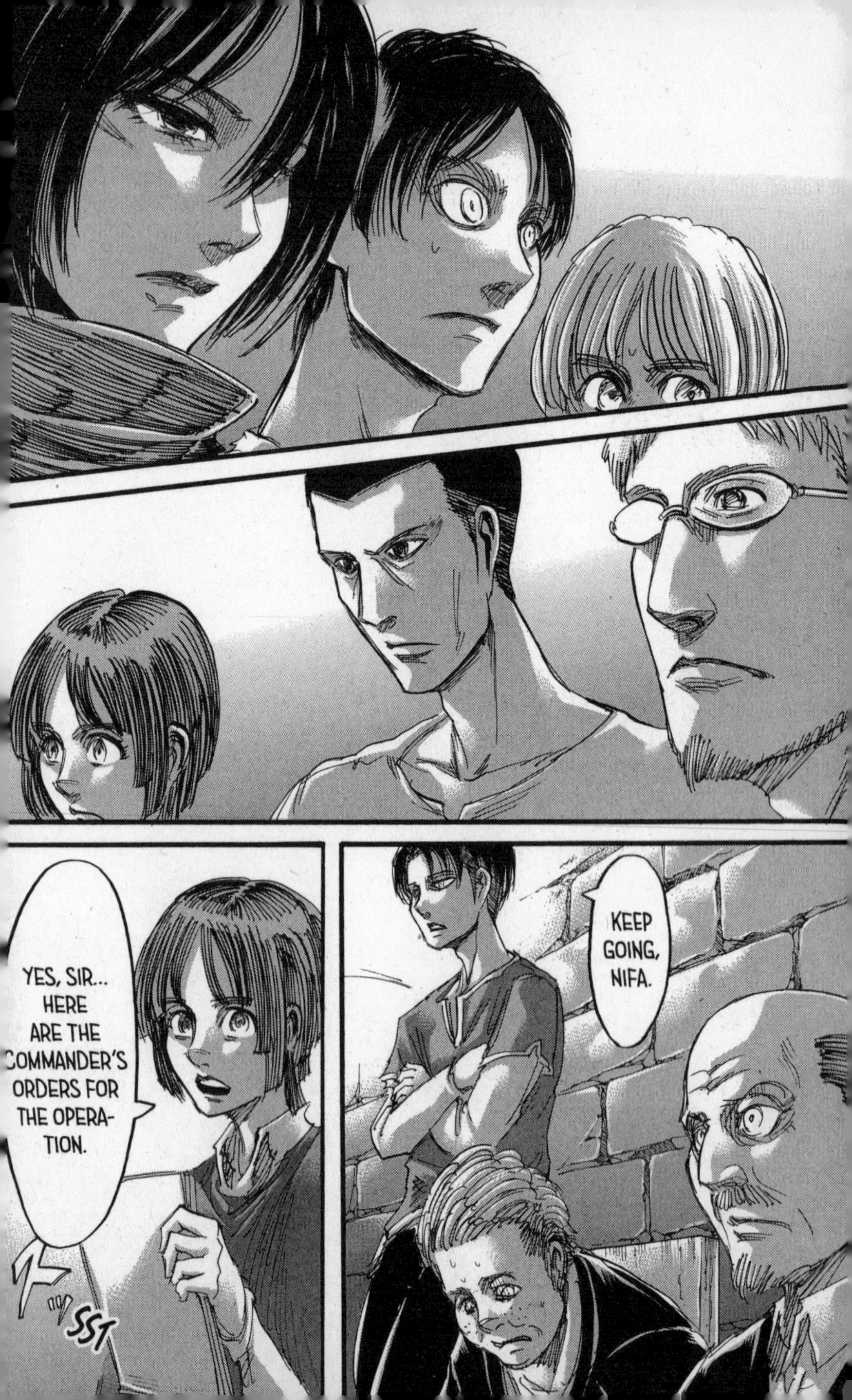
KEEP GOING, NIFA.
YES, SIR... HERE ARE THE COMMANDER'S ORDERS FOR THE OPERA- TION.
SST

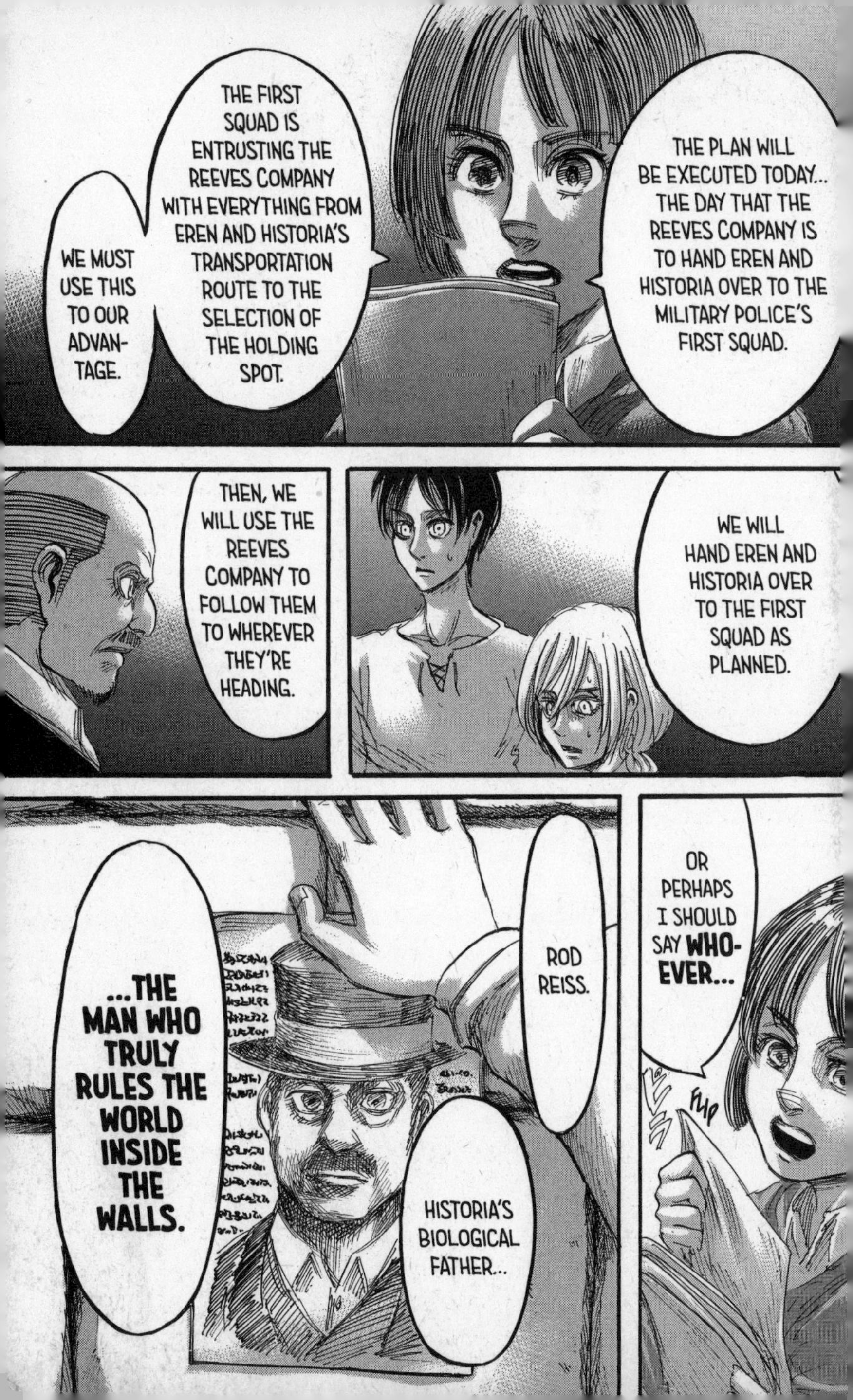
THE PLAN WILL BE EXECUTED TODAY... THE DAY THAT THE REEVES COMPANY IS TO HAND EREN AND HISTORIA OVER TO THE MILITARY POLICE'S FIRST SQUAD.
THE FIRST SQUAD IS ENTRUSTING THE REEVES COMPANY WITH EVERYTHING FROM EREN AND HISTORIA'S TRANSPORTATION ROUTE TO THE SELECTION OF THE HOLDING SPOT.
WE MUST USE THIS TO OUR ADVAN-TAGE.
WE WILL HAND EREN AND HISTORIA OVER TO THE FIRST SQUAD AS PLANNED.
THEN, WE WILL USE THE REEVES COMPANY TO FOLLOW THEM TO WHEREVER THEY'RE HEADING.
OR PERHAPS I SHOULD SAY **WHO-EVER...**
FLIP
ROD REISS.
HISTORIA'S BIOLOGICAL FATHER...
...THE MAN WHO TRULY RULES THE WORLD INSIDE THE WALLS.

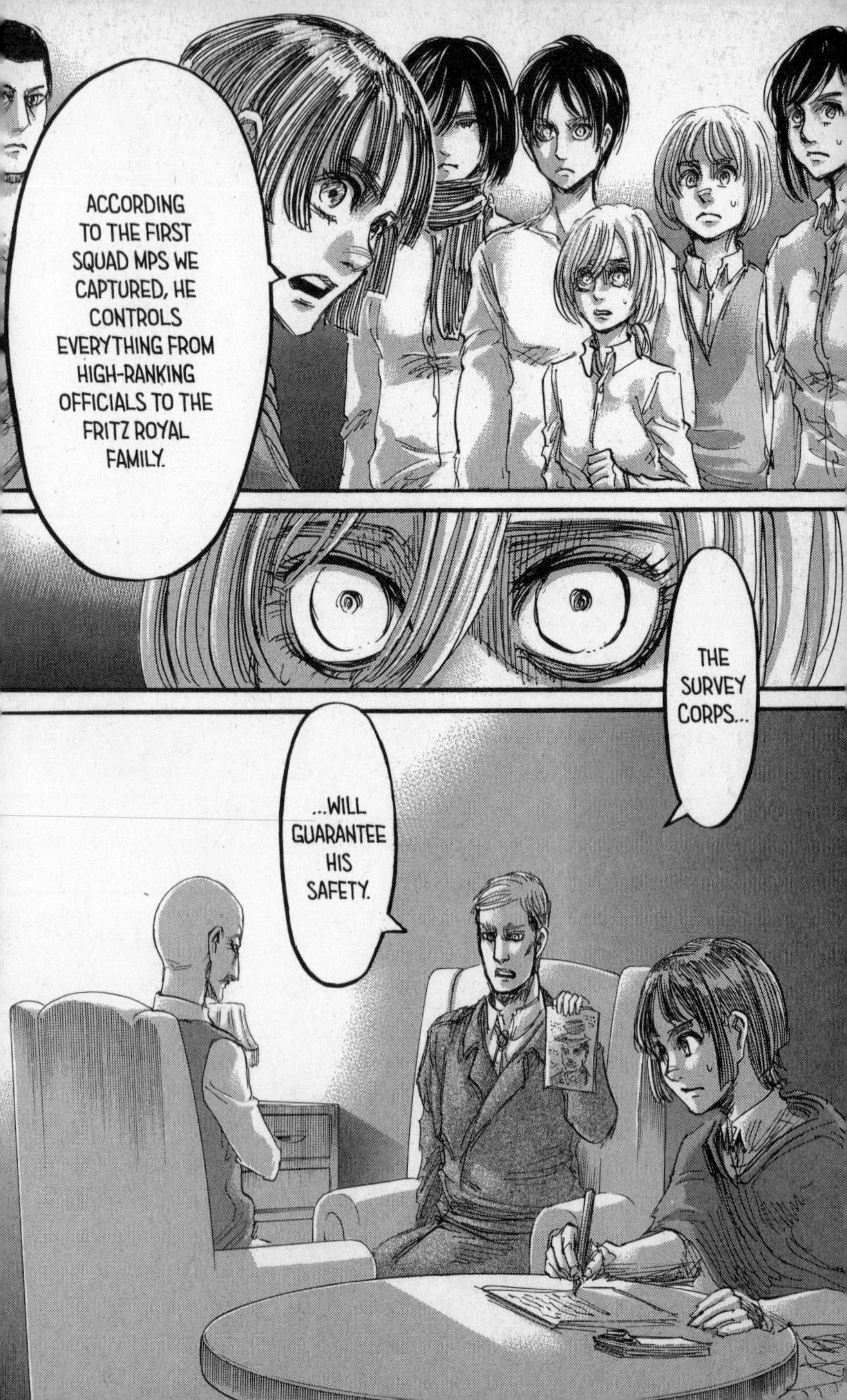
ACCORDING TO THE FIRST SQUAD MPS WE CAPTURED, HE CONTROLS EVERYTHING FROM HIGH-RANKING OFFICIALS TO THE FRITZ ROYAL FAMILY.
THE SURVEY CORPS...
...WILL GUARANTEE HIS SAFETY.

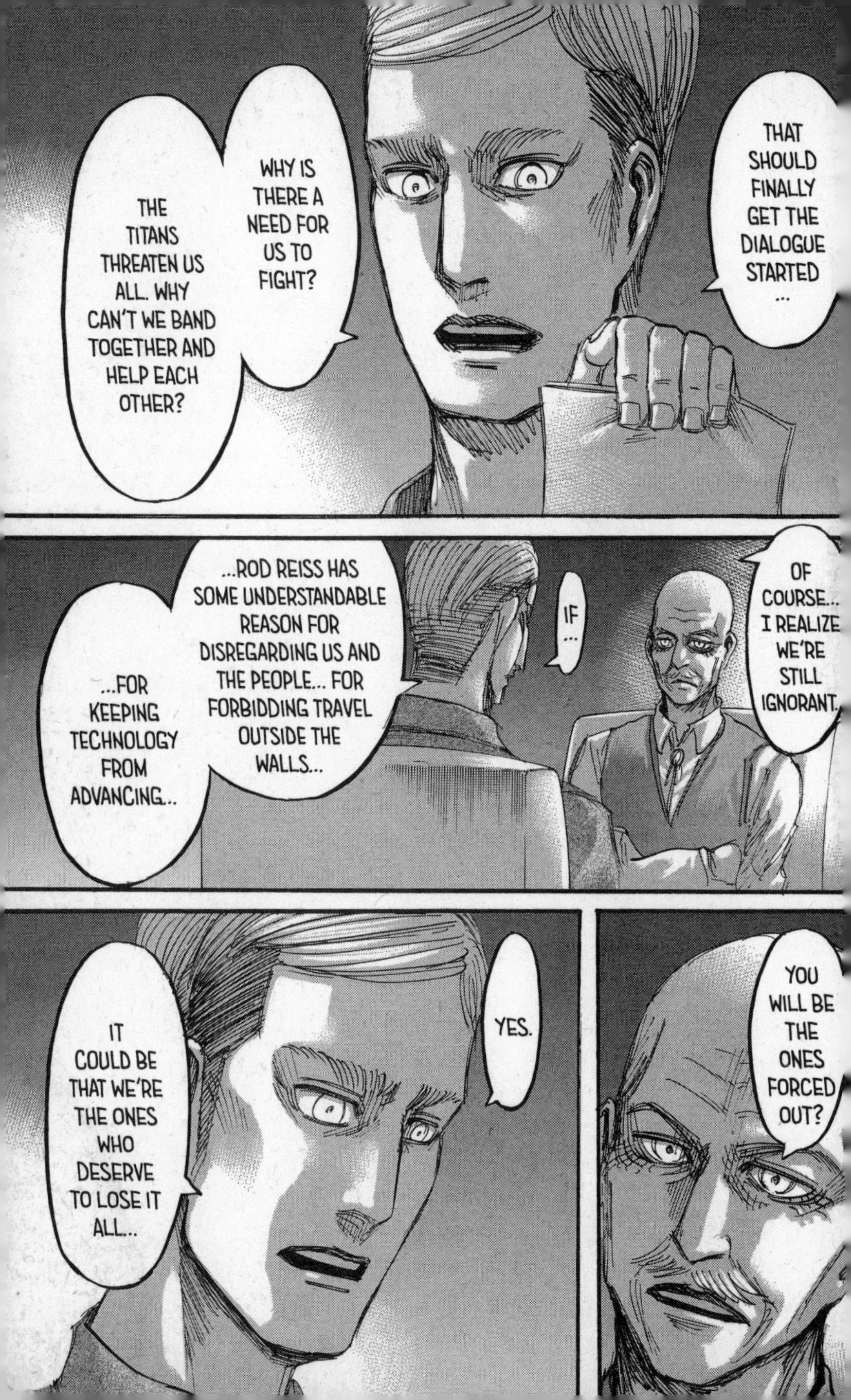
THAT SHOULD FINALLY GET THE DIALOGUE STARTED...
WHY IS THERE A NEED FOR US TO FIGHT?
THE TITANS THREATEN US ALL. WHY CAN'T WE BAND TOGETHER AND HELP EACH OTHER?
OF COURSE... I REALIZE WE'RE STILL IGNORANT.
IF...
...ROD REISS HAS SOME UNDERSTANDABLE REASON FOR DISREGARDING US AND THE PEOPLE... FOR FORBIDDING TRAVEL OUTSIDE THE WALLS...
...FOR KEEPING TECHNOLOGY FROM ADVANCING...
YOU WILL BE THE ONES FORCED OUT?
YES.
IT COULD BE THAT WE'RE THE ONES WHO DESERVE TO LOSE IT ALL...

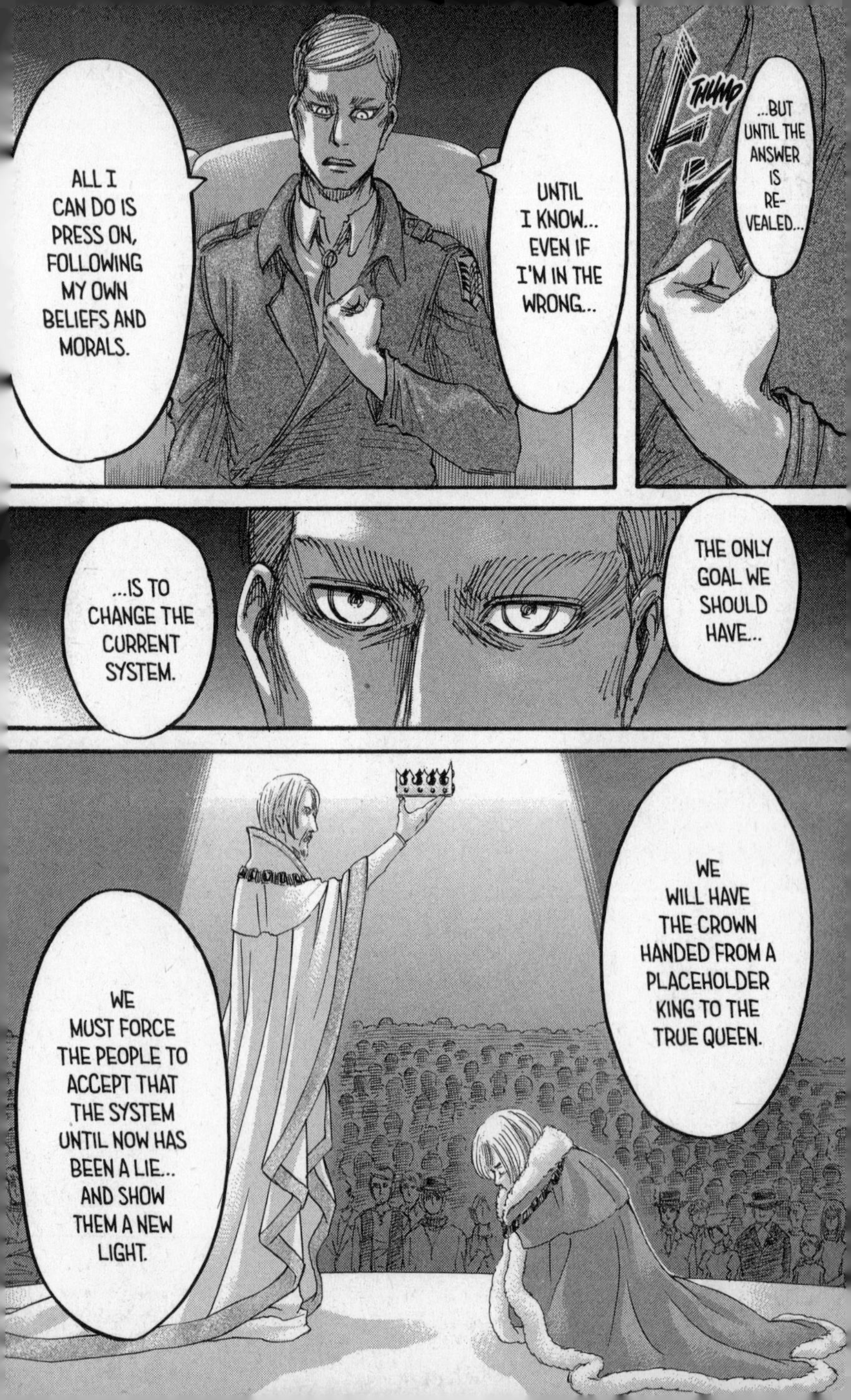
THUMP
...BUT UNTIL THE ANSWER IS RE- VEALED...
UNTIL I KNOW... EVEN IF I'M IN THE WRONG...
ALL I CAN DO IS PRESS ON, FOLLOWING MY OWN BELIEFS AND MORALS.
THE ONLY GOAL WE SHOULD HAVE...
...IS TO CHANGE THE CURRENT SYSTEM.
WE WILL HAVE THE CROWN HANDED FROM A PLACEHOLDER KING TO THE TRUE QUEEN.
WE MUST FORCE THE PEOPLE TO ACCEPT THAT THE SYSTEM UNTIL NOW HAS BEEN A LIE... AND SHOW THEM A NEW LIGHT.

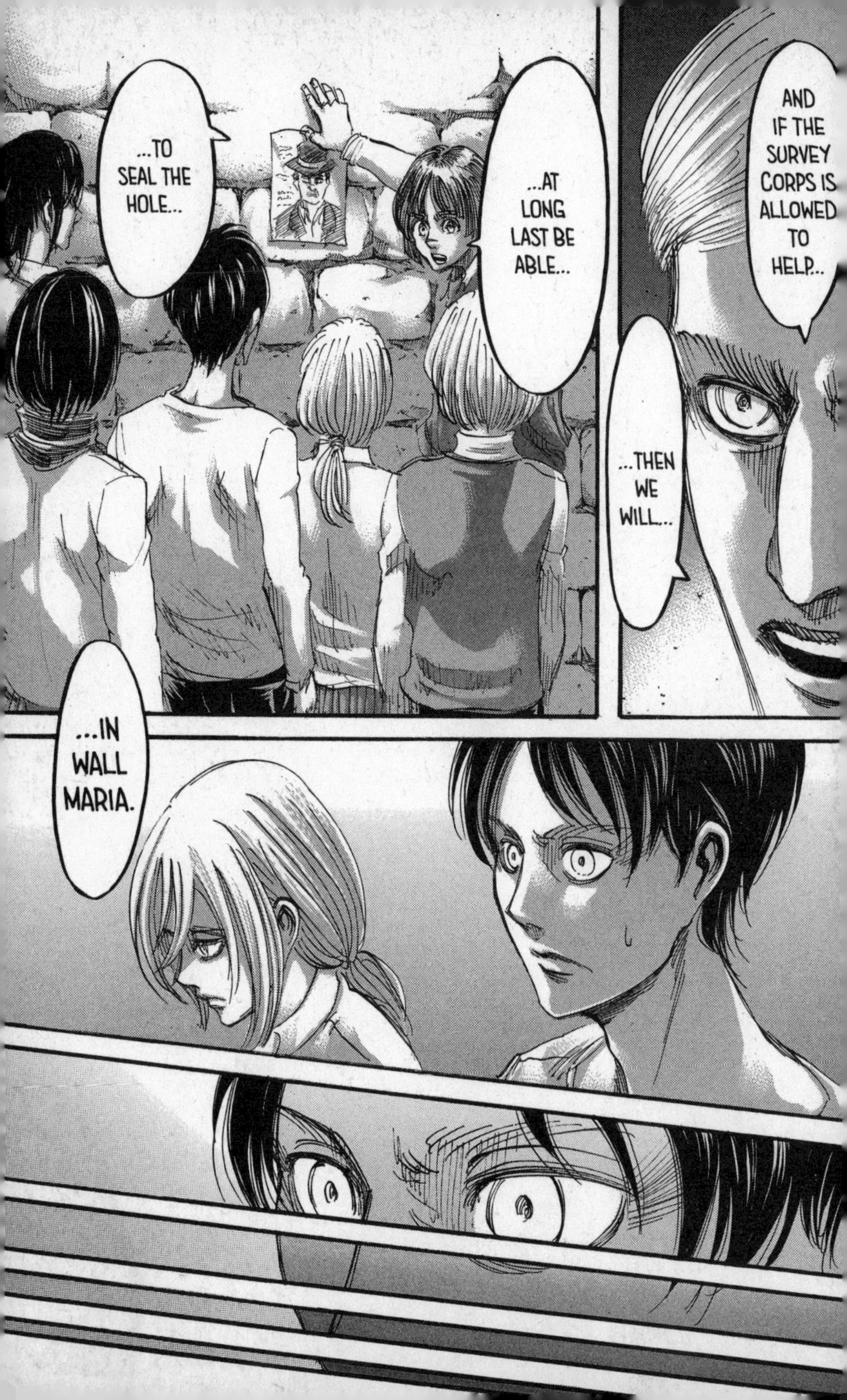
AND IF THE SURVEY CORPS IS ALLOWED TO HELP...
...THEN WE WILL...
...AT LONG LAST BE ABLE...
...TO SEAL THE HOLE...
...IN WALL MARIA.

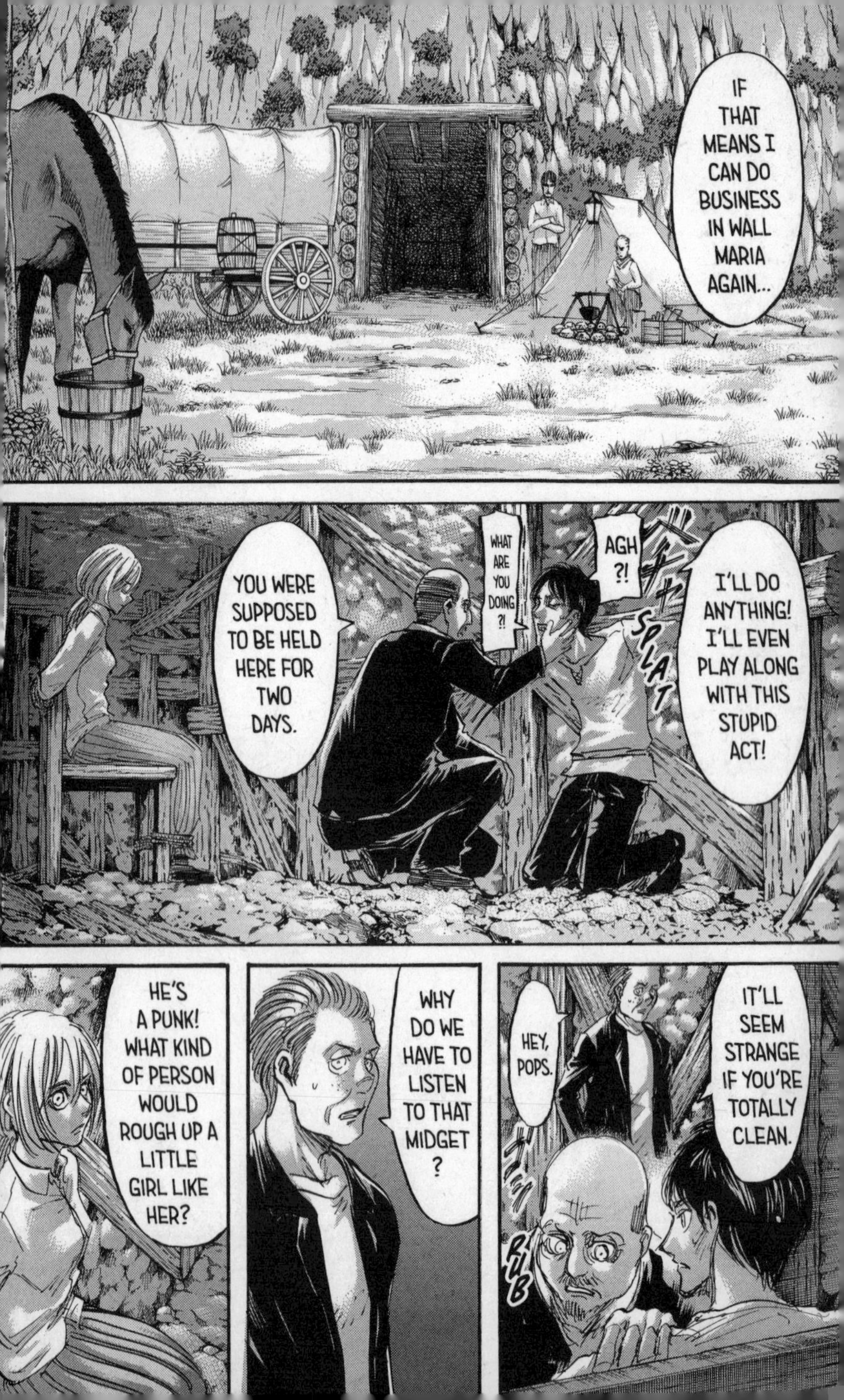
IF THAT MEANS I CAN DO BUSINESS IN WALL MARIA AGAIN...
I'LL DO ANYTHING! I'LL EVEN PLAY ALONG WITH THIS STUPID ACT!
SPLAT
AGH?!
WHAT ARE YOU DOING?!
YOU WERE SUPPOSED TO BE HELD HERE FOR TWO DAYS.
IT'LL SEEM STRANGE IF YOU'RE TOTALLY CLEAN.
HEY, POPS.
RUB
WHY DO WE HAVE TO LISTEN TO THAT MIDGET?
HE'S A PUNK! WHAT KIND OF PERSON WOULD ROUGH UP A LITTLE GIRL LIKE HER?

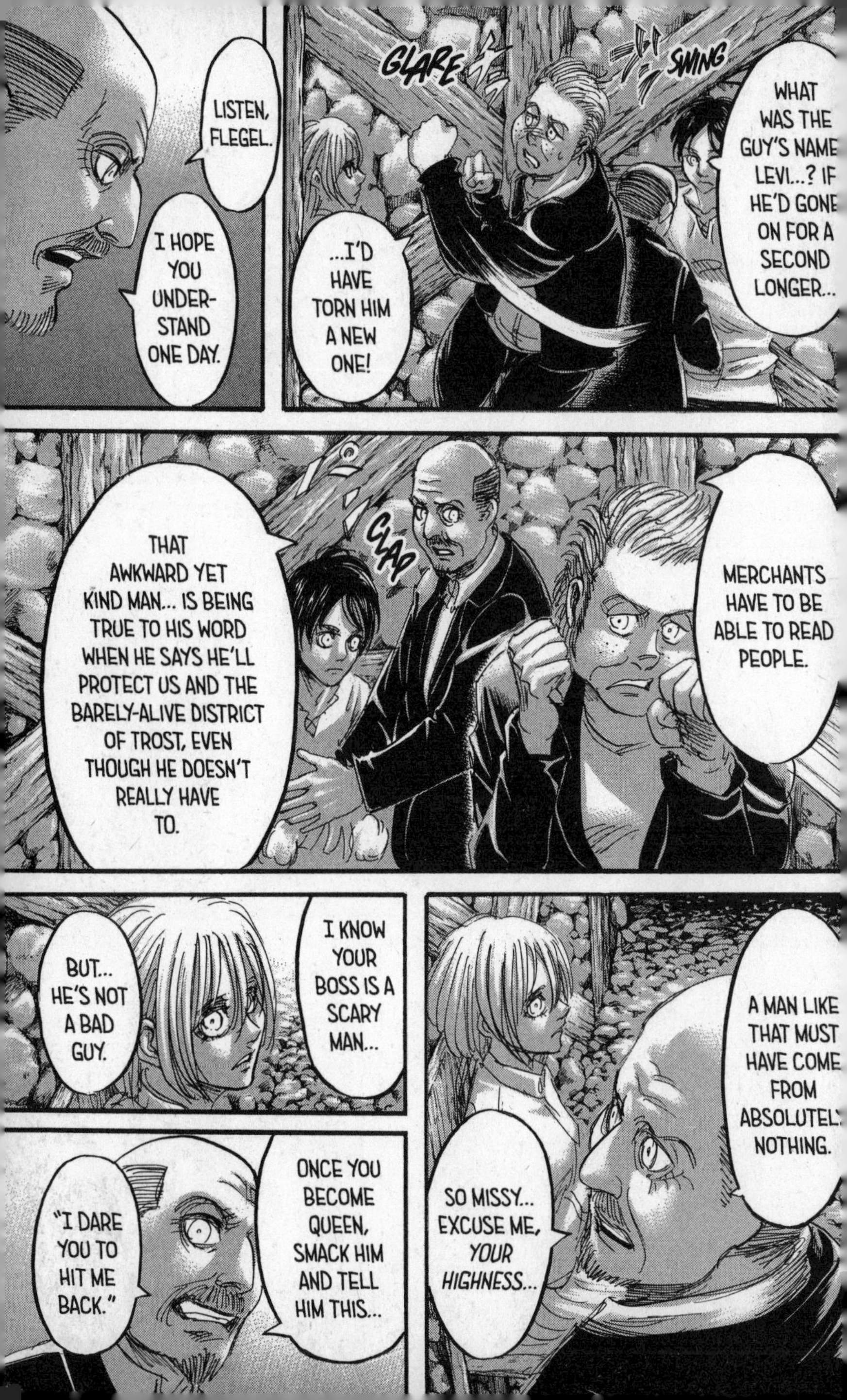
GLARE
SWING
WHAT WAS THE GUY'S NAME LEVI...? IF HE'D GONE ON FOR A SECOND LONGER...
...I'D HAVE TORN HIM A NEW ONE!
LISTEN, FLEGEL.
I HOPE YOU UNDER-STAND ONE DAY.
MERCHANTS HAVE TO BE ABLE TO READ PEOPLE.
CLAP
THAT AWKWARD YET KIND MAN... IS BEING TRUE TO HIS WORD WHEN HE SAYS HE'LL PROTECT US AND THE BARELY-ALIVE DISTRICT OF TROST, EVEN THOUGH HE DOESN'T REALLY HAVE TO.
A MAN LIKE THAT MUST HAVE COME FROM ABSOLUTEL NOTHING.
SO MISSY... EXCUSE ME, *YOUR HIGHNESS*...
I KNOW YOUR BOSS IS A SCARY MAN...
BUT... HE'S NOT A BAD GUY.
ONCE YOU BECOME QUEEN, SMACK HIM AND TELL HIM THIS...
"I DARE YOU TO HIT ME BACK."

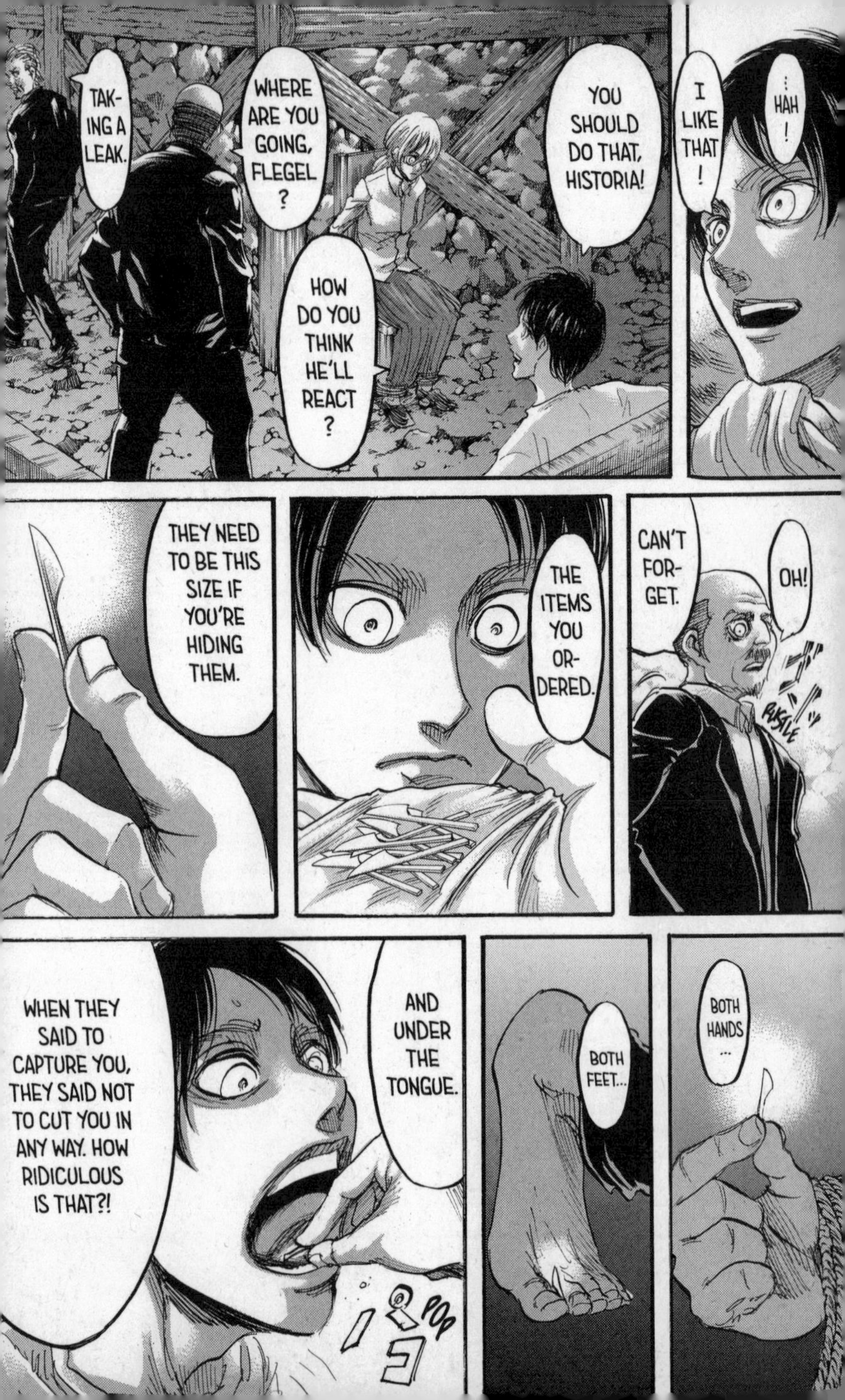
...HAH!
I LIKE THAT!
YOU SHOULD DO THAT, HISTORIA!
HOW DO YOU THINK HE'LL REACT?
WHERE ARE YOU GOING, FLEGEL?
TAK-ING A LEAK.
OH!
CAN'T FOR-GET.
THE ITEMS YOU OR-DERED.
THEY NEED TO BE THIS SIZE IF YOU'RE HIDING THEM.
BOTH HANDS...
BOTH FEET...
AND UNDER THE TONGUE.
WHEN THEY SAID TO CAPTURE YOU, THEY SAID NOT TO CUT YOU IN ANY WAY. HOW RIDICULOUS IS THAT?!
POP

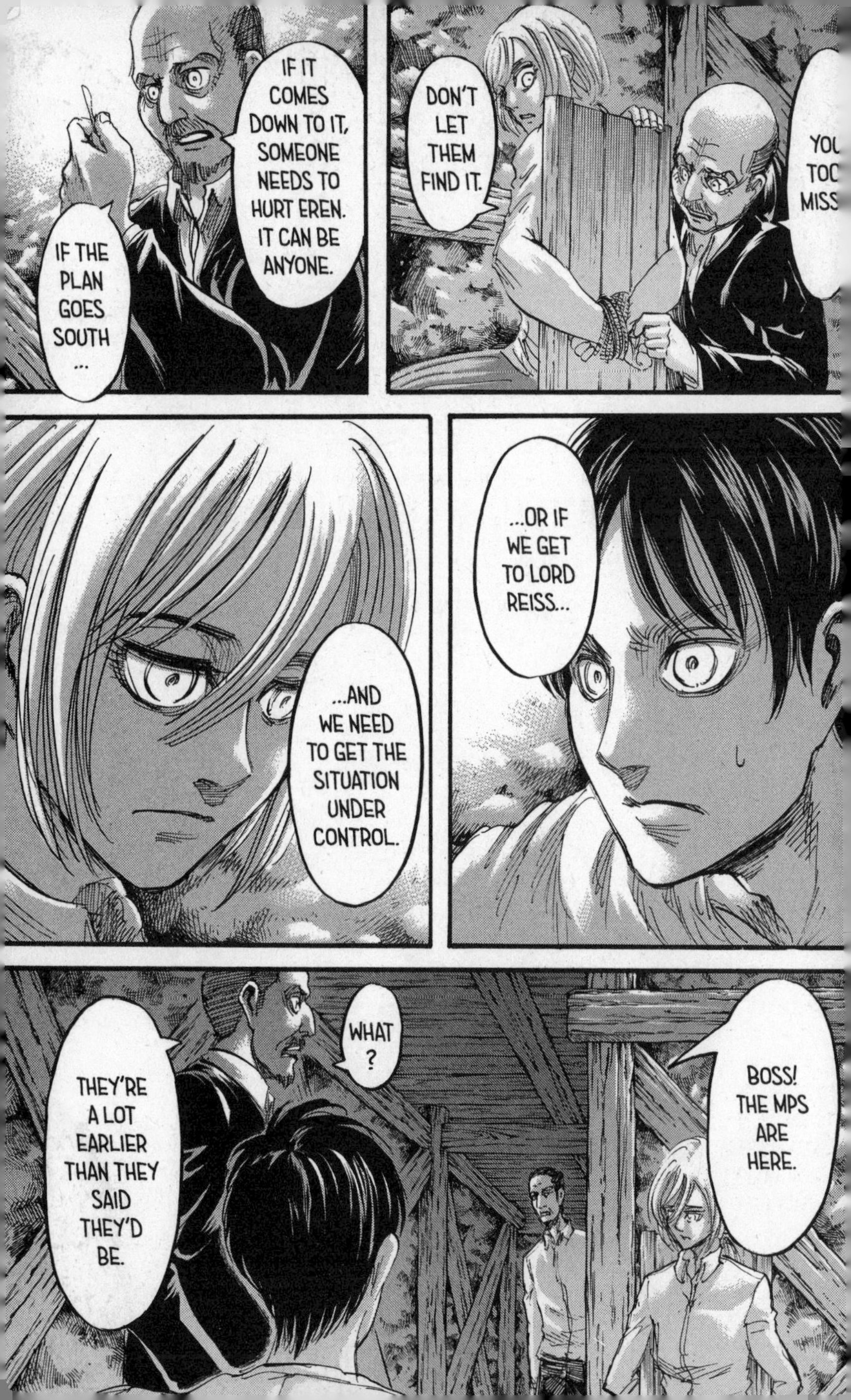
YOU TOO MISS
DON'T LET THEM FIND IT.
IF IT COMES DOWN TO IT, SOMEONE NEEDS TO HURT EREN. IT CAN BE ANYONE.
IF THE PLAN GOES SOUTH ...
...OR IF WE GET TO LORD REISS...
...AND WE NEED TO GET THE SITUATION UNDER CONTROL.
BOSS! THE MPS ARE HERE.
WHAT ?
THEY'RE A LOT EARLIER THAN THEY SAID THEY'D BE.

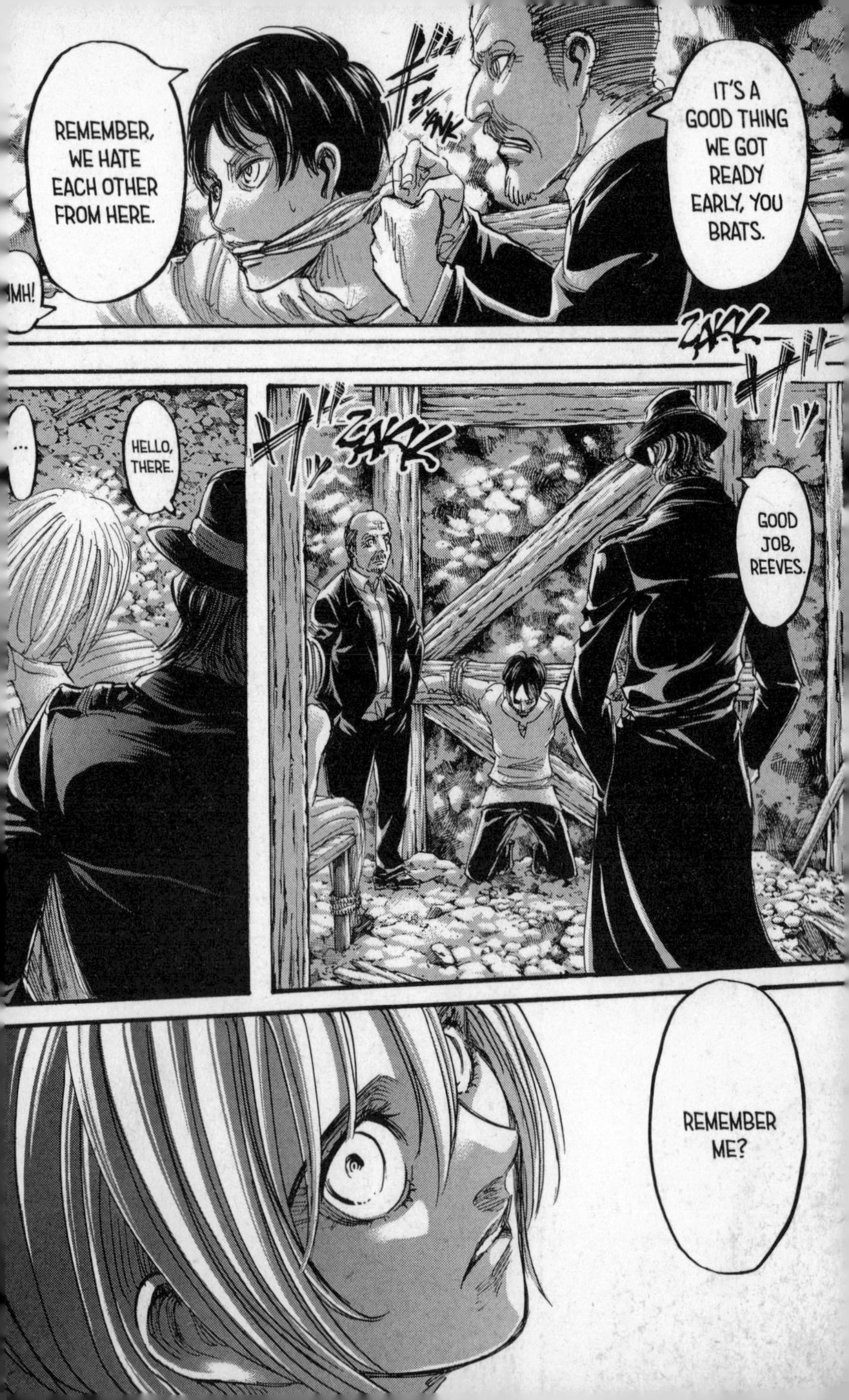
IT'S A GOOD THING WE GOT READY EARLY, YOU BRATS.
YANK
REMEMBER, WE HATE EACH OTHER FROM HERE.
MH!
ZAKK
GOOD JOB, REEVES.
ZAKK
HELLO, THERE.
...
REMEMBER ME?

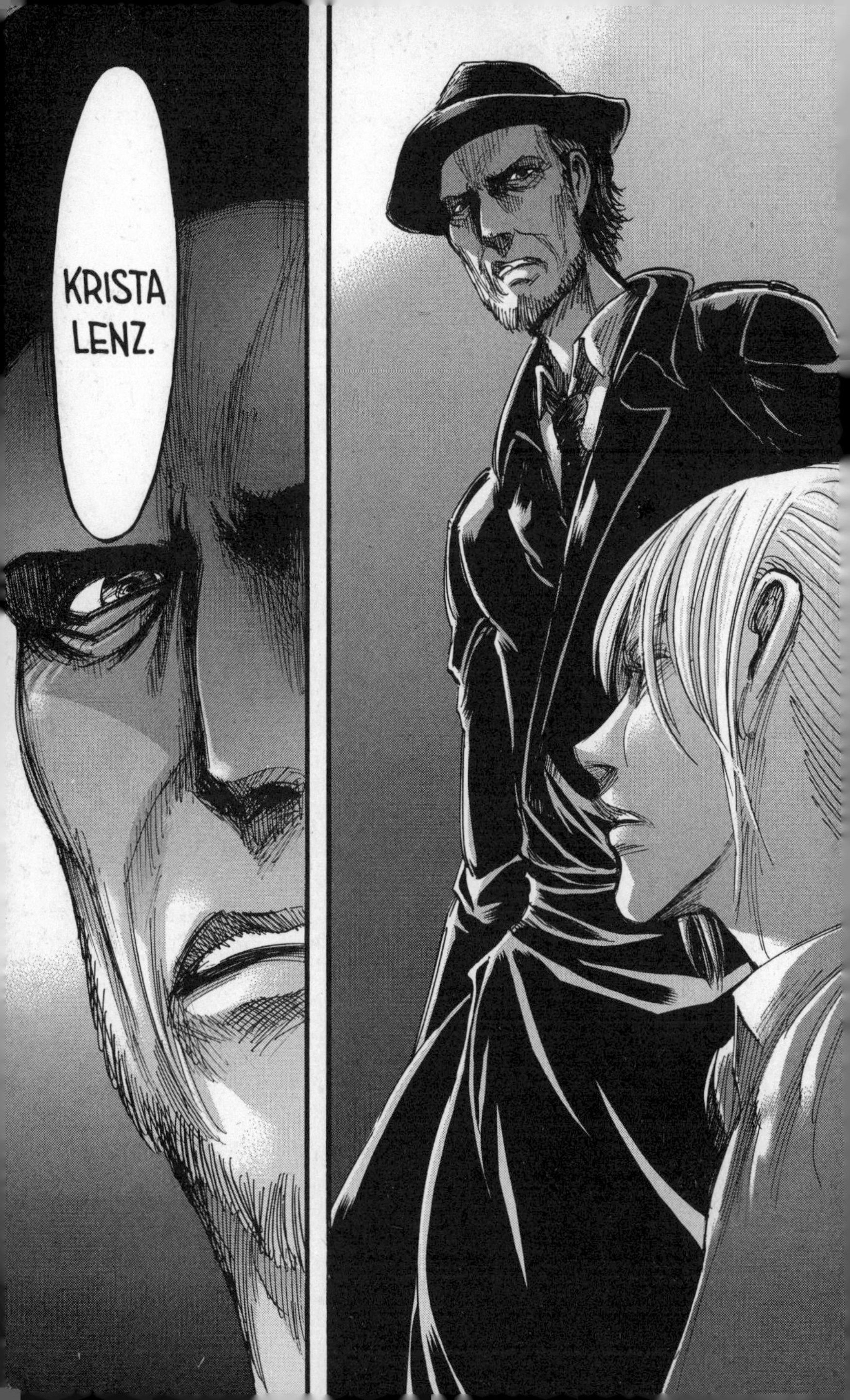
KRISTA LENZ.

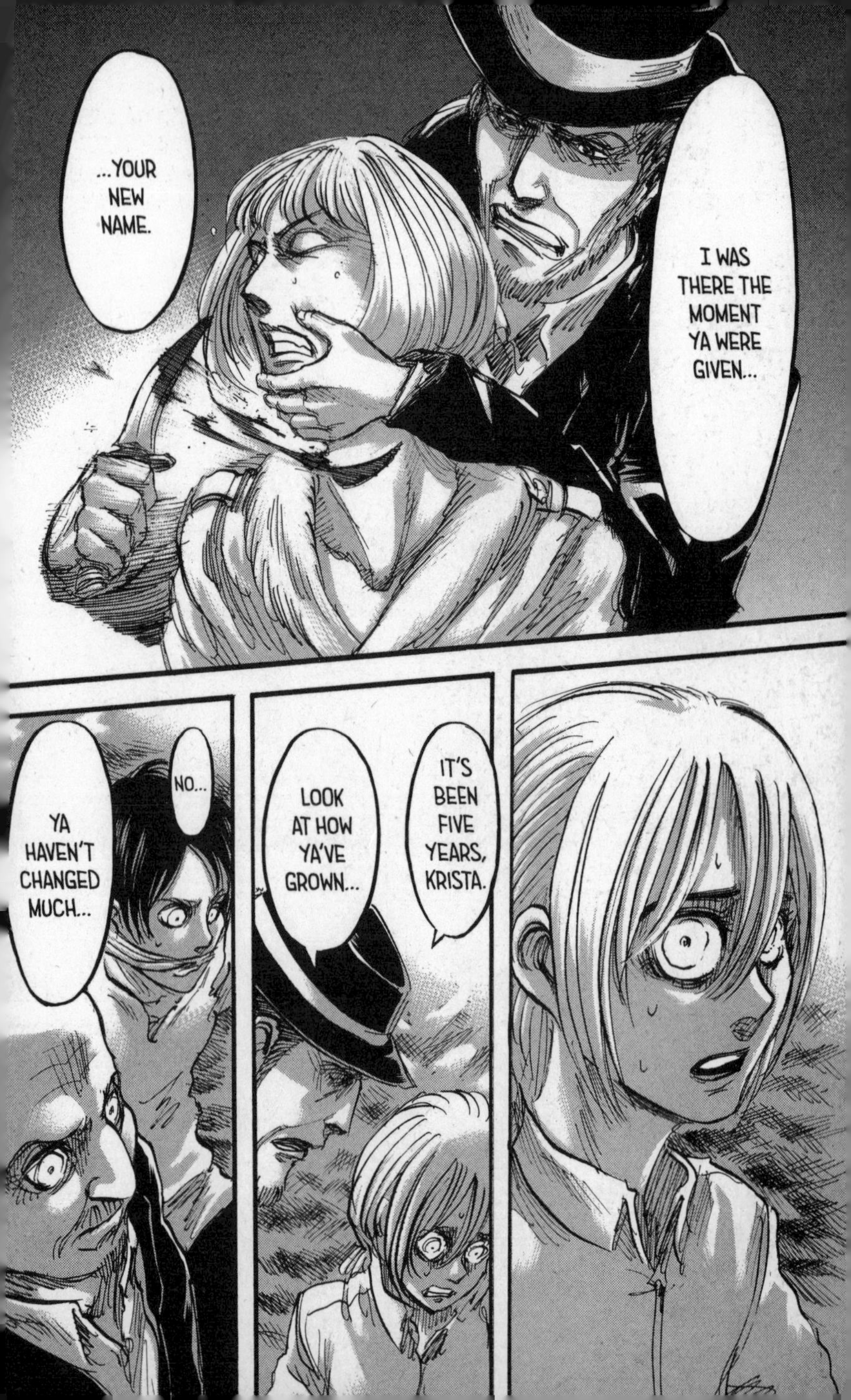
I WAS THERE THE MOMENT YA WERE GIVEN...
...YOUR NEW NAME.
IT'S BEEN FIVE YEARS, KRISTA.
LOOK AT HOW YA'VE GROWN...
NO...
YA HAVEN'T CHANGED MUCH...

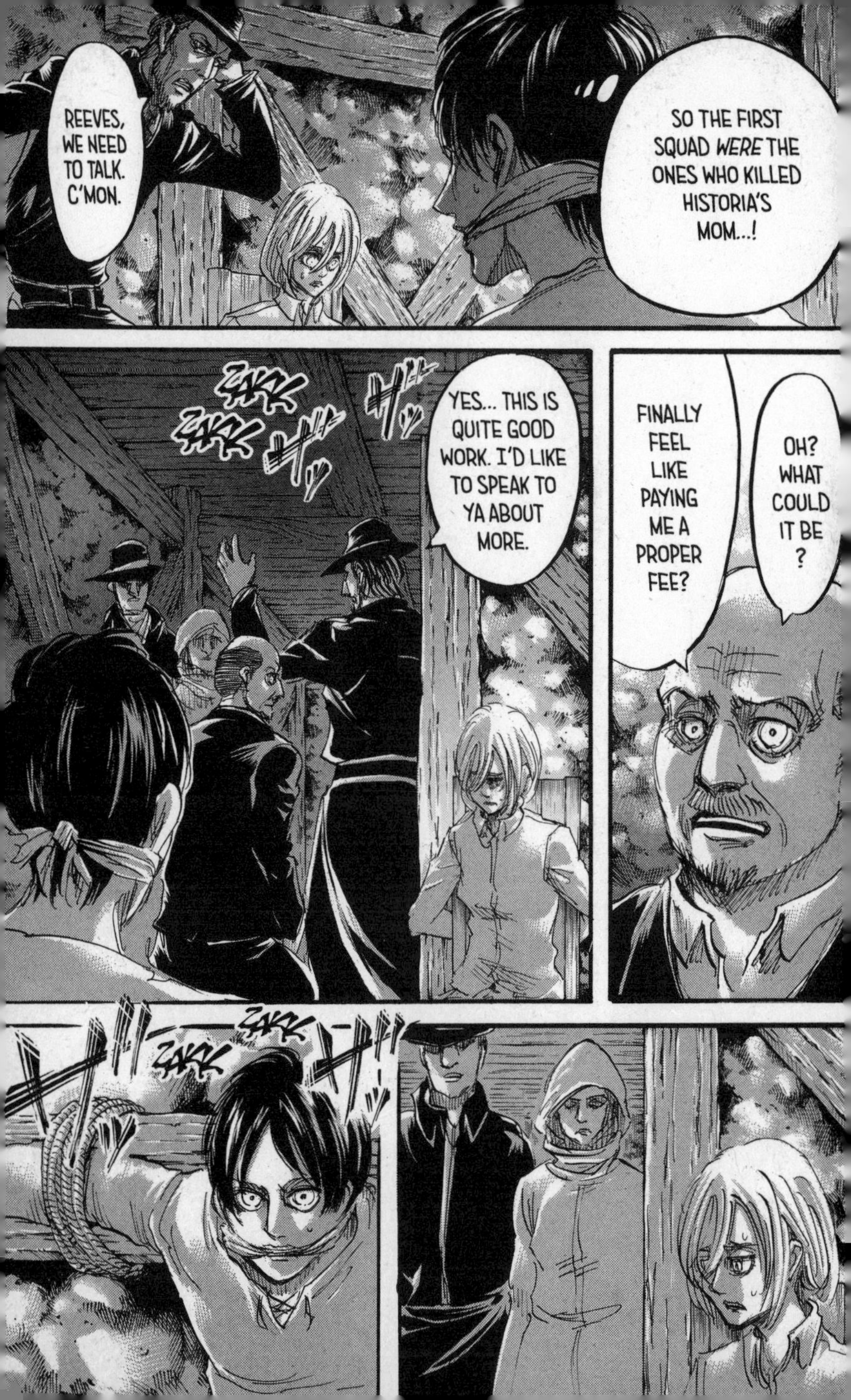

SO THE FIRST SQUAD *WERE* THE ONES WHO KILLED HISTORIA'S MOM...!
REEVES, WE NEED TO TALK. C'MON.
OH? WHAT COULD IT BE?
FINALLY FEEL LIKE PAYING ME A PROPER FEE?
YES... THIS IS QUITE GOOD WORK. I'D LIKE TO SPEAK TO YA ABOUT MORE.

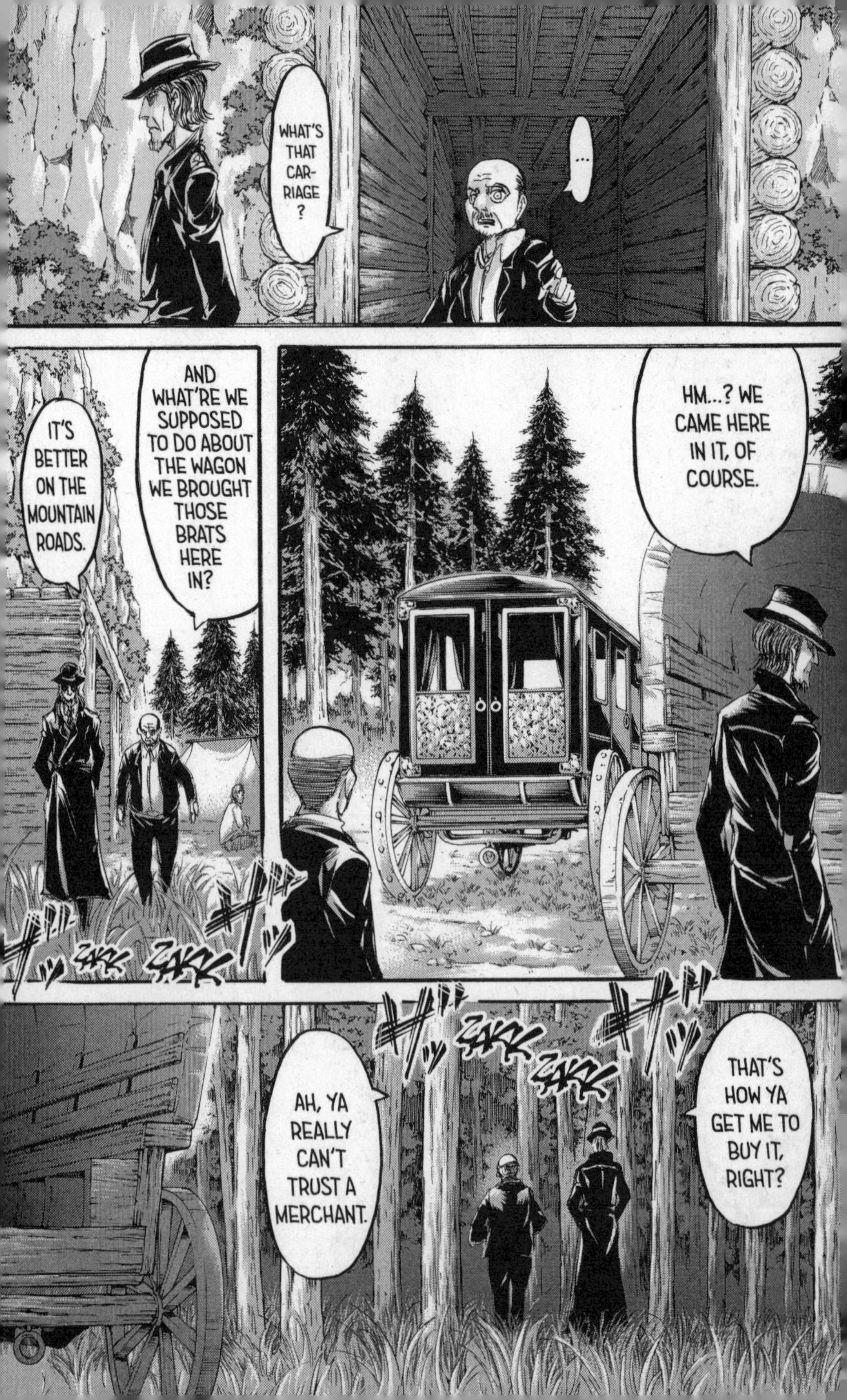
...
WHAT'S THAT CAR-RIAGE?
HM...? WE CAME HERE IN IT, OF COURSE.
AND WHAT'RE WE SUPPOSED TO DO ABOUT THE WAGON WE BROUGHT THOSE BRATS HERE IN?
IT'S BETTER ON THE MOUNTAIN ROADS.
ZAKK
ZAKK
THAT'S HOW YA GET ME TO BUY IT, RIGHT?
ZAKK
ZAKK
AH, YA REALLY CAN'T TRUST A MERCHANT.

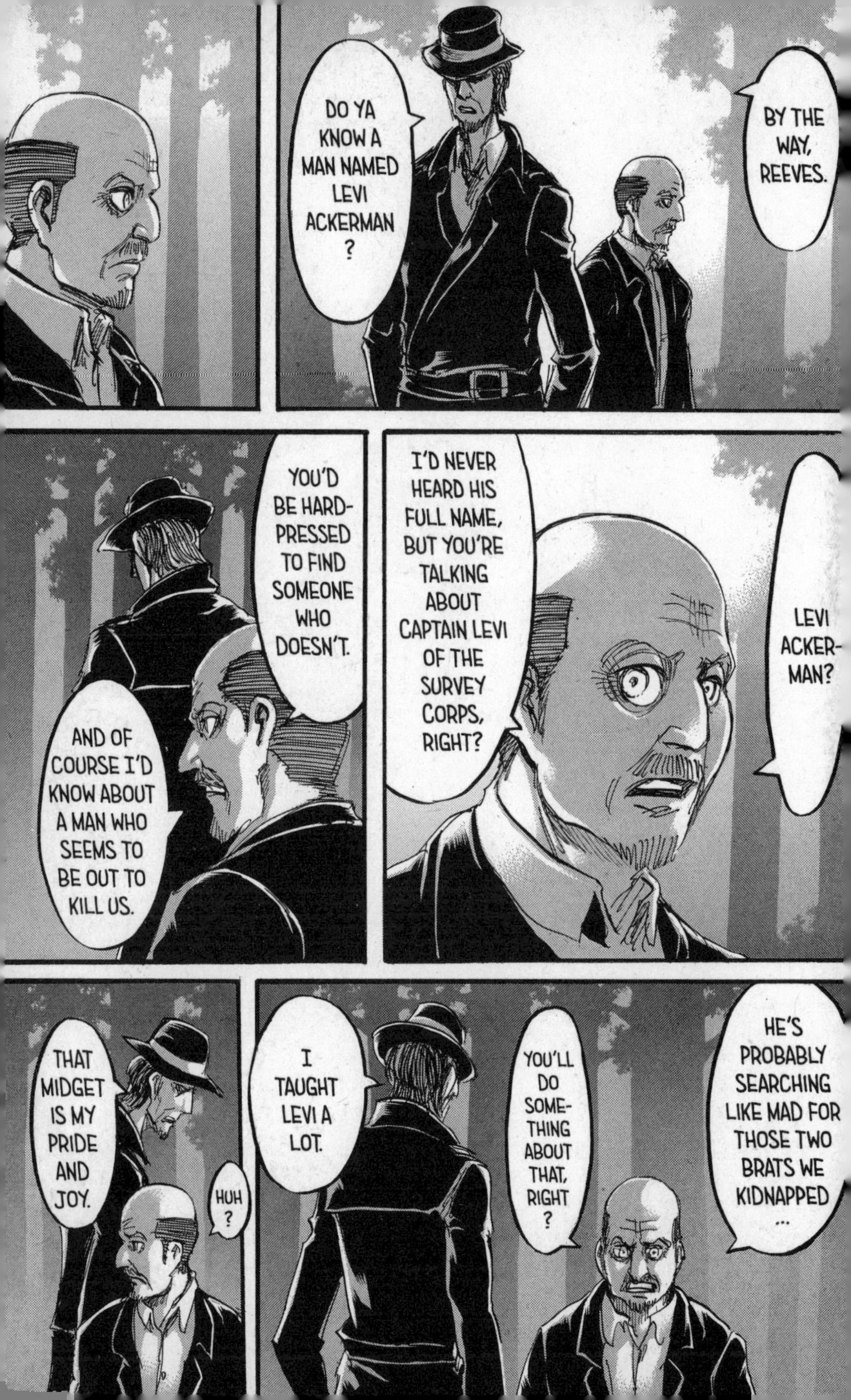
BY THE WAY, REEVES.
DO YA KNOW A MAN NAMED LEVI ACKERMAN?
LEVI ACKERMAN?
I'D NEVER HEARD HIS FULL NAME, BUT YOU'RE TALKING ABOUT CAPTAIN LEVI OF THE SURVEY CORPS, RIGHT?
YOU'D BE HARD-PRESSED TO FIND SOMEONE WHO DOESN'T.
AND OF COURSE I'D KNOW ABOUT A MAN WHO SEEMS TO BE OUT TO KILL US.
HE'S PROBABLY SEARCHING LIKE MAD FOR THOSE TWO BRATS WE KIDNAPPED...
YOU'LL DO SOMETHING ABOUT THAT, RIGHT?
I TAUGHT LEVI A LOT.
THAT MIDGET IS MY PRIDE AND JOY.
HUH?

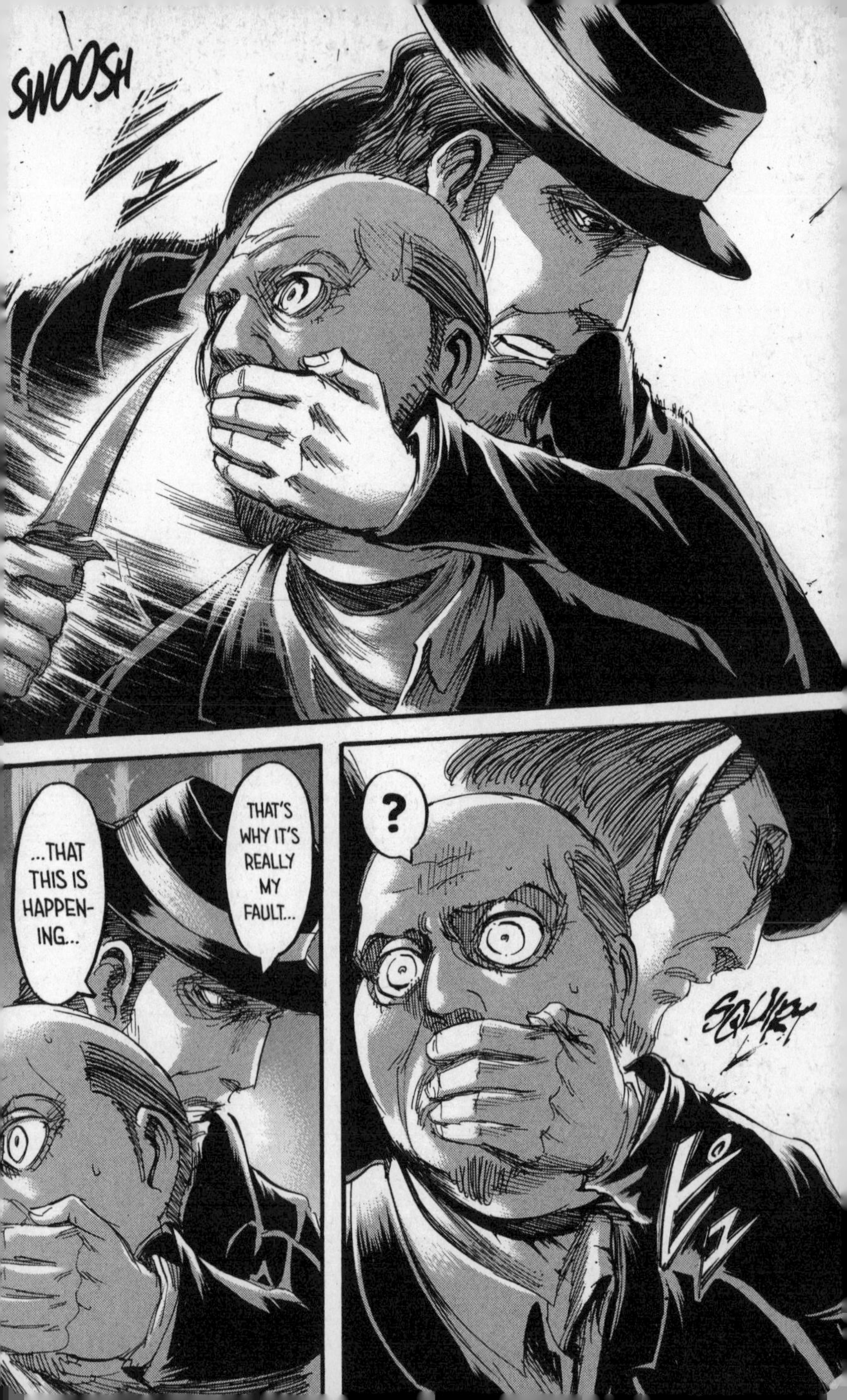
SWOOSH
?
SQUIRT
THAT'S WHY IT'S REALLY MY FAULT...
...THAT THIS IS HAPPEN-ING...

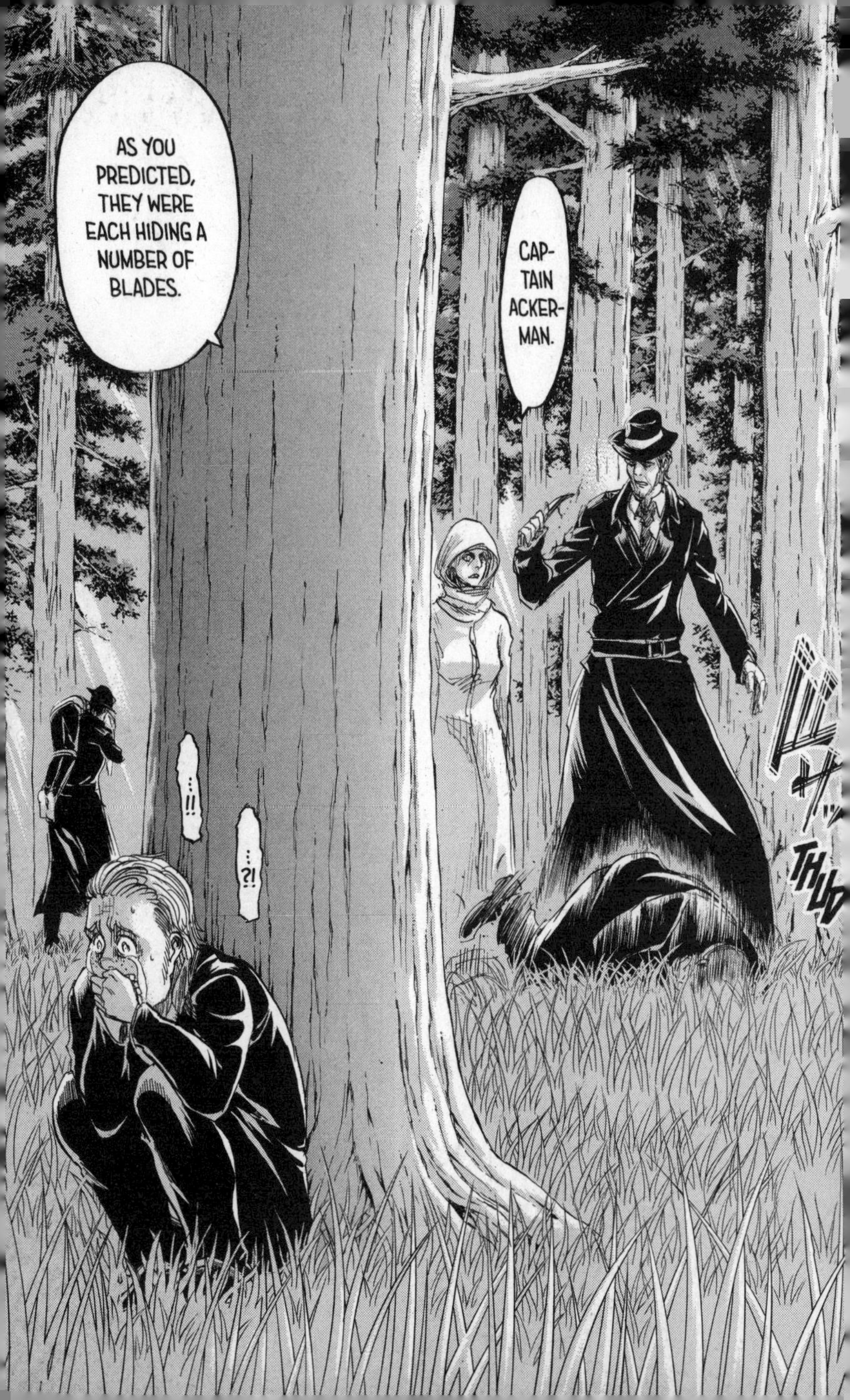
CAP-TAIN ACKER-MAN.
AS YOU PREDICTED, THEY WERE EACH HIDING A NUMBER OF BLADES.
THUD
...!!
...?!

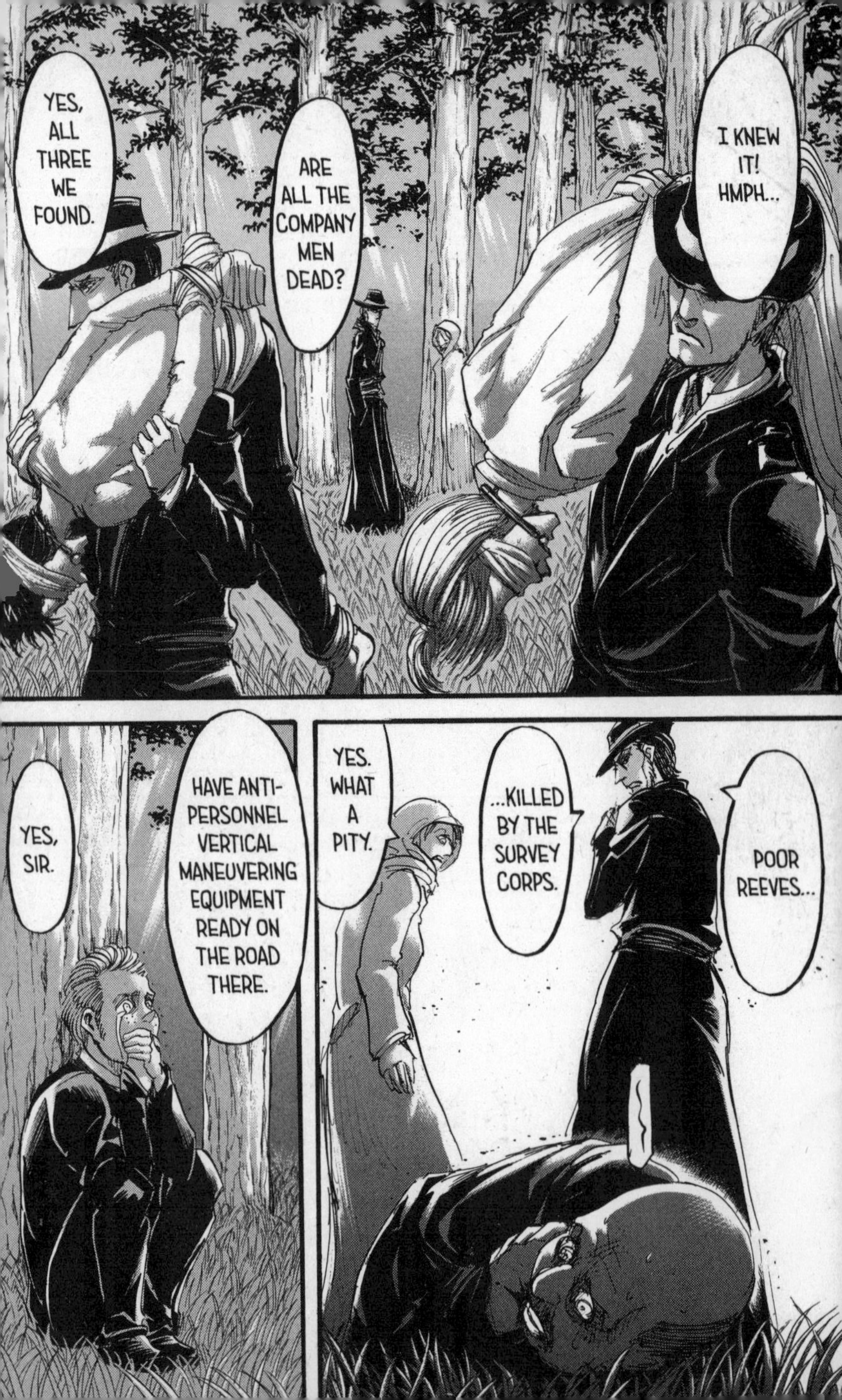
I KNEW IT! HMPH...
ARE ALL THE COMPANY MEN DEAD?
YES, ALL THREE WE FOUND.
POOR REEVES...
...KILLED BY THE SURVEY CORPS.
YES. WHAT A PITY.
HAVE ANTI-PERSONNEL VERTICAL MANEUVERING EQUIPMENT READY ON THE ROAD THERE.
YES, SIR.

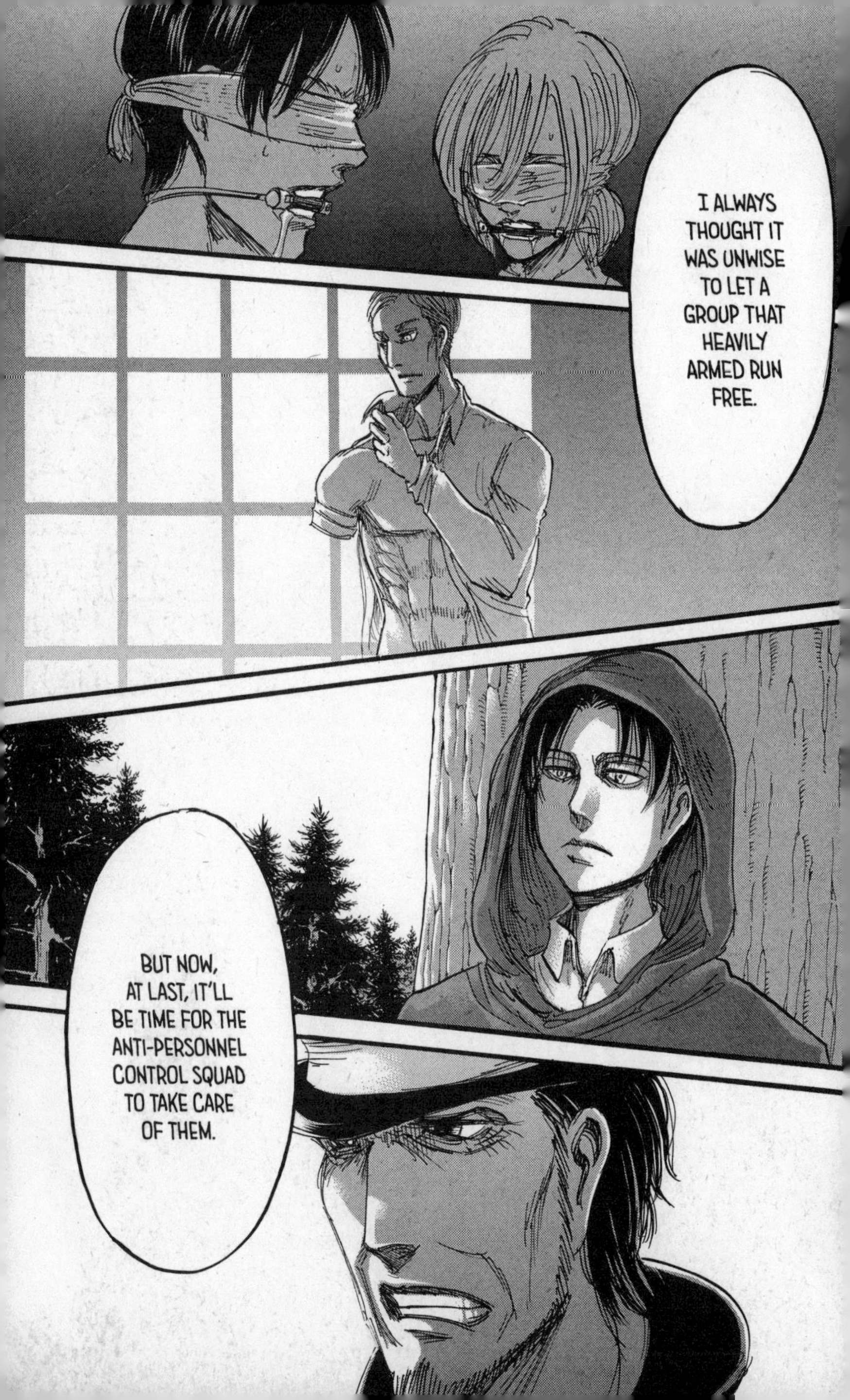
I ALWAYS THOUGHT IT WAS UNWISE TO LET A GROUP THAT HEAVILY ARMED RUN FREE.
BUT NOW, AT LAST, IT'LL BE TIME FOR THE ANTI-PERSONNEL CONTROL SQUAD TO TAKE CARE OF THEM.

ATTACK on TITAN

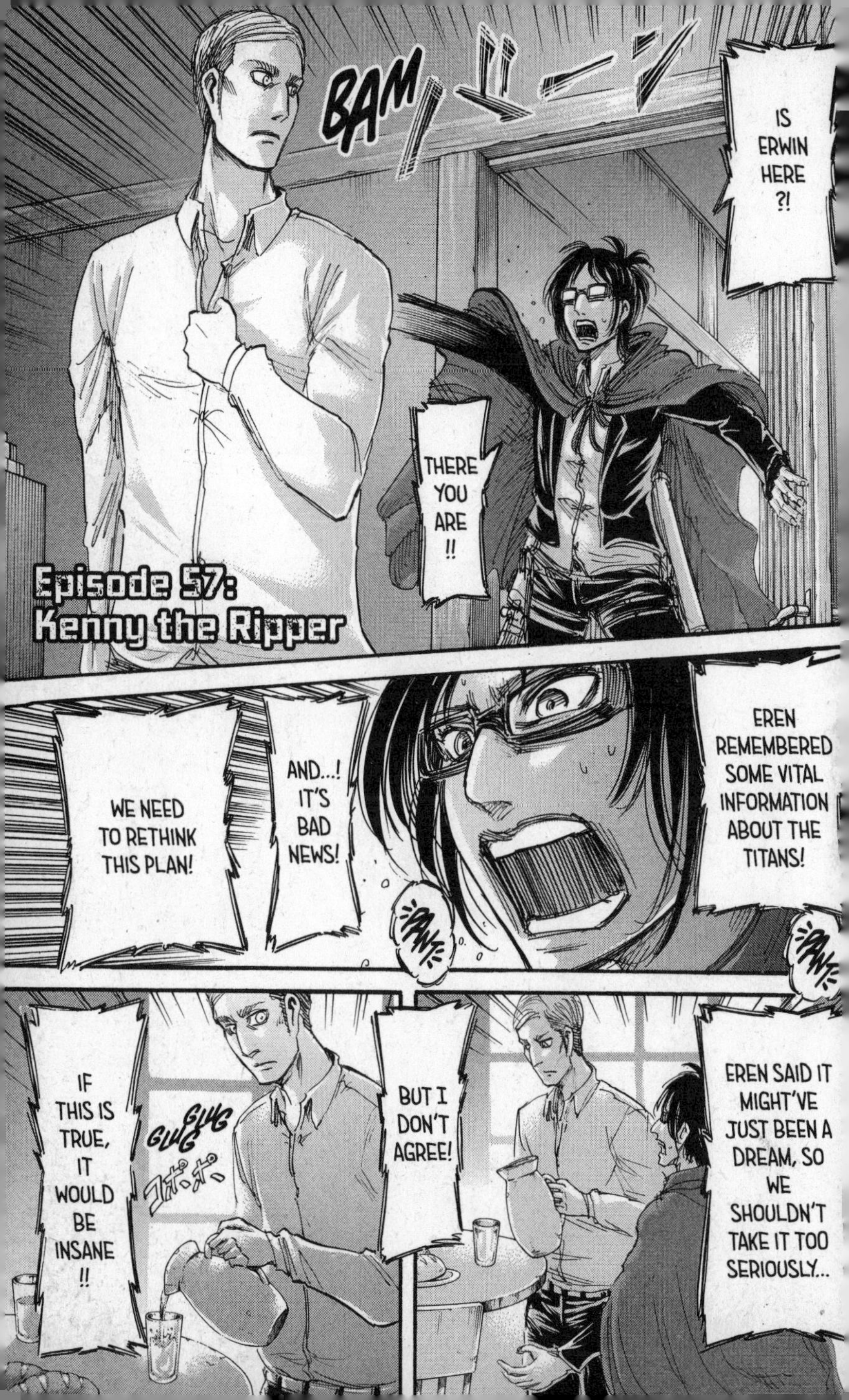
IS ERWIN HERE ?!
BAM
THERE YOU ARE !!
Episode 57:
Kenny the Ripper
EREN REMEMBERED SOME VITAL INFORMATION ABOUT THE TITANS!
PANT
AND...! IT'S BAD NEWS!
WE NEED TO RETHINK THIS PLAN!
PANT
EREN SAID IT MIGHT'VE JUST BEEN A DREAM, SO WE SHOULDN'T TAKE IT TOO SERIOUSLY...
BUT I DON'T AGREE!
IF THIS IS TRUE, IT WOULD BE INSANE !!
GLUG GLUG
コポ、ポ、

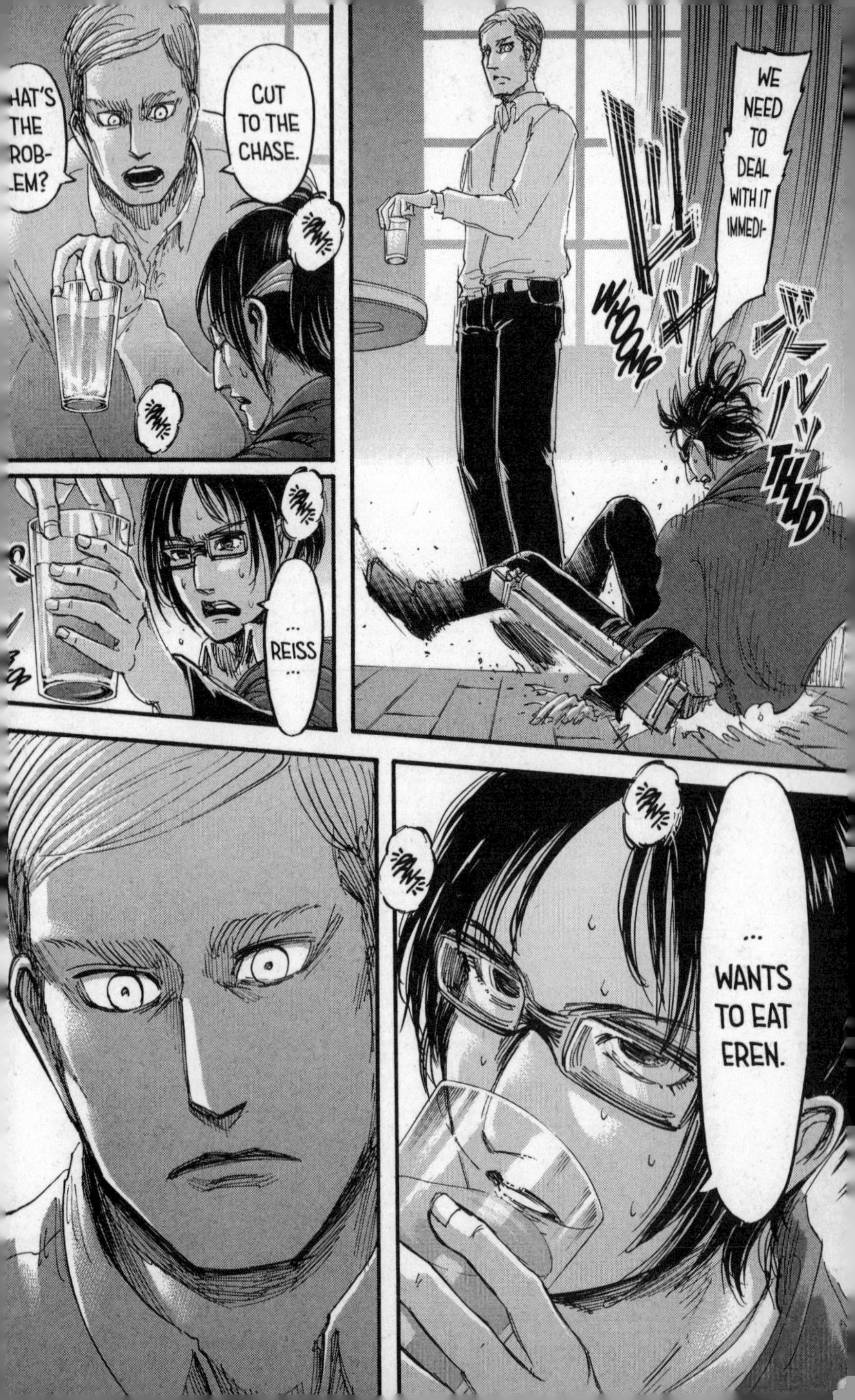
WE NEED TO DEAL WITH IT IMMEDI-
WHOOMP
THUD
CUT TO THE CHASE.
PANT
HAT'S THE ROB- LEM?
PANT
PANT
... REISS ...
PANT
PANT
... WANTS TO EAT EREN.

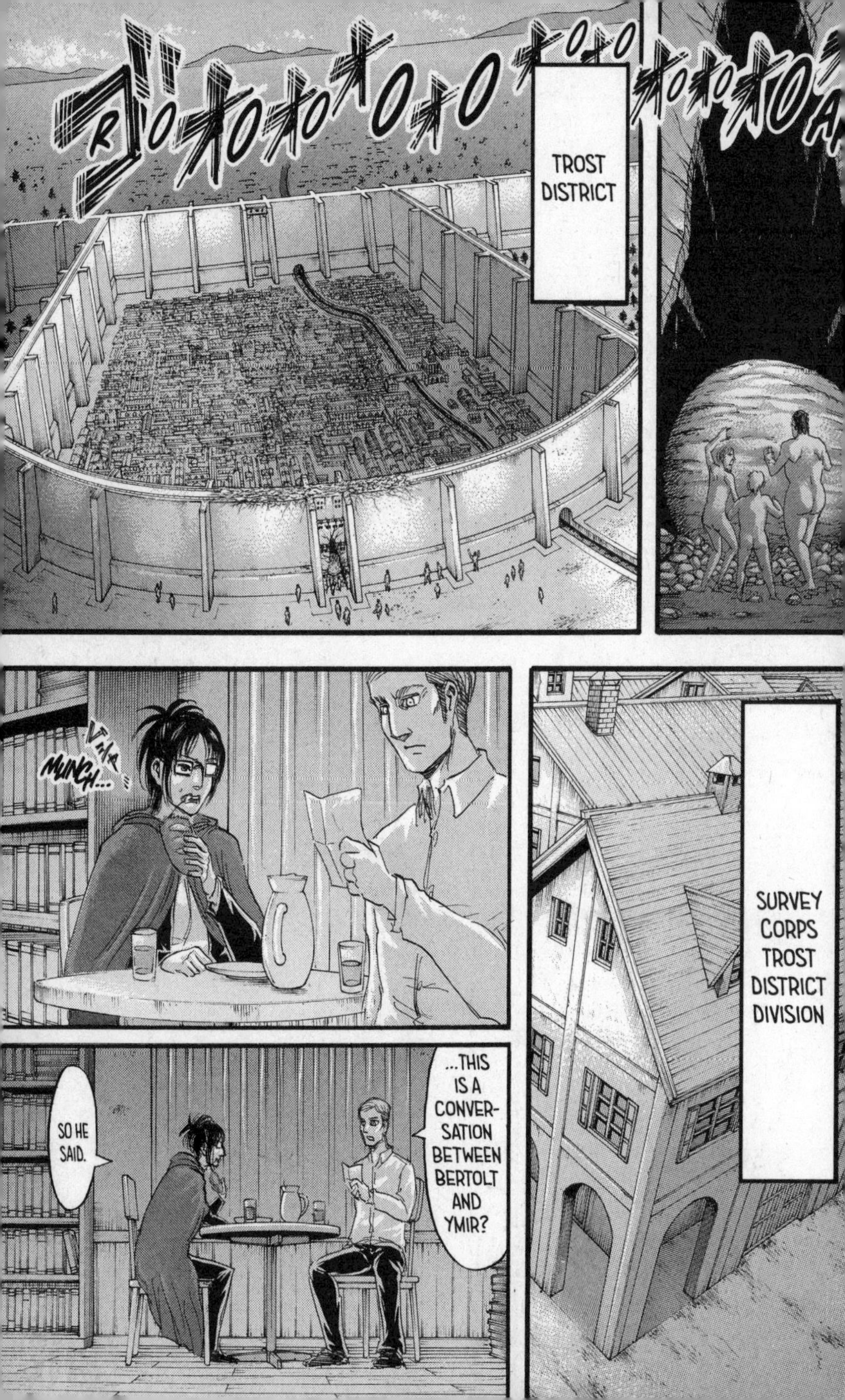
TROST DISTRICT
SURVEY CORPS TROST DISTRICT DIVISION
MUNCH...
...THIS IS A CONVER-SATION BETWEEN BERTOLT AND YMIR?
SO HE SAID.

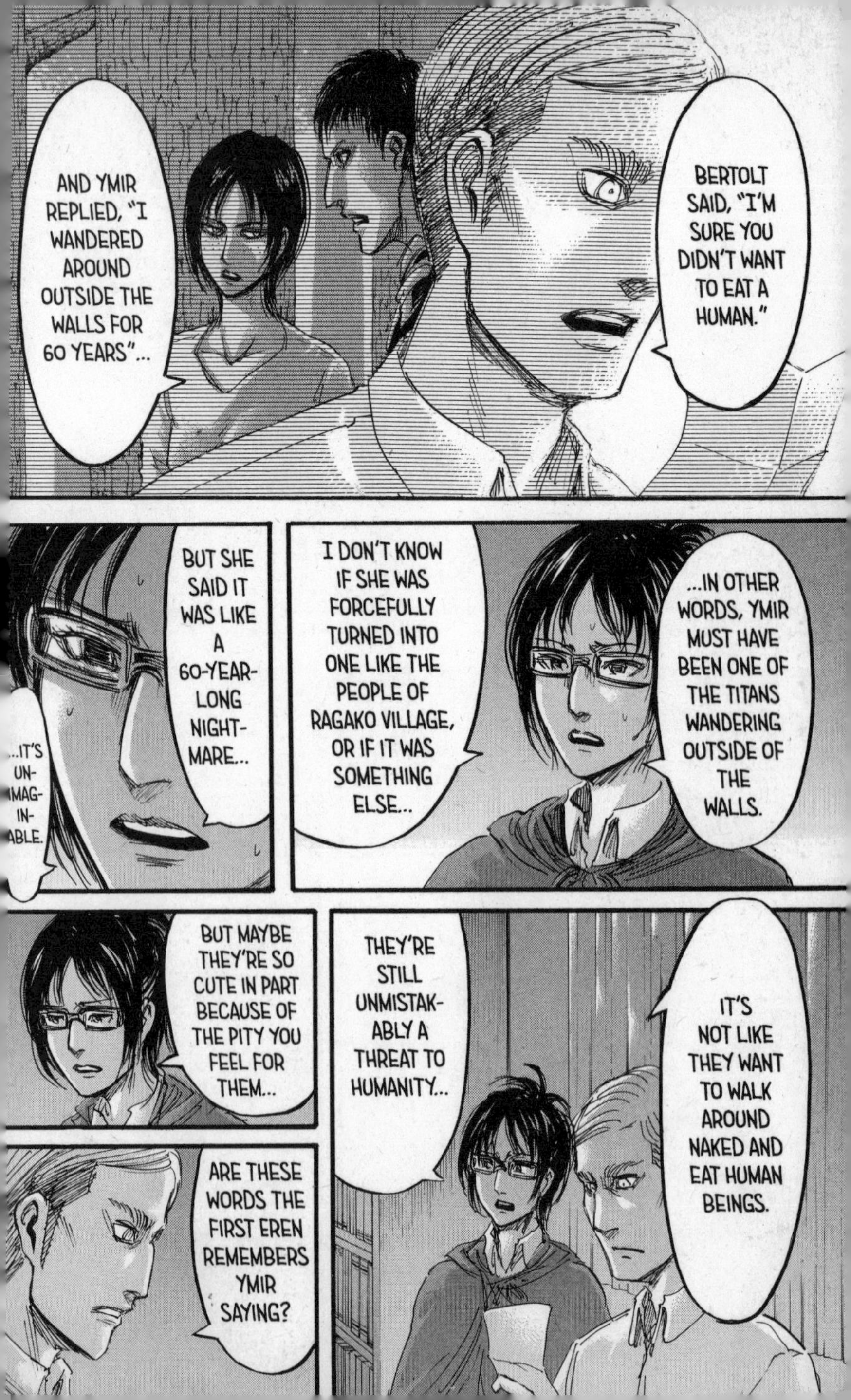
BERTOLT SAID, "I'M SURE YOU DIDN'T WANT TO EAT A HUMAN."
AND YMIR REPLIED, "I WANDERED AROUND OUTSIDE THE WALLS FOR 60 YEARS"...
...IN OTHER WORDS, YMIR MUST HAVE BEEN ONE OF THE TITANS WANDERING OUTSIDE OF THE WALLS.
I DON'T KNOW IF SHE WAS FORCEFULLY TURNED INTO ONE LIKE THE PEOPLE OF RAGAKO VILLAGE, OR IF IT WAS SOMETHING ELSE...
BUT SHE SAID IT WAS LIKE A 60-YEAR-LONG NIGHTMARE...
...IT'S UNIMAGINABLE.
IT'S NOT LIKE THEY WANT TO WALK AROUND NAKED AND EAT HUMAN BEINGS.
THEY'RE STILL UNMISTAKABLY A THREAT TO HUMANITY...
BUT MAYBE THEY'RE SO CUTE IN PART BECAUSE OF THE PITY YOU FEEL FOR THEM...
ARE THESE WORDS THE FIRST EREN REMEMBERS YMIR SAYING?

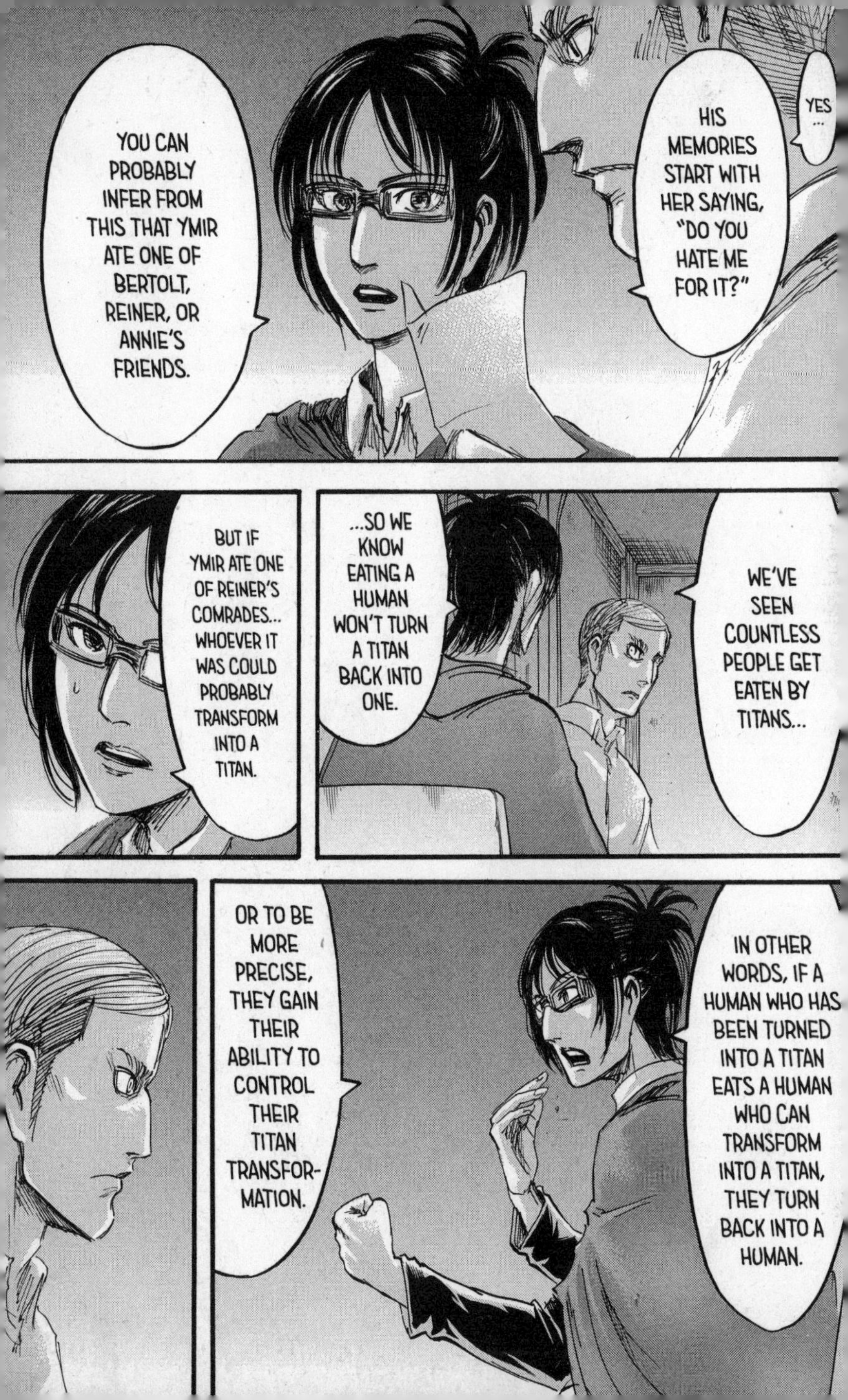
YES...
HIS MEMORIES START WITH HER SAYING, "DO YOU HATE ME FOR IT?"
YOU CAN PROBABLY INFER FROM THIS THAT YMIR ATE ONE OF BERTOLT, REINER, OR ANNIE'S FRIENDS.
WE'VE SEEN COUNTLESS PEOPLE GET EATEN BY TITANS...
...SO WE KNOW EATING A HUMAN WON'T TURN A TITAN BACK INTO ONE.
BUT IF YMIR ATE ONE OF REINER'S COMRADES... WHOEVER IT WAS COULD PROBABLY TRANSFORM INTO A TITAN.
IN OTHER WORDS, IF A HUMAN WHO HAS BEEN TURNED INTO A TITAN EATS A HUMAN WHO CAN TRANSFORM INTO A TITAN, THEY TURN BACK INTO A HUMAN.
OR TO BE MORE PRECISE, THEY GAIN THEIR ABILITY TO CONTROL THEIR TITAN TRANSFOR-MATION.

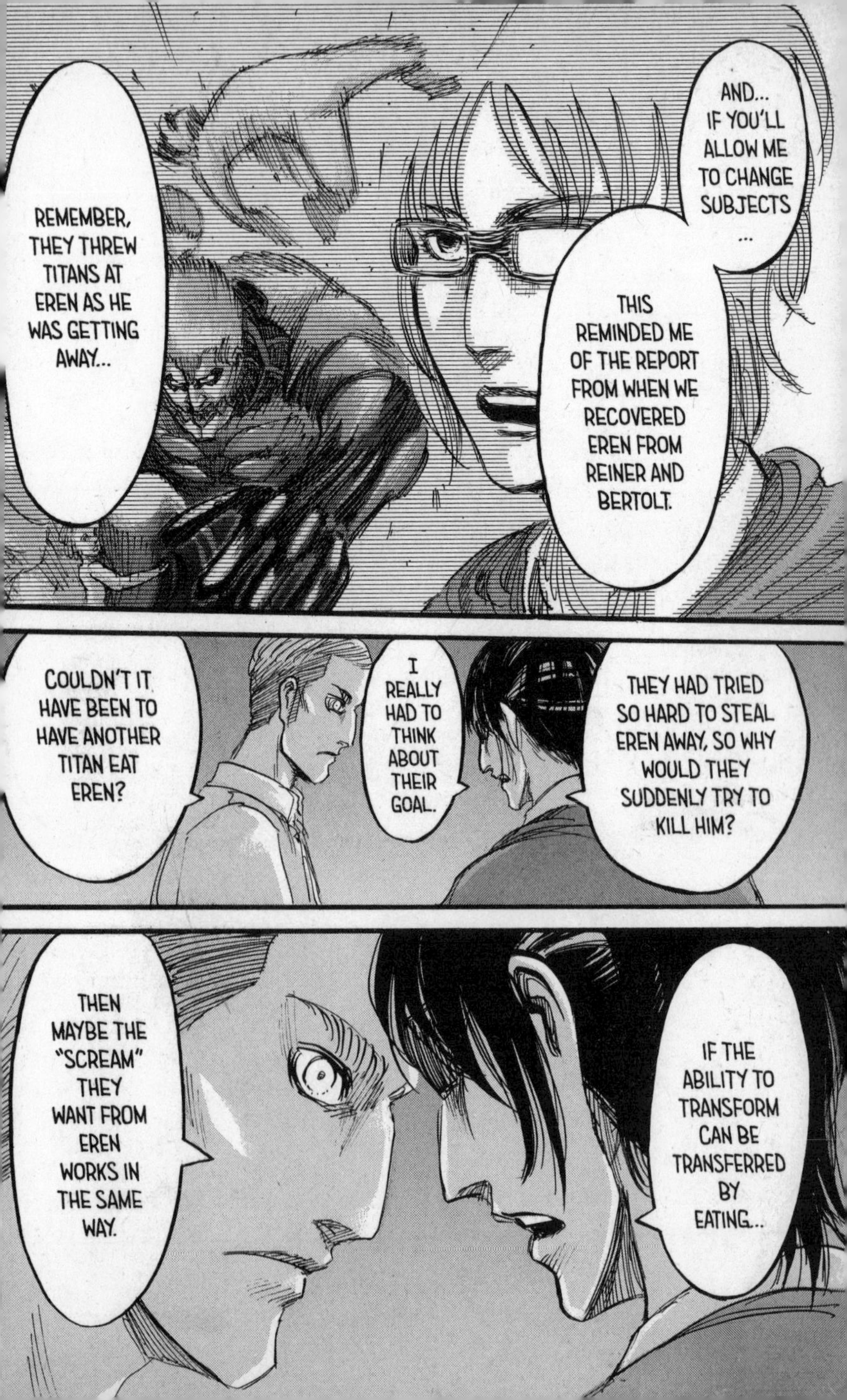
AND... IF YOU'LL ALLOW ME TO CHANGE SUBJECTS ...
THIS REMINDED ME OF THE REPORT FROM WHEN WE RECOVERED EREN FROM REINER AND BERTOLT.
REMEMBER, THEY THREW TITANS AT EREN AS HE WAS GETTING AWAY...
THEY HAD TRIED SO HARD TO STEAL EREN AWAY, SO WHY WOULD THEY SUDDENLY TRY TO KILL HIM?
I REALLY HAD TO THINK ABOUT THEIR GOAL.
COULDN'T IT HAVE BEEN TO HAVE ANOTHER TITAN EAT EREN?
IF THE ABILITY TO TRANSFORM CAN BE TRANSFERRED BY EATING...
THEN MAYBE THE "SCREAM" THEY WANT FROM EREN WORKS IN THE SAME WAY.

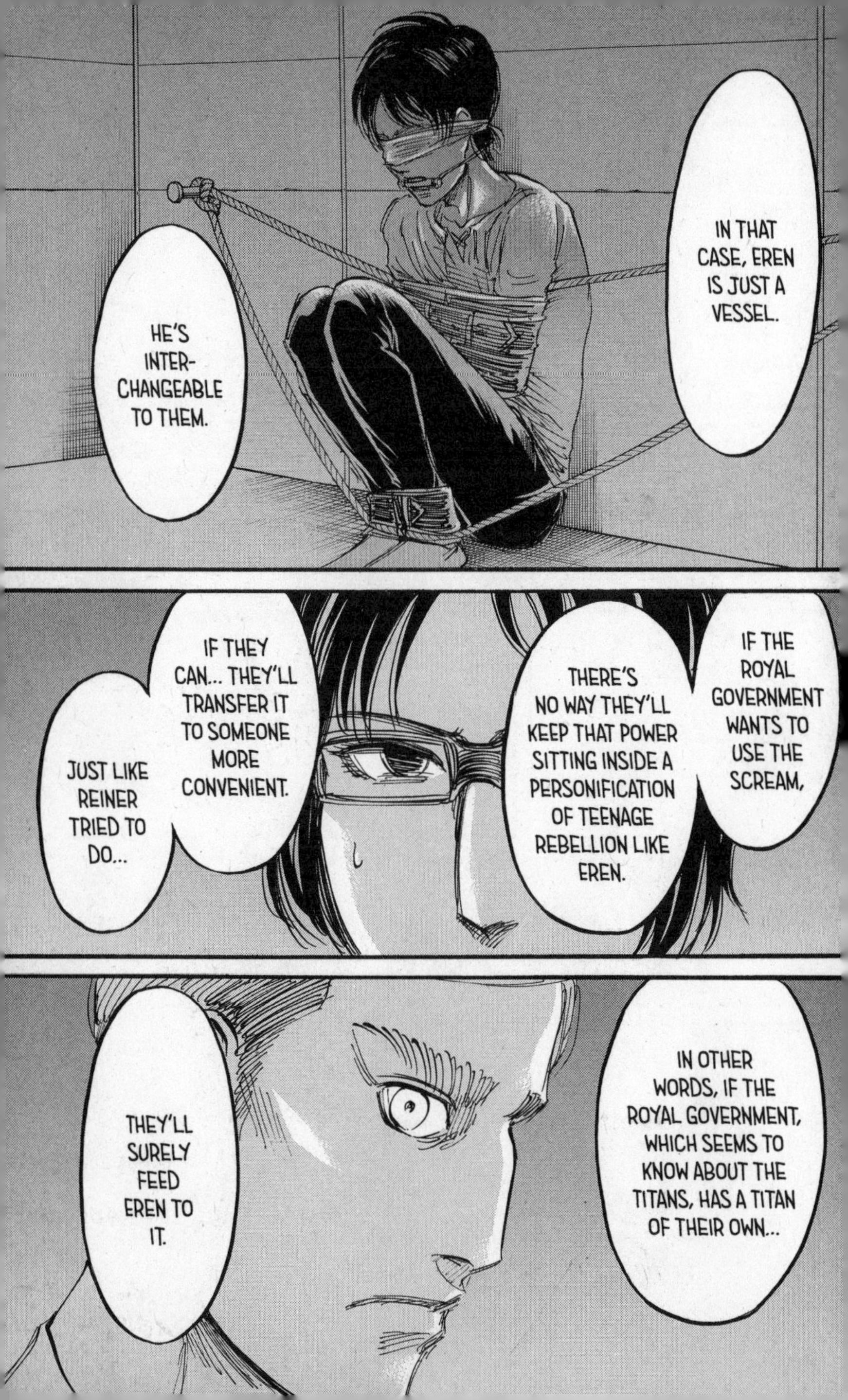
IN THAT CASE, EREN IS JUST A VESSEL.
HE'S INTER-CHANGEABLE TO THEM.
IF THE ROYAL GOVERNMENT WANTS TO USE THE SCREAM,
THERE'S NO WAY THEY'LL KEEP THAT POWER SITTING INSIDE A PERSONIFICATION OF TEENAGE REBELLION LIKE EREN.
IF THEY CAN... THEY'LL TRANSFER IT TO SOMEONE MORE CONVENIENT.
JUST LIKE REINER TRIED TO DO...
IN OTHER WORDS, IF THE ROYAL GOVERNMENT, WHICH SEEMS TO KNOW ABOUT THE TITANS, HAS A TITAN OF THEIR OWN...
THEY'LL SURELY FEED EREN TO IT.

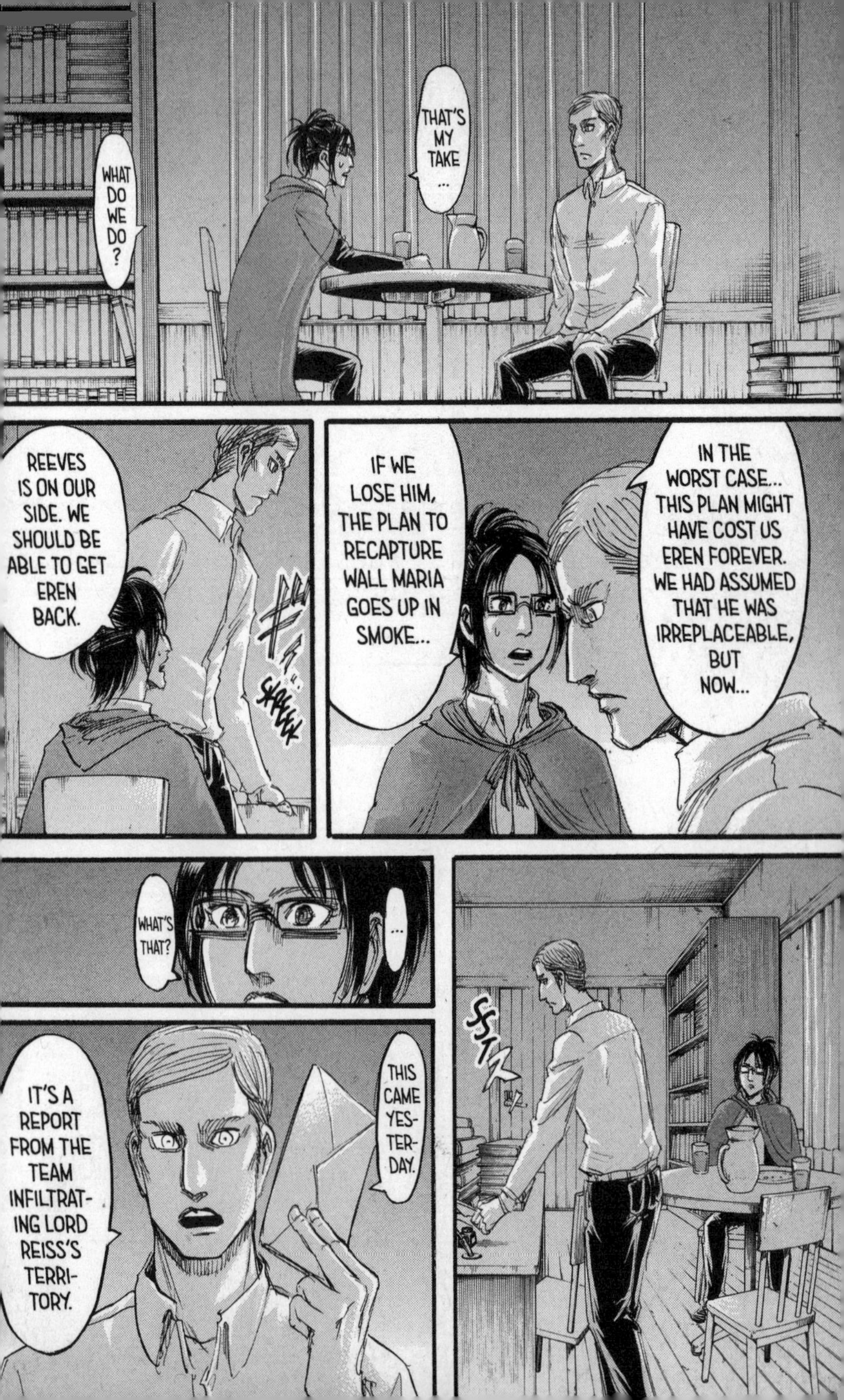
THAT'S MY TAKE ...
WHAT DO WE DO?
IN THE WORST CASE... THIS PLAN MIGHT HAVE COST US EREN FOREVER. WE HAD ASSUMED THAT HE WAS IRREPLACEABLE, BUT NOW...
IF WE LOSE HIM, THE PLAN TO RECAPTURE WALL MARIA GOES UP IN SMOKE...
REEVES IS ON OUR SIDE. WE SHOULD BE ABLE TO GET EREN BACK.
...
WHAT'S THAT?
THIS CAME YES-TER-DAY.
IT'S A REPORT FROM THE TEAM INFILTRAT-ING LORD REISS'S TERRI-TORY.

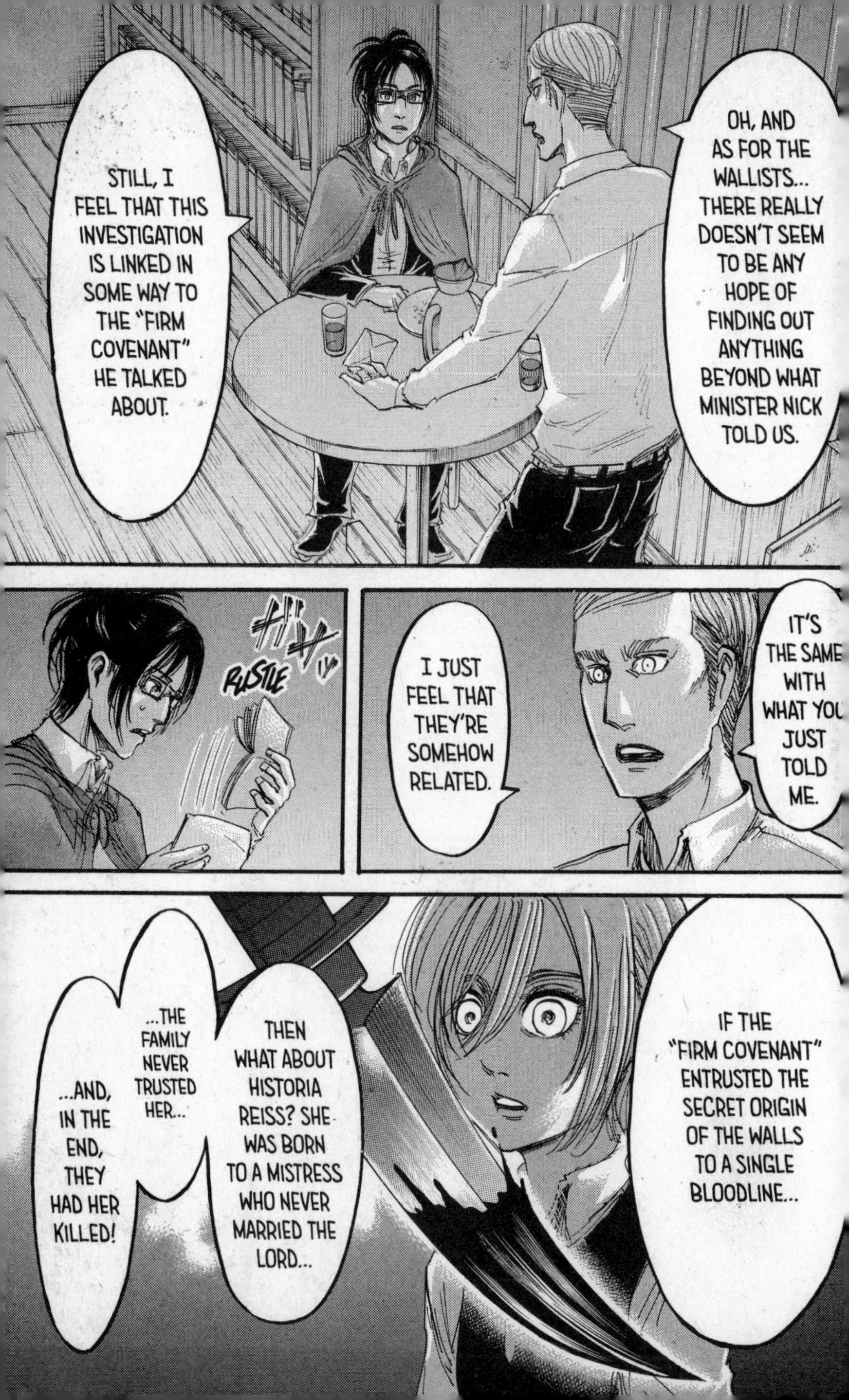
OH, AND AS FOR THE WALLISTS... THERE REALLY DOESN'T SEEM TO BE ANY HOPE OF FINDING OUT ANYTHING BEYOND WHAT MINISTER NICK TOLD US.
STILL, I FEEL THAT THIS INVESTIGATION IS LINKED IN SOME WAY TO THE "FIRM COVENANT" HE TALKED ABOUT.
IT'S THE SAME WITH WHAT YOU JUST TOLD ME.
I JUST FEEL THAT THEY'RE SOMEHOW RELATED.
RUSTLE
IF THE "FIRM COVENANT" ENTRUSTED THE SECRET ORIGIN OF THE WALLS TO A SINGLE BLOODLINE...
THEN WHAT ABOUT HISTORIA REISS? SHE WAS BORN TO A MISTRESS WHO NEVER MARRIED THE LORD...
...THE FAMILY NEVER TRUSTED HER...
...AND, IN THE END, THEY HAD HER KILLED!

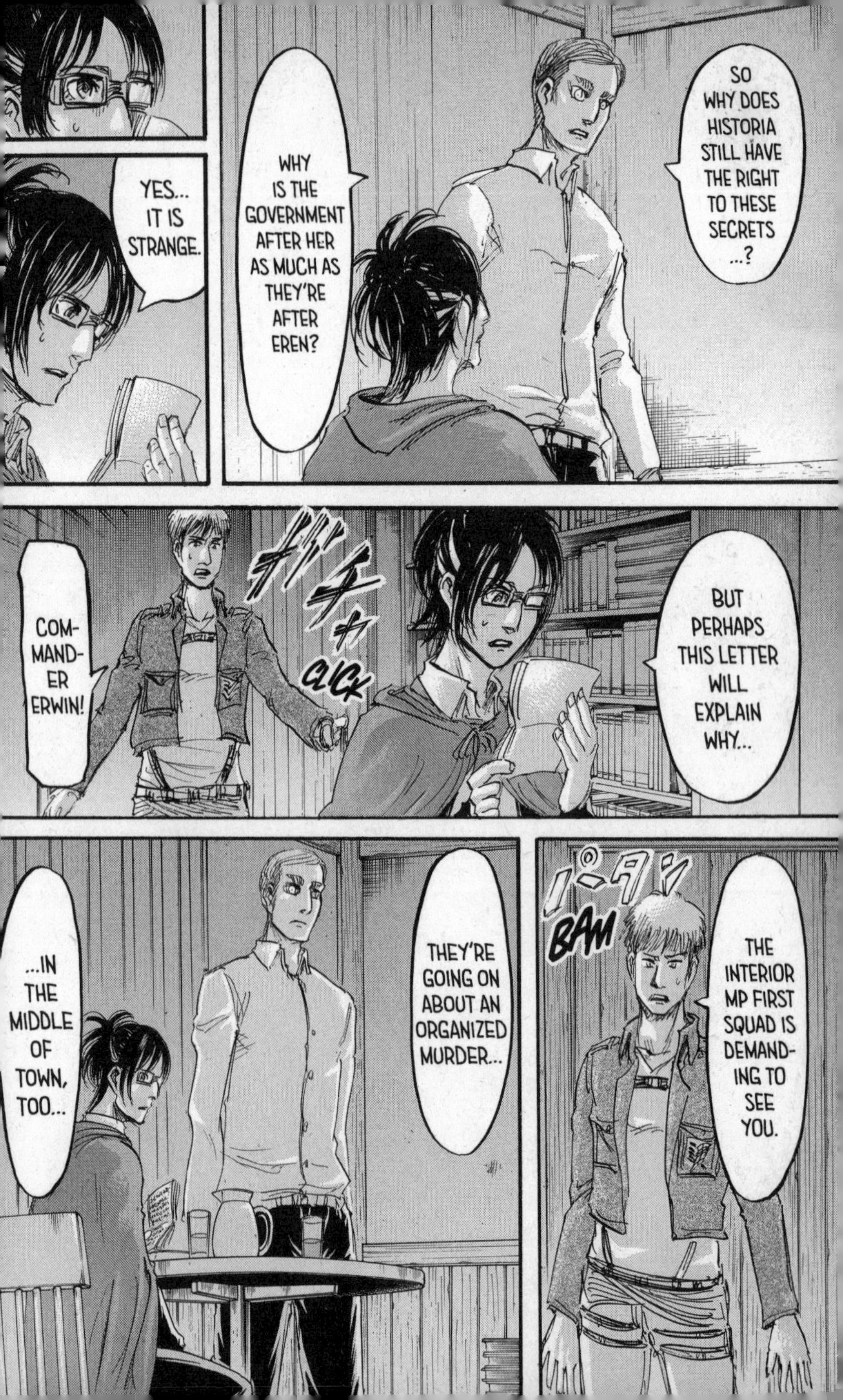
SO WHY DOES HISTORIA STILL HAVE THE RIGHT TO THESE SECRETS ...?
WHY IS THE GOVERNMENT AFTER HER AS MUCH AS THEY'RE AFTER EREN?
YES... IT IS STRANGE.
BUT PERHAPS THIS LETTER WILL EXPLAIN WHY...
ガチャ
CLICK
COM-MAND-ER ERWIN!
パタン
BAM
THE INTERIOR MP FIRST SQUAD IS DEMAND-ING TO SEE YOU.
THEY'RE GOING ON ABOUT AN ORGANIZED MURDER...
...IN THE MIDDLE OF TOWN, TOO...

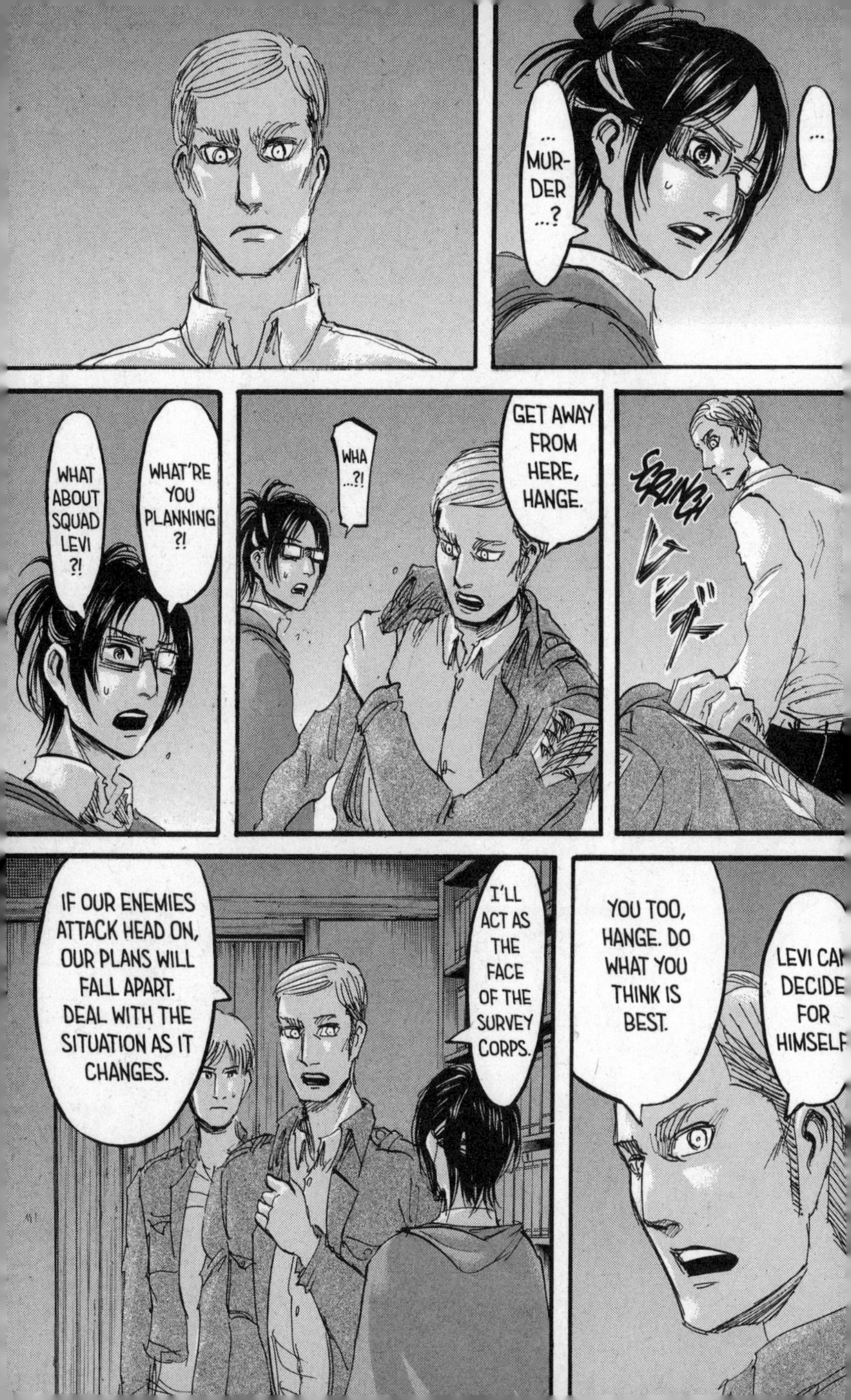
...
... MURDER ...?
SCRUNCH
GET AWAY FROM HERE, HANGE.
WHA ...?!
WHAT'RE YOU PLANNING ?!
WHAT ABOUT SQUAD LEVI ?!
LEVI CAN DECIDE FOR HIMSELF
YOU TOO, HANGE. DO WHAT YOU THINK IS BEST.
I'LL ACT AS THE FACE OF THE SURVEY CORPS.
IF OUR ENEMIES ATTACK HEAD ON, OUR PLANS WILL FALL APART. DEAL WITH THE SITUATION AS IT CHANGES.

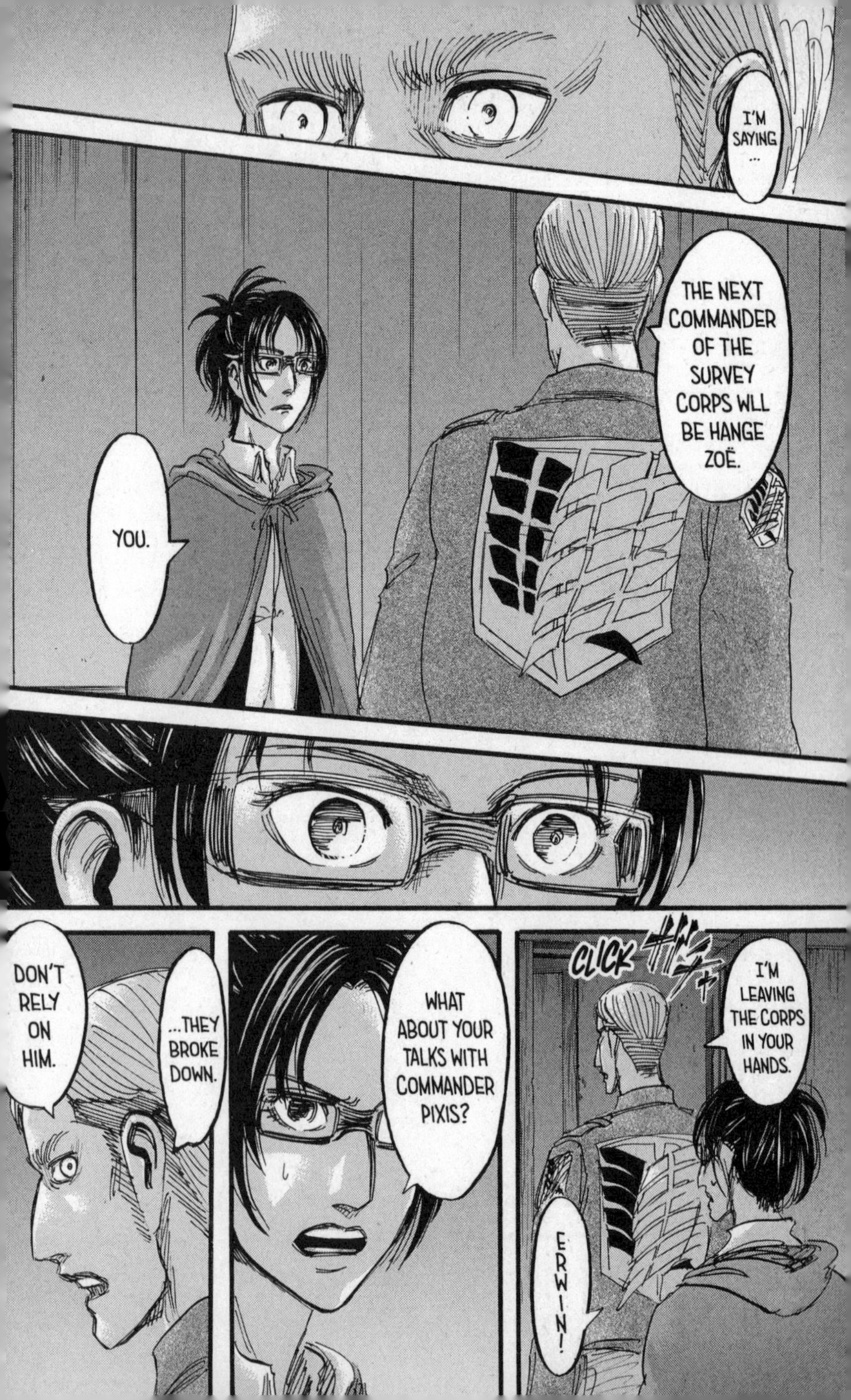
I'M SAYING ...
THE NEXT COMMANDER OF THE SURVEY CORPS WLL BE HANGE ZOË.
YOU.
I'M LEAVING THE CORPS IN YOUR HANDS.
CLICK
ERWIN!
WHAT ABOUT YOUR TALKS WITH COMMANDER PIXIS?
...THEY BROKE DOWN.
DON'T RELY ON HIM.

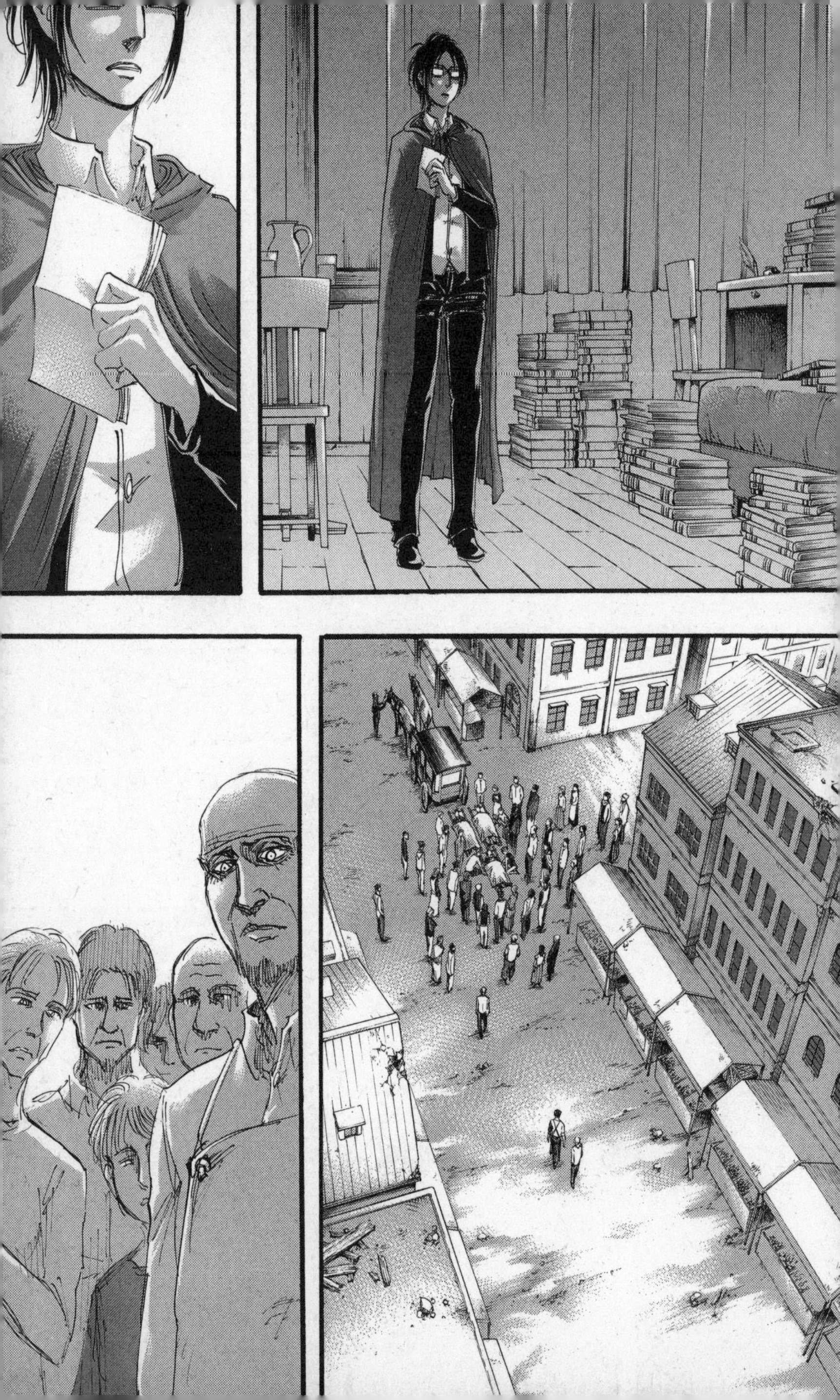

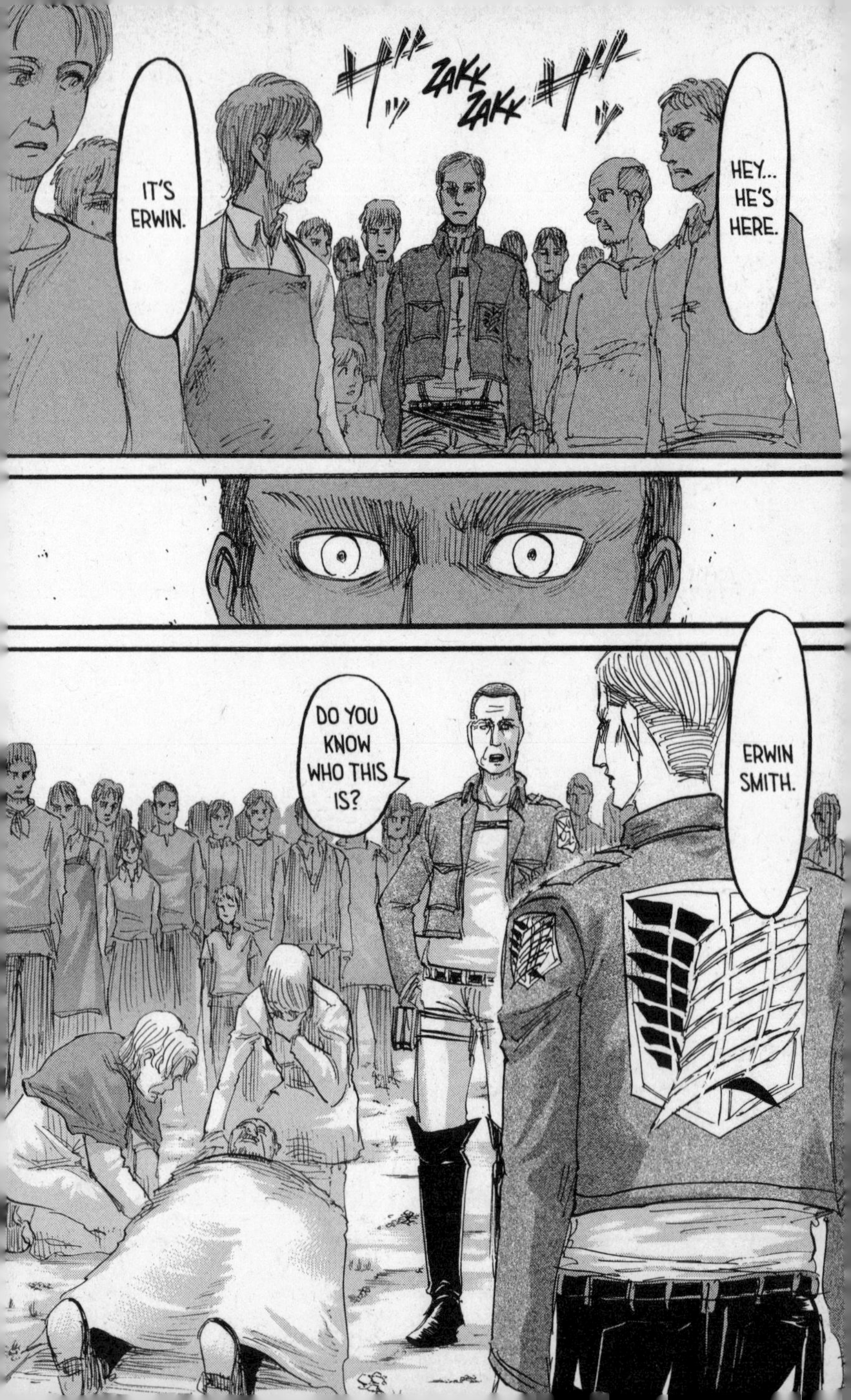
HEY... HE'S HERE.
ZAKK ZAKK
IT'S ERWIN.
ERWIN SMITH.
DO YOU KNOW WHO THIS IS?

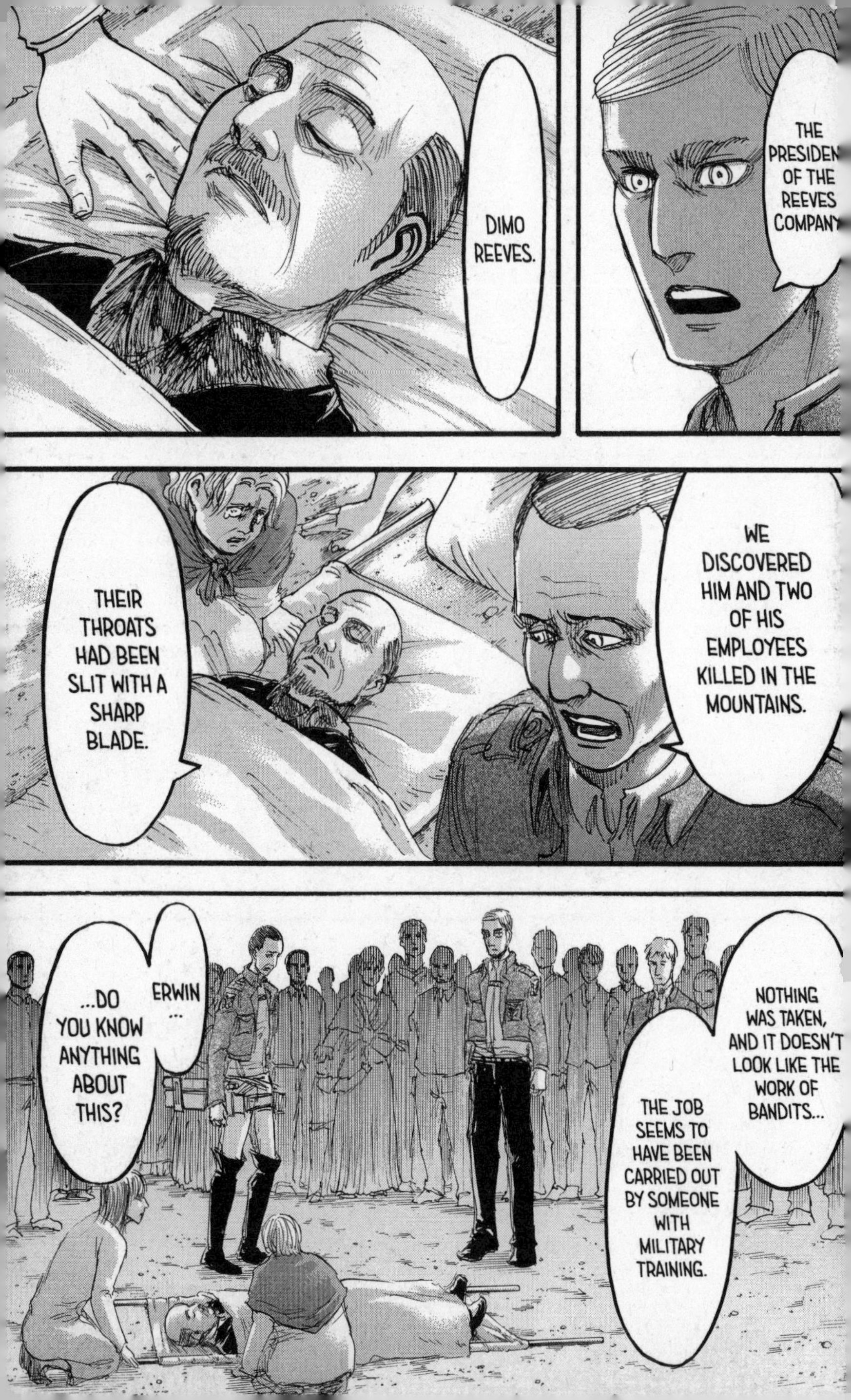
THE PRESIDEN OF THE REEVES COMPANY
DIMO REEVES.
WE DISCOVERED HIM AND TWO OF HIS EMPLOYEES KILLED IN THE MOUNTAINS.
THEIR THROATS HAD BEEN SLIT WITH A SHARP BLADE.
NOTHING WAS TAKEN, AND IT DOESN'T LOOK LIKE THE WORK OF BANDITS...
THE JOB SEEMS TO HAVE BEEN CARRIED OUT BY SOMEONE WITH MILITARY TRAINING.
ERWIN ...
...DO YOU KNOW ANYTHING ABOUT THIS?

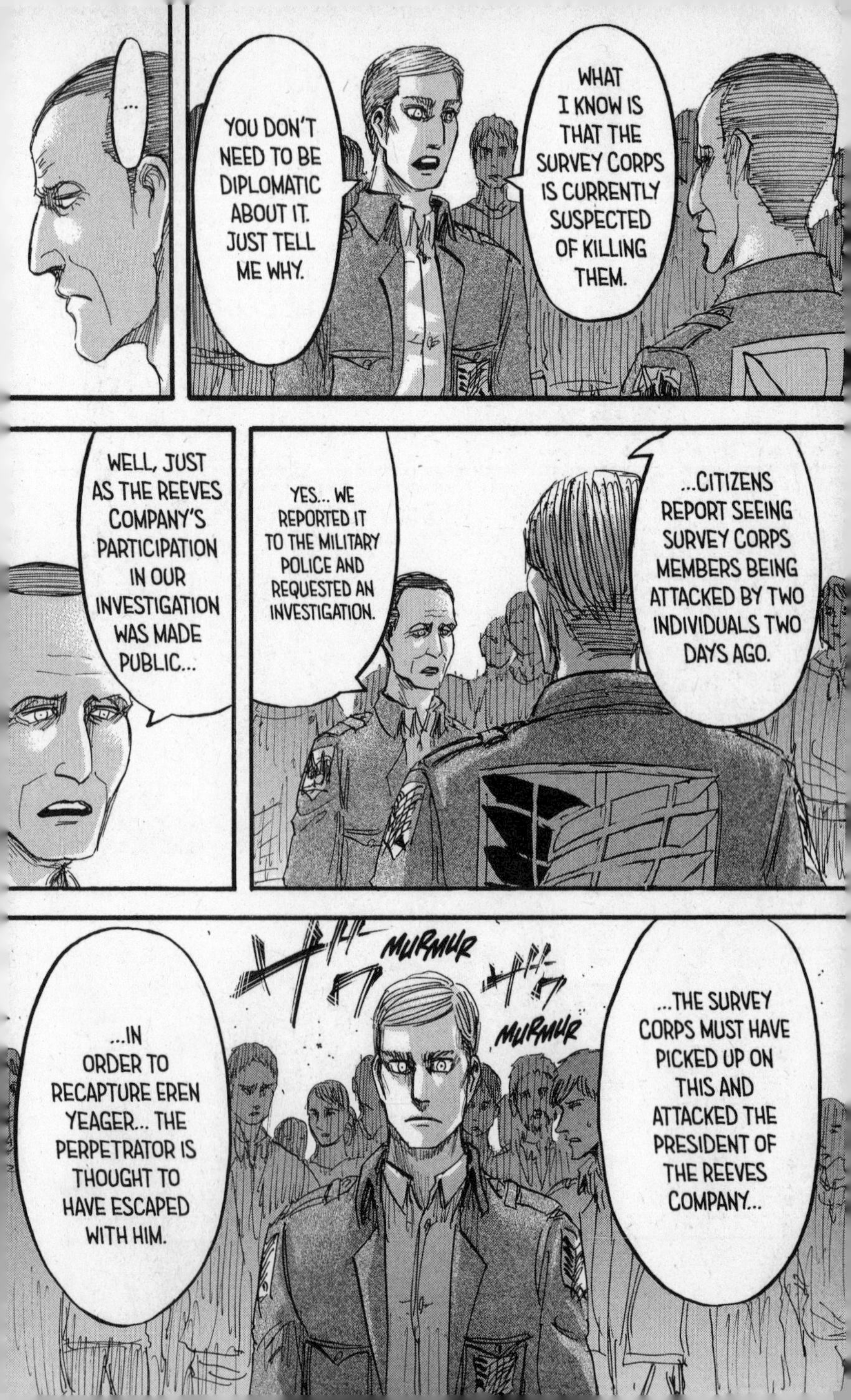
WHAT I KNOW IS THAT THE SURVEY CORPS IS CURRENTLY SUSPECTED OF KILLING THEM.
YOU DON'T NEED TO BE DIPLOMATIC ABOUT IT. JUST TELL ME WHY.
...
...CITIZENS REPORT SEEING SURVEY CORPS MEMBERS BEING ATTACKED BY TWO INDIVIDUALS TWO DAYS AGO.
YES... WE REPORTED IT TO THE MILITARY POLICE AND REQUESTED AN INVESTIGATION.
WELL, JUST AS THE REEVES COMPANY'S PARTICIPATION IN OUR INVESTIGATION WAS MADE PUBLIC...
...THE SURVEY CORPS MUST HAVE PICKED UP ON THIS AND ATTACKED THE PRESIDENT OF THE REEVES COMPANY...
MURMUR
MURMUR
...IN ORDER TO RECAPTURE EREN YEAGER... THE PERPETRATOR IS THOUGHT TO HAVE ESCAPED WITH HIM.

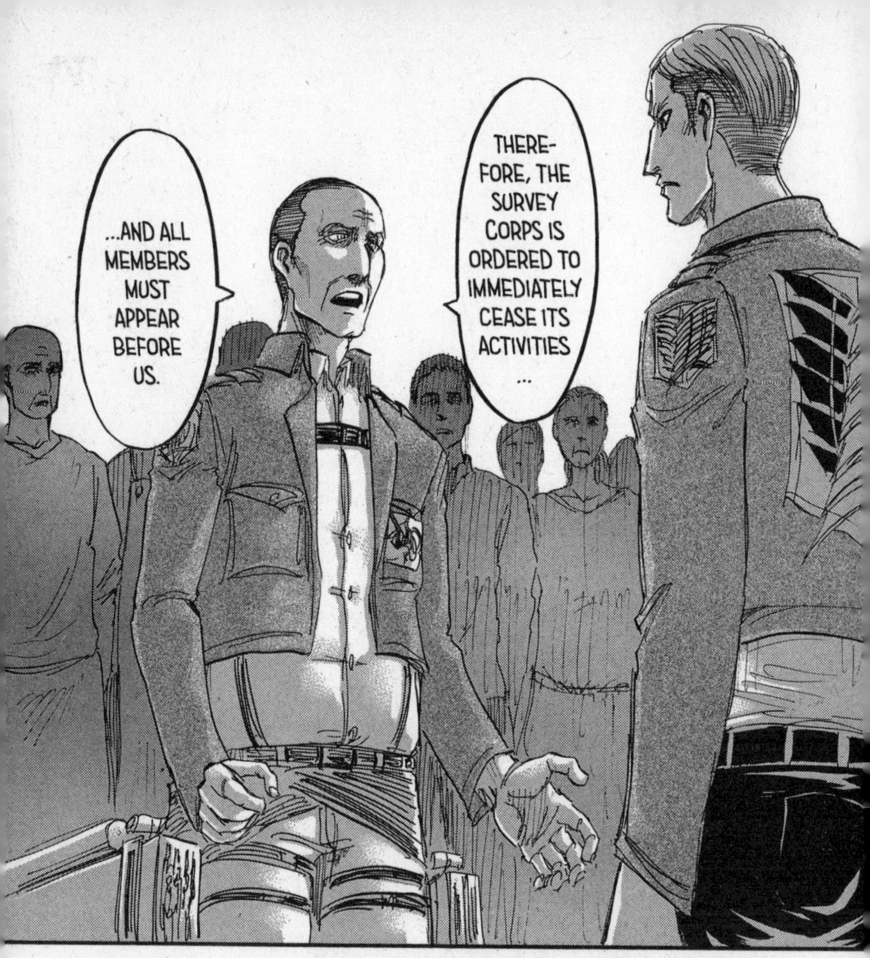
THERE-FORE, THE SURVEY CORPS IS ORDERED TO IMMEDIATELY CEASE ITS ACTIVITIES ...
...AND ALL MEMBERS MUST APPEAR BEFORE US.

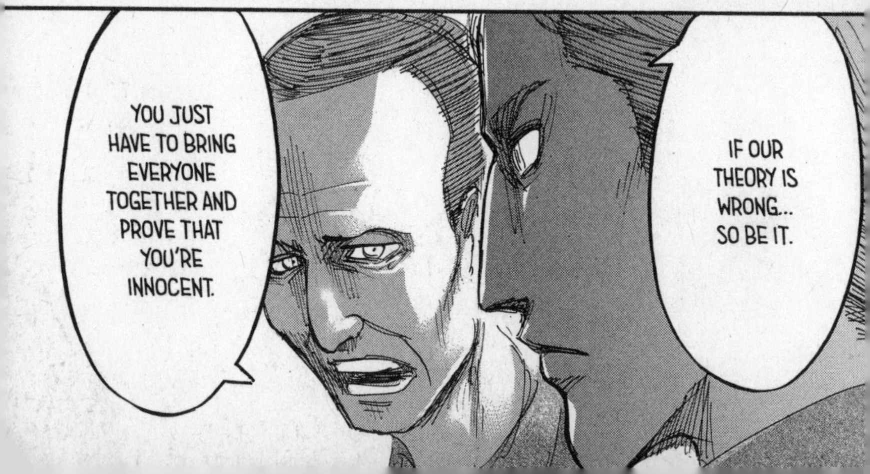
IF OUR THEORY IS WRONG... SO BE IT.
YOU JUST HAVE TO BRING EVERYONE TOGETHER AND PROVE THAT YOU'RE INNOCENT.

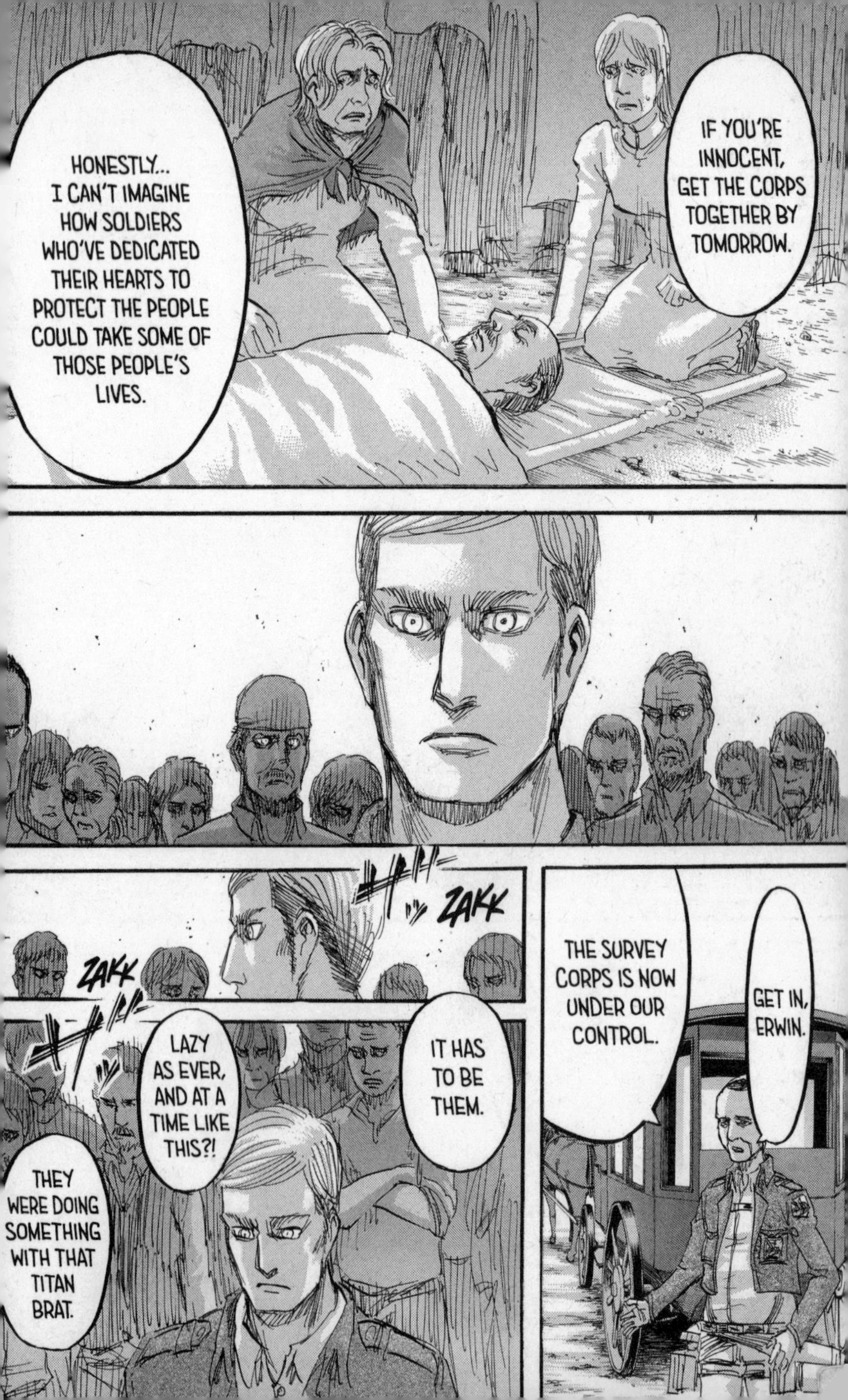

IF YOU'RE INNOCENT, GET THE CORPS TOGETHER BY TOMORROW.
HONESTLY... I CAN'T IMAGINE HOW SOLDIERS WHO'VE DEDICATED THEIR HEARTS TO PROTECT THE PEOPLE COULD TAKE SOME OF THOSE PEOPLE'S LIVES.
GET IN, ERWIN.
THE SURVEY CORPS IS NOW UNDER OUR CONTROL.
ZAKK
ZAKK
IT HAS TO BE THEM.
LAZY AS EVER, AND AT A TIME LIKE THIS?!
THEY WERE DOING SOMETHING WITH THAT TITAN BRAT.

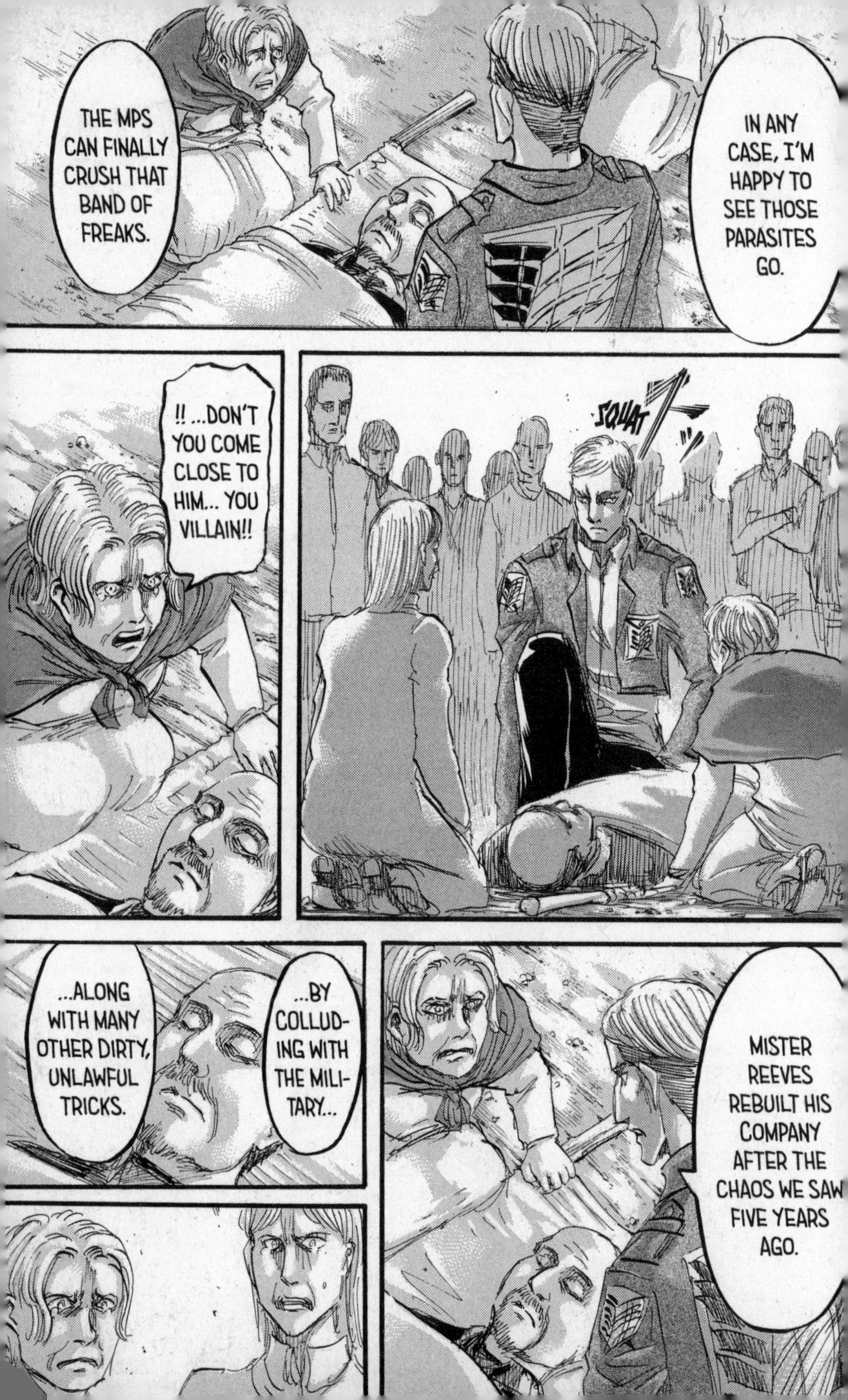
IN ANY CASE, I'M HAPPY TO SEE THOSE PARASITES GO.
THE MPS CAN FINALLY CRUSH THAT BAND OF FREAKS.
SQUAT
!! ...DON'T YOU COME CLOSE TO HIM... YOU VILLAIN!!
MISTER REEVES REBUILT HIS COMPANY AFTER THE CHAOS WE SAW FIVE YEARS AGO.
...BY COLLUDING WITH THE MILITARY...
...ALONG WITH MANY OTHER DIRTY, UNLAWFUL TRICKS.

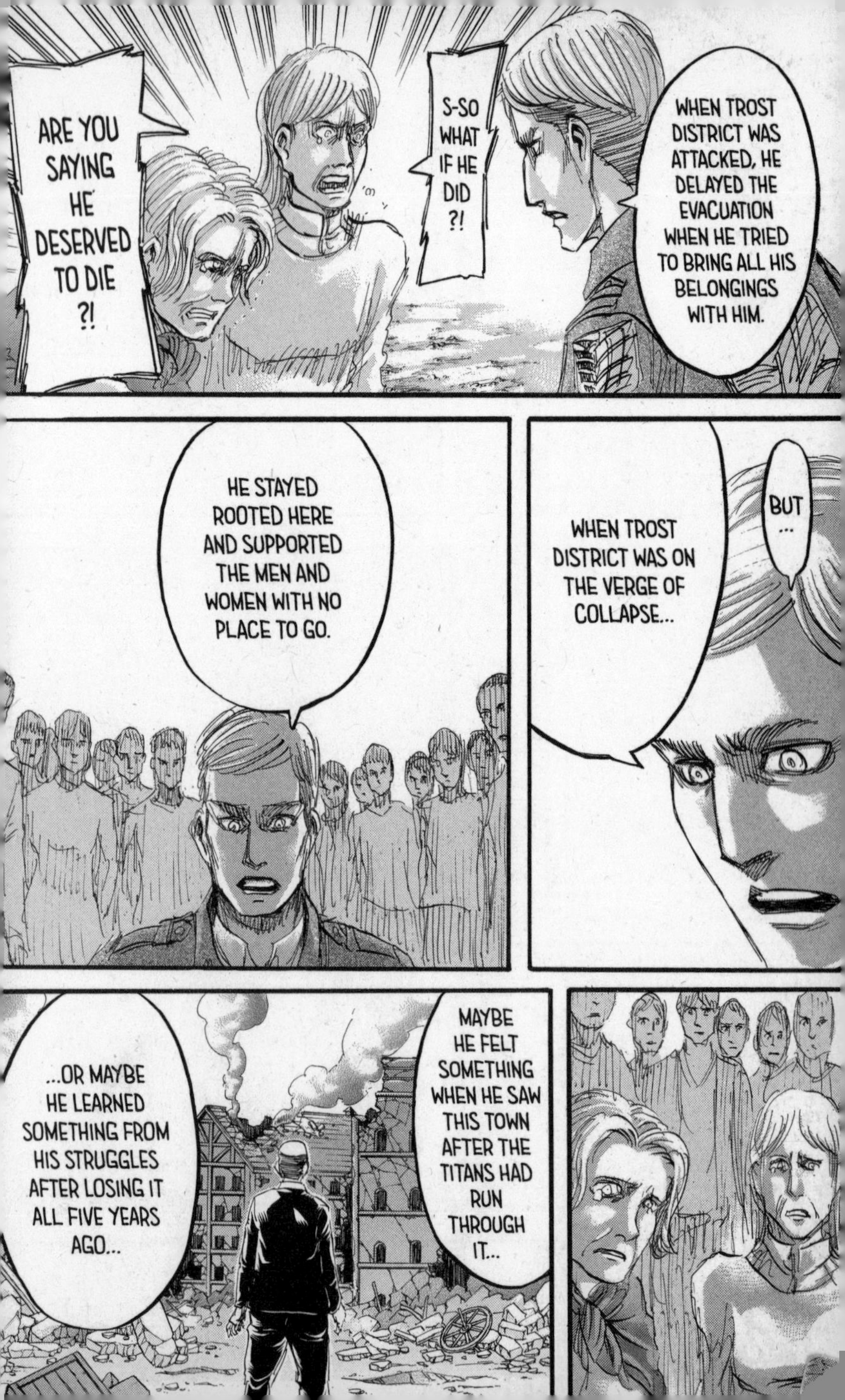
WHEN TROST DISTRICT WAS ATTACKED, HE DELAYED THE EVACUATION WHEN HE TRIED TO BRING ALL HIS BELONGINGS WITH HIM.
S-SO WHAT IF HE DID?!
ARE YOU SAYING HE DESERVED TO DIE?!
BUT ...
WHEN TROST DISTRICT WAS ON THE VERGE OF COLLAPSE...
HE STAYED ROOTED HERE AND SUPPORTED THE MEN AND WOMEN WITH NO PLACE TO GO.
MAYBE HE FELT SOMETHING WHEN HE SAW THIS TOWN AFTER THE TITANS HAD RUN THROUGH IT...
...OR MAYBE HE LEARNED SOMETHING FROM HIS STRUGGLES AFTER LOSING IT ALL FIVE YEARS AGO...

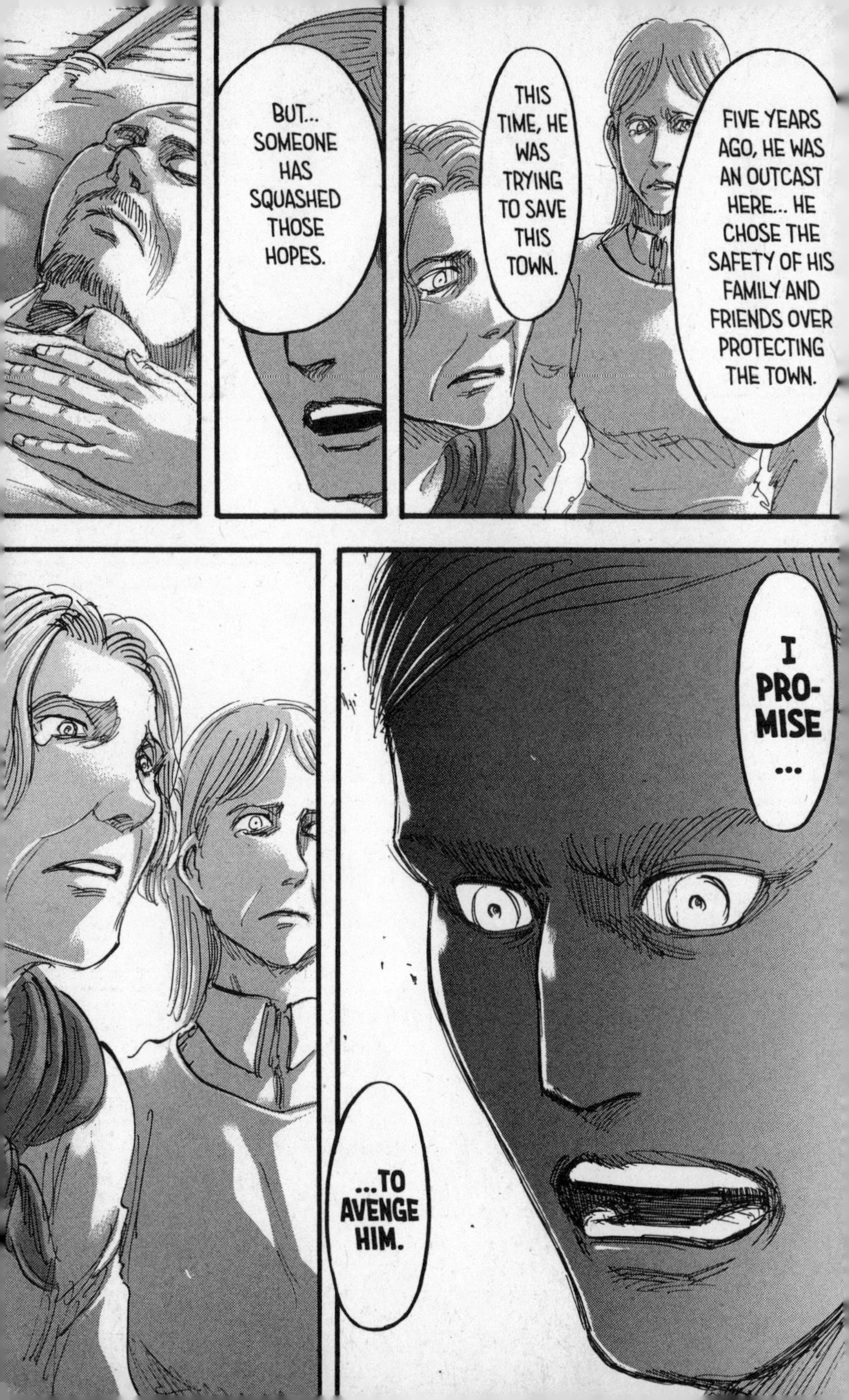
FIVE YEARS AGO, HE WAS AN OUTCAST HERE... HE CHOSE THE SAFETY OF HIS FAMILY AND FRIENDS OVER PROTECTING THE TOWN.
THIS TIME, HE WAS TRYING TO SAVE THIS TOWN.
BUT... SOMEONE HAS SQUASHED THOSE HOPES.
I PROMISE...
...TO AVENGE HIM.

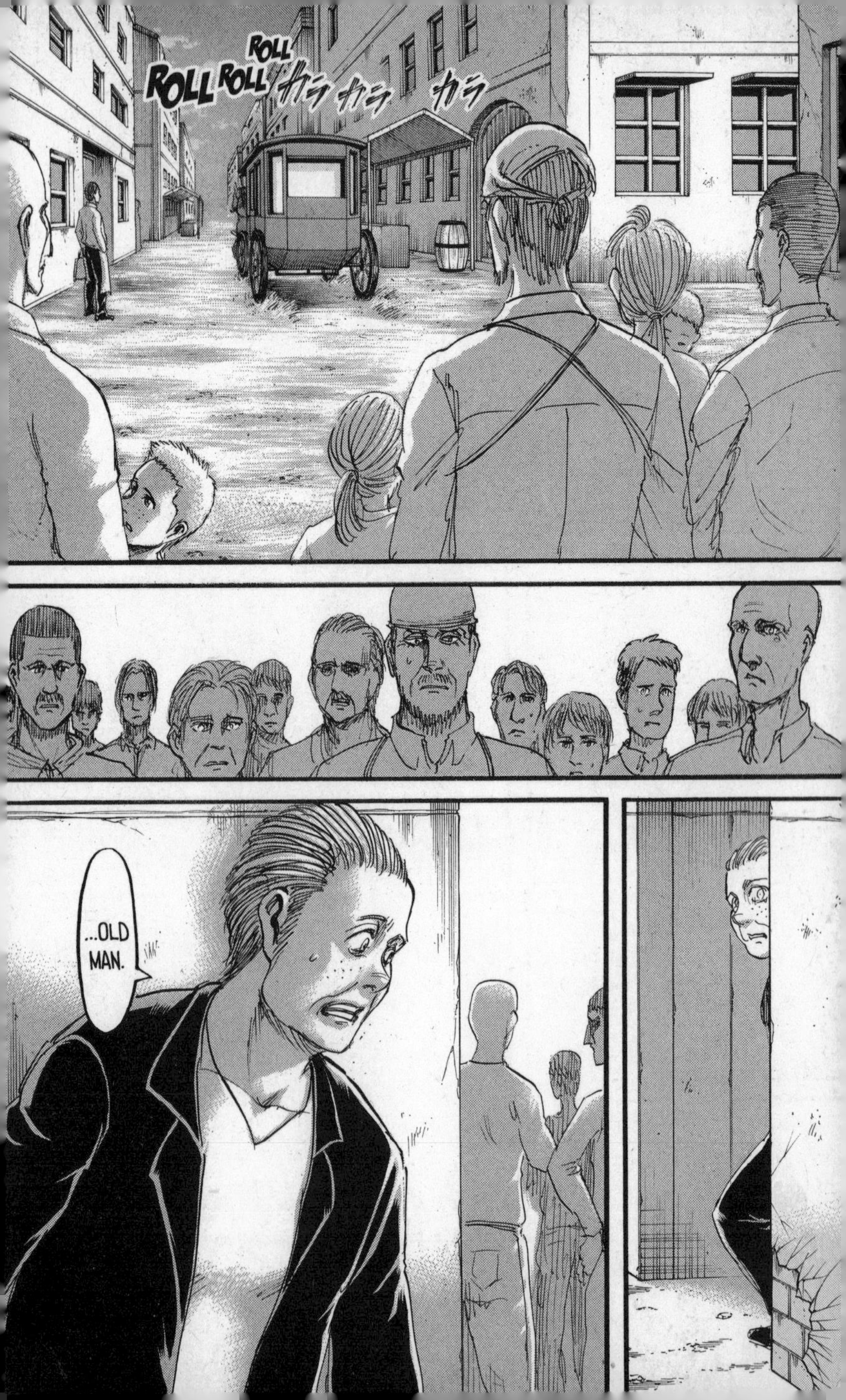
ROLL ROLL ROLL
カラ カラ カラ
...OLD MAN.

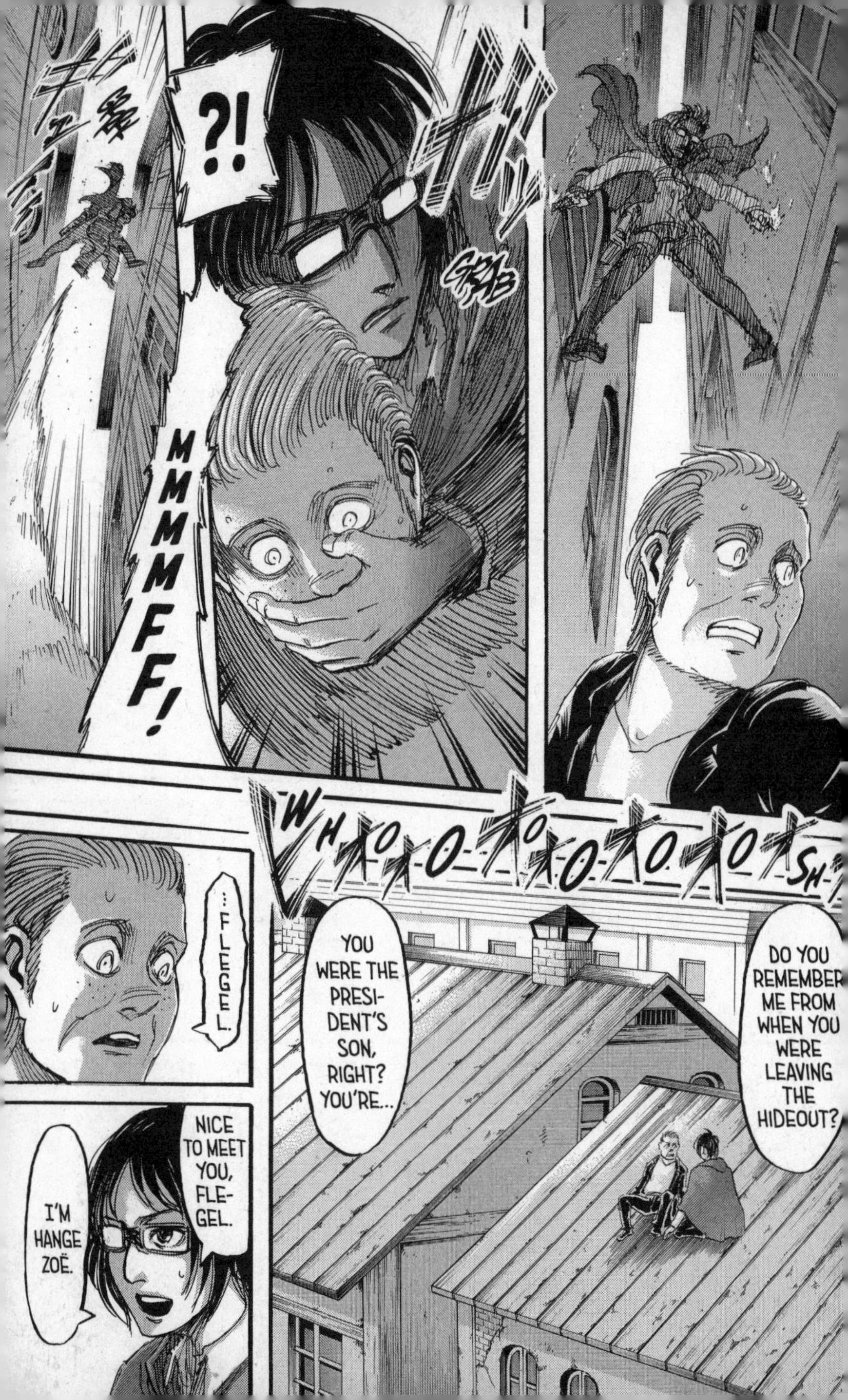
?!
GRAB
MMMMFF!
WHOOOOOOOOOOSH
DO YOU REMEMBER ME FROM WHEN YOU WERE LEAVING THE HIDEOUT?
YOU WERE THE PRESIDENT'S SON, RIGHT? YOU'RE...
...FLEGEL.
NICE TO MEET YOU, FLEGEL.
I'M HANGE ZOË.

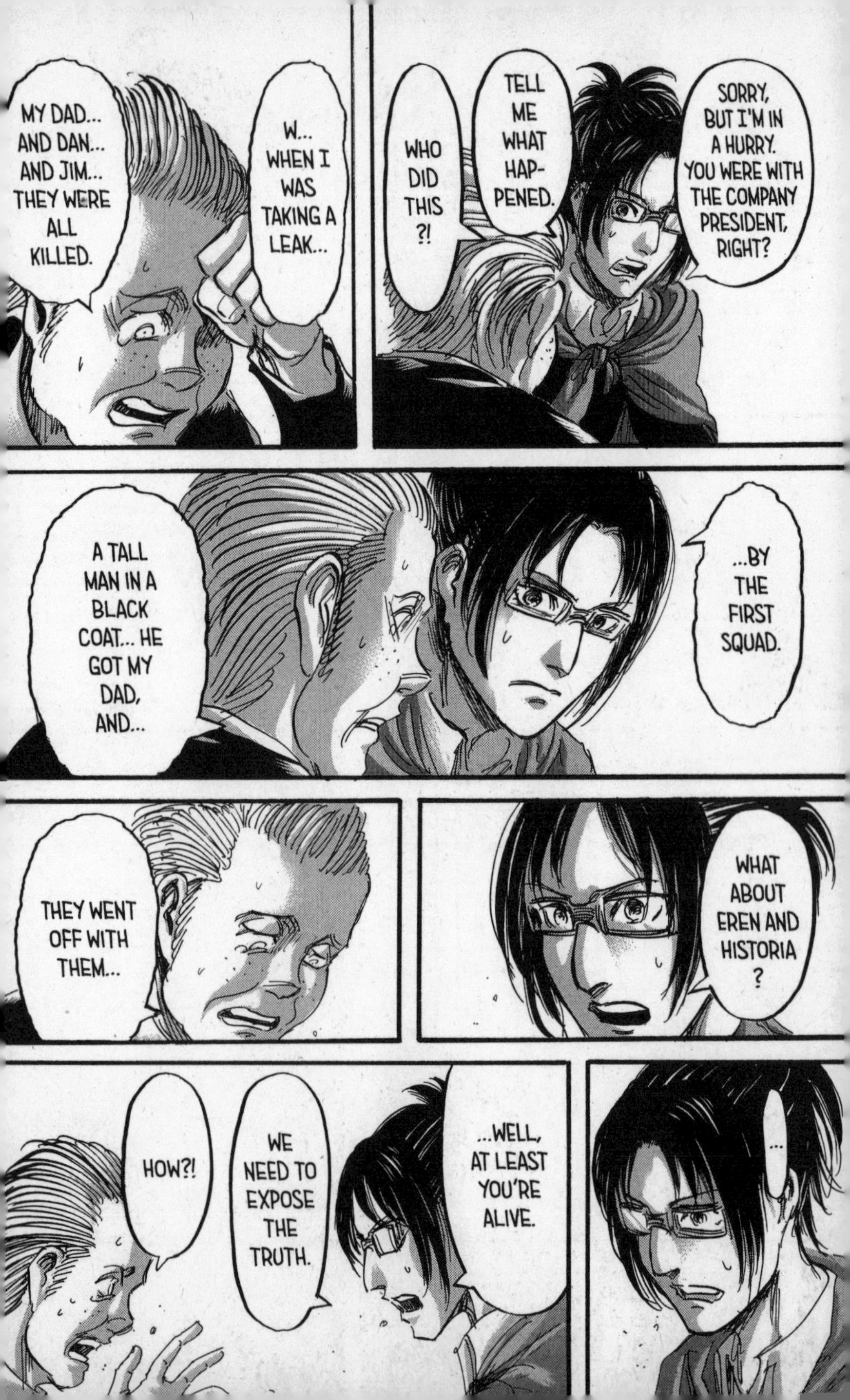
SORRY, BUT I'M IN A HURRY. YOU WERE WITH THE COMPANY PRESIDENT, RIGHT?
TELL ME WHAT HAPPENED.
WHO DID THIS?!
W... WHEN I WAS TAKING A LEAK...
MY DAD... AND DAN... AND JIM... THEY WERE ALL KILLED.
...BY THE FIRST SQUAD.
A TALL MAN IN A BLACK COAT... HE GOT MY DAD, AND...
WHAT ABOUT EREN AND HISTORIA?
THEY WENT OFF WITH THEM...
...
...WELL, AT LEAST YOU'RE ALIVE.
WE NEED TO EXPOSE THE TRUTH.
HOW?!

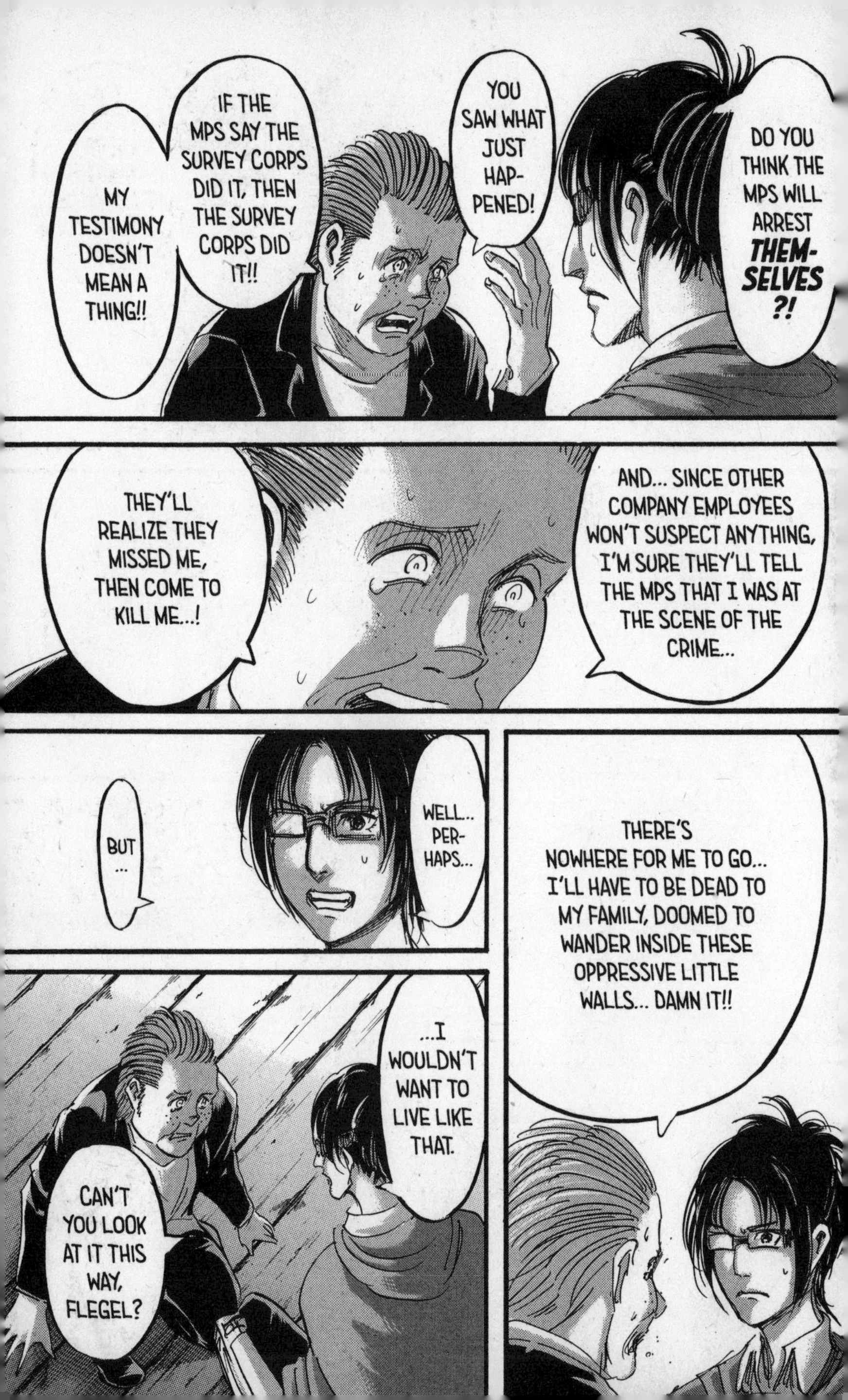
DO YOU THINK THE MPS WILL ARREST **THEMSELVES?!**
YOU SAW WHAT JUST HAPPENED!
IF THE MPS SAY THE SURVEY CORPS DID IT, THEN THE SURVEY CORPS DID IT!!
MY TESTIMONY DOESN'T MEAN A THING!!
AND... SINCE OTHER COMPANY EMPLOYEES WON'T SUSPECT ANYTHING, I'M SURE THEY'LL TELL THE MPS THAT I WAS AT THE SCENE OF THE CRIME...
THEY'LL REALIZE THEY MISSED ME, THEN COME TO KILL ME...!
THERE'S NOWHERE FOR ME TO GO... I'LL HAVE TO BE DEAD TO MY FAMILY, DOOMED TO WANDER INSIDE THESE OPPRESSIVE LITTLE WALLS... DAMN IT!!
WELL.. PERHAPS...
BUT ...
...I WOULDN'T WANT TO LIVE LIKE THAT.
CAN'T YOU LOOK AT IT THIS WAY, FLEGEL?

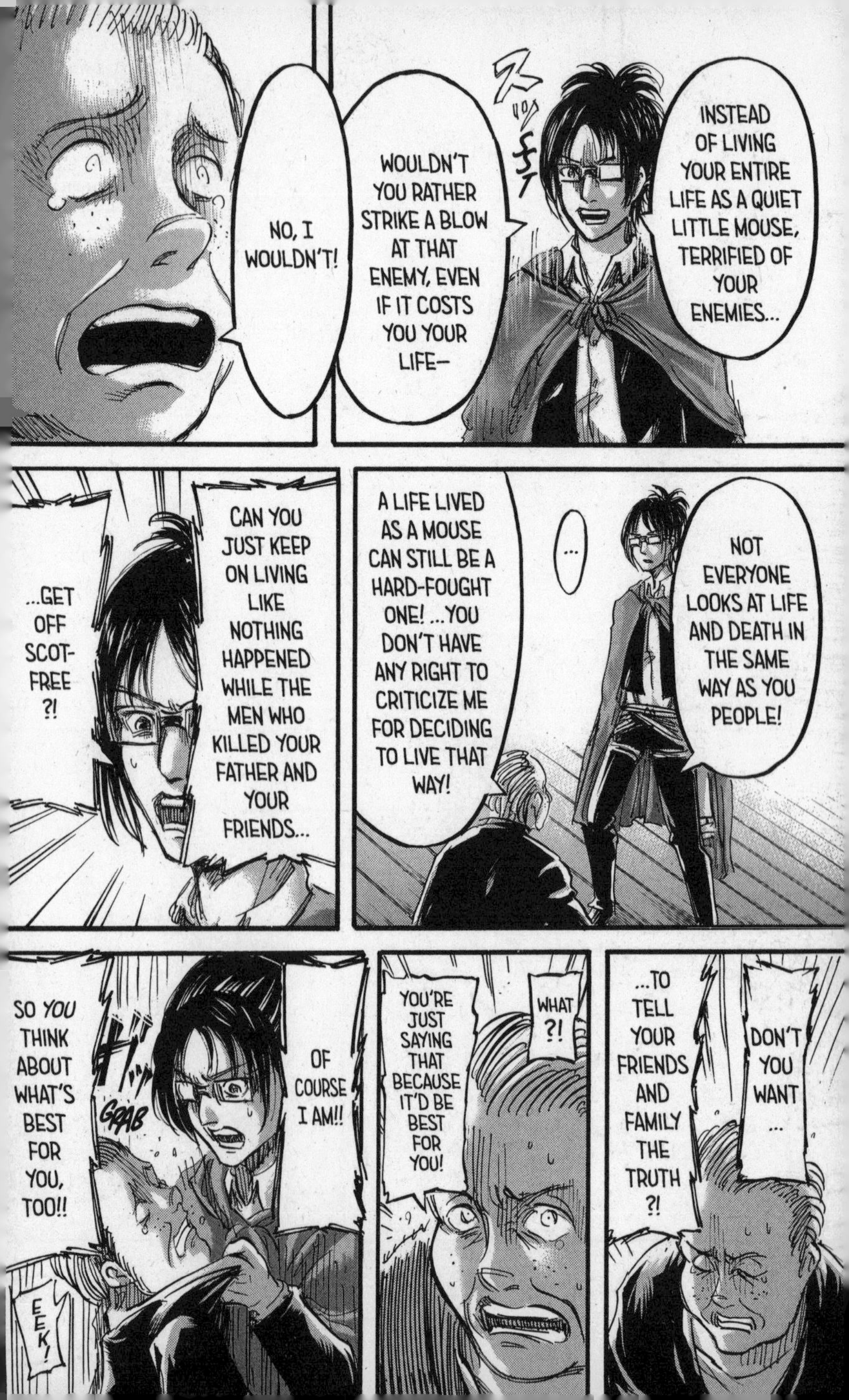
INSTEAD OF LIVING YOUR ENTIRE LIFE AS A QUIET LITTLE MOUSE, TERRIFIED OF YOUR ENEMIES...
WOULDN'T YOU RATHER STRIKE A BLOW AT THAT ENEMY, EVEN IF IT COSTS YOU YOUR LIFE—
NO, I WOULDN'T!
NOT EVERYONE LOOKS AT LIFE AND DEATH IN THE SAME WAY AS YOU PEOPLE!
...
A LIFE LIVED AS A MOUSE CAN STILL BE A HARD-FOUGHT ONE! ...YOU DON'T HAVE ANY RIGHT TO CRITICIZE ME FOR DECIDING TO LIVE THAT WAY!
CAN YOU JUST KEEP ON LIVING LIKE NOTHING HAPPENED WHILE THE MEN WHO KILLED YOUR FATHER AND YOUR FRIENDS...
...GET OFF SCOT-FREE?!
DON'T YOU WANT...
...TO TELL YOUR FRIENDS AND FAMILY THE TRUTH?!
WHAT?!
YOU'RE JUST SAYING THAT BECAUSE IT'D BE BEST FOR YOU!
OF COURSE I AM!!
GRAB
SO *YOU* THINK ABOUT WHAT'S BEST FOR YOU, TOO!!
EEK!

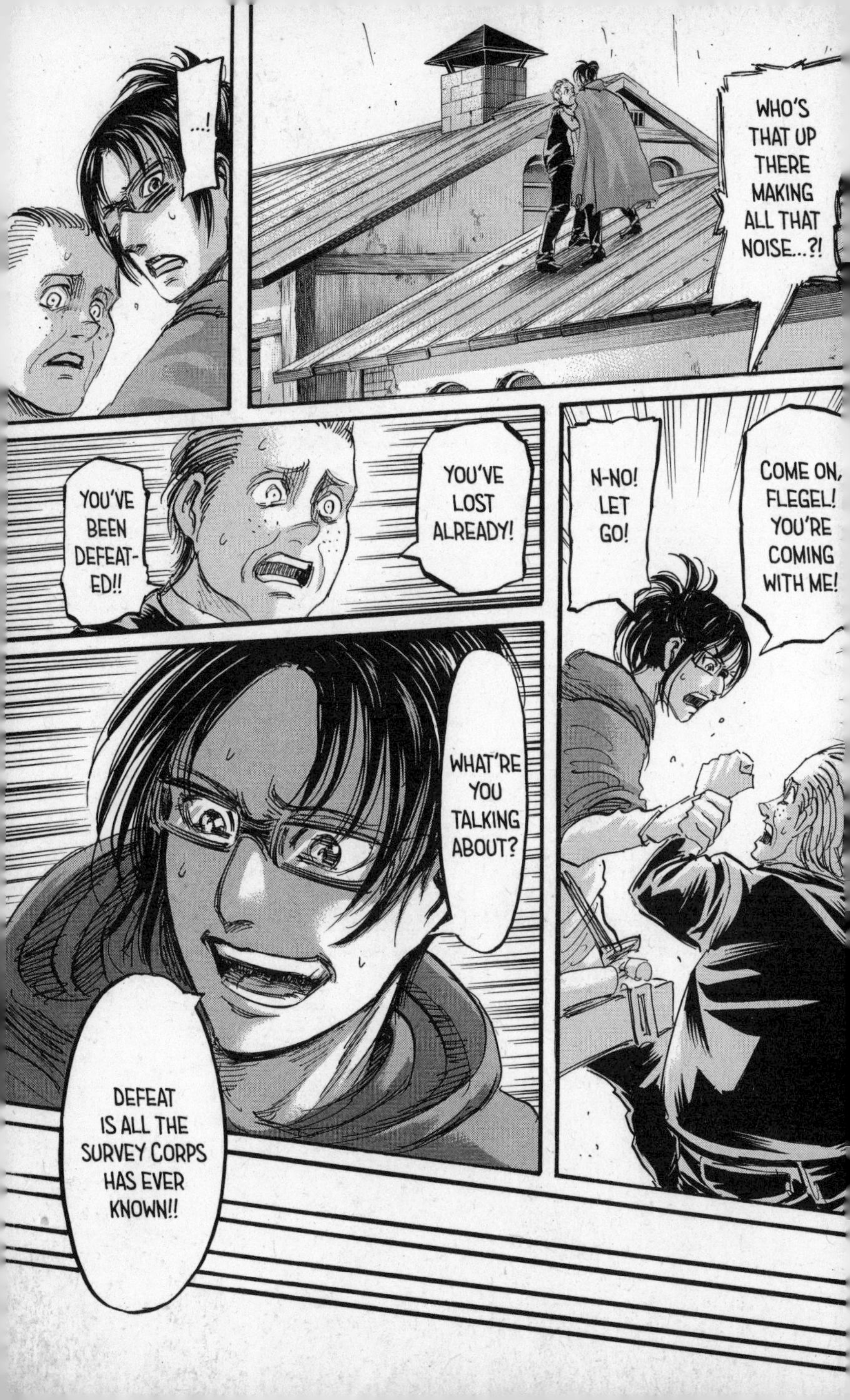
WHO'S THAT UP THERE MAKING ALL THAT NOISE...?!
...!
COME ON, FLEGEL! YOU'RE COMING WITH ME!
N-NO! LET GO!
YOU'VE LOST ALREADY!
YOU'VE BEEN DEFEAT-ED!!
WHAT'RE YOU TALKING ABOUT?
DEFEAT IS ALL THE SURVEY CORPS HAS EVER KNOWN!!

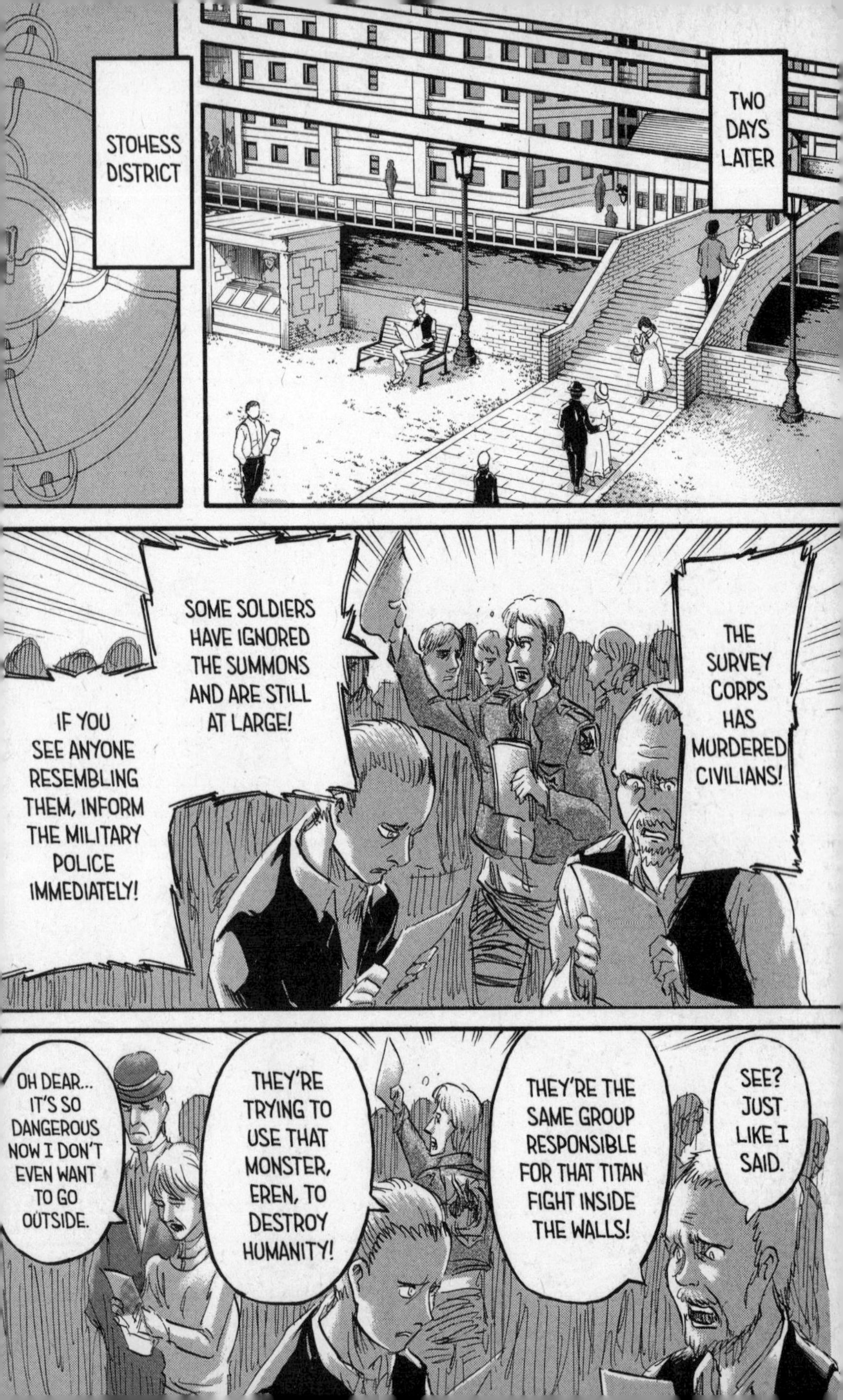
TWO DAYS LATER
STOHESS DISTRICT
THE SURVEY CORPS HAS MURDERED CIVILIANS!
SOME SOLDIERS HAVE IGNORED THE SUMMONS AND ARE STILL AT LARGE!
IF YOU SEE ANYONE RESEMBLING THEM, INFORM THE MILITARY POLICE IMMEDIATELY!
SEE? JUST LIKE I SAID.
THEY'RE THE SAME GROUP RESPONSIBLE FOR THAT TITAN FIGHT INSIDE THE WALLS!
THEY'RE TRYING TO USE THAT MONSTER, EREN, TO DESTROY HUMANITY!
OH DEAR... IT'S SO DANGEROUS NOW I DON'T EVEN WANT TO GO OUTSIDE.

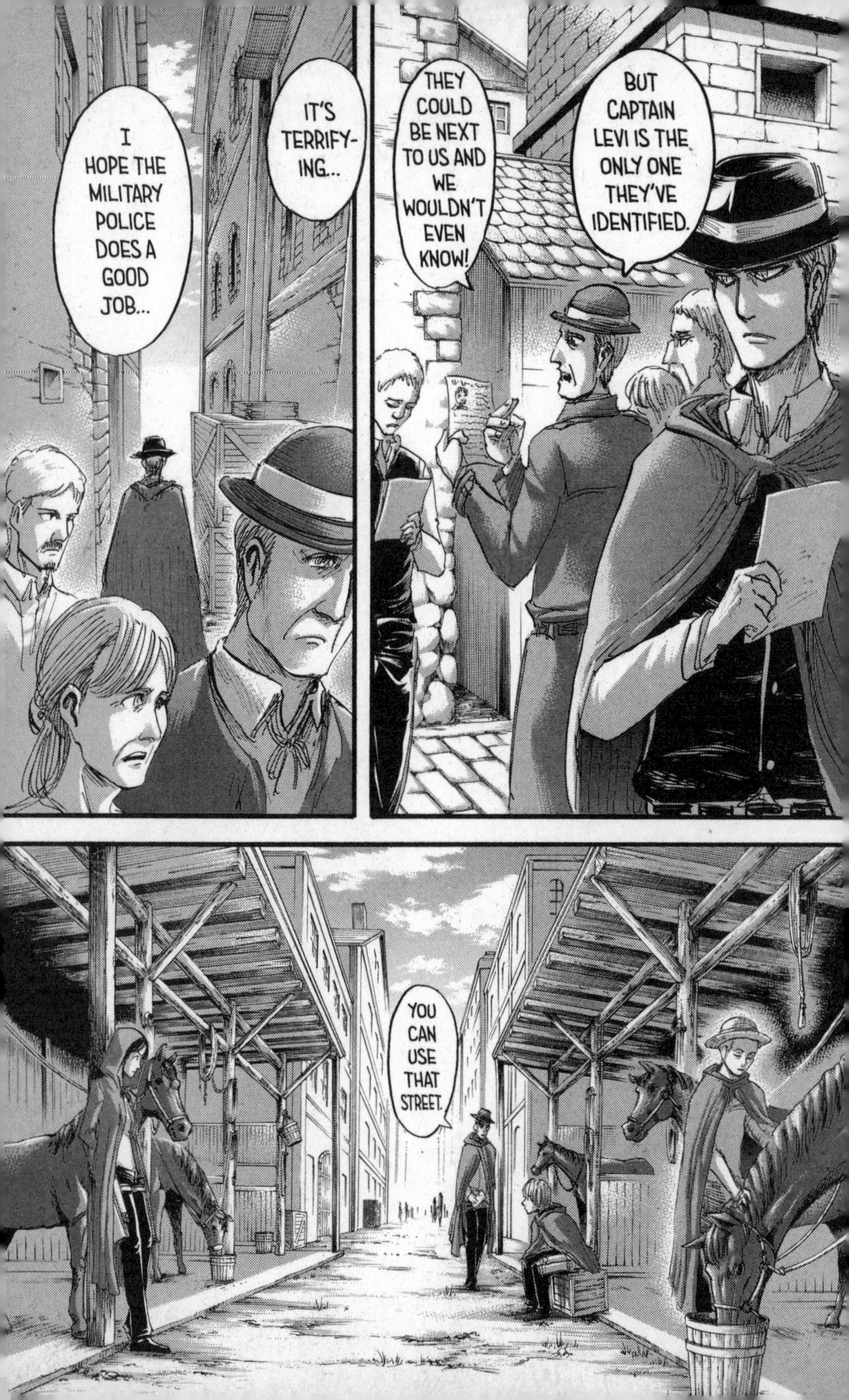
BUT CAPTAIN LEVI IS THE ONLY ONE THEY'VE IDENTIFIED.
THEY COULD BE NEXT TO US AND WE WOULDN'T EVEN KNOW!
IT'S TERRIFY-ING...
I HOPE THE MILITARY POLICE DOES A GOOD JOB...
YOU CAN USE THAT STREET.

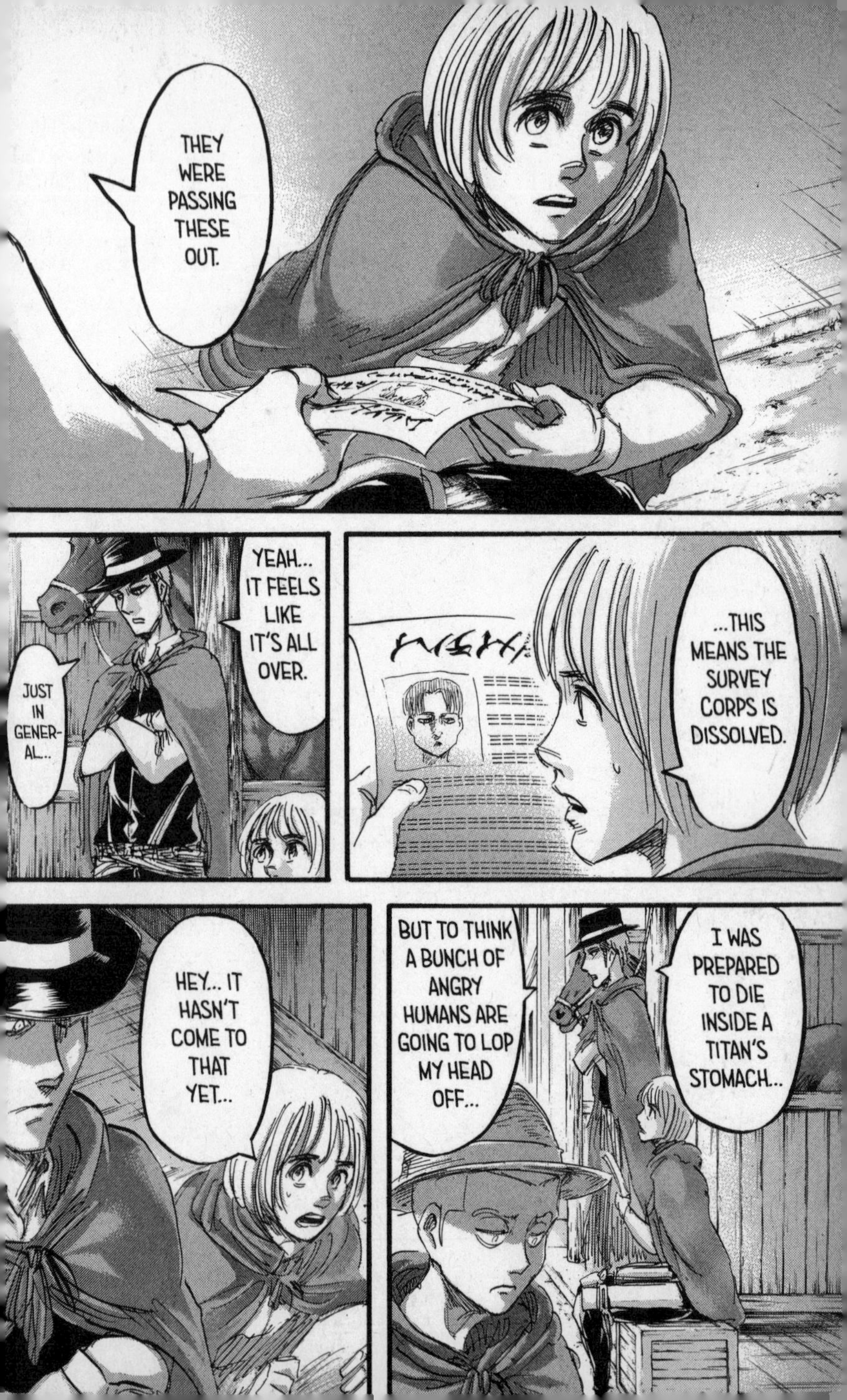
THEY WERE PASSING THESE OUT.
...THIS MEANS THE SURVEY CORPS IS DISSOLVED.
YEAH... IT FEELS LIKE IT'S ALL OVER.
JUST IN GENERAL...
I WAS PREPARED TO DIE INSIDE A TITAN'S STOMACH...
BUT TO THINK A BUNCH OF ANGRY HUMANS ARE GOING TO LOP MY HEAD OFF...
HEY... IT HASN'T COME TO THAT YET...

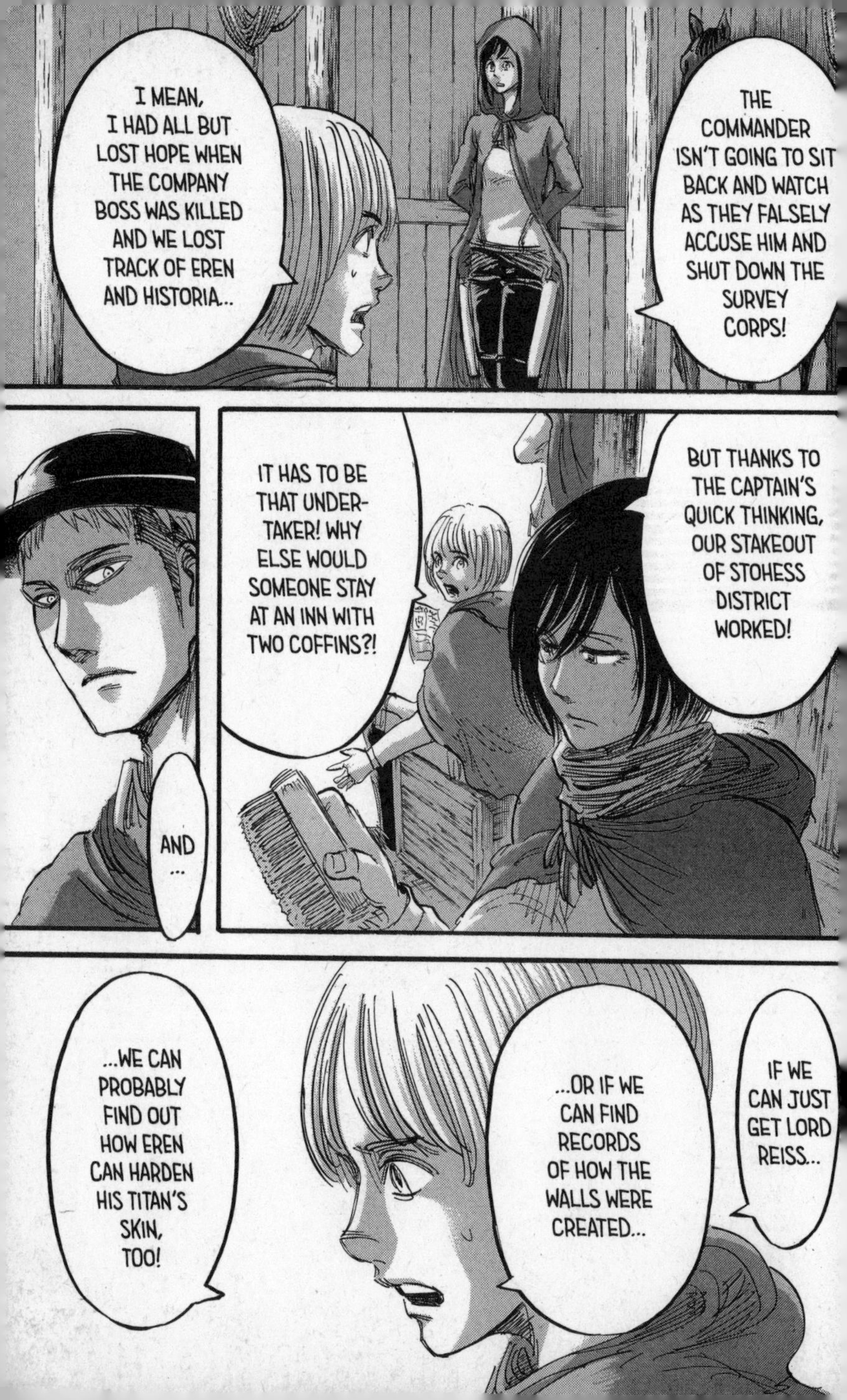
THE COMMANDER ISN'T GOING TO SIT BACK AND WATCH AS THEY FALSELY ACCUSE HIM AND SHUT DOWN THE SURVEY CORPS!
I MEAN, I HAD ALL BUT LOST HOPE WHEN THE COMPANY BOSS WAS KILLED AND WE LOST TRACK OF EREN AND HISTORIA...
BUT THANKS TO THE CAPTAIN'S QUICK THINKING, OUR STAKEOUT OF STOHESS DISTRICT WORKED!
IT HAS TO BE THAT UNDER-TAKER! WHY ELSE WOULD SOMEONE STAY AT AN INN WITH TWO COFFINS?!
AND ...
IF WE CAN JUST GET LORD REISS...
...OR IF WE CAN FIND RECORDS OF HOW THE WALLS WERE CREATED...
...WE CAN PROBABLY FIND OUT HOW EREN CAN HARDEN HIS TITAN'S SKIN, TOO!

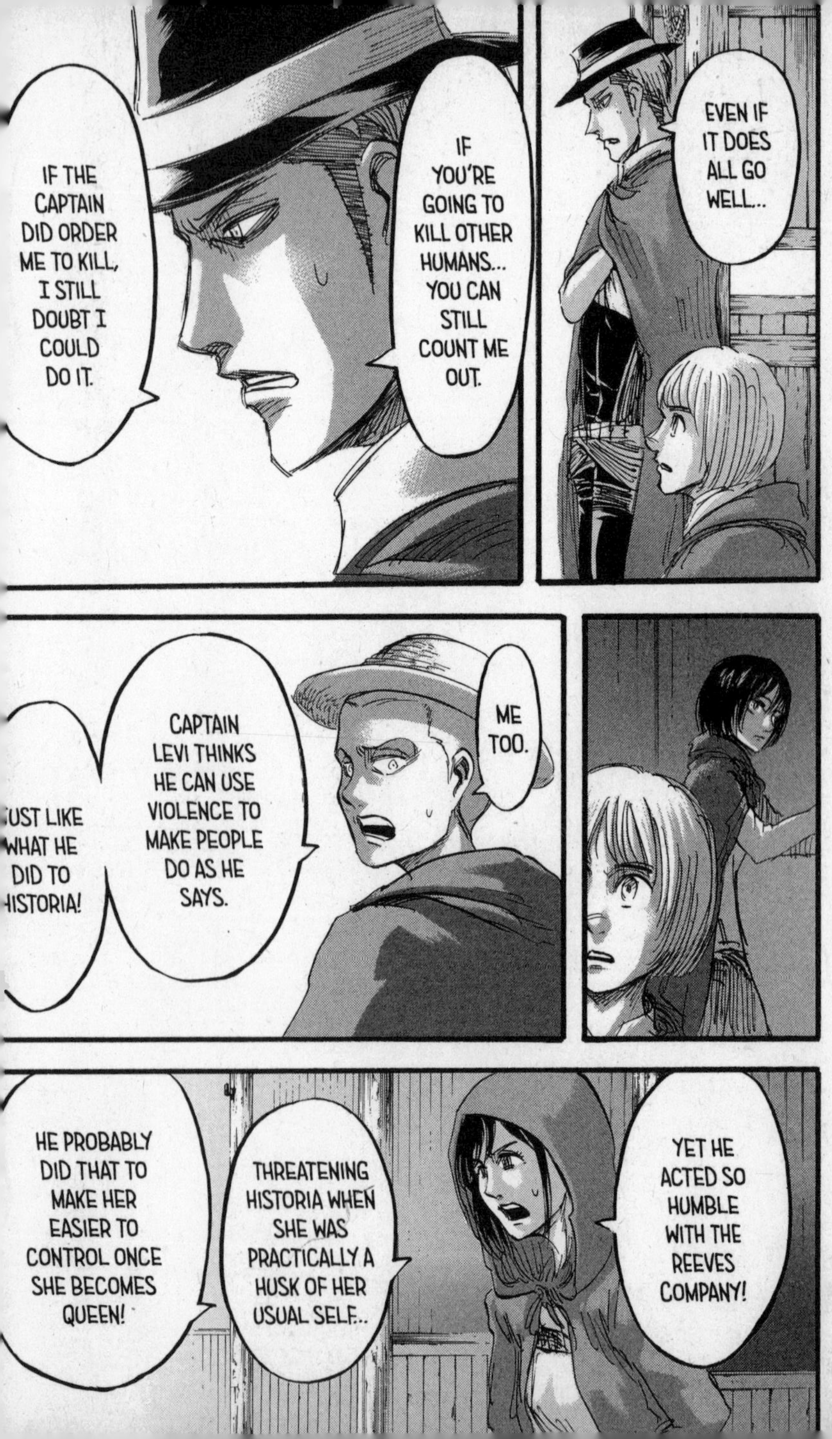
EVEN IF IT DOES ALL GO WELL...
IF YOU'RE GOING TO KILL OTHER HUMANS... YOU CAN STILL COUNT ME OUT.
IF THE CAPTAIN DID ORDER ME TO KILL, I STILL DOUBT I COULD DO IT.
ME TOO.
CAPTAIN LEVI THINKS HE CAN USE VIOLENCE TO MAKE PEOPLE DO AS HE SAYS.
JUST LIKE WHAT HE DID TO HISTORIA!
YET HE ACTED SO HUMBLE WITH THE REEVES COMPANY!
THREATENING HISTORIA WHEN SHE WAS PRACTICALLY A HUSK OF HER USUAL SELF...
HE PROBABLY DID THAT TO MAKE HER EASIER TO CONTROL ONCE SHE BECOMES QUEEN!

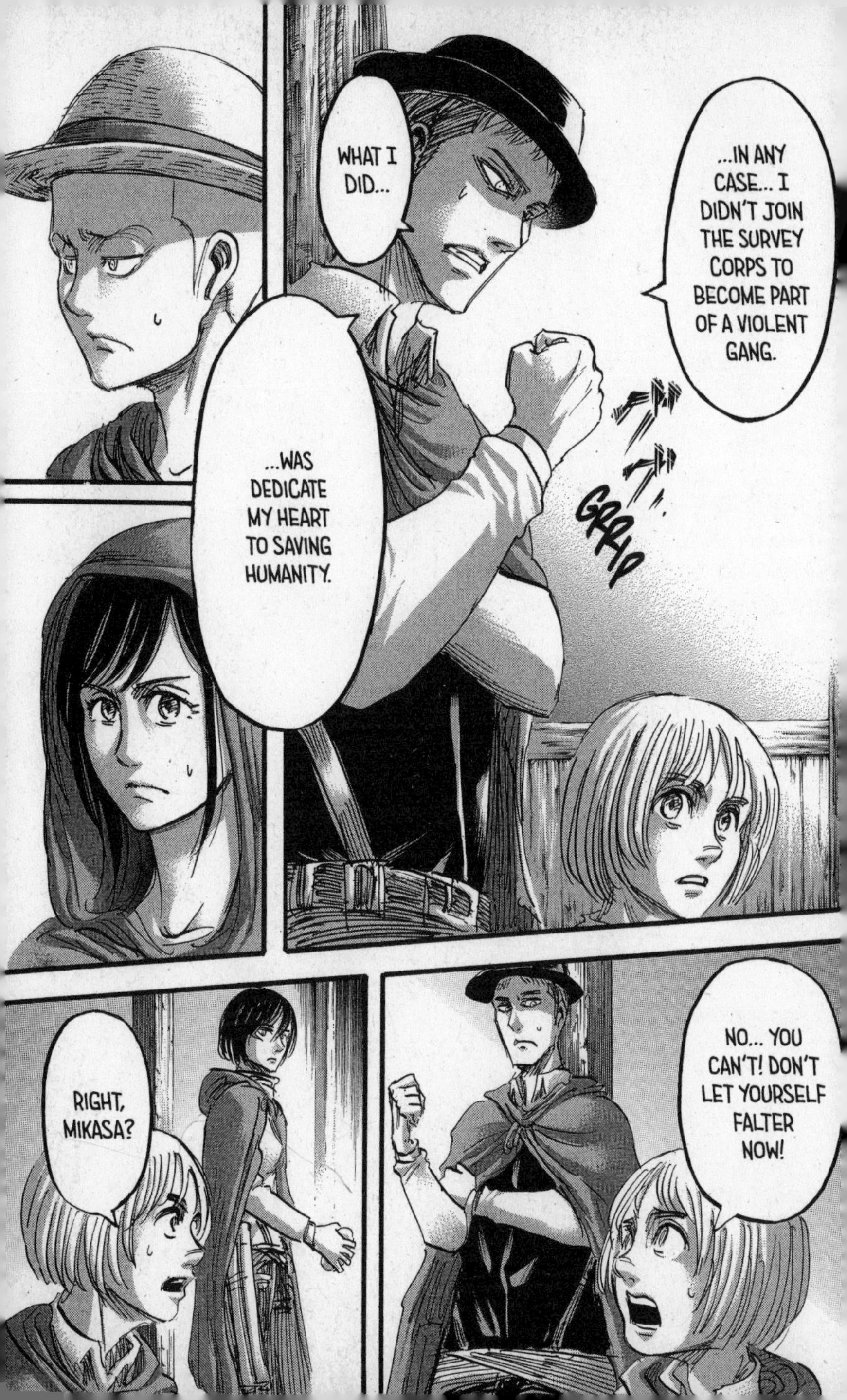
...IN ANY CASE... I DIDN'T JOIN THE SURVEY CORPS TO BECOME PART OF A VIOLENT GANG.
WHAT I DID...
GRRIP
...WAS DEDICATE MY HEART TO SAVING HUMANITY.
NO... YOU CAN'T! DON'T LET YOURSELF FALTER NOW!
RIGHT, MIKASA?

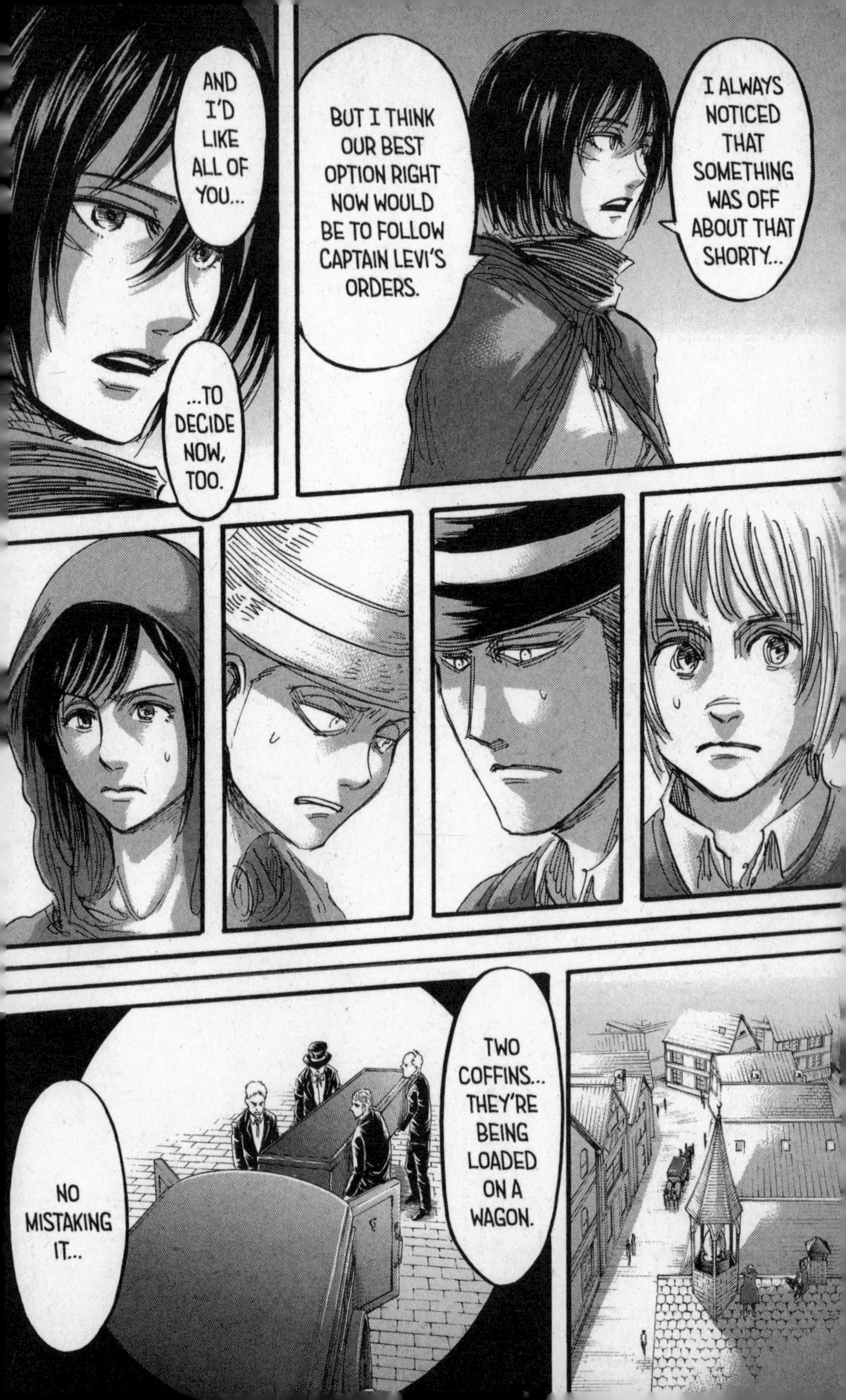
I ALWAYS NOTICED THAT SOMETHING WAS OFF ABOUT THAT SHORTY...
BUT I THINK OUR BEST OPTION RIGHT NOW WOULD BE TO FOLLOW CAPTAIN LEVI'S ORDERS.
AND I'D LIKE ALL OF YOU...
...TO DECIDE NOW, TOO.
TWO COFFINS... THEY'RE BEING LOADED ON A WAGON.
NO MISTAKING IT...

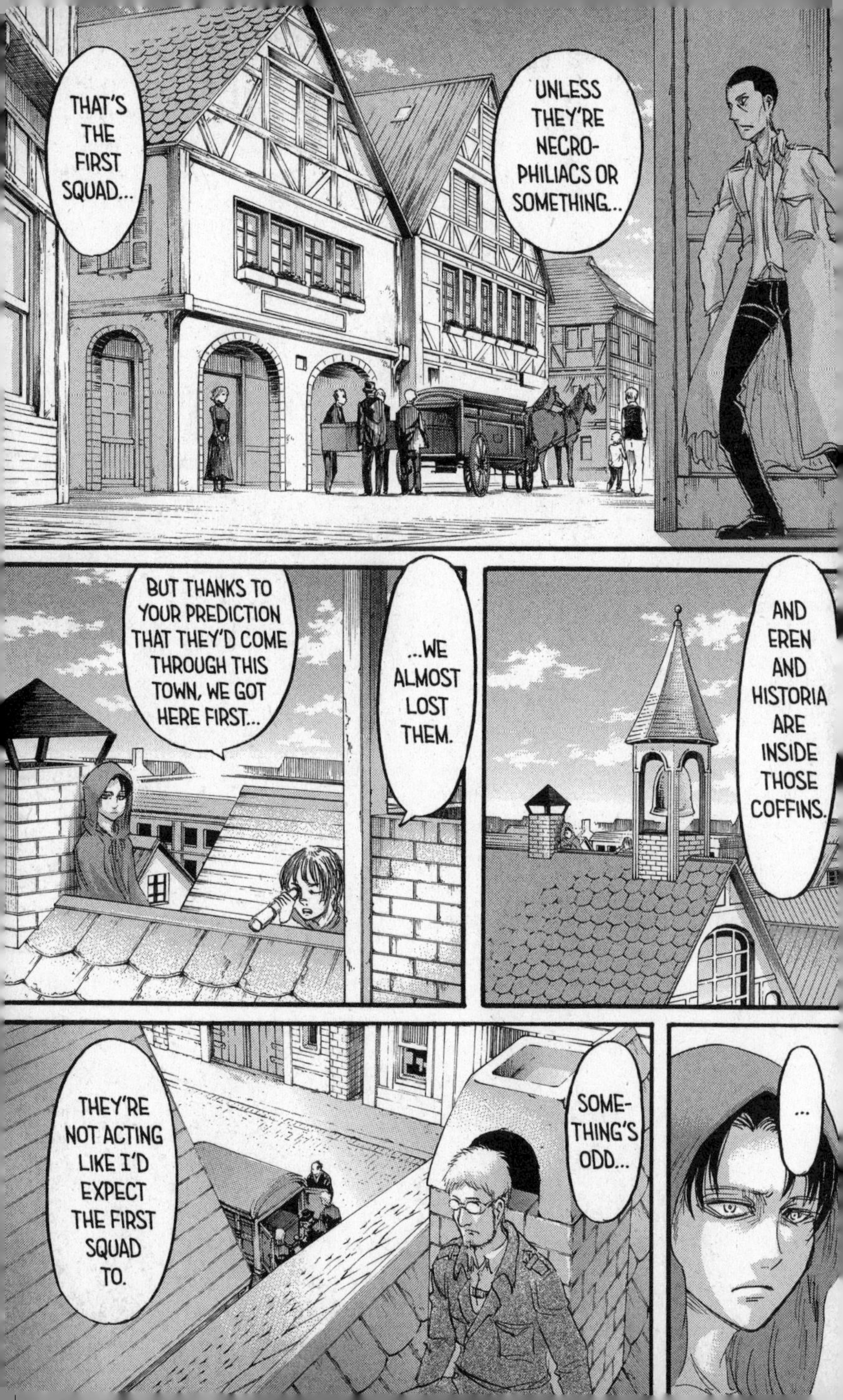
UNLESS THEY'RE NECRO-PHILIACS OR SOMETHING...
THAT'S THE FIRST SQUAD...
AND EREN AND HISTORIA ARE INSIDE THOSE COFFINS.
BUT THANKS TO YOUR PREDICTION THAT THEY'D COME THROUGH THIS TOWN, WE GOT HERE FIRST...
...WE ALMOST LOST THEM.
...
SOME-THING'S ODD...
THEY'RE NOT ACTING LIKE I'D EXPECT THE FIRST SQUAD TO.

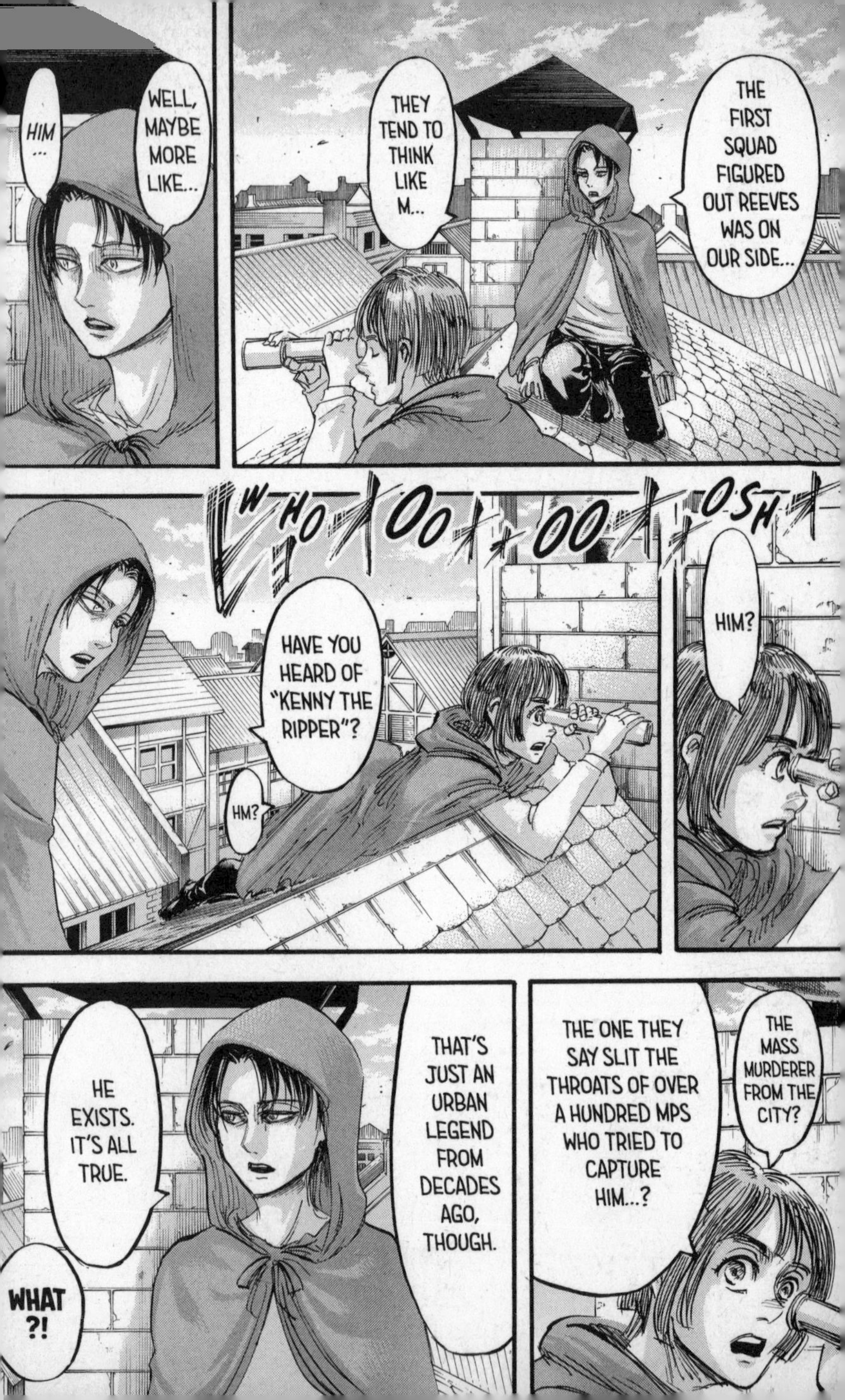
THE FIRST SQUAD FIGURED OUT REEVES WAS ON OUR SIDE...
THEY TEND TO THINK LIKE M...
WELL, MAYBE MORE LIKE...
HIM...
HIM?
WHOOOOOSH
HAVE YOU HEARD OF "KENNY THE RIPPER"?
HM?
THE MASS MURDERER FROM THE CITY?
THE ONE THEY SAY SLIT THE THROATS OF OVER A HUNDRED MPS WHO TRIED TO CAPTURE HIM...?
THAT'S JUST AN URBAN LEGEND FROM DECADES AGO, THOUGH.
HE EXISTS. IT'S ALL TRUE.
WHAT?!

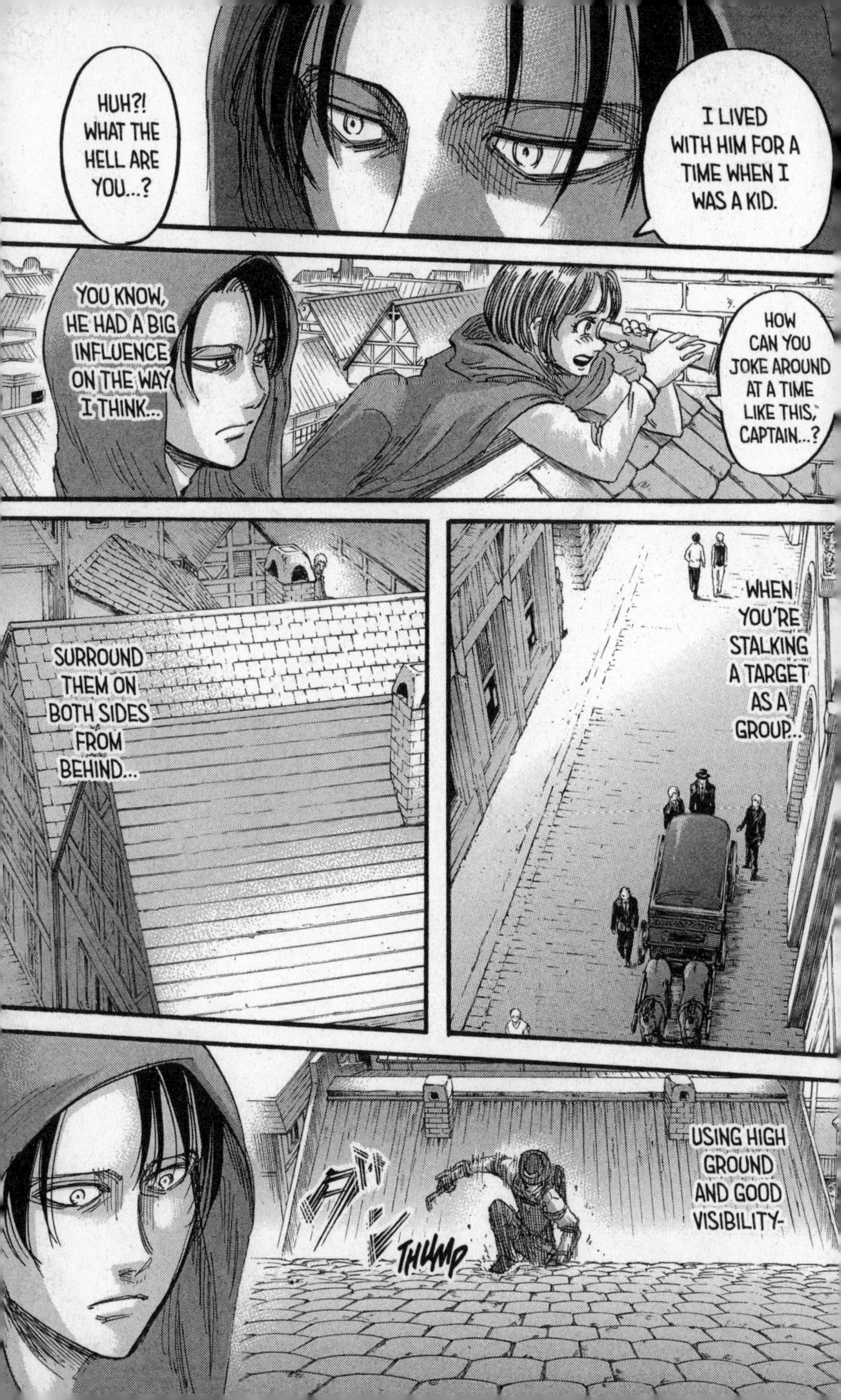
I LIVED WITH HIM FOR A TIME WHEN I WAS A KID.
HUH?! WHAT THE HELL ARE YOU...?
HOW CAN YOU JOKE AROUND AT A TIME LIKE THIS, CAPTAIN...?
YOU KNOW, HE HAD A BIG INFLUENCE ON THE WAY I THINK...
WHEN YOU'RE STALKING A TARGET AS A GROUP...
SURROUND THEM ON BOTH SIDES FROM BEHIND...
USING HIGH GROUND AND GOOD VISIBILITY-
THUMP

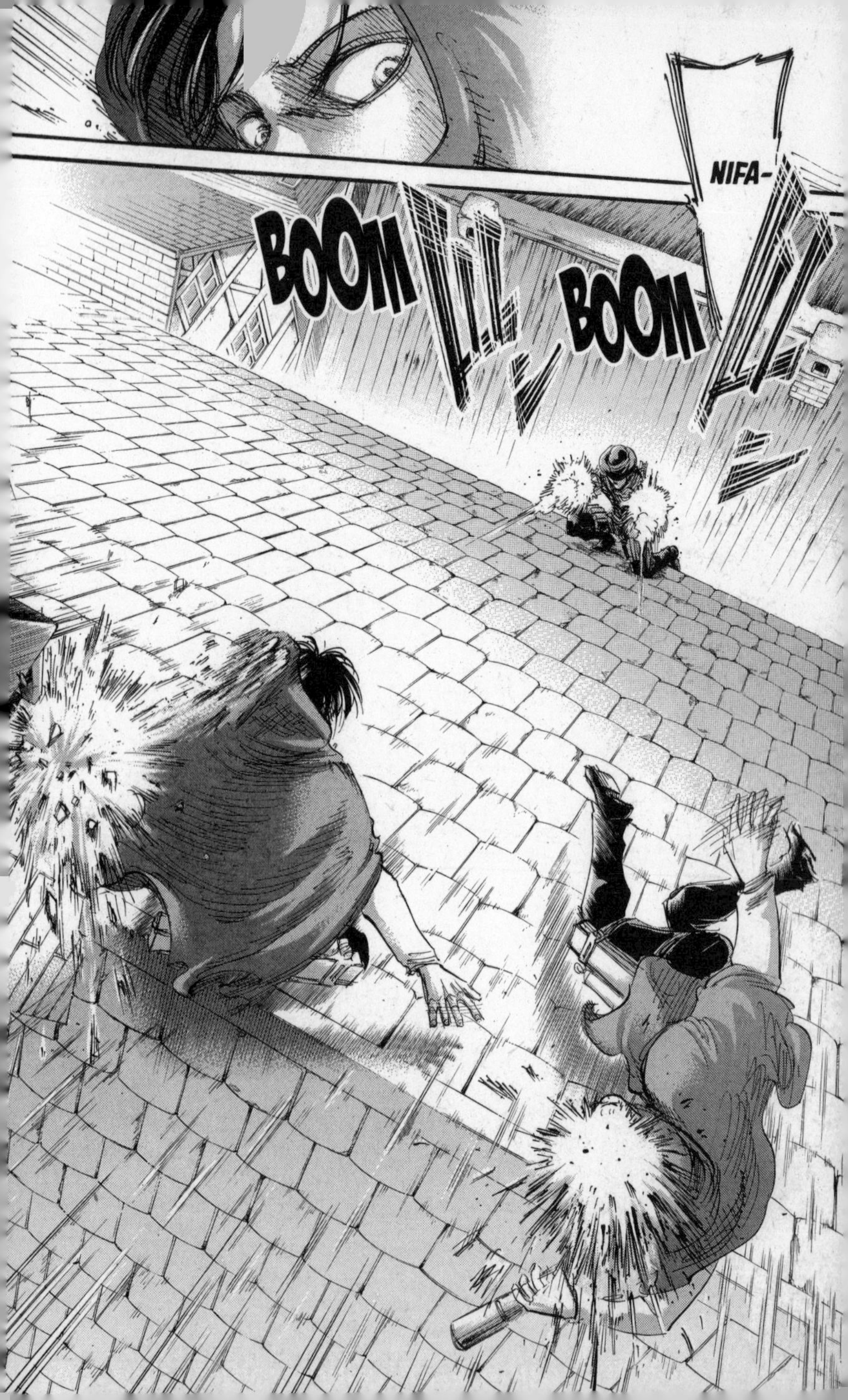
NIFA-
BOOM
BOOM

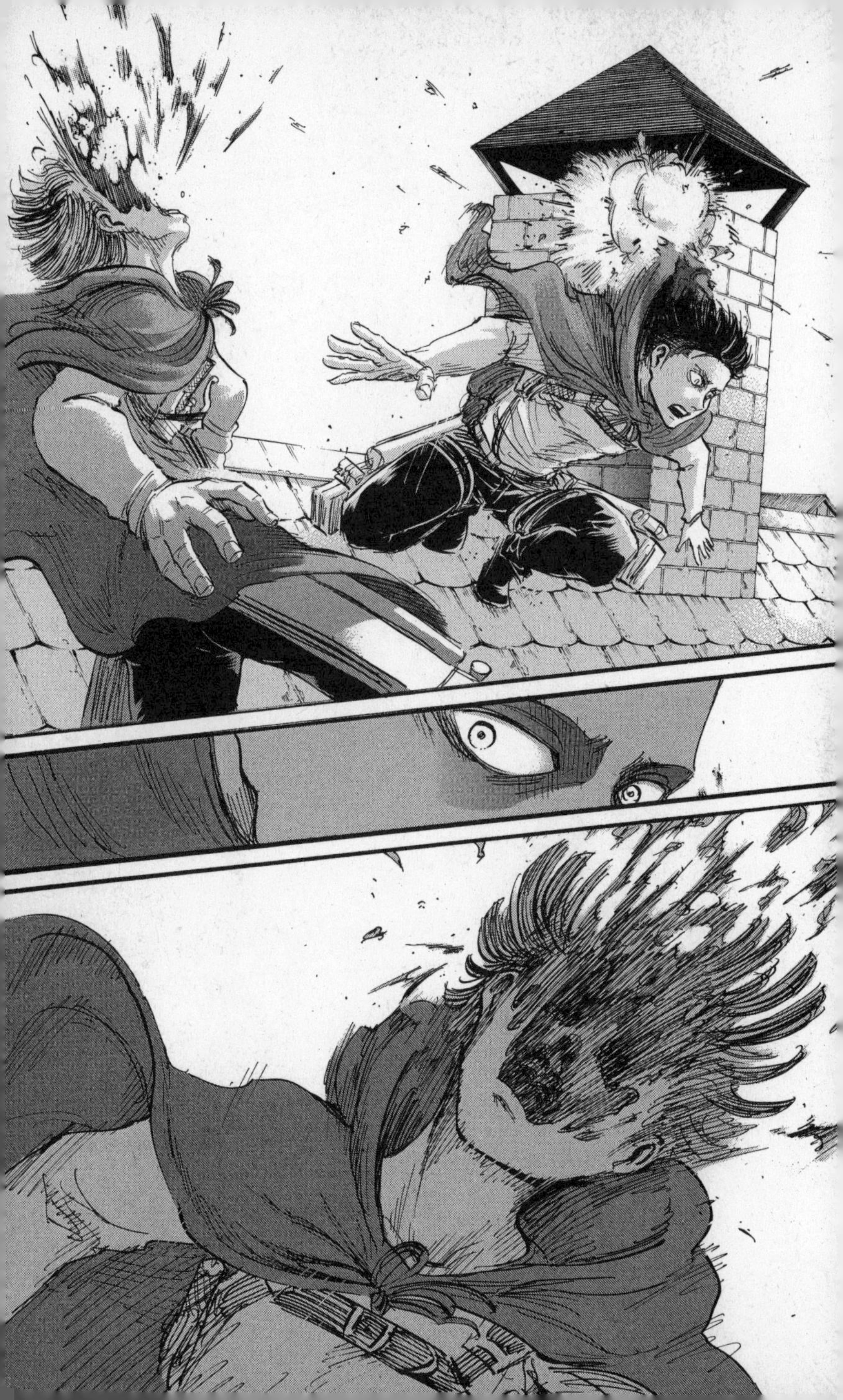

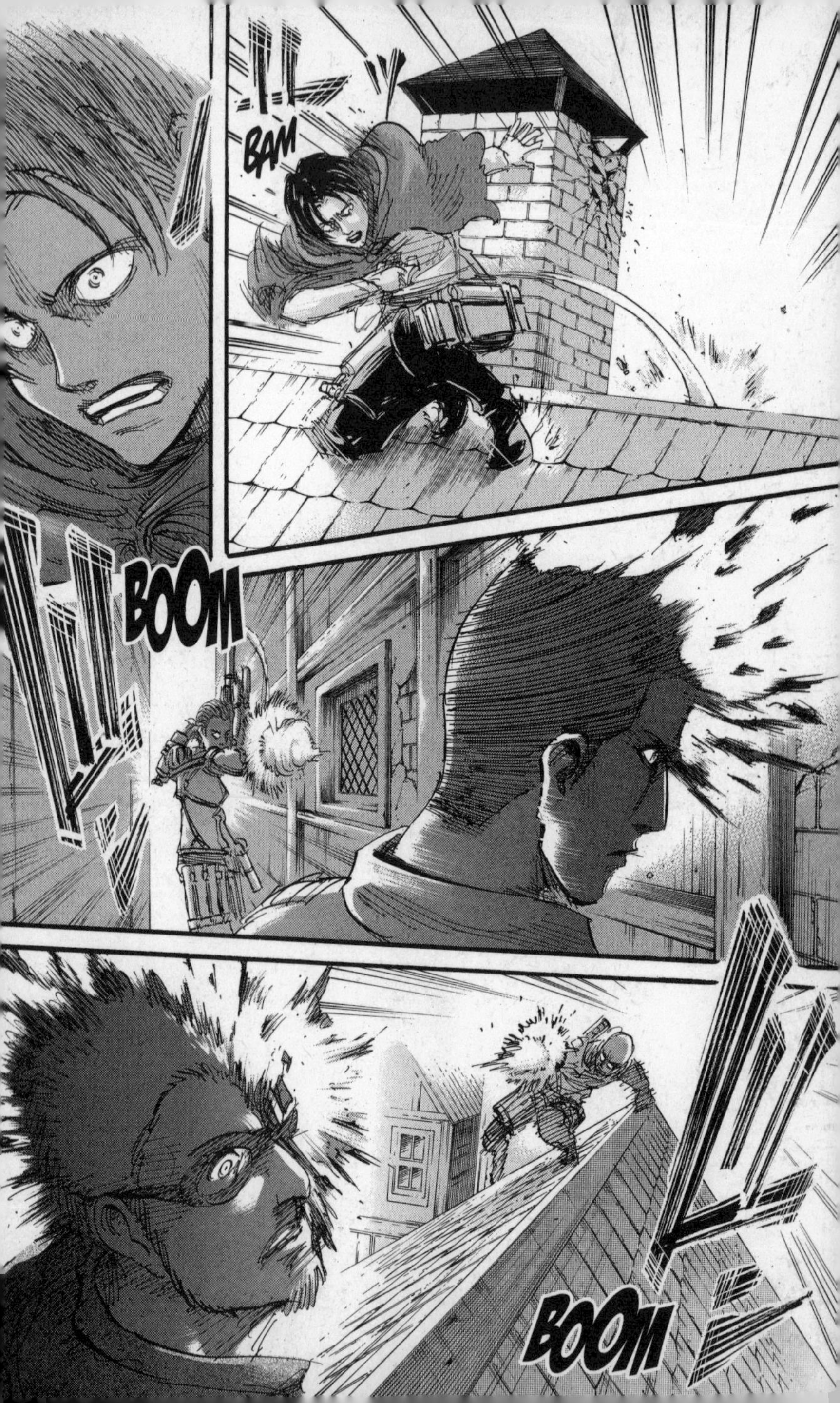
BAM
BOOM
BOOM

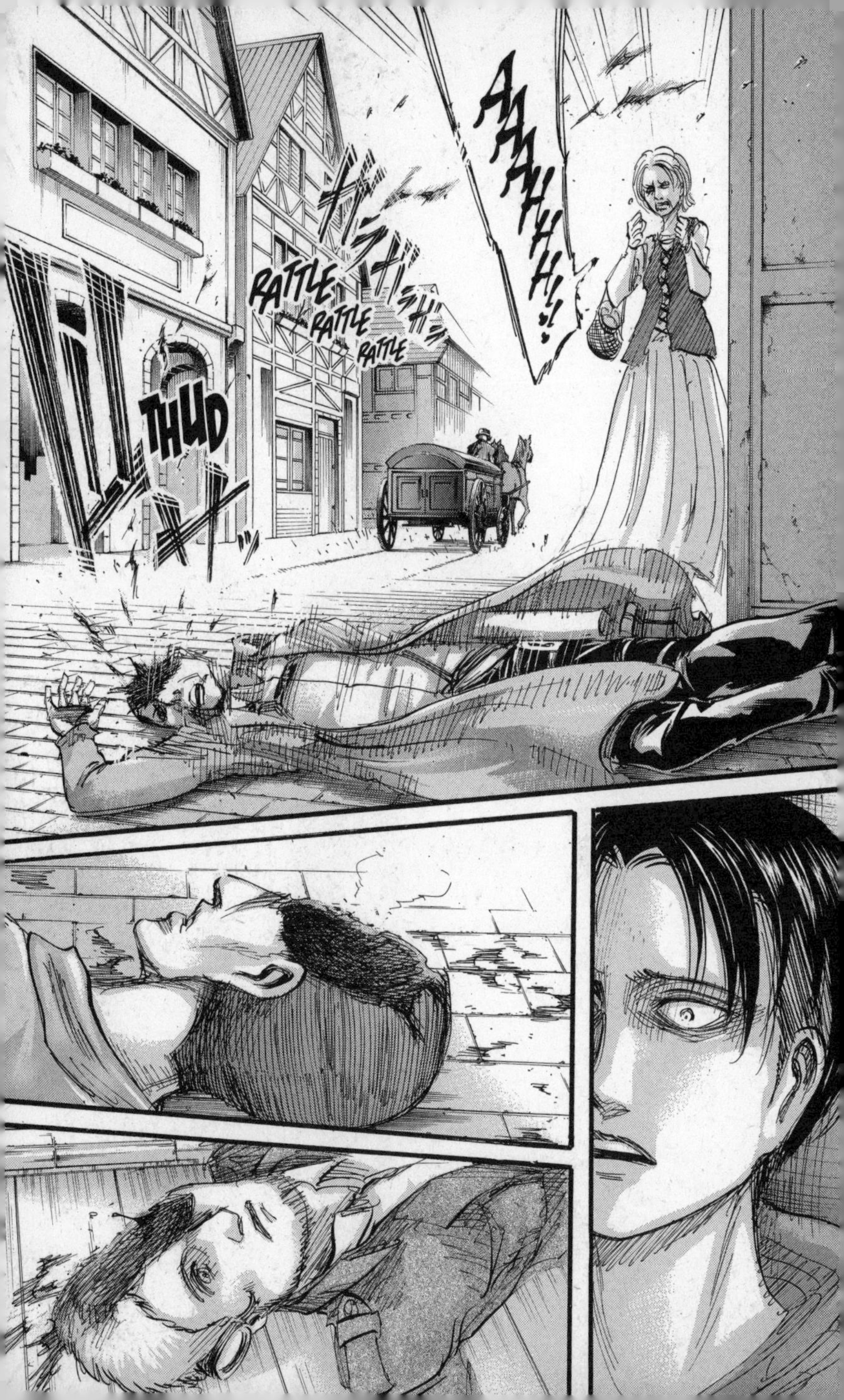
AAAHHH!!
RATTLE
RATTLE
RATTLE
THUD

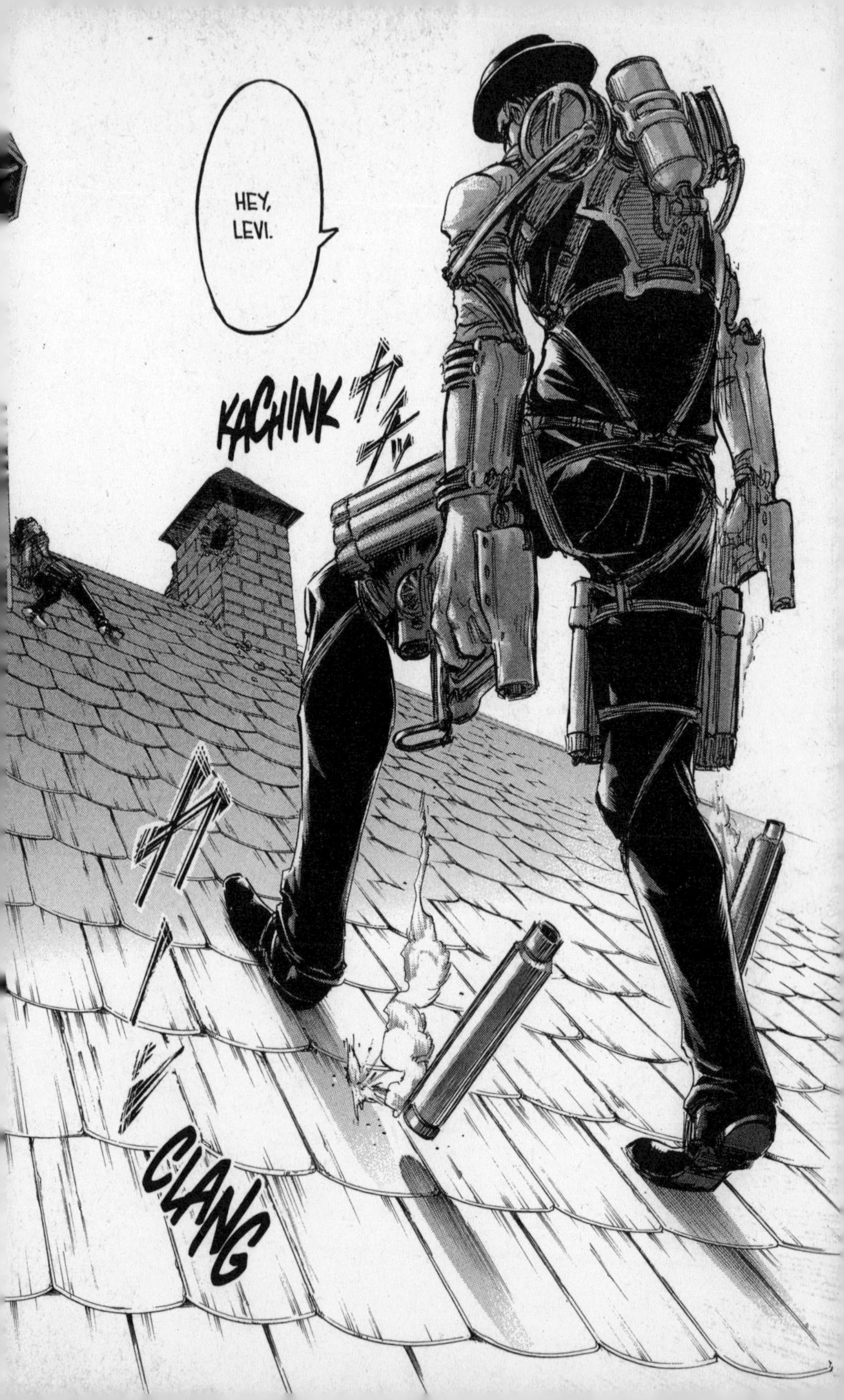
HEY, LEVI.
KACHINK
CLANG

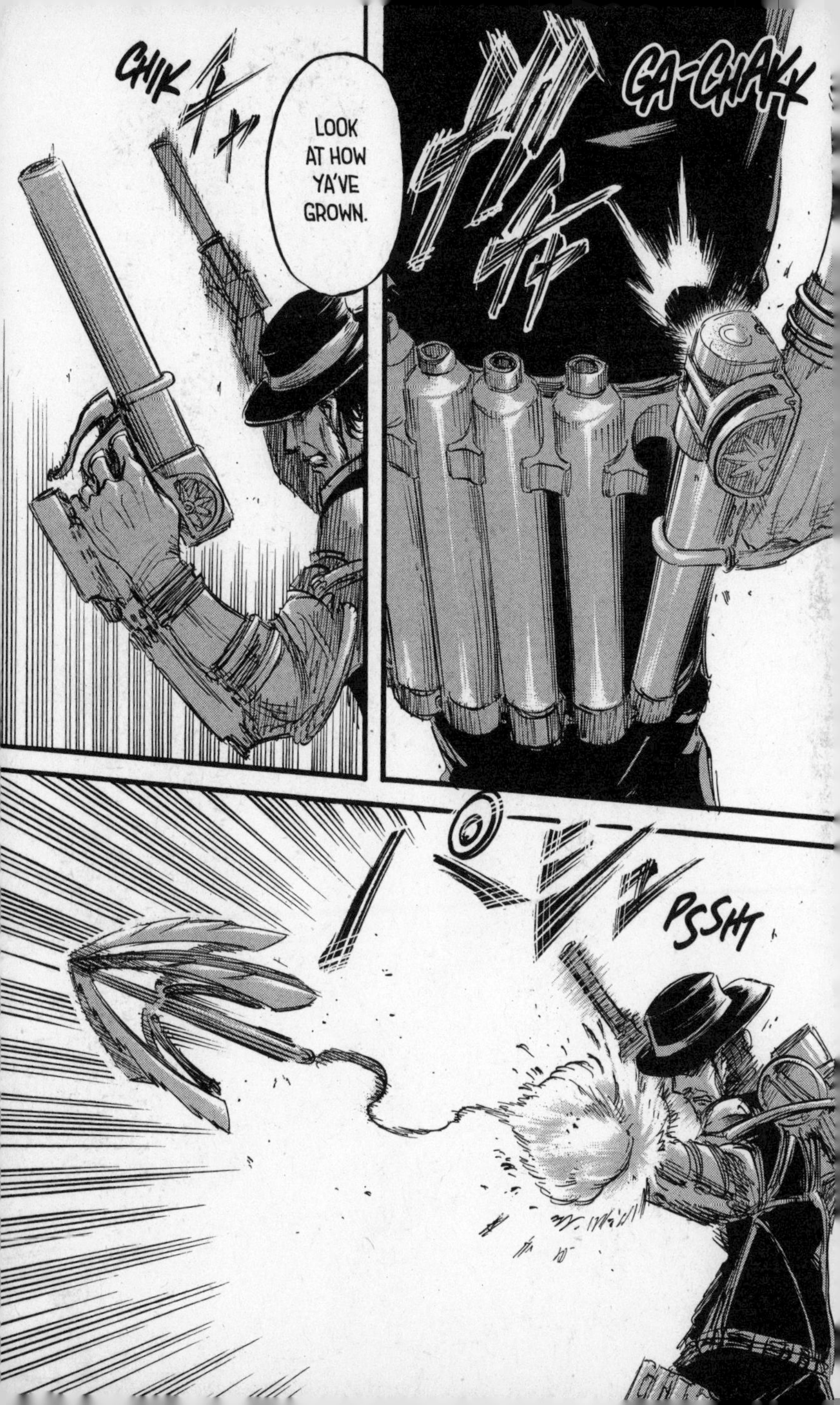
GA-CHAKK
CHIK
LOOK AT HOW YA'VE GROWN.
PSSHT

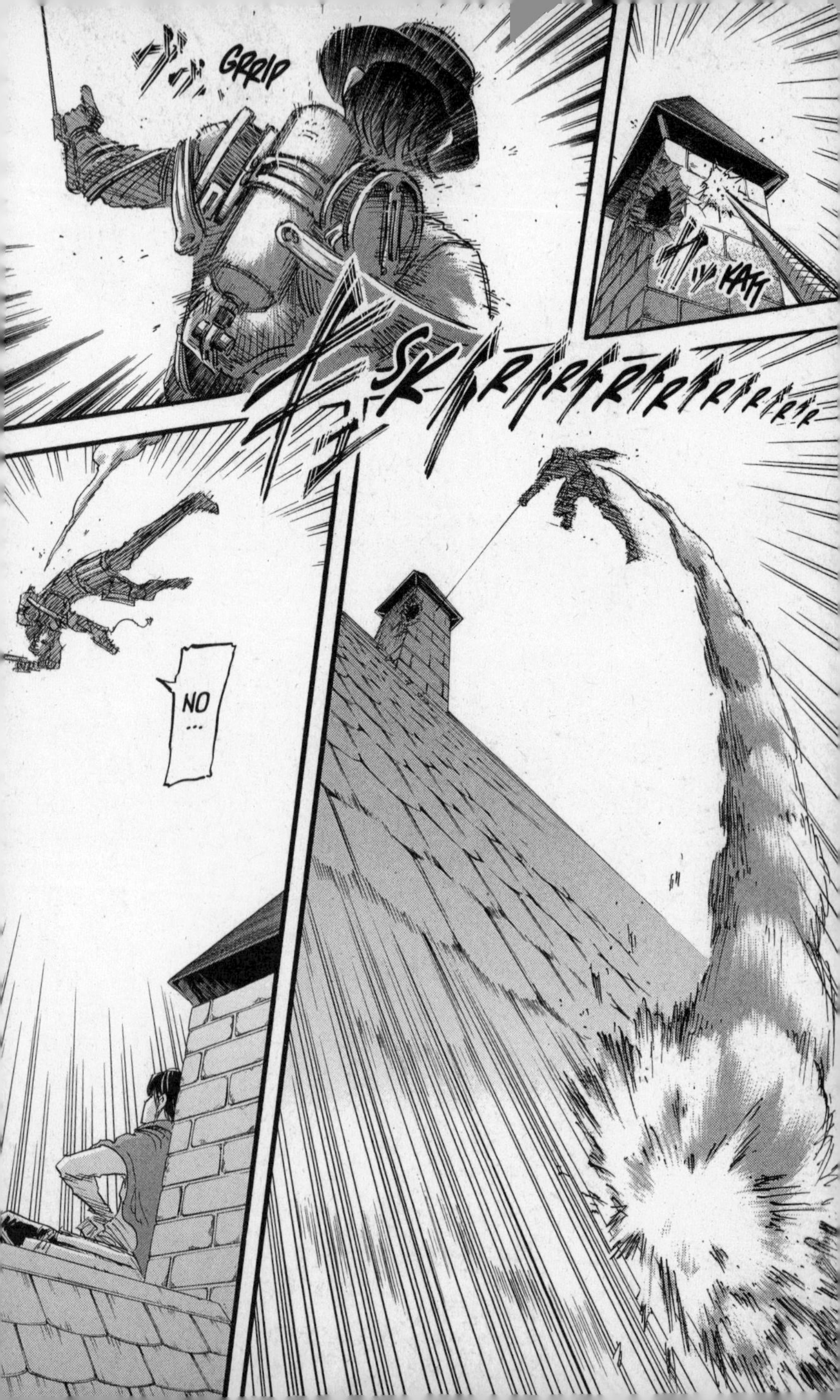
KATT
GRRIP
SKRRRRRRRRRRRRRRRRR
NO ...

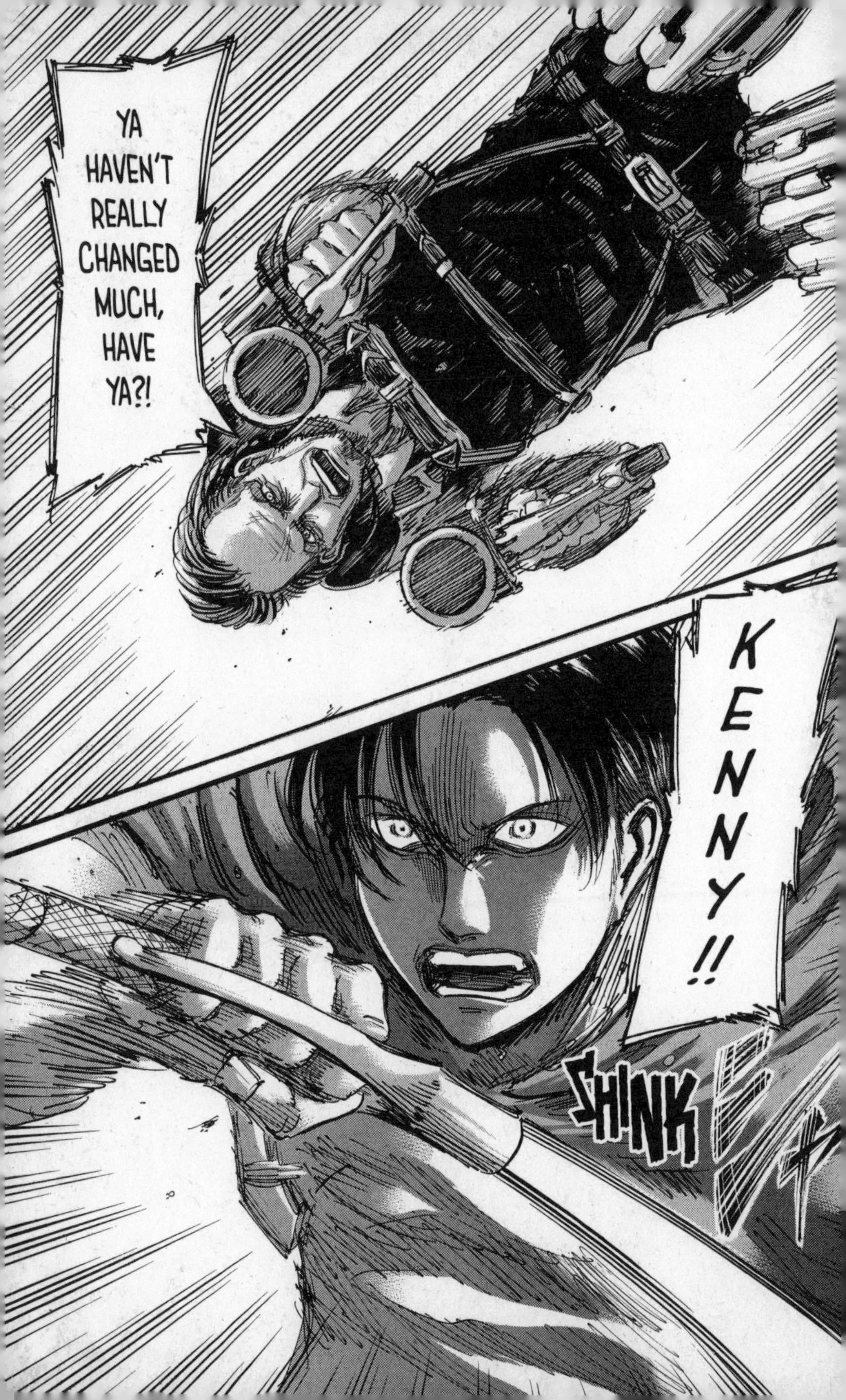
YA HAVEN'T REALLY CHANGED MUCH, HAVE YA?!
KENNY!!
SHINK

ATTACK on TITAN

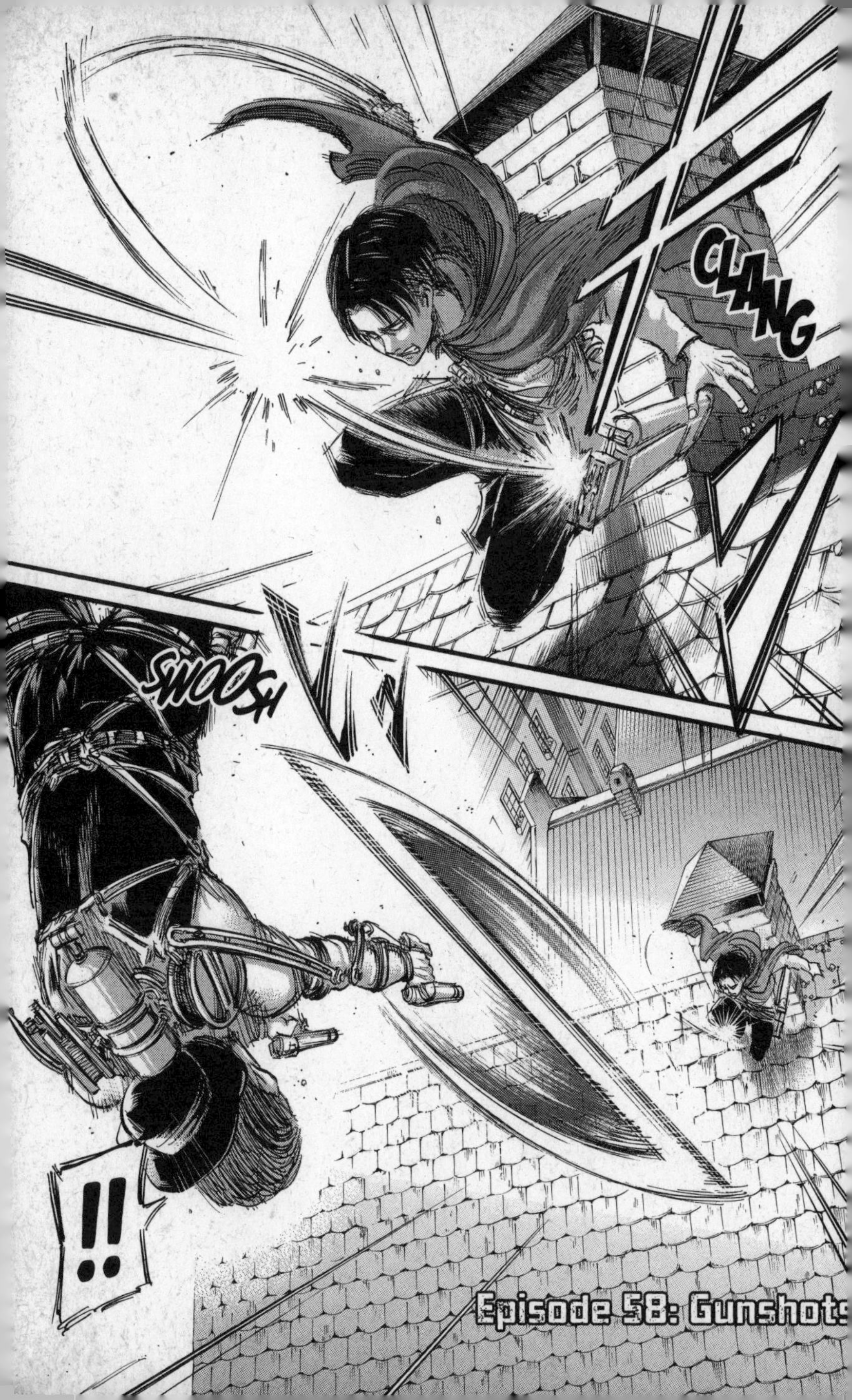
CLANG
SWOOSH
!!
Episode 58: Gunshots

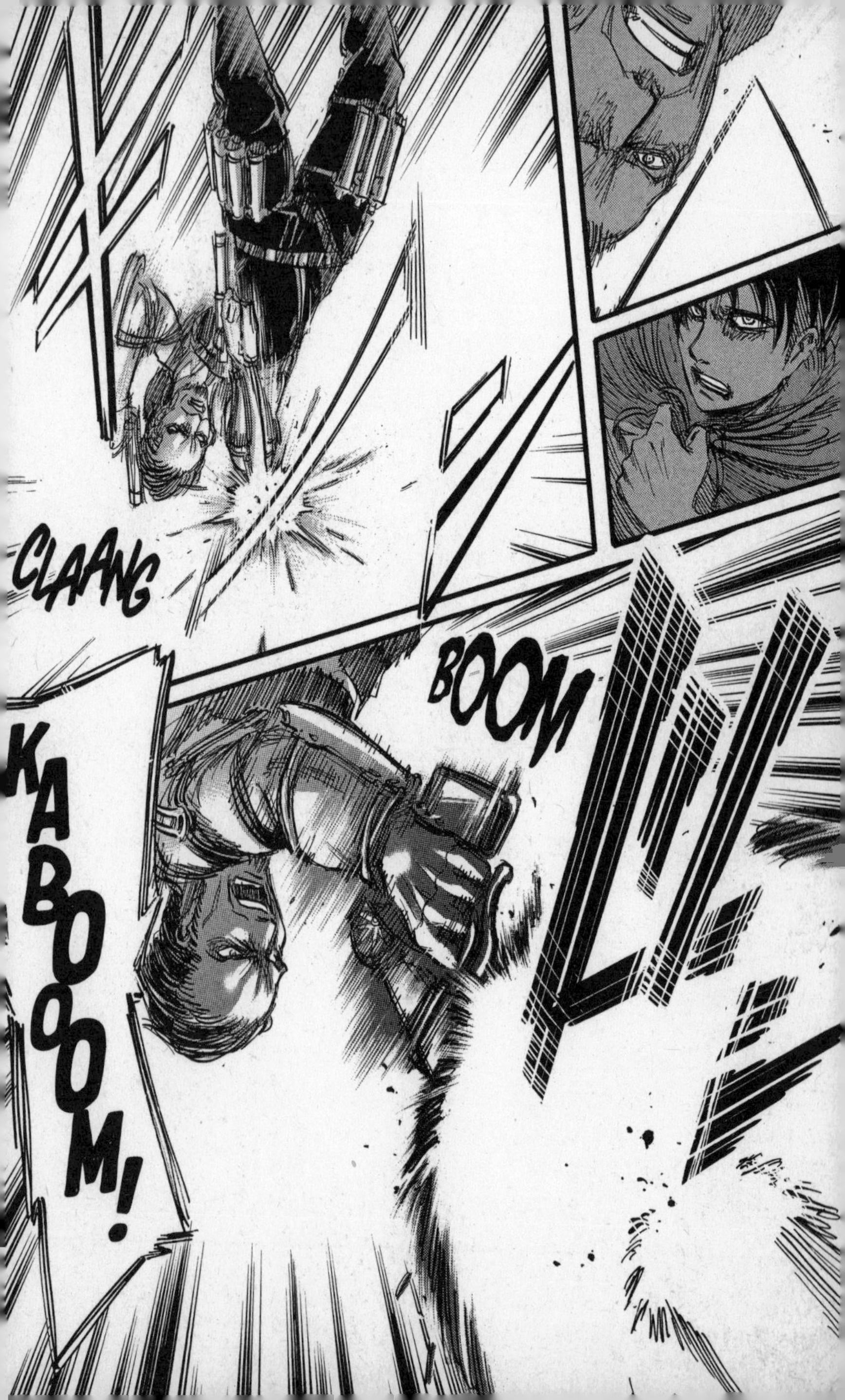
CLAANG
BOOM
KABOOOM!

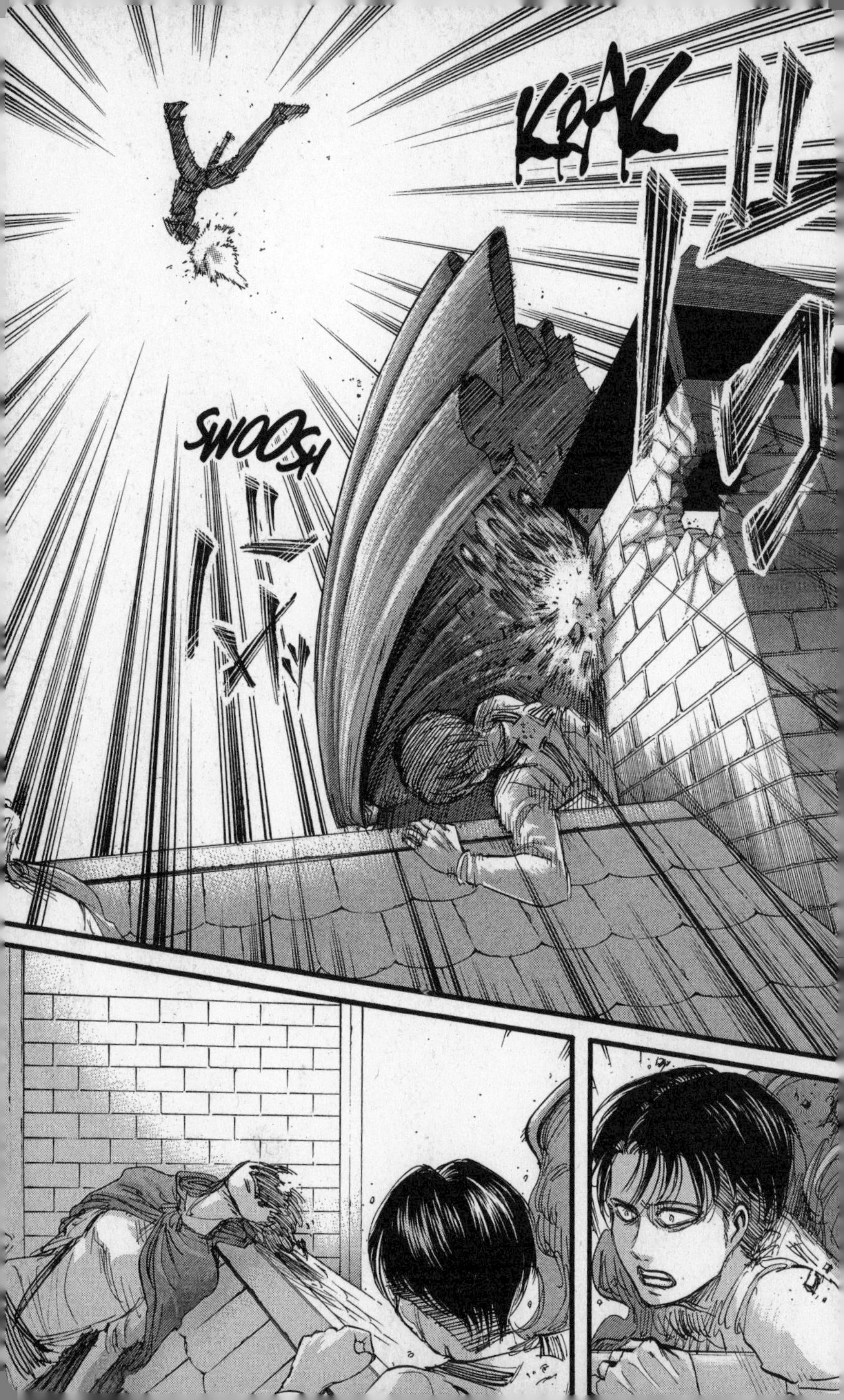
KRAK
SWOOSH

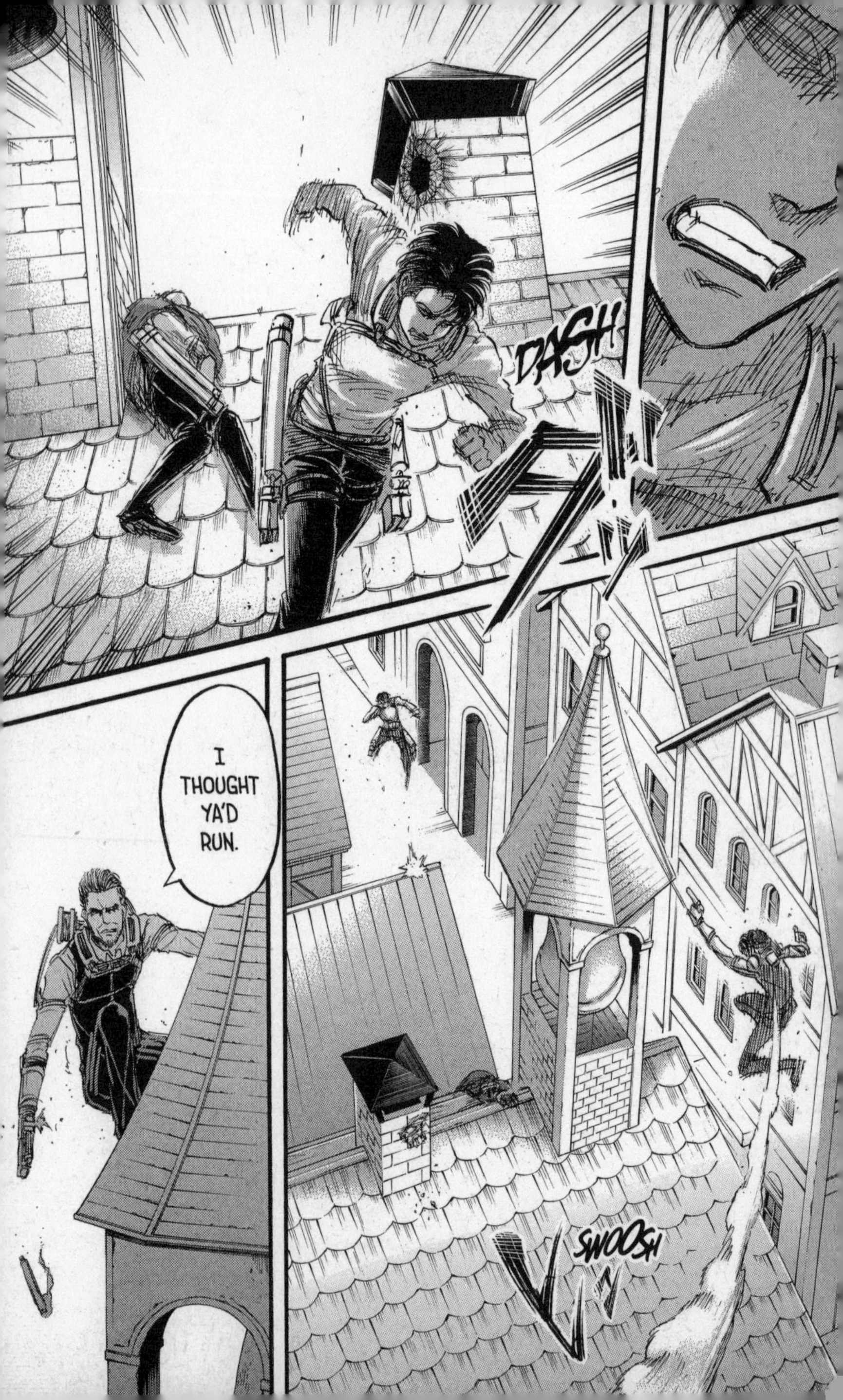
DASH!
SWOOSH
I THOUGHT YA'D RUN.

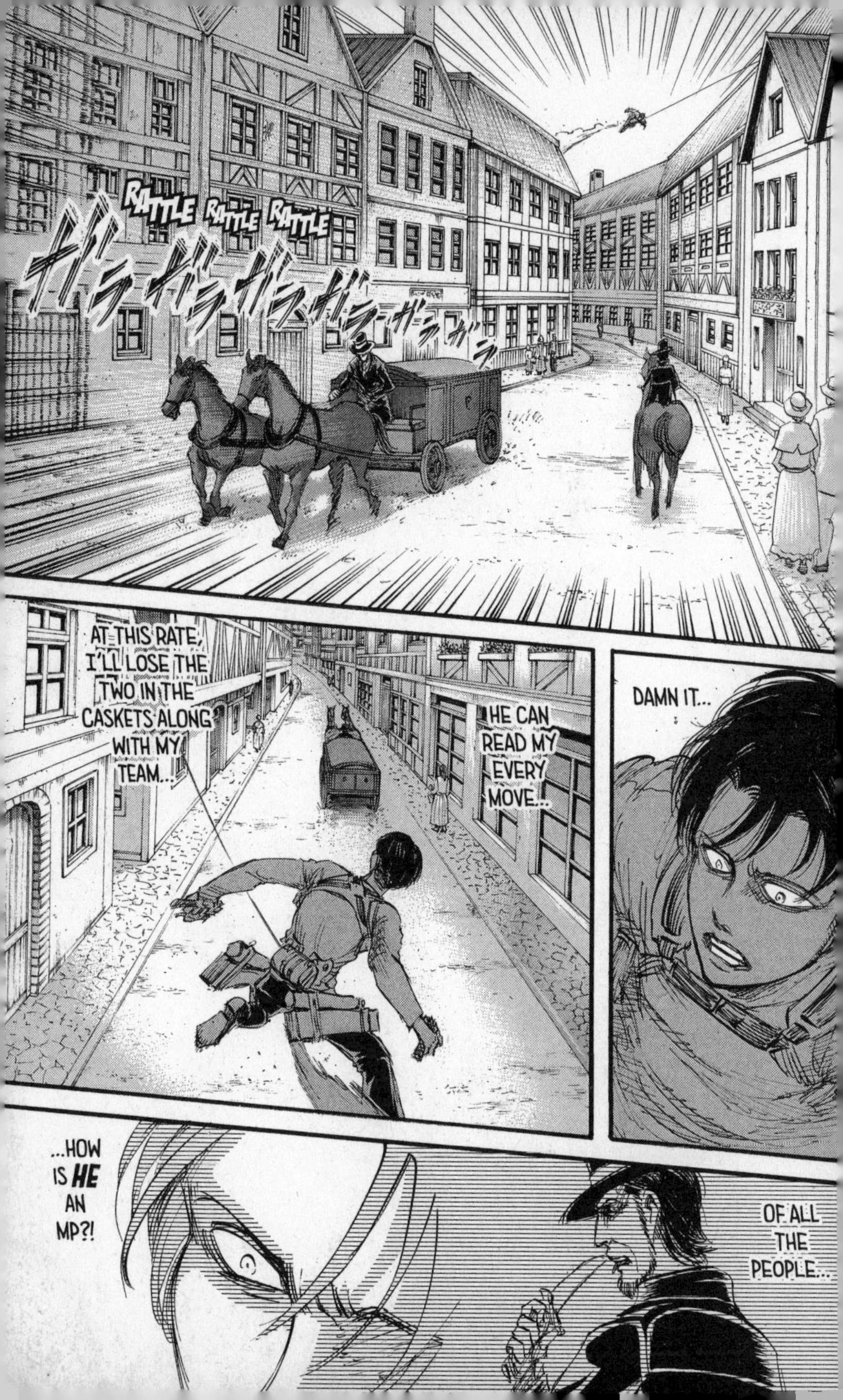
RATTLE RATTLE RATTLE
ガラ ガラ ガラ ガラ ガラ ガラ
DAMN IT...
HE CAN READ MY EVERY MOVE...
AT THIS RATE, I'LL LOSE THE TWO IN THE CASKETS ALONG WITH MY TEAM...
OF ALL THE PEOPLE...
...HOW IS **HE** AN MP?!

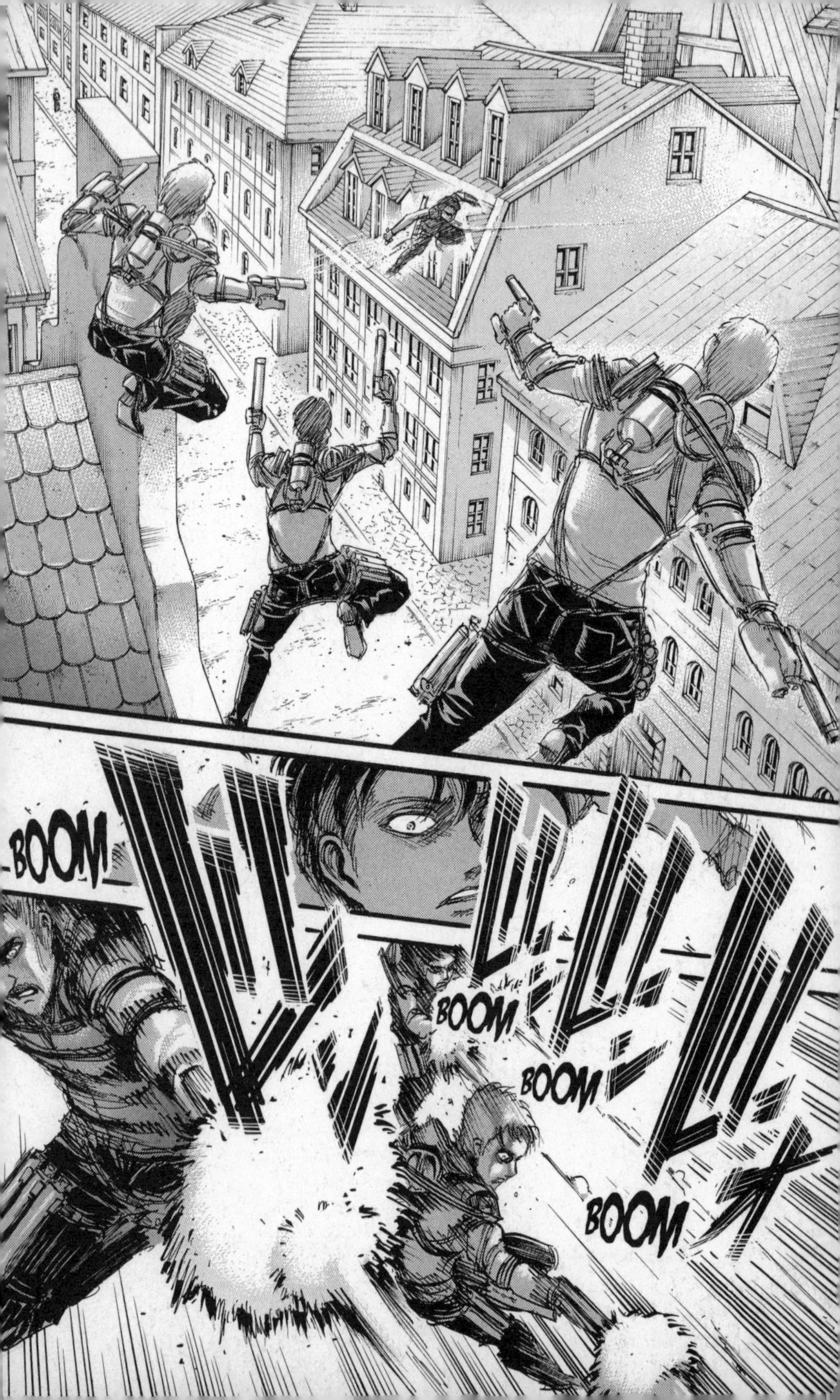
BOOM
BOOM
BOOM
BOOM

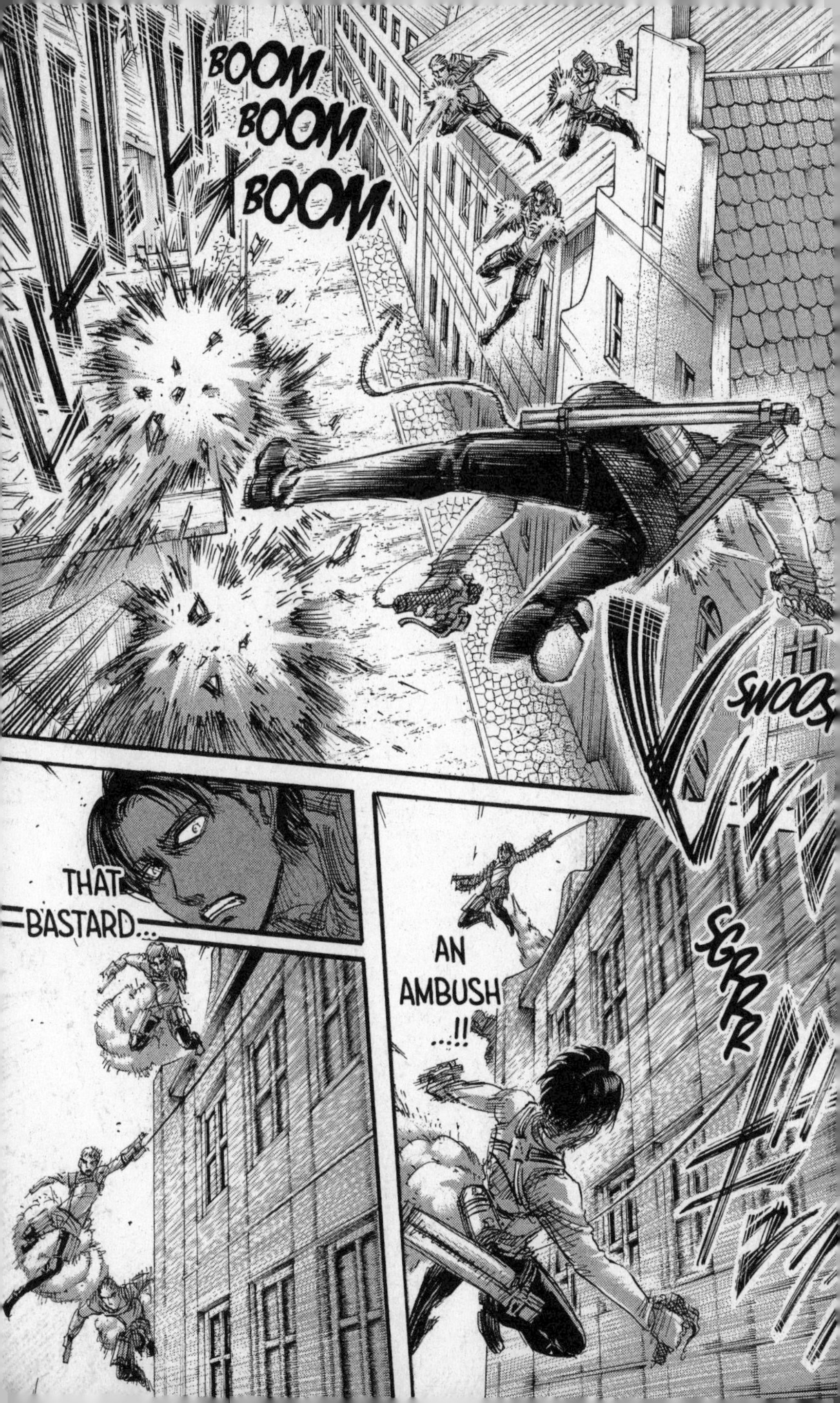
BOOM
BOOM
BOOM
SWOOS
AN AMBUSH ...!!
SCRRR
THAT BASTARD...

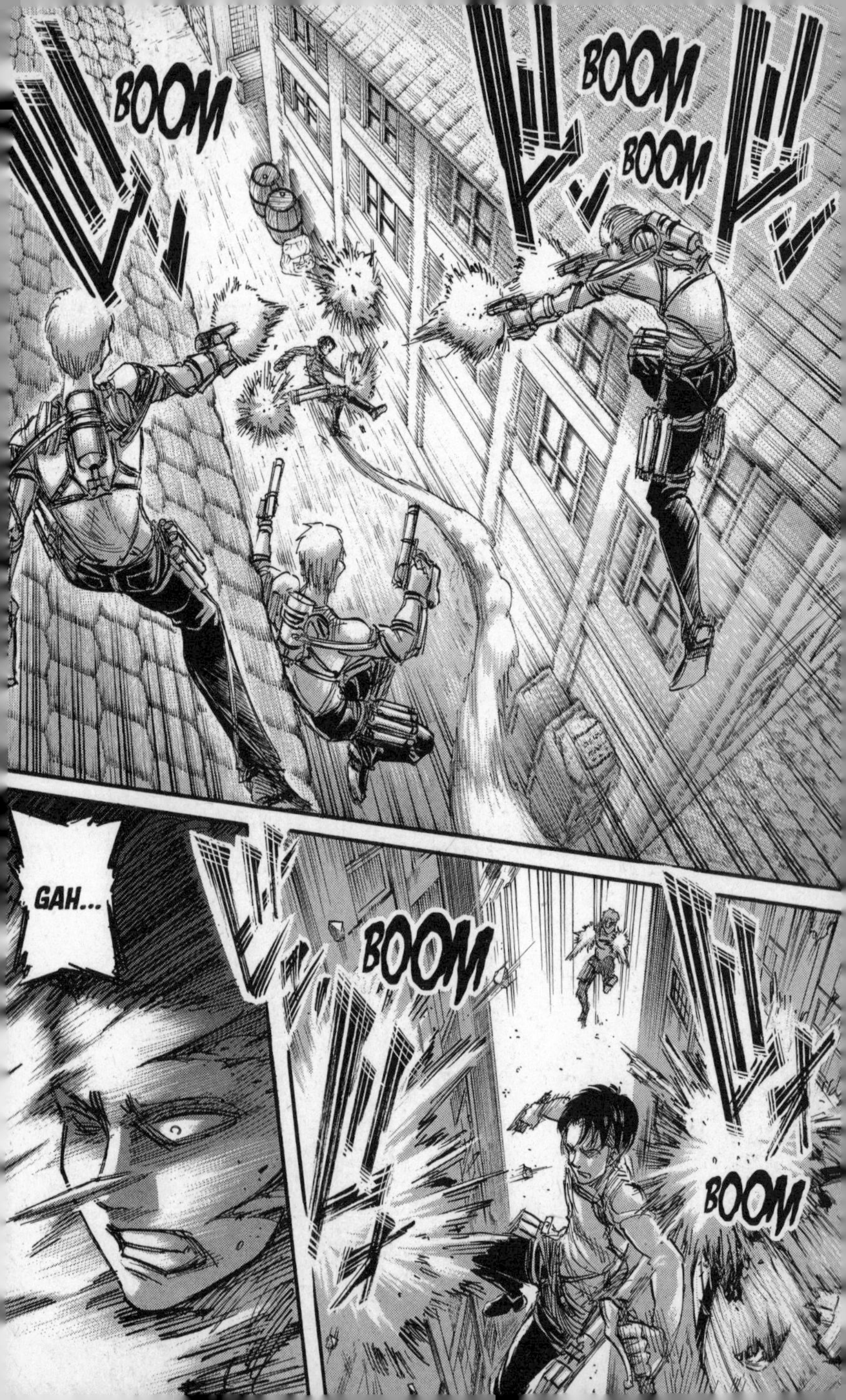
BOOM
BOOM
BOOM
BOOM
BOOM
GAH...

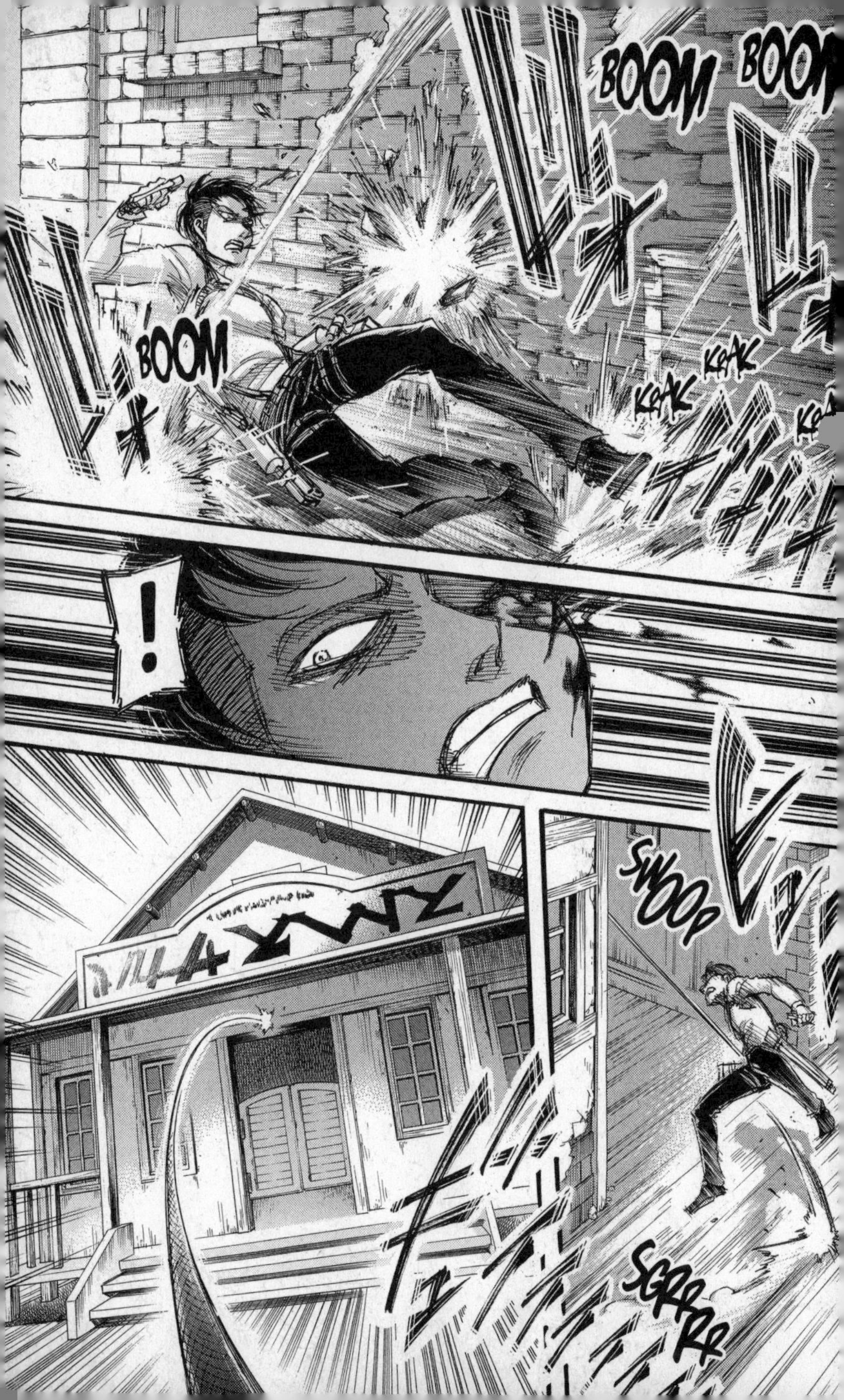
BOOM BOOM
KRAK KRAK
BOOM
!
SWOOP
SGRRRR

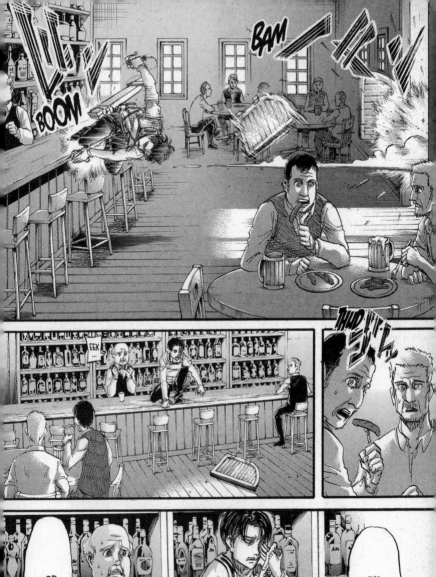

...OF THE SURVEY CORPS...

IT'S L... LEVI...

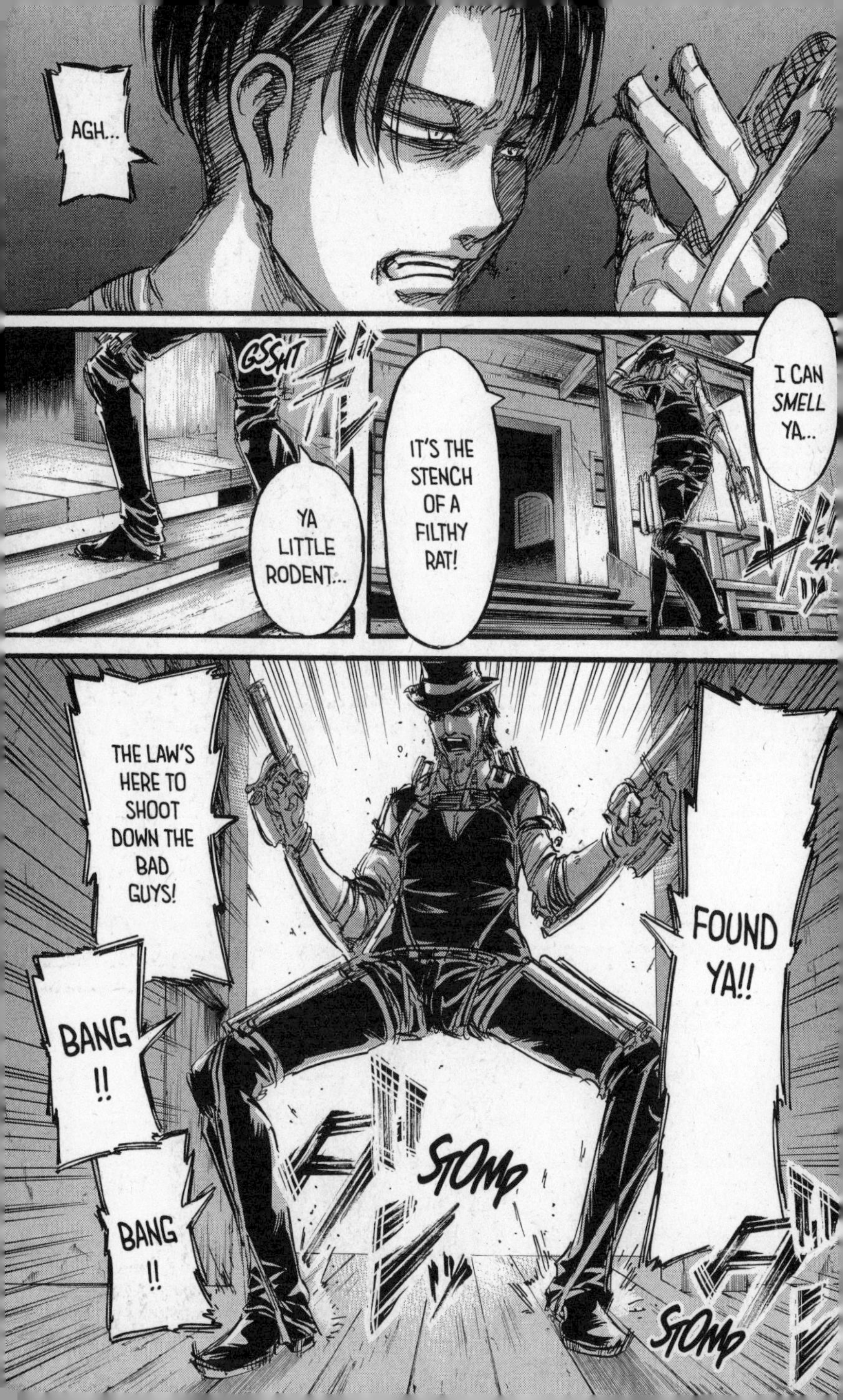
AGH...
I CAN SMELL YA...
IT'S THE STENCH OF A FILTHY RAT!
GSSHT
YA LITTLE RODENT...
FOUND YA!!
THE LAW'S HERE TO SHOOT DOWN THE BAD GUYS!
BANG !!
STOMP
BANG !!
STOMP

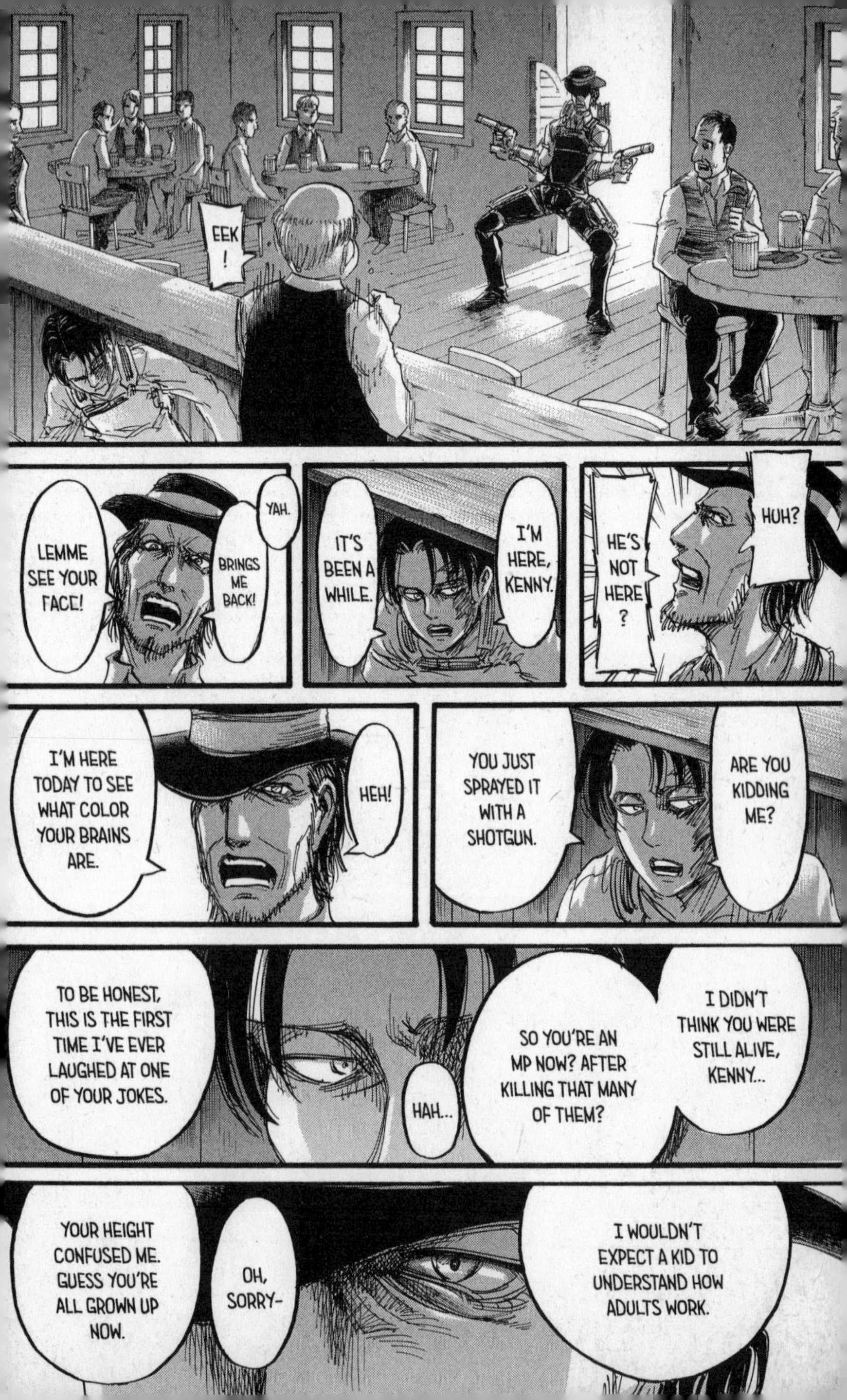
EEK!
HUH?
HE'S NOT HERE?
I'M HERE, KENNY.
IT'S BEEN A WHILE.
YAH.
BRINGS ME BACK!
LEMME SEE YOUR FACE!
ARE YOU KIDDING ME?
YOU JUST SPRAYED IT WITH A SHOTGUN.
HEH!
I'M HERE TODAY TO SEE WHAT COLOR YOUR BRAINS ARE.
I DIDN'T THINK YOU WERE STILL ALIVE, KENNY...
SO YOU'RE AN MP NOW? AFTER KILLING THAT MANY OF THEM?
HAH...
TO BE HONEST, THIS IS THE FIRST TIME I'VE EVER LAUGHED AT ONE OF YOUR JOKES.
I WOULDN'T EXPECT A KID TO UNDERSTAND HOW ADULTS WORK.
OH, SORRY-
YOUR HEIGHT CONFUSED ME. GUESS YOU'RE ALL GROWN UP NOW.

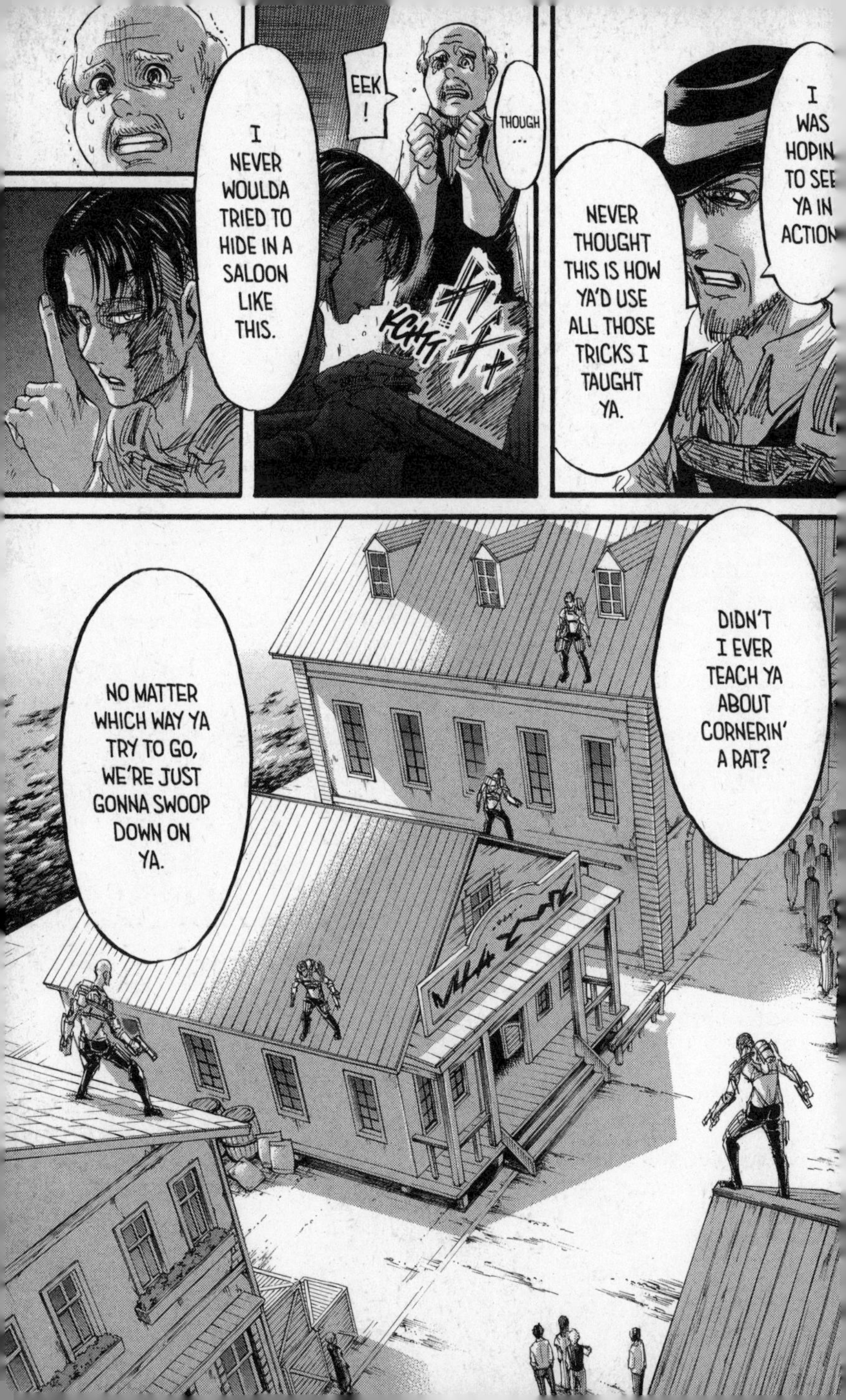
I WAS HOPIN TO SEE YA IN ACTION
NEVER THOUGHT THIS IS HOW YA'D USE ALL THOSE TRICKS I TAUGHT YA.
THOUGH ...
EEK!
KCHT
I NEVER WOULDA TRIED TO HIDE IN A SALOON LIKE THIS.
DIDN'T I EVER TEACH YA ABOUT CORNERIN' A RAT?
NO MATTER WHICH WAY YA TRY TO GO, WE'RE JUST GONNA SWOOP DOWN ON YA.

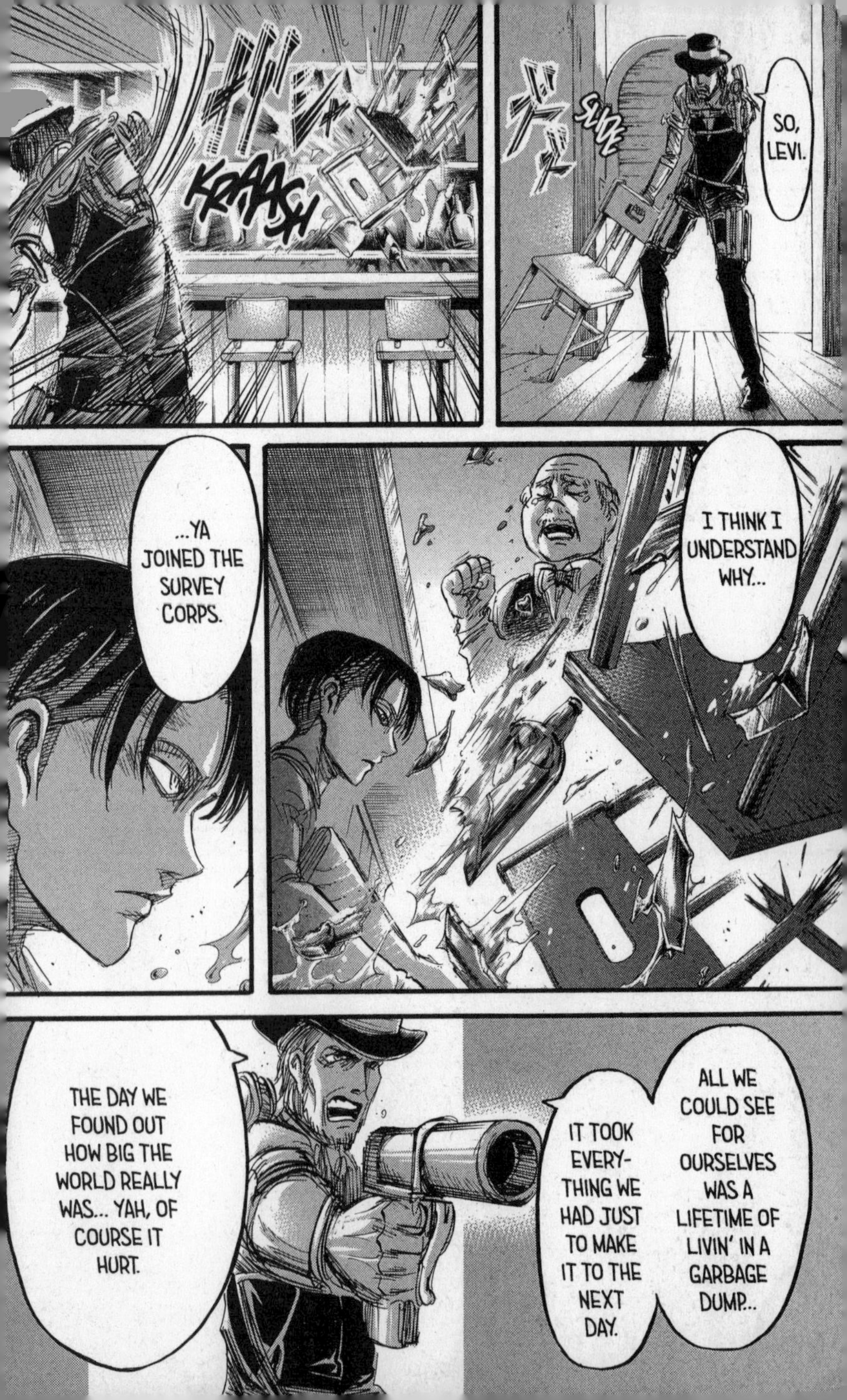
SLIDE
SO, LEVI.
KRAASH
I THINK I UNDERSTAND WHY...
...YA JOINED THE SURVEY CORPS.
ALL WE COULD SEE FOR OURSELVES WAS A LIFETIME OF LIVIN' IN A GARBAGE DUMP...
IT TOOK EVERY-THING WE HAD JUST TO MAKE IT TO THE NEXT DAY.
THE DAY WE FOUND OUT HOW BIG THE WORLD REALLY WAS... YAH, OF COURSE IT HURT.

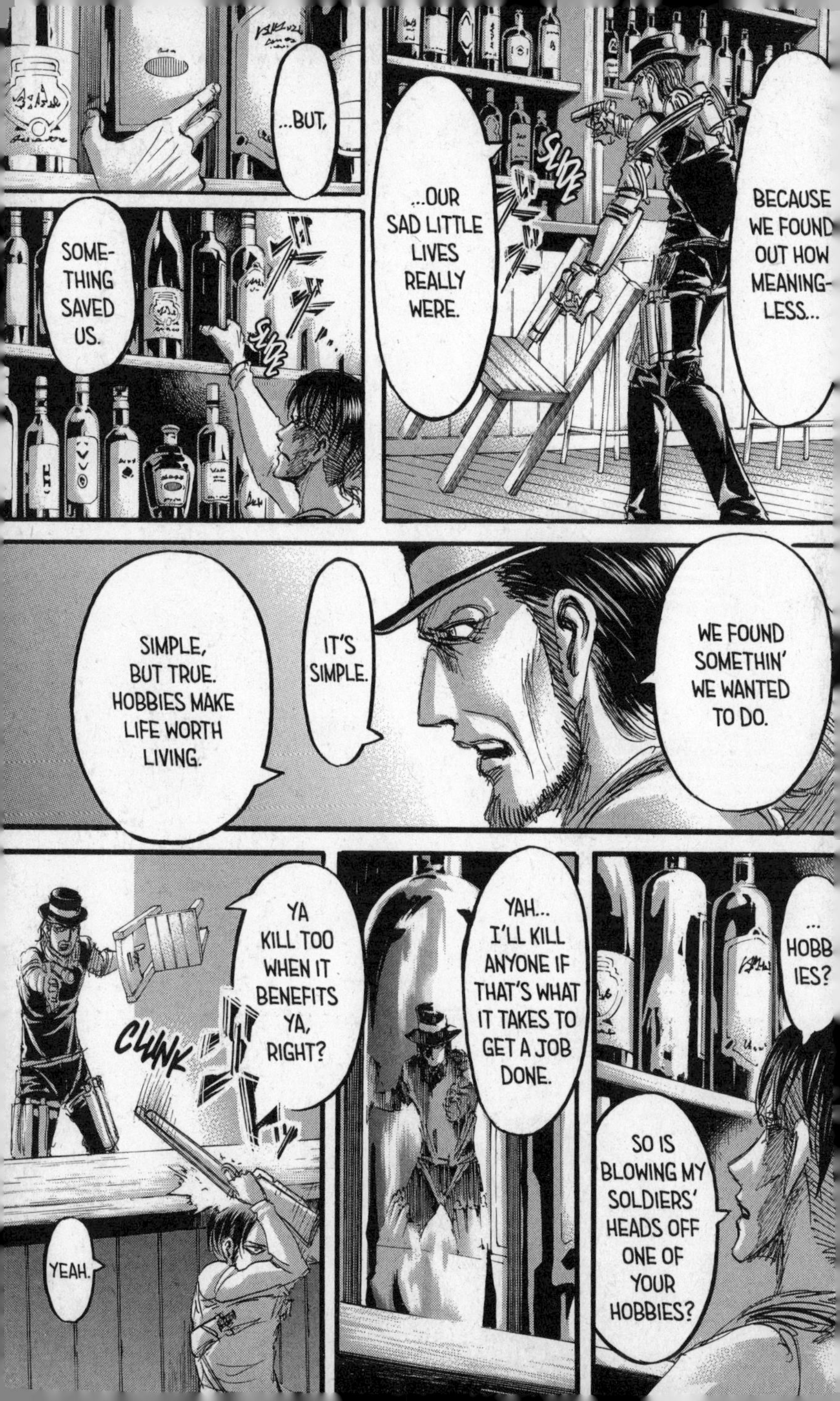
BECAUSE WE FOUND OUT HOW MEANING-LESS...
SLIDE
...OUR SAD LITTLE LIVES REALLY WERE.
...BUT,
SOME-THING SAVED US.
SLIDE
WE FOUND SOMETHIN' WE WANTED TO DO.
IT'S SIMPLE.
SIMPLE, BUT TRUE. HOBBIES MAKE LIFE WORTH LIVING.
...HOBBIES?
SO IS BLOWING MY SOLDIERS' HEADS OFF ONE OF YOUR HOBBIES?
YAH... I'LL KILL ANYONE IF THAT'S WHAT IT TAKES TO GET A JOB DONE.
YA KILL TOO WHEN IT BENEFITS YA, RIGHT?
CLUNK
YEAH.

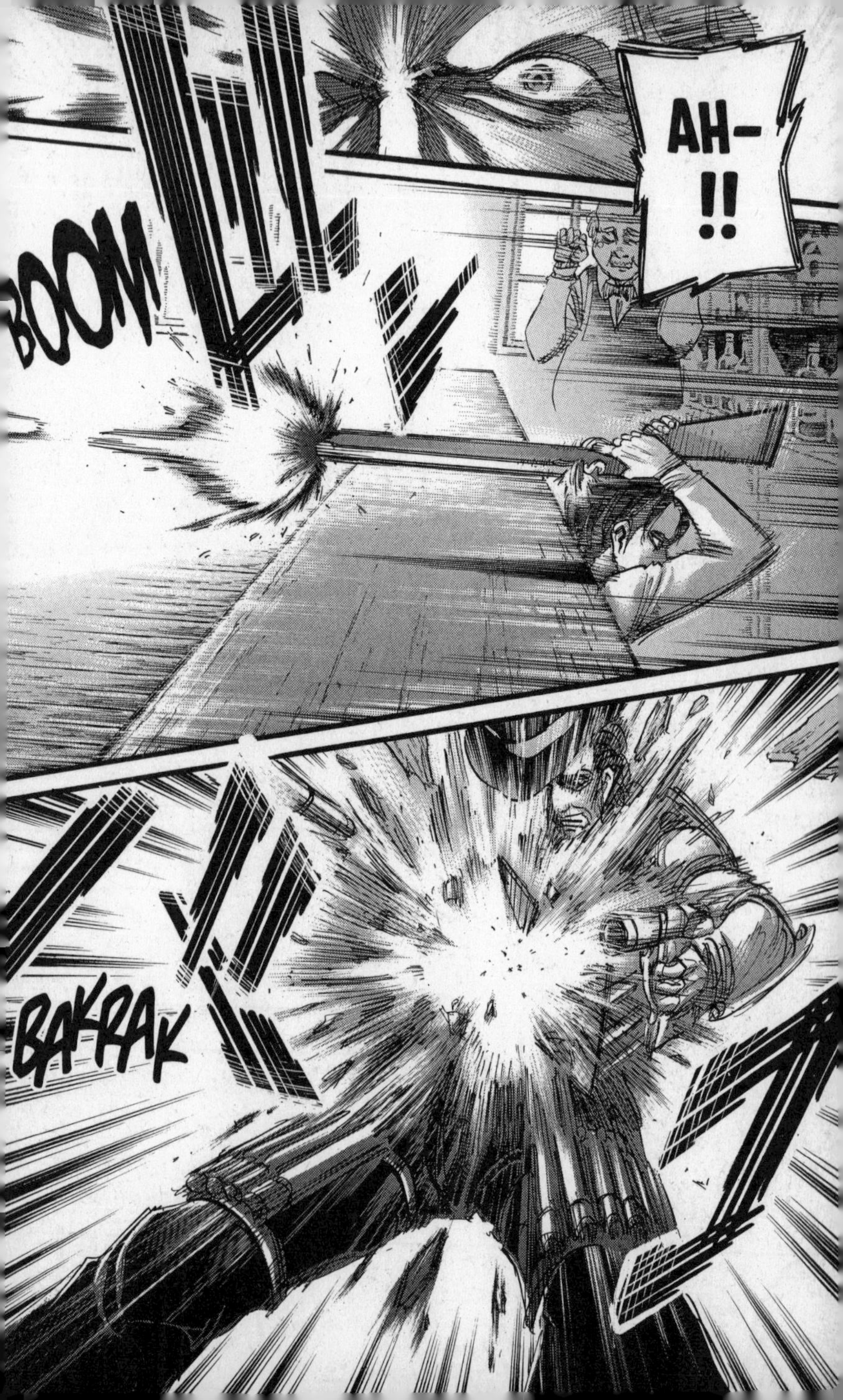
AH-
!!
BOOM
BAKRAK

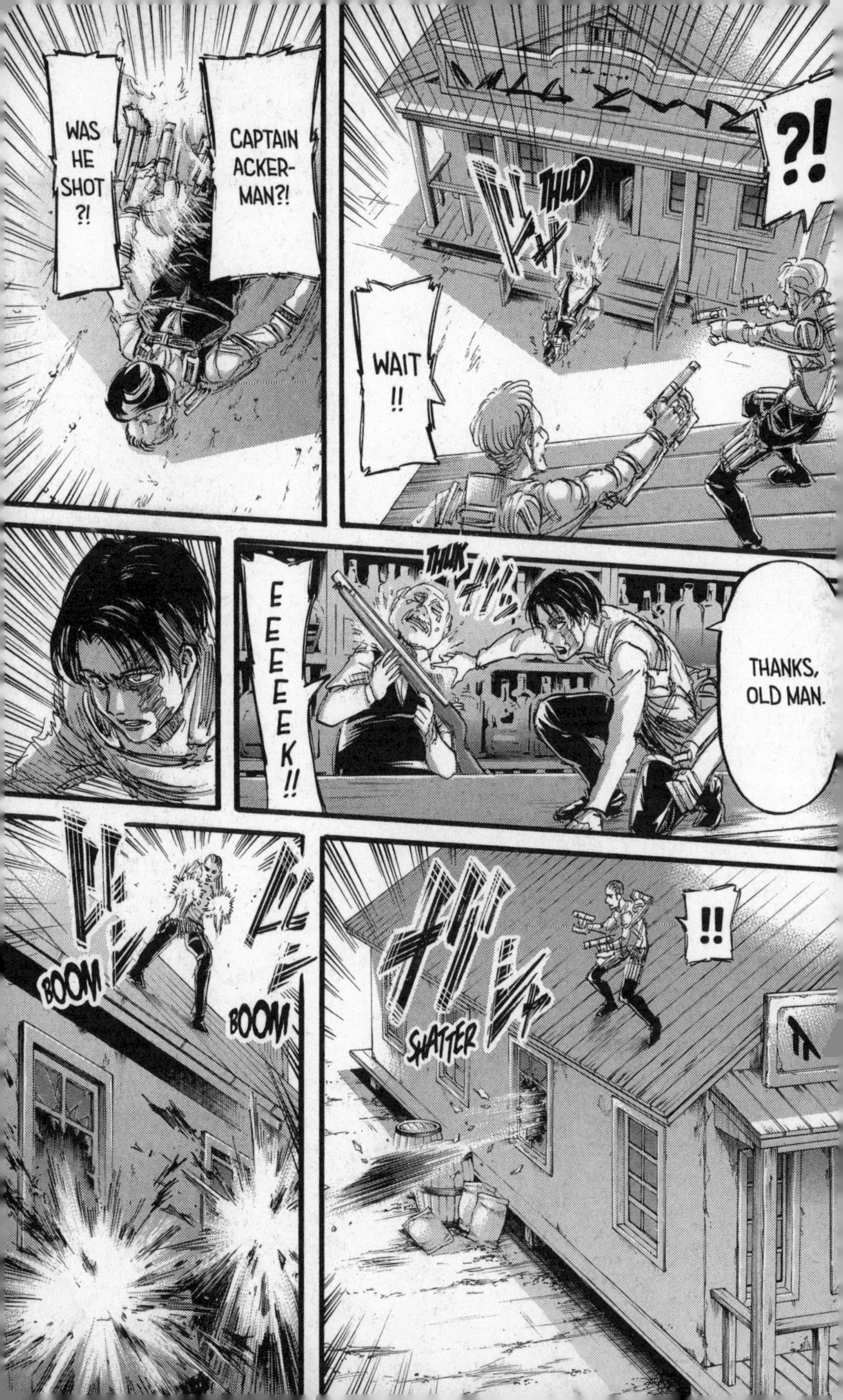
?!
THUD
WAIT !!
CAPTAIN ACKER-MAN?!
WAS HE SHOT ?!
THANKS, OLD MAN.
THUK
EEEEEEK!!
!!
SHATTER
BOOM
BOOM

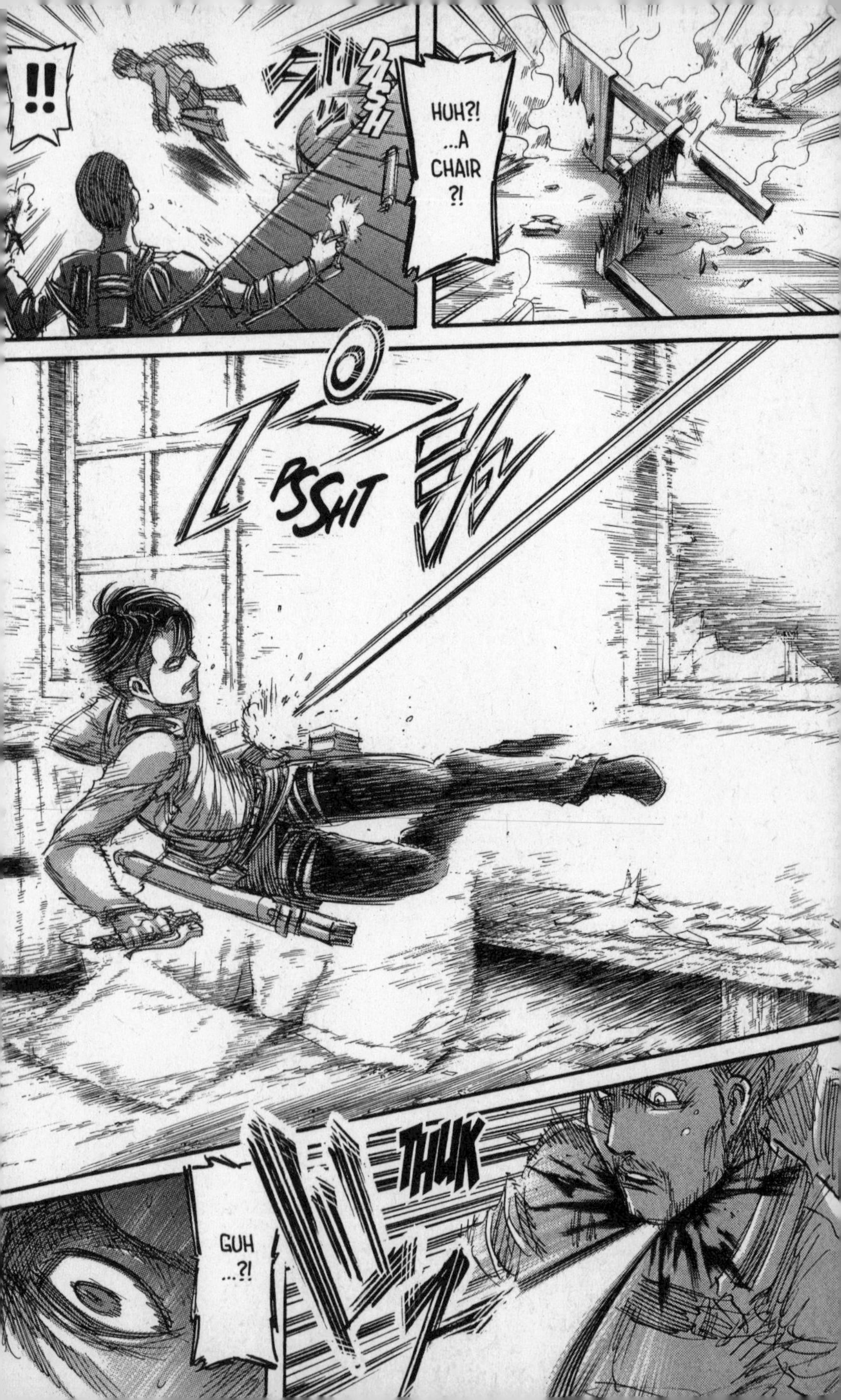

HUH?! ...A CHAIR ?!
DASH
!!
PSSHT
THUK
GUH ...?!

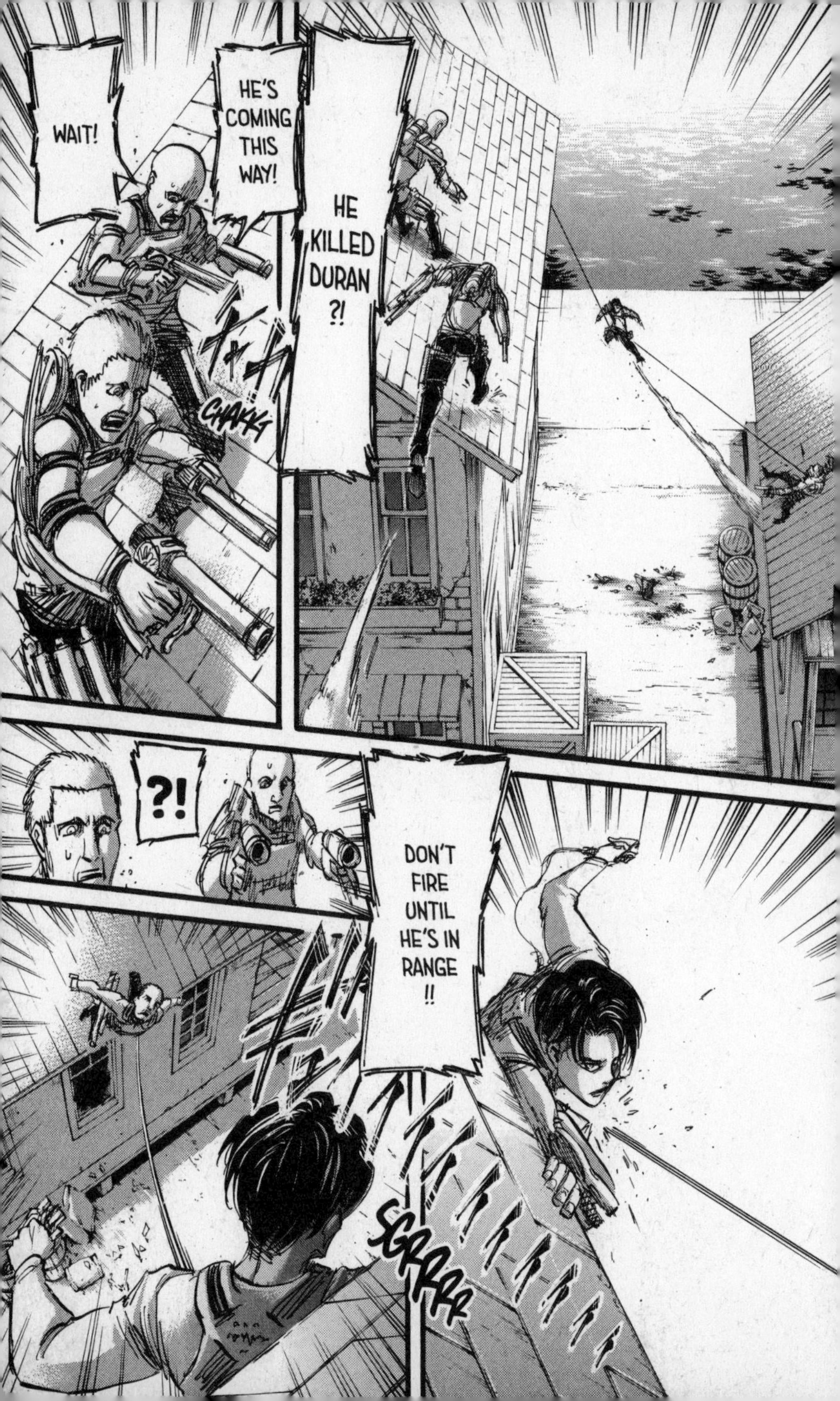
HE KILLED DURAN ?!
HE'S COMING THIS WAY!
WAIT!
CHAKK
DON'T FIRE UNTIL HE'S IN RANGE !!
?!
SGRRRR

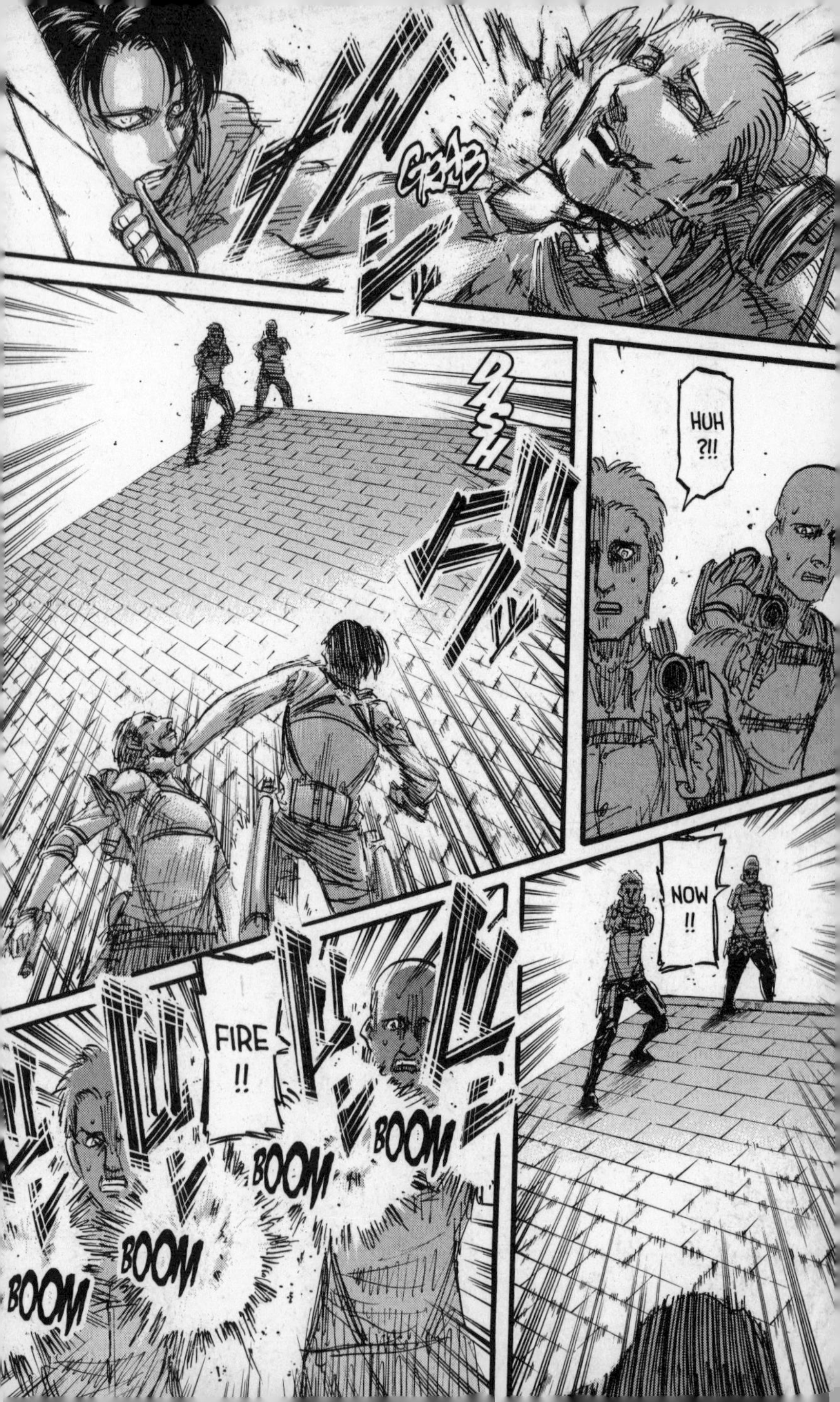
GRAB
HUH ?!!
DASH
NOW !!
FIRE !!
BOOM
BOOM
BOOM
BOOM

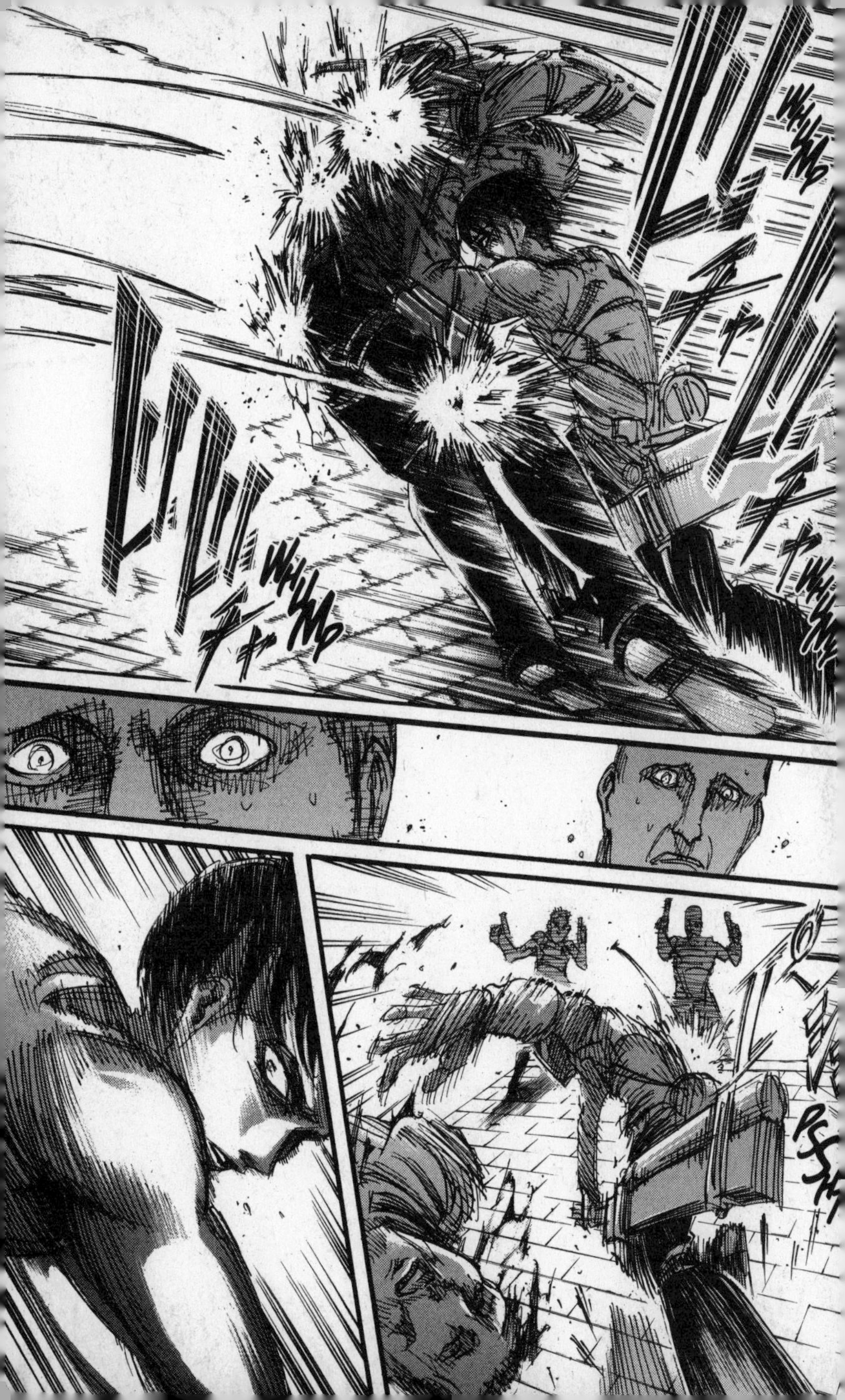
WHUMP
WHUMP
PSSH

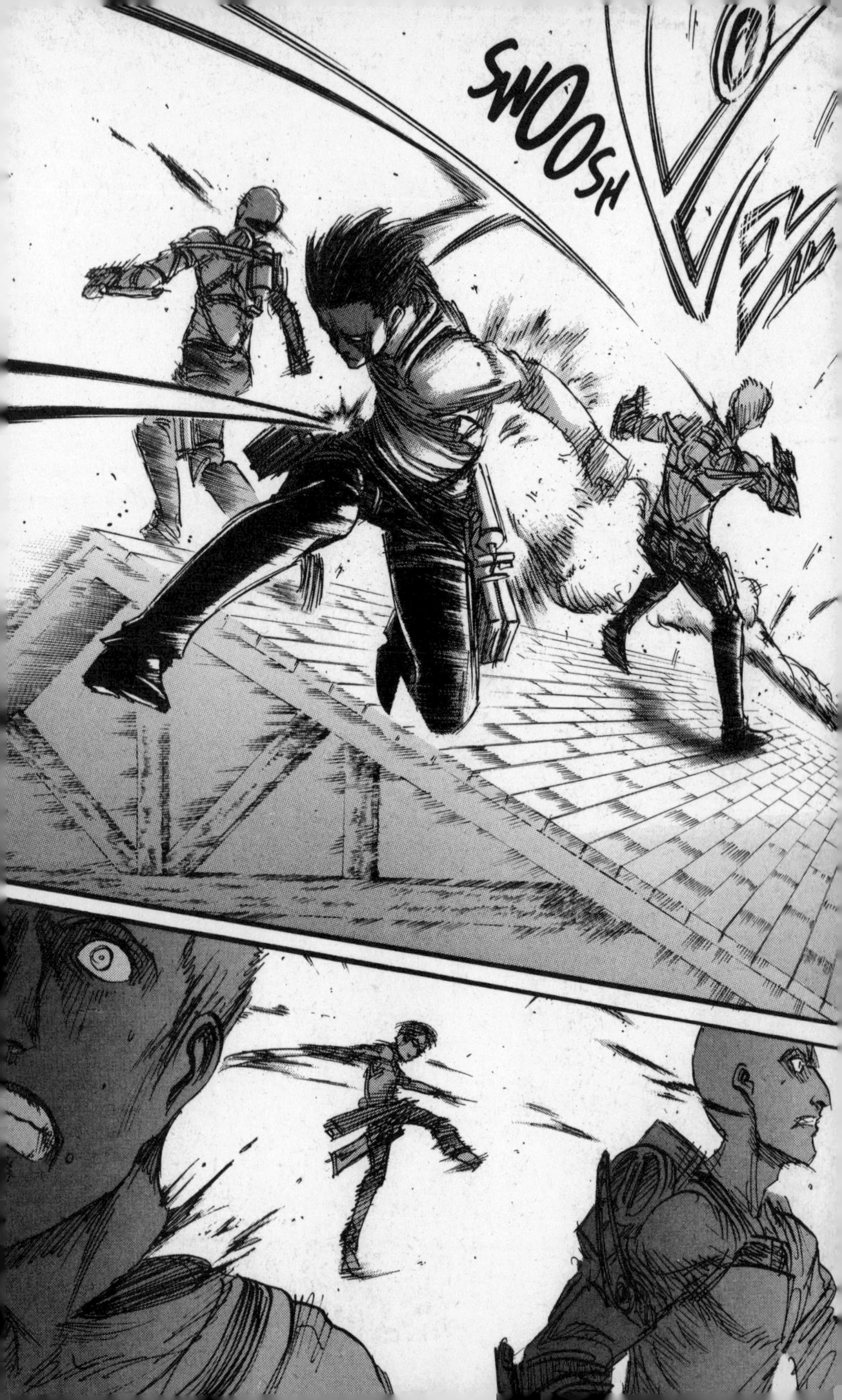
SWOOSH

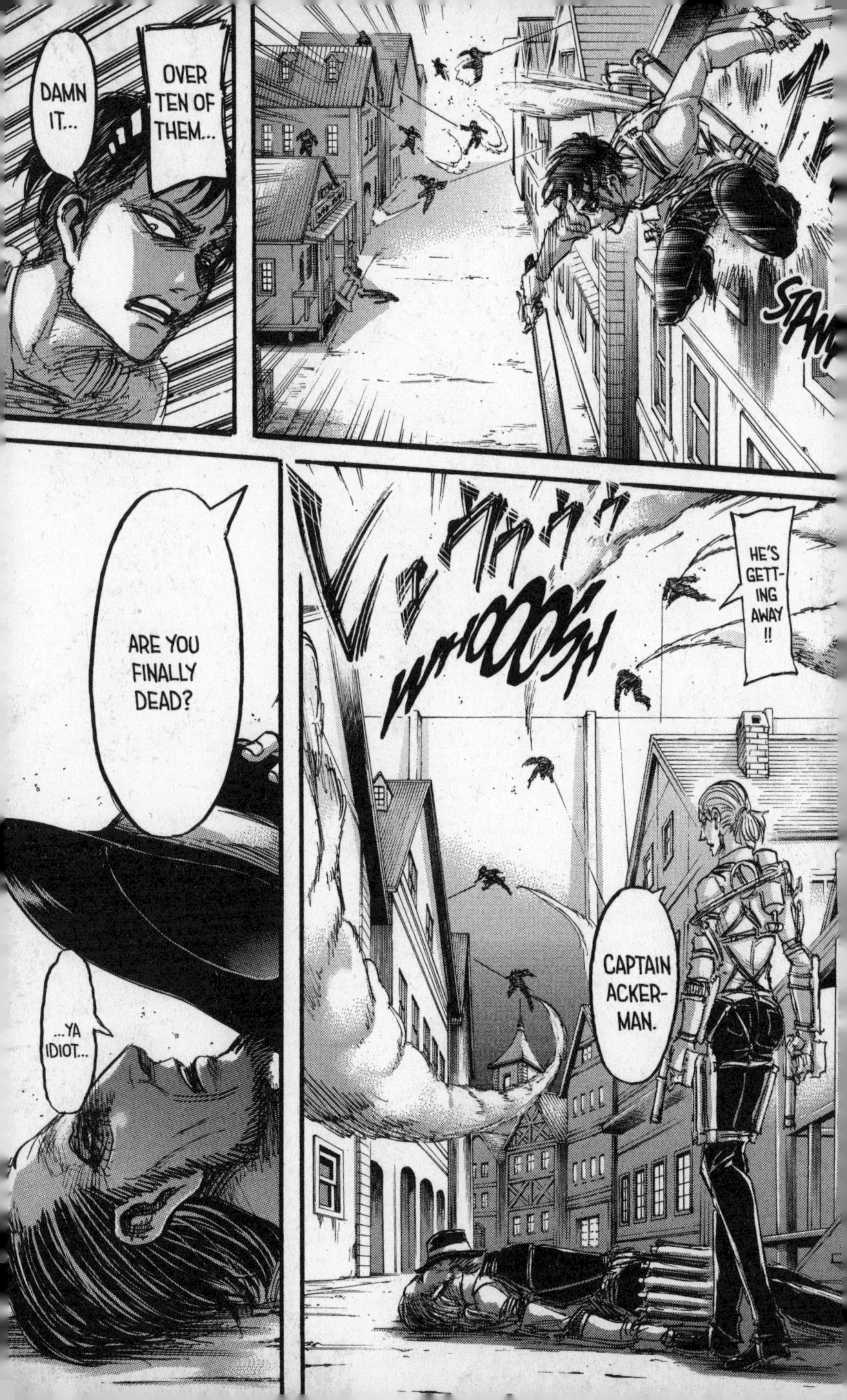

OVER TEN OF THEM...
DAMN IT...
WHOOOSH
HE'S GETT- ING AWAY !!
CAPTAIN ACKER- MAN.
ARE YOU FINALLY DEAD?
...YA IDIOT...

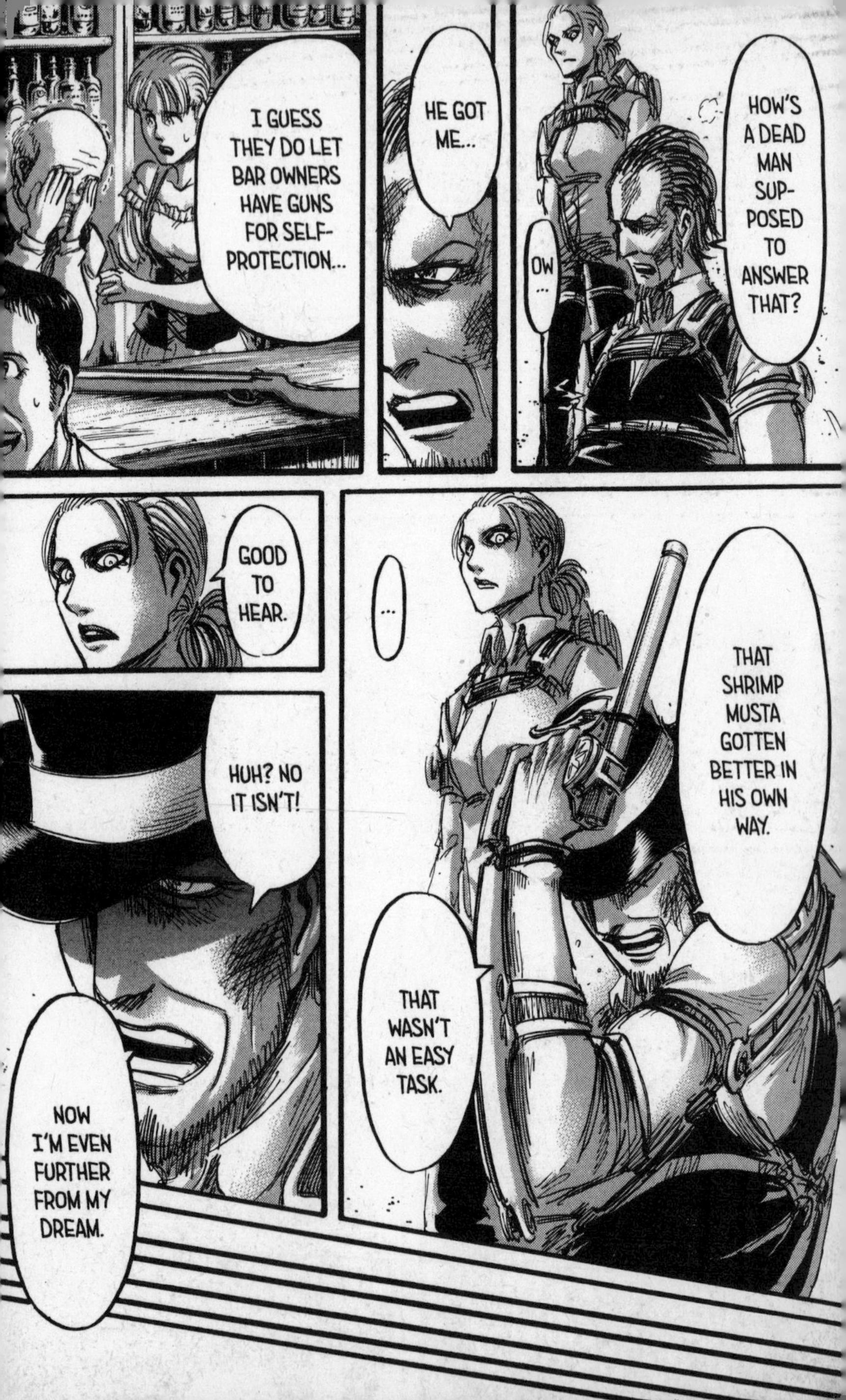
HOW'S A DEAD MAN SUPPOSED TO ANSWER THAT?
OW...
HE GOT ME...
I GUESS THEY DO LET BAR OWNERS HAVE GUNS FOR SELF-PROTECTION...
THAT SHRIMP MUSTA GOTTEN BETTER IN HIS OWN WAY.
...
THAT WASN'T AN EASY TASK.
GOOD TO HEAR.
HUH? NO IT ISN'T!
NOW I'M EVEN FURTHER FROM MY DREAM.

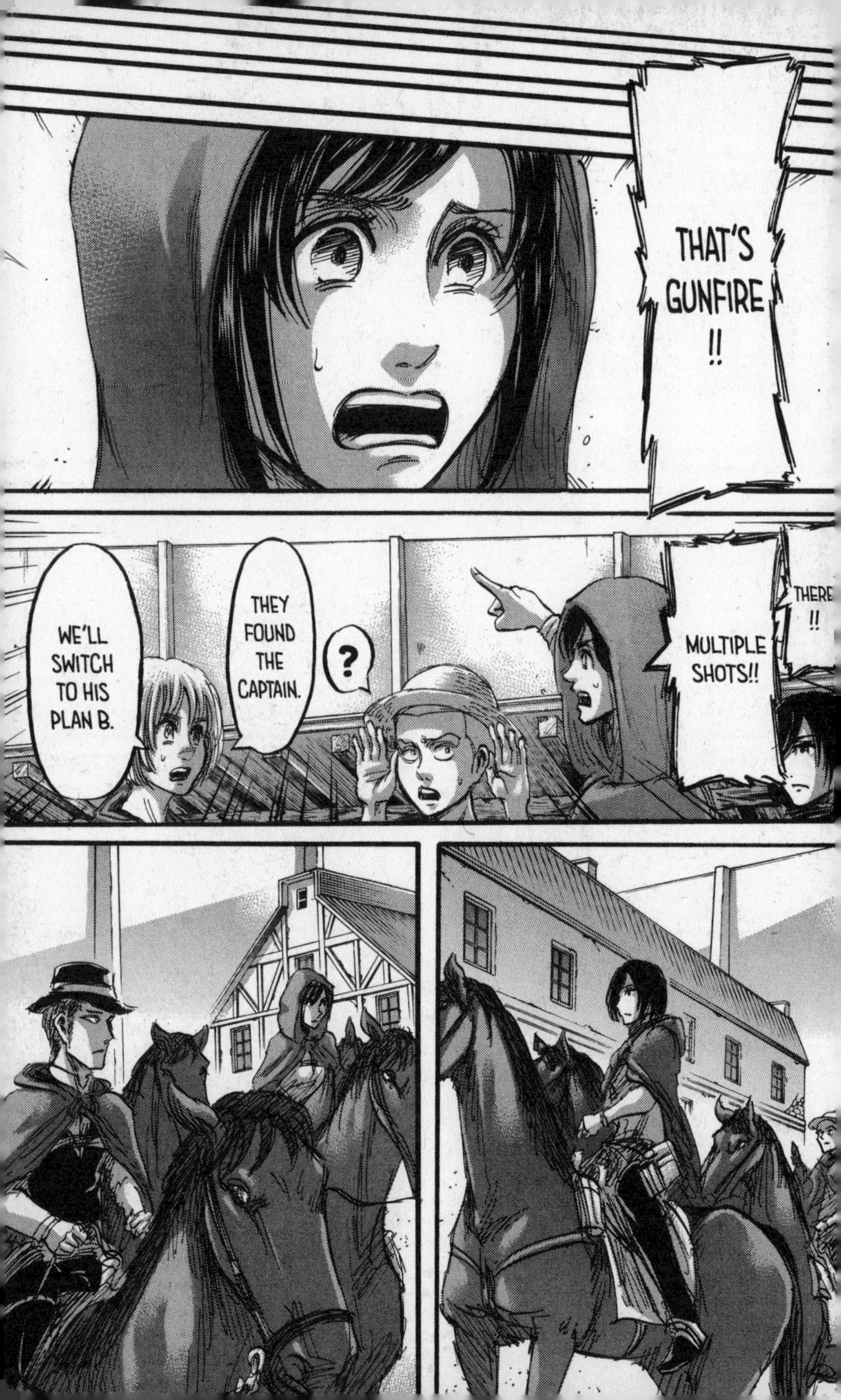

THAT'S GUNFIRE !!
THERE !!
MULTIPLE SHOTS!!
?
THEY FOUND THE CAPTAIN.
WE'LL SWITCH TO HIS PLAN B.

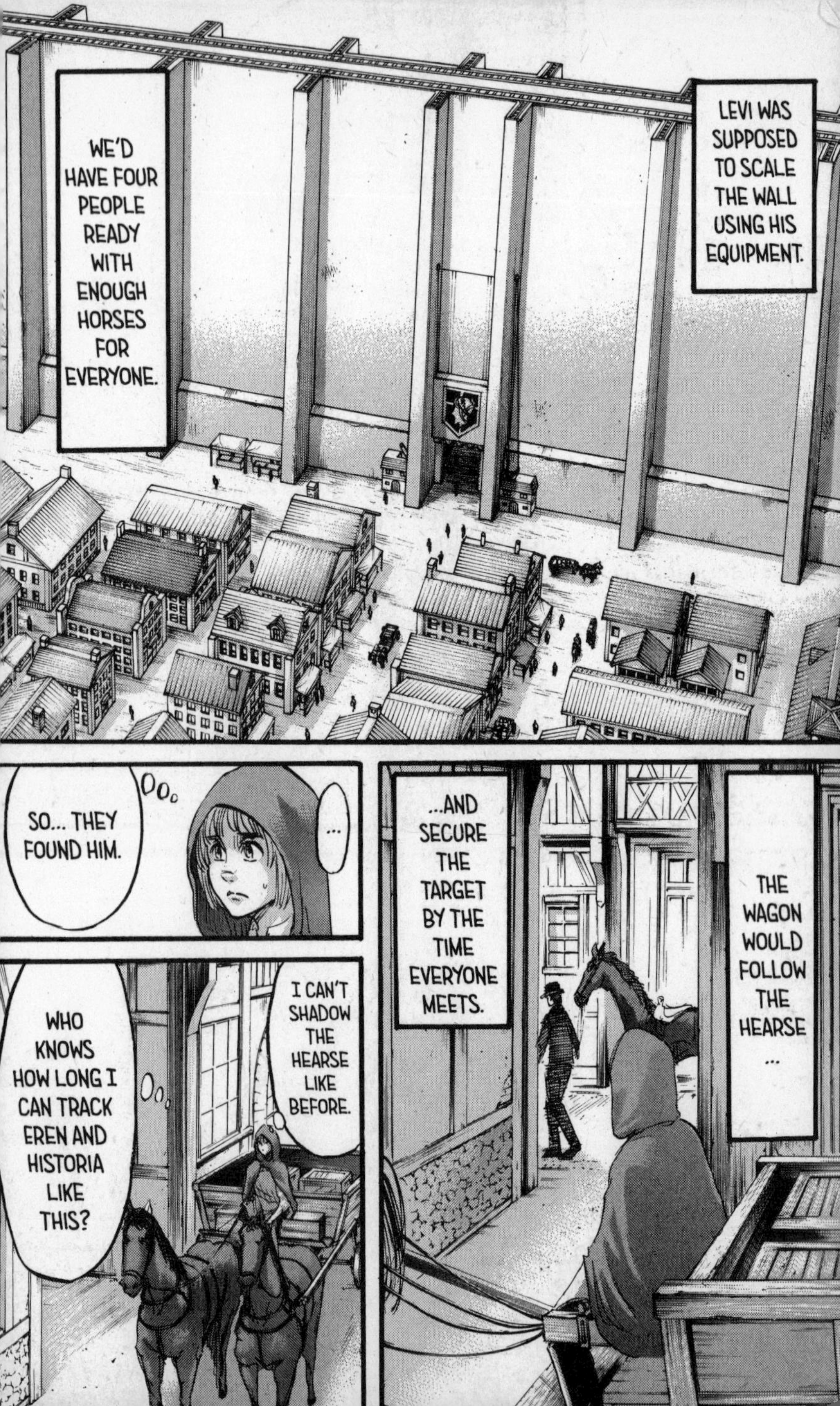
LEVI WAS SUPPOSED TO SCALE THE WALL USING HIS EQUIPMENT.
WE'D HAVE FOUR PEOPLE READY WITH ENOUGH HORSES FOR EVERYONE.
THE WAGON WOULD FOLLOW THE HEARSE...
...AND SECURE THE TARGET BY THE TIME EVERYONE MEETS.
...
SO... THEY FOUND HIM.
I CAN'T SHADOW THE HEARSE LIKE BEFORE.
WHO KNOWS HOW LONG I CAN TRACK EREN AND HISTORIA LIKE THIS?

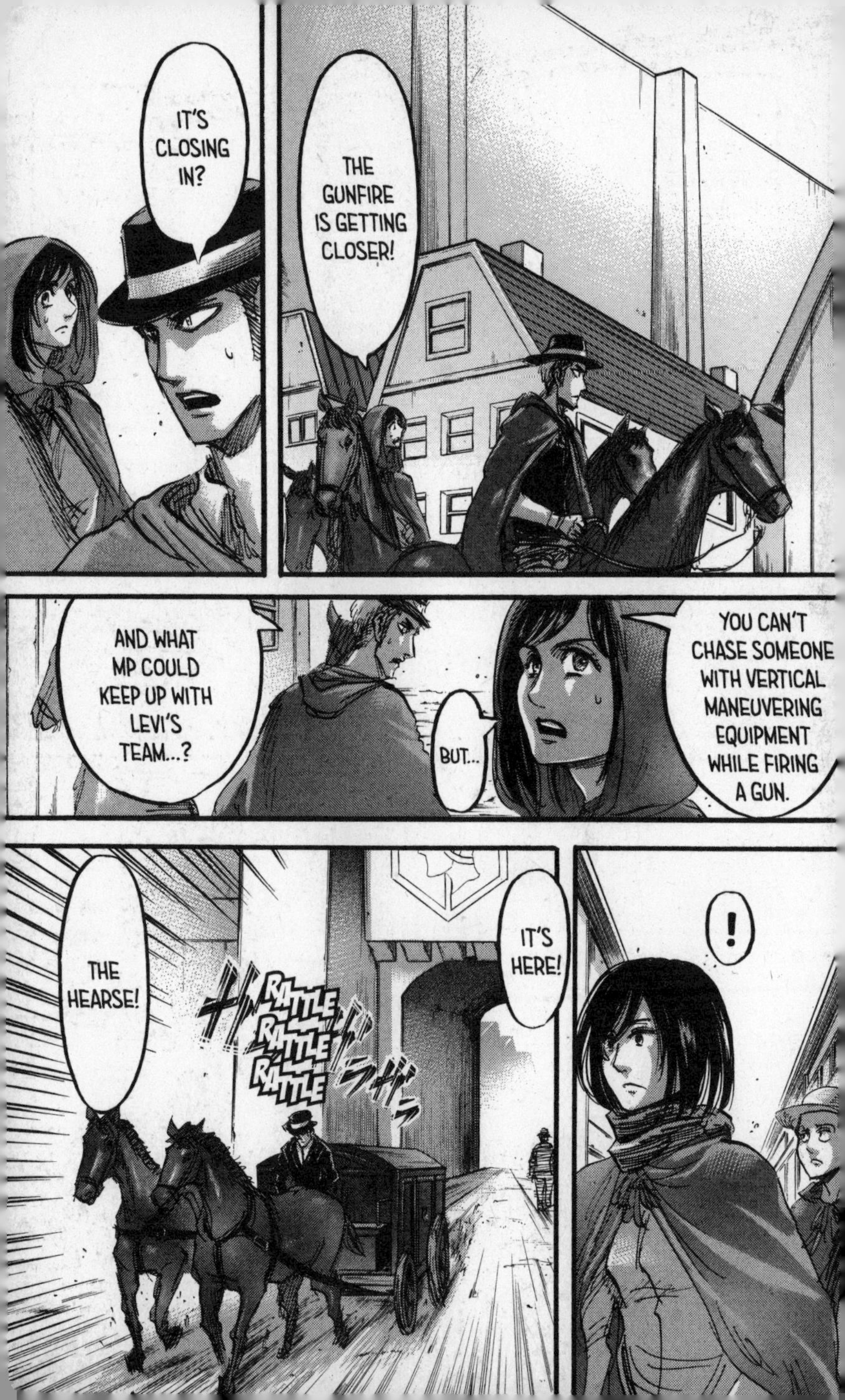
THE GUNFIRE IS GETTING CLOSER!
IT'S CLOSING IN?
YOU CAN'T CHASE SOMEONE WITH VERTICAL MANEUVERING EQUIPMENT WHILE FIRING A GUN.
BUT...
AND WHAT MP COULD KEEP UP WITH LEVI'S TEAM...?
!
IT'S HERE!
RATTLE RATTLE RATTLE
THE HEARSE!

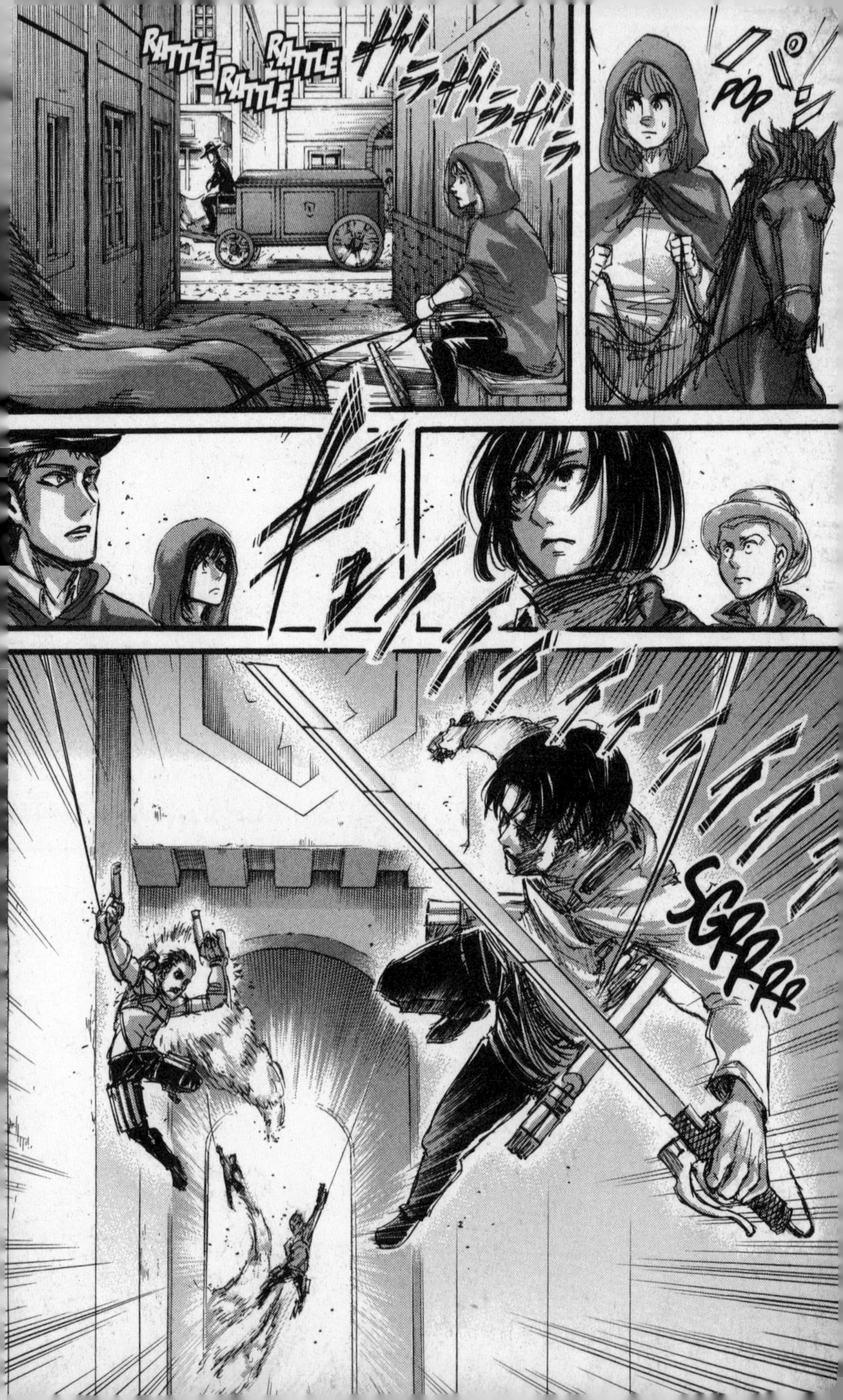
POP
RATTLE
RATTLE
RATTLE
SGRRRR

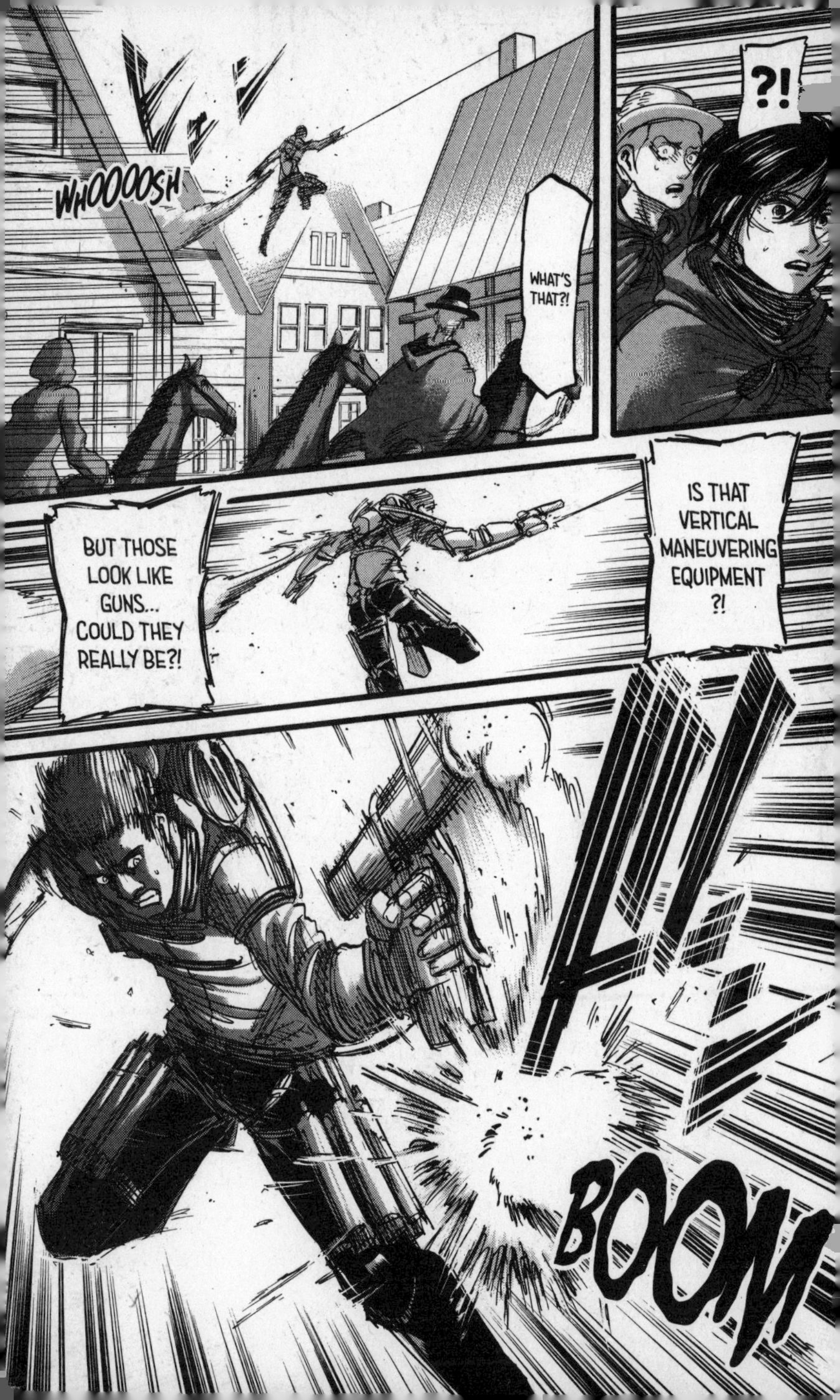
?!
WHAT'S THAT?!
WHOOOOSH
IS THAT VERTICAL MANEUVERING EQUIPMENT ?!
BUT THOSE LOOK LIKE GUNS... COULD THEY REALLY BE?!
BOOM

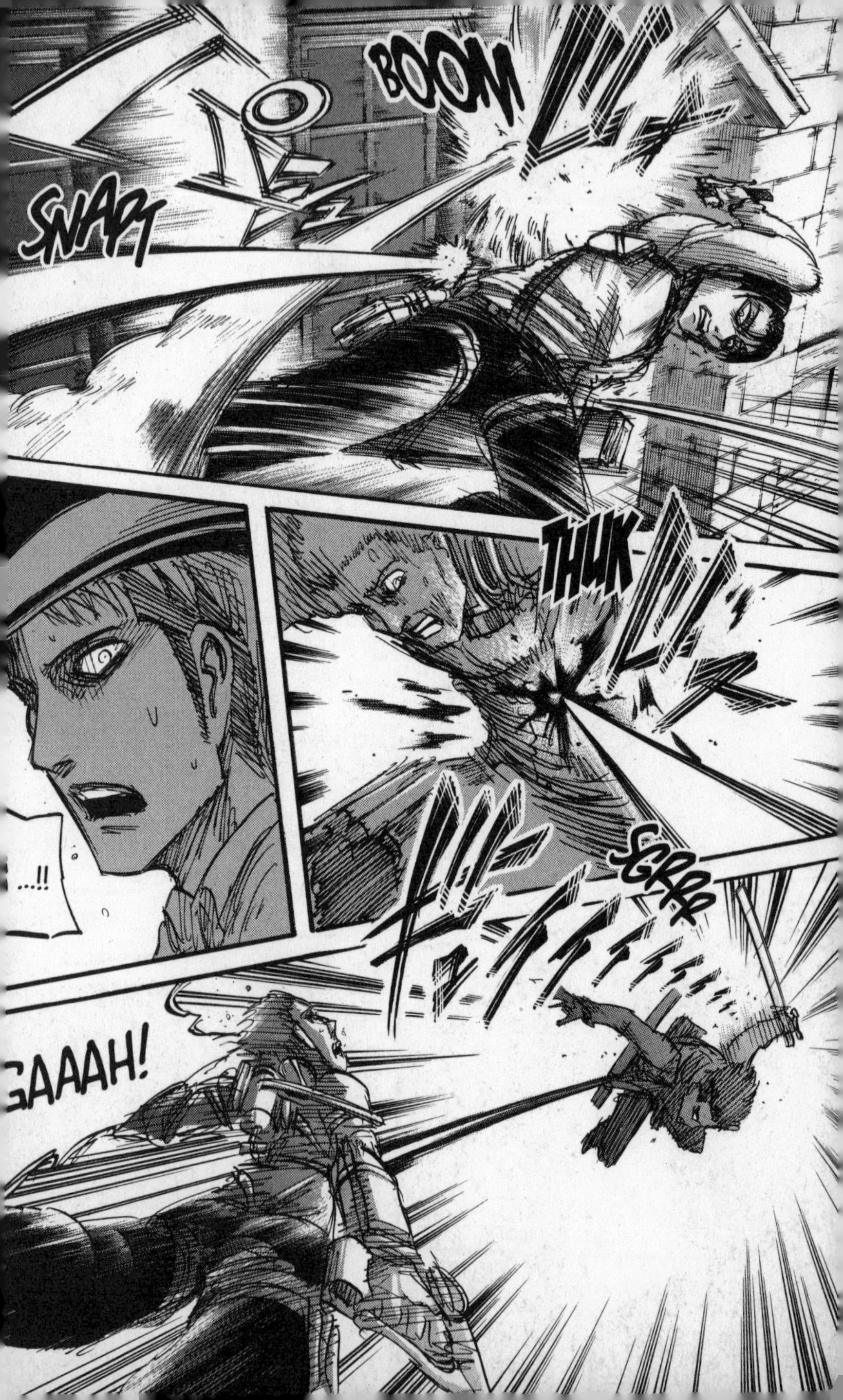
BOOM
SNAP
THUK
...!!
SCRRR
GAAAH!

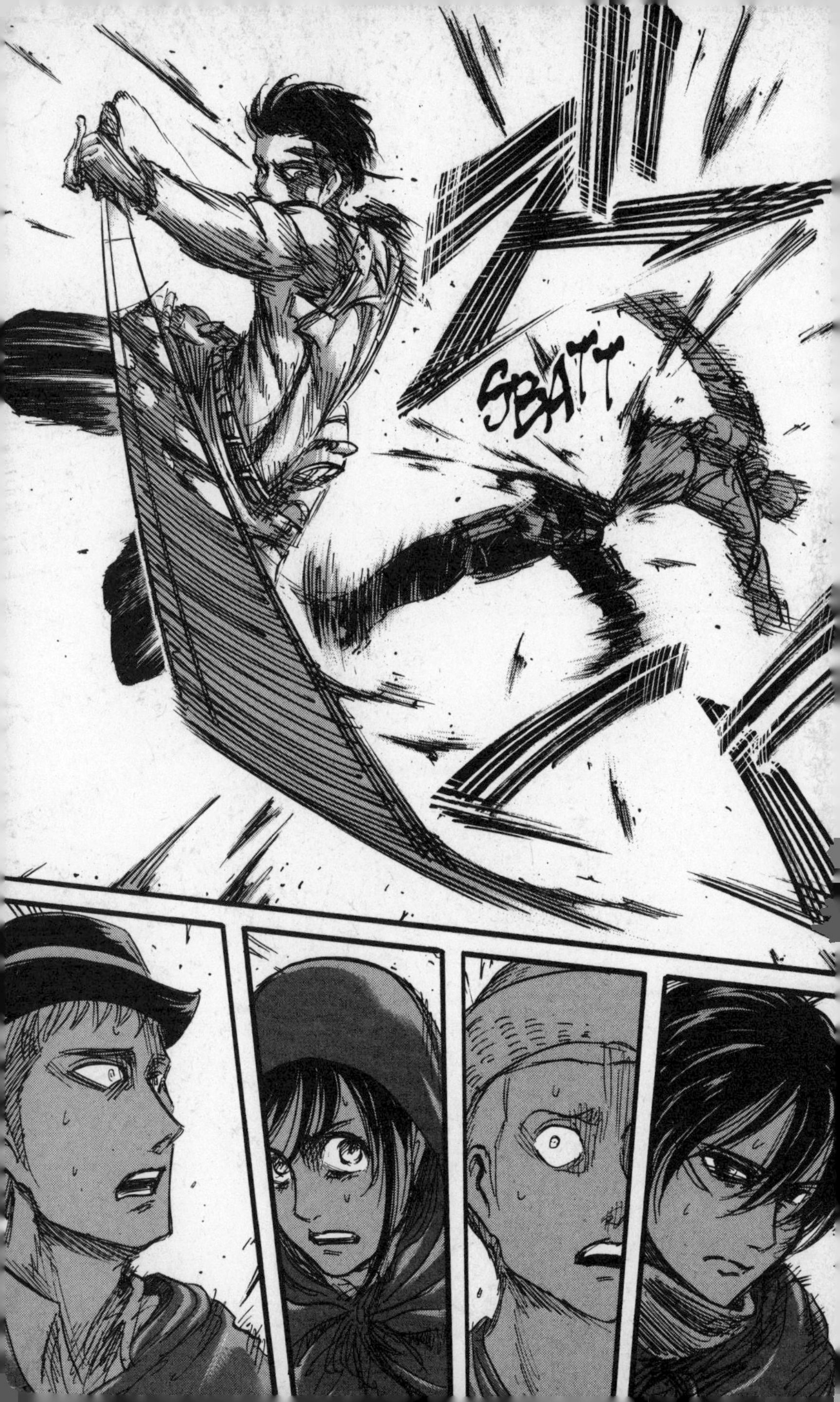
SBATT

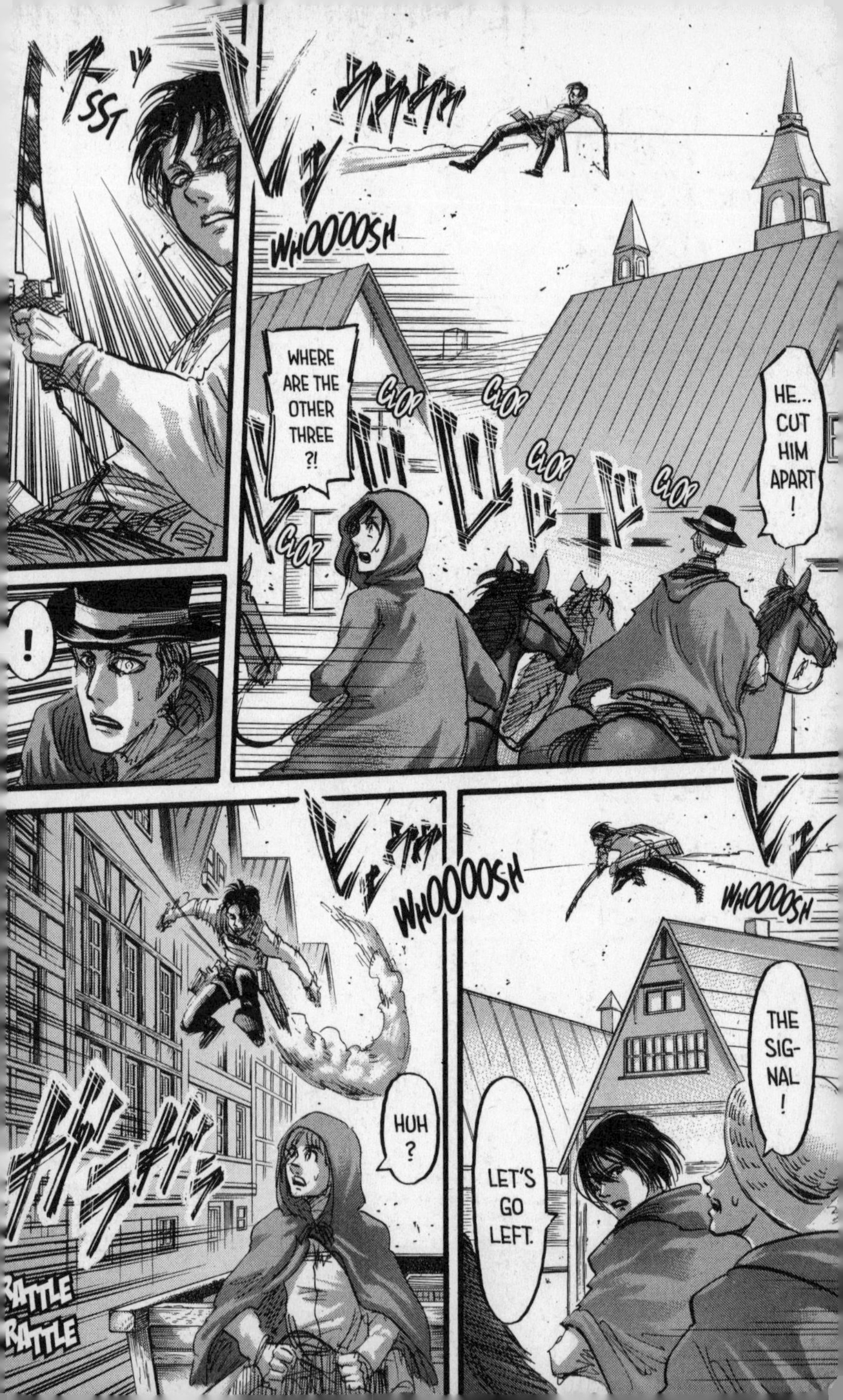

WHOOOOSH
HE... CUT HIM APART !
CLOP
CLOP
CLOP
CLOP
WHERE ARE THE OTHER THREE ?!
CLOP
SSST
!
WHOOOOSH
THE SIGNAL !
LET'S GO LEFT.
WHOOOOSH
HUH ?
RATTLE
RATTLE

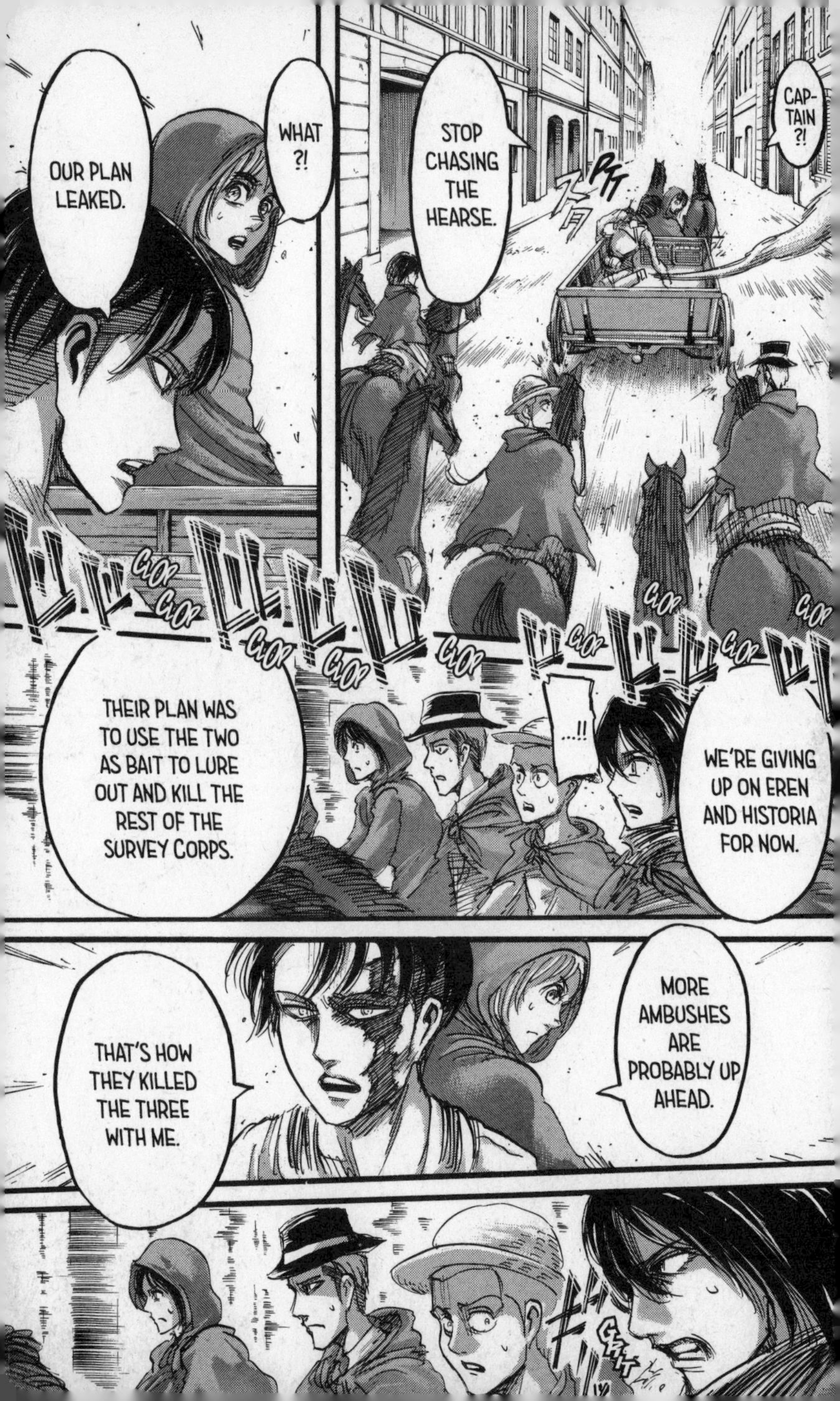
CAP-TAIN ?!
STOP CHASING THE HEARSE.
WHAT ?!
OUR PLAN LEAKED.
CLOP CLOP CLOP CLOP CLOP CLOP CLOP CLOP CLOP CLOP
WE'RE GIVING UP ON EREN AND HISTORIA FOR NOW.
...!!
THEIR PLAN WAS TO USE THE TWO AS BAIT TO LURE OUT AND KILL THE REST OF THE SURVEY CORPS.
MORE AMBUSHES ARE PROBABLY UP AHEAD.
THAT'S HOW THEY KILLED THE THREE WITH ME.
GRIT

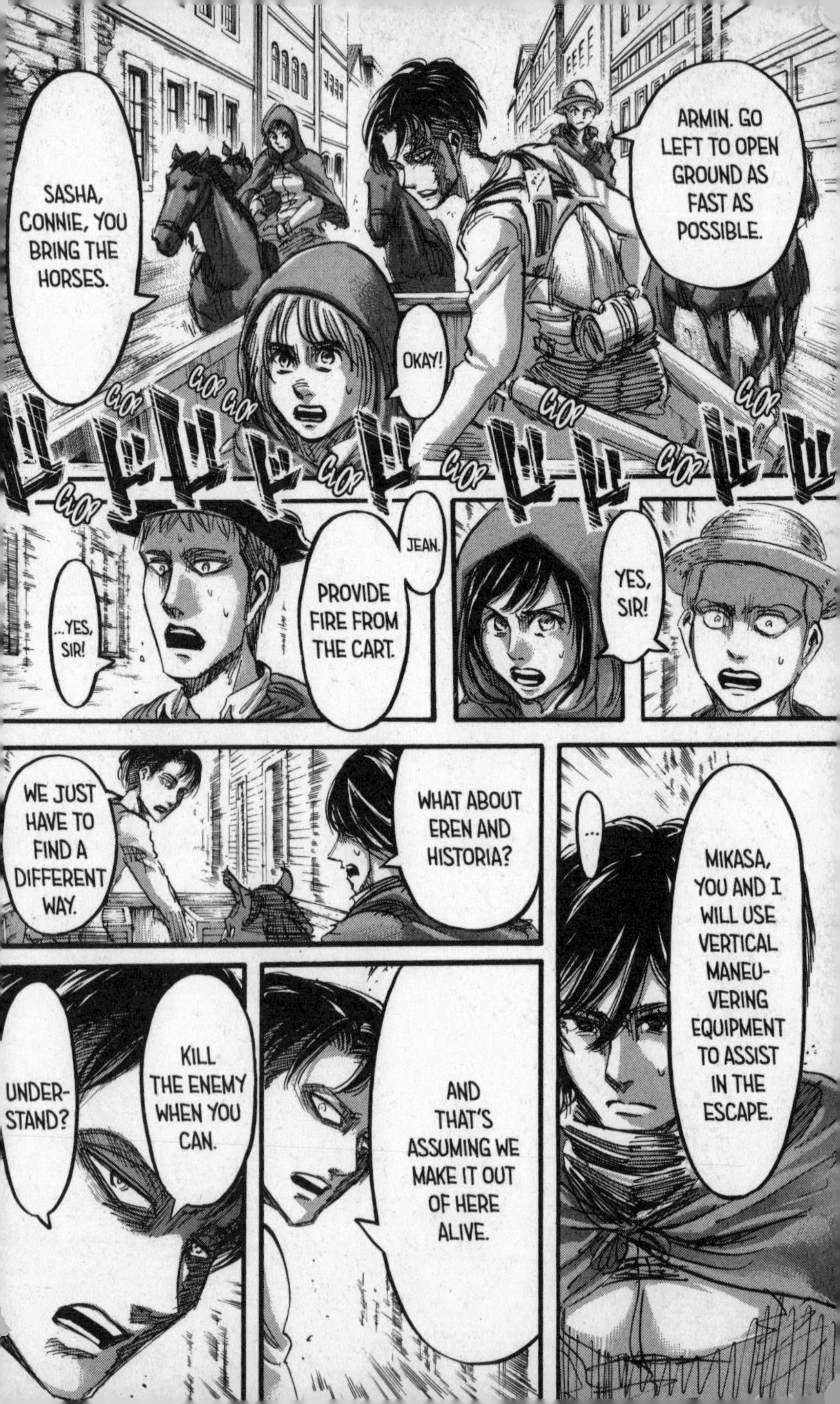
ARMIN. GO LEFT TO OPEN GROUND AS FAST AS POSSIBLE.
OKAY!
SASHA, CONNIE, YOU BRING THE HORSES.
CLOP CLOP CLOP CLOP CLOP CLOP CLOP CLOP CLOP
YES, SIR!
JEAN.
PROVIDE FIRE FROM THE CART.
...YES, SIR!
...
MIKASA, YOU AND I WILL USE VERTICAL MANEU-VERING EQUIPMENT TO ASSIST IN THE ESCAPE.
WHAT ABOUT EREN AND HISTORIA?
WE JUST HAVE TO FIND A DIFFERENT WAY.
AND THAT'S ASSUMING WE MAKE IT OUT OF HERE ALIVE.
KILL THE ENEMY WHEN YOU CAN.
UNDER-STAND?

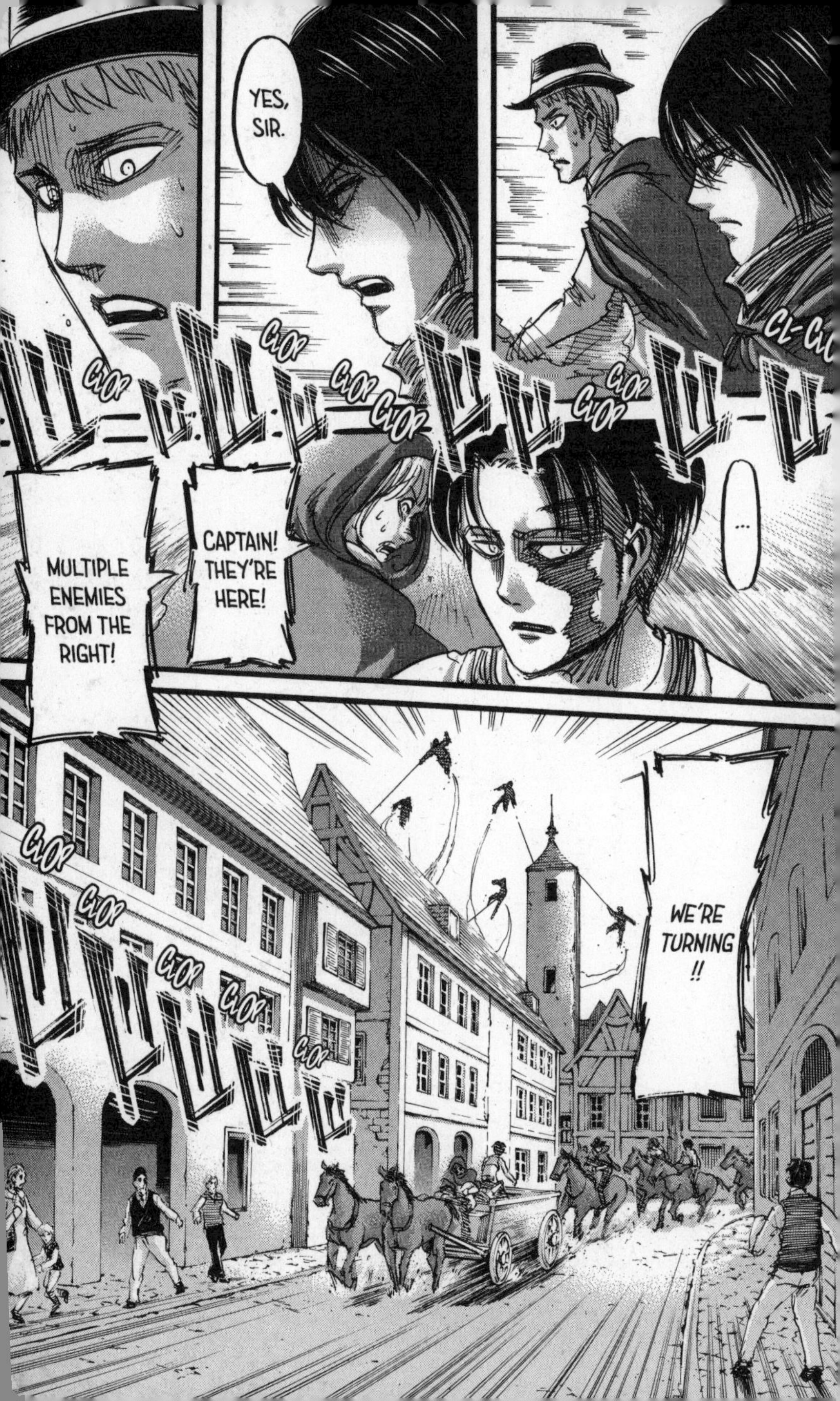
CL-CLOP
CLOP
CLOP
YES, SIR.
CLOP
CLOP
CLOP
CLOP
...
CAPTAIN! THEY'RE HERE!
MULTIPLE ENEMIES FROM THE RIGHT!
WE'RE TURNING !!
CLOP
CLOP
CLOP
CLOP
CLOP

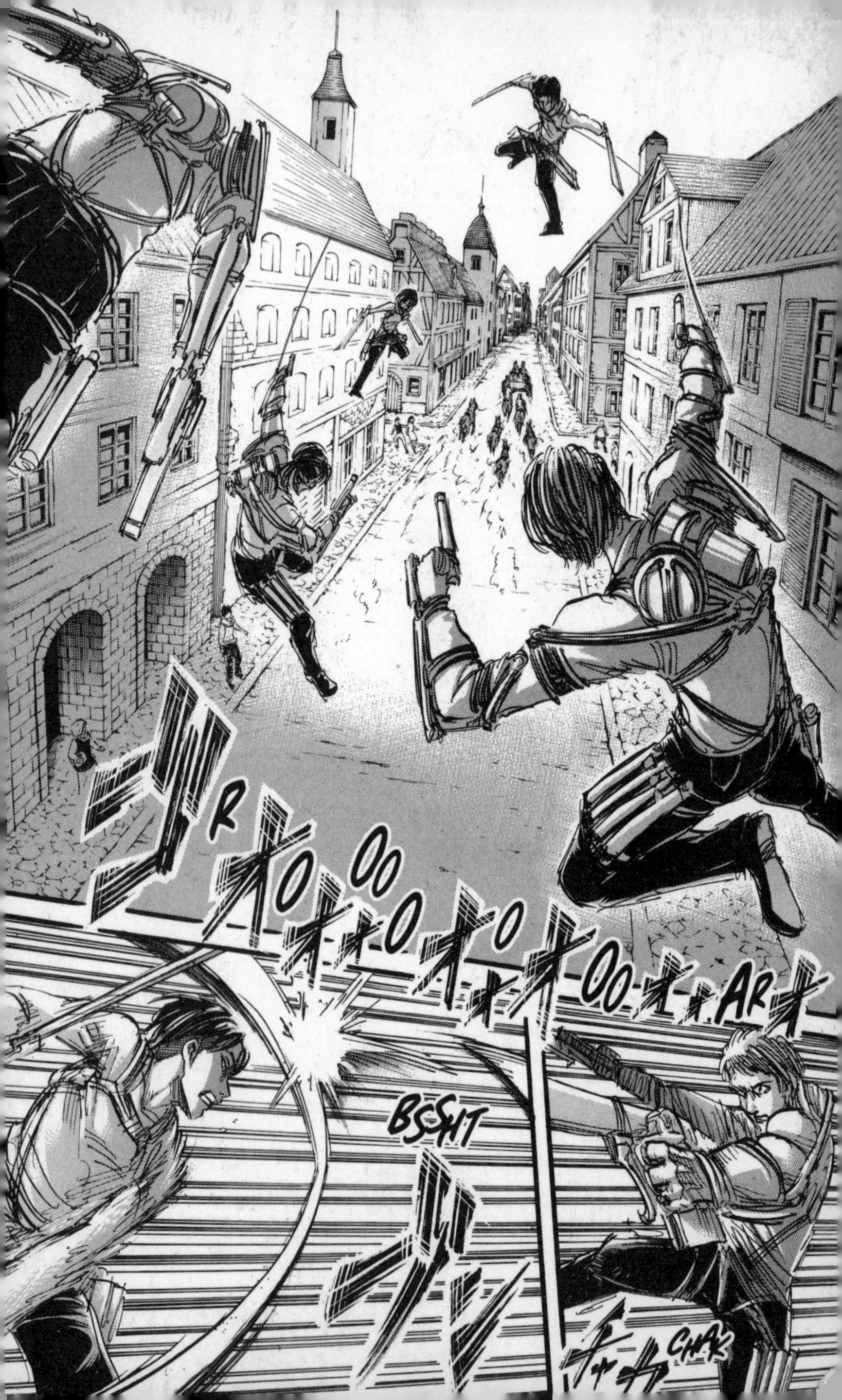
ROOOOOOOOAR
BSSHT
CHAK

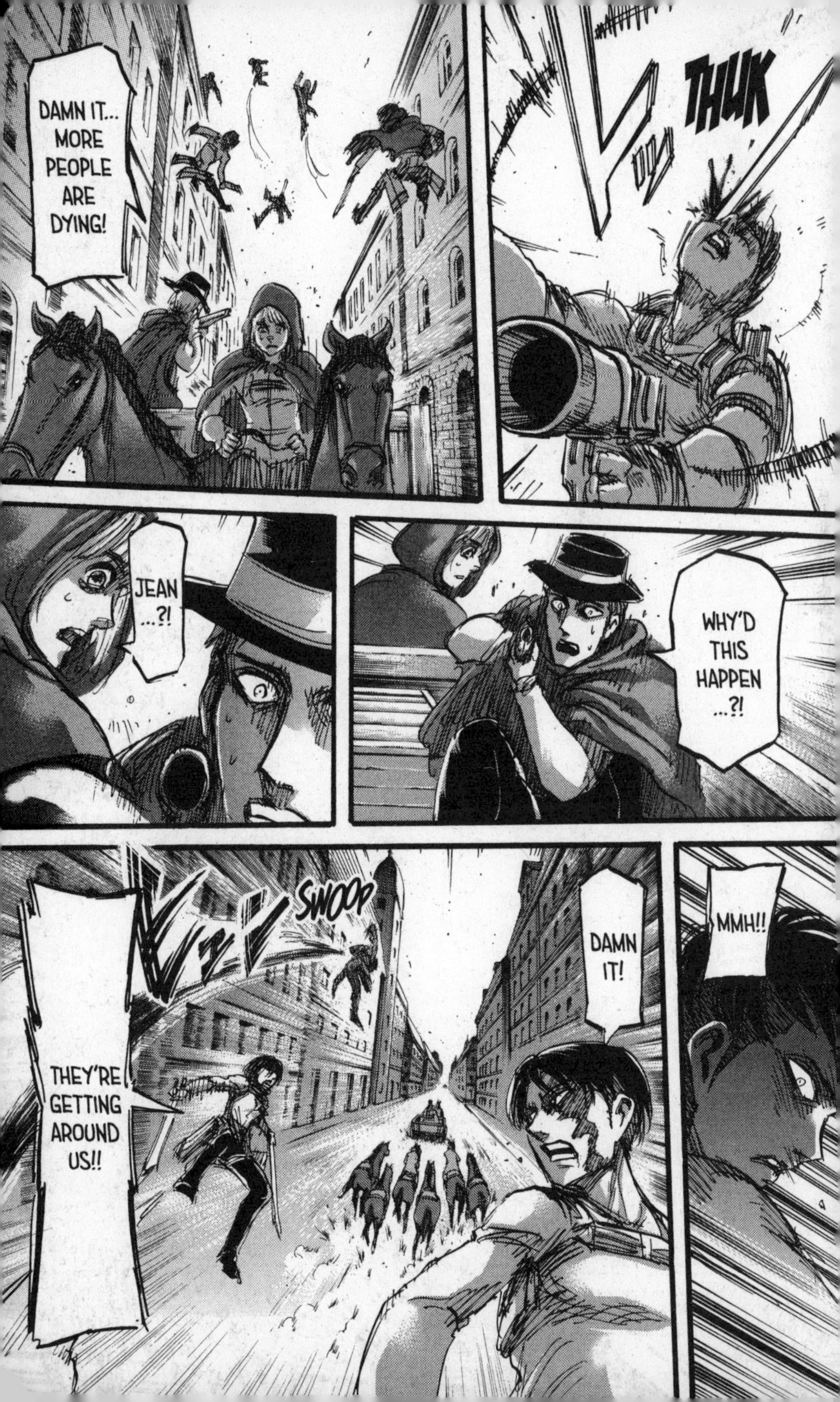
THUK
DAMN IT... MORE PEOPLE ARE DYING!
WHY'D THIS HAPPEN ...?!
JEAN ...?!
MMH!!
DAMN IT!
SWOOP
THEY'RE GETTING AROUND US!!

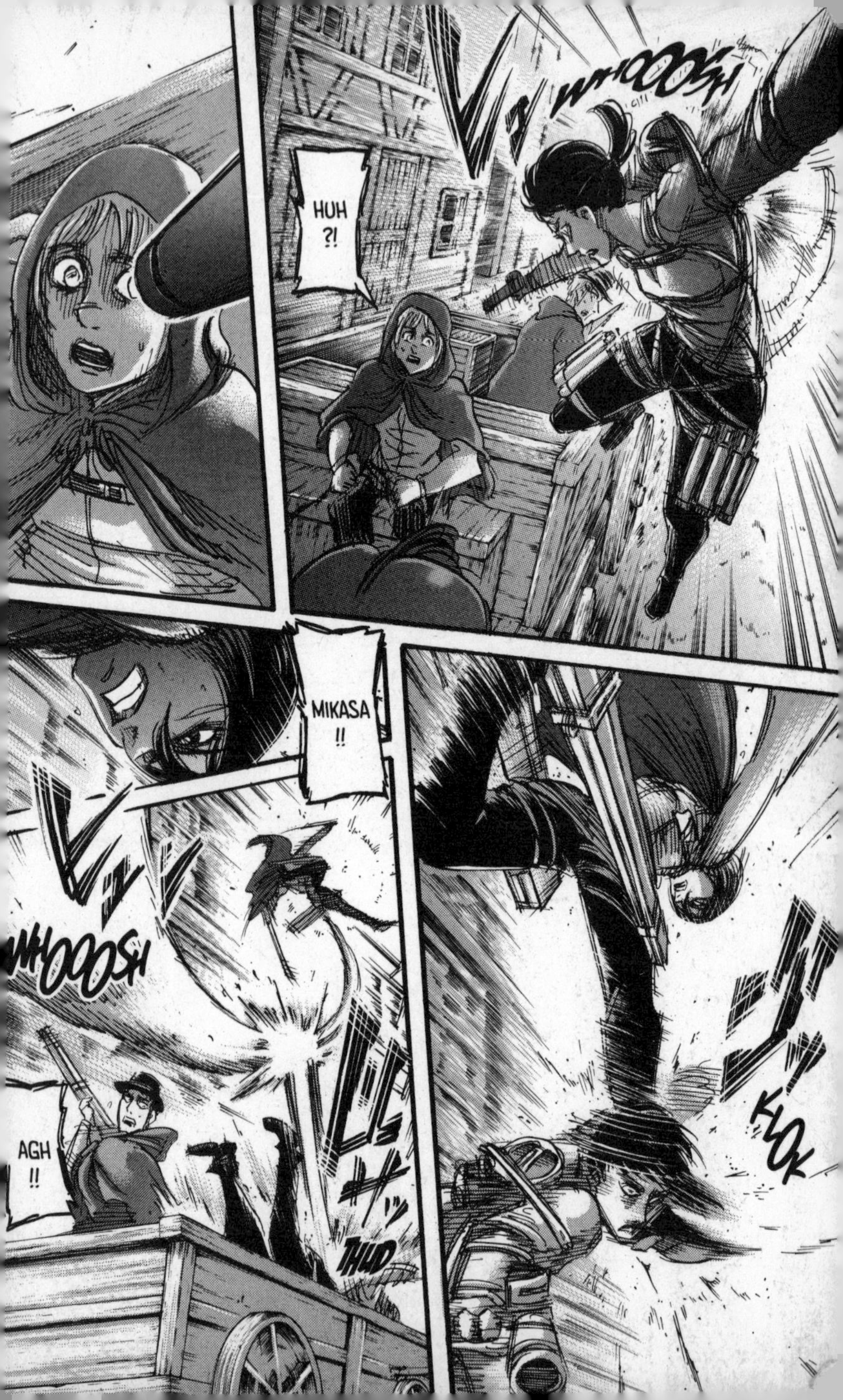
HUH ?!
KLOK
MIKASA !!
WHOOOSH
AGH !!
THUD

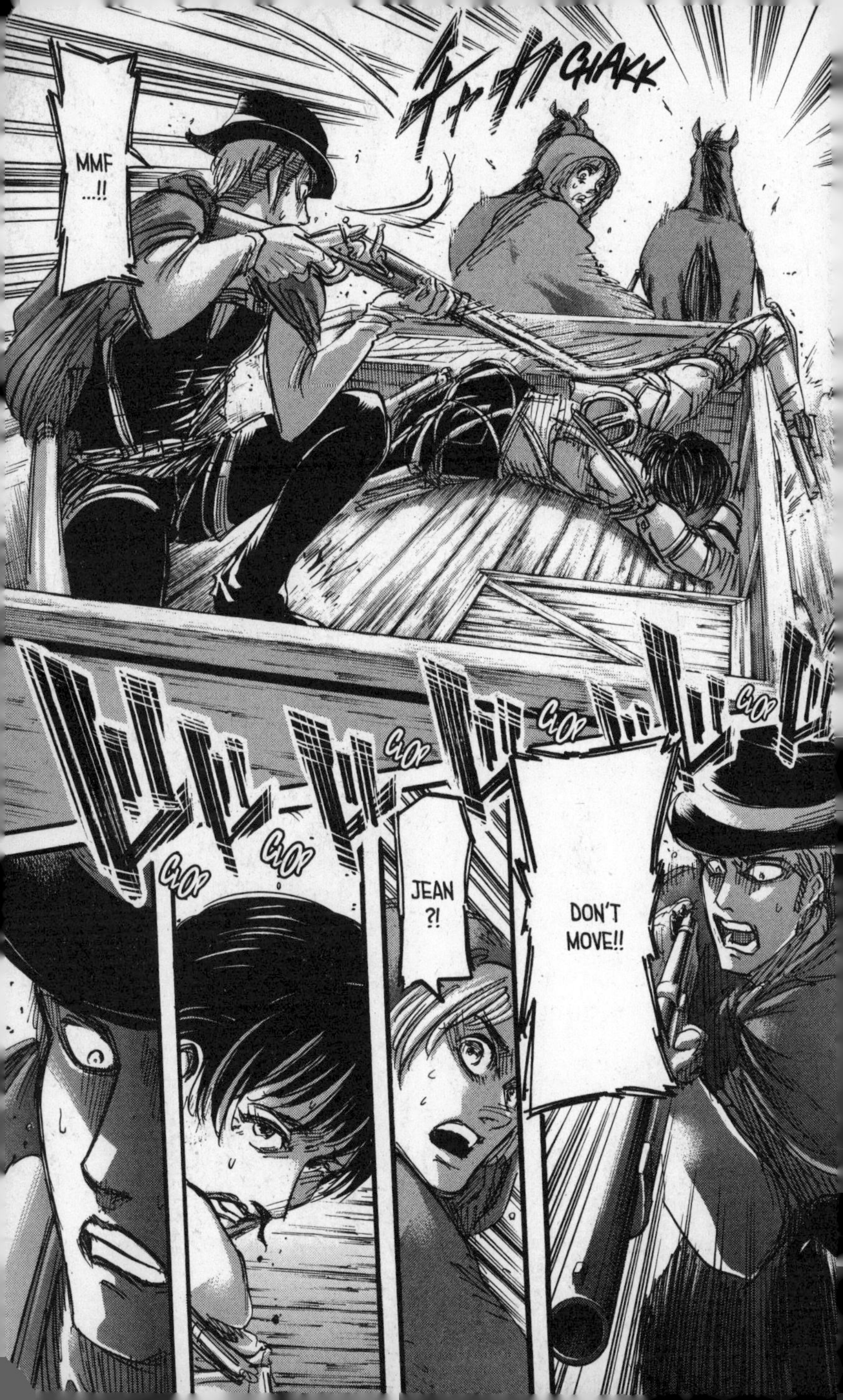
GIAKK
MMF ...!!
CLOP
CLOP
CLOP
DON'T MOVE!!
JEAN ?!
CLOP
CLOP

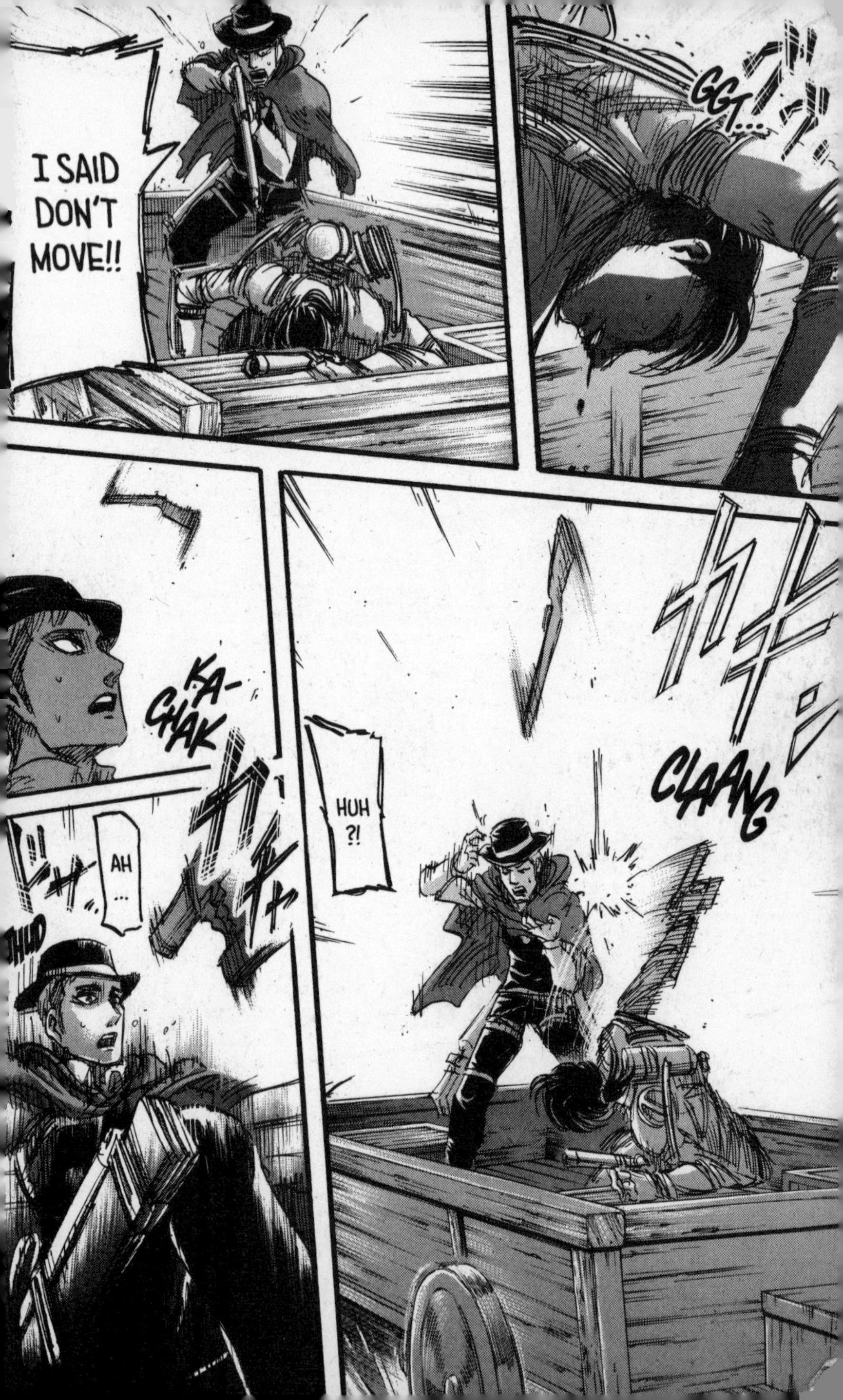
GGT...
I SAID DON'T MOVE!!
CLAANG
HUH ?!
KA-CHAK
AH ...
THUD

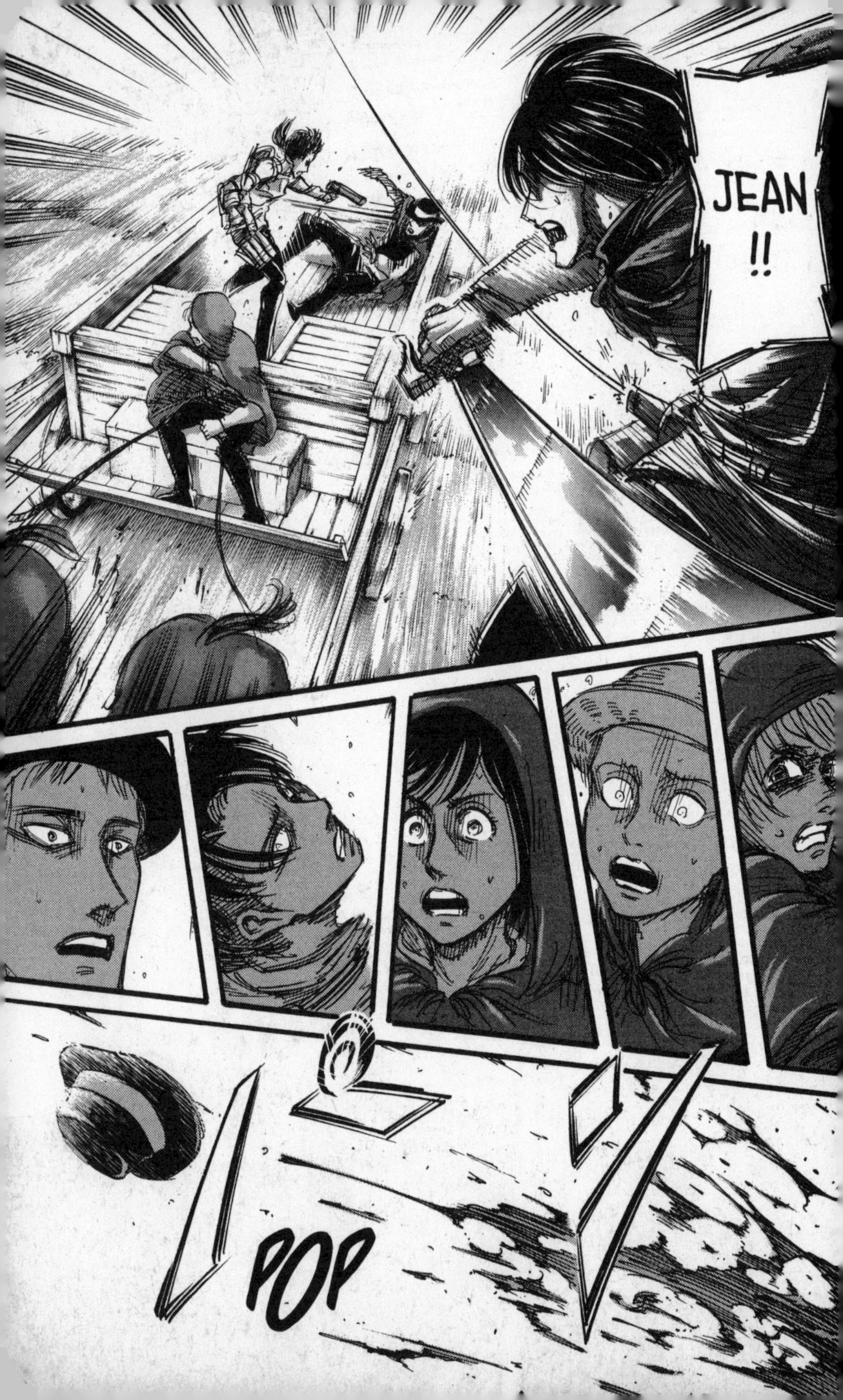
JEAN !!
POP

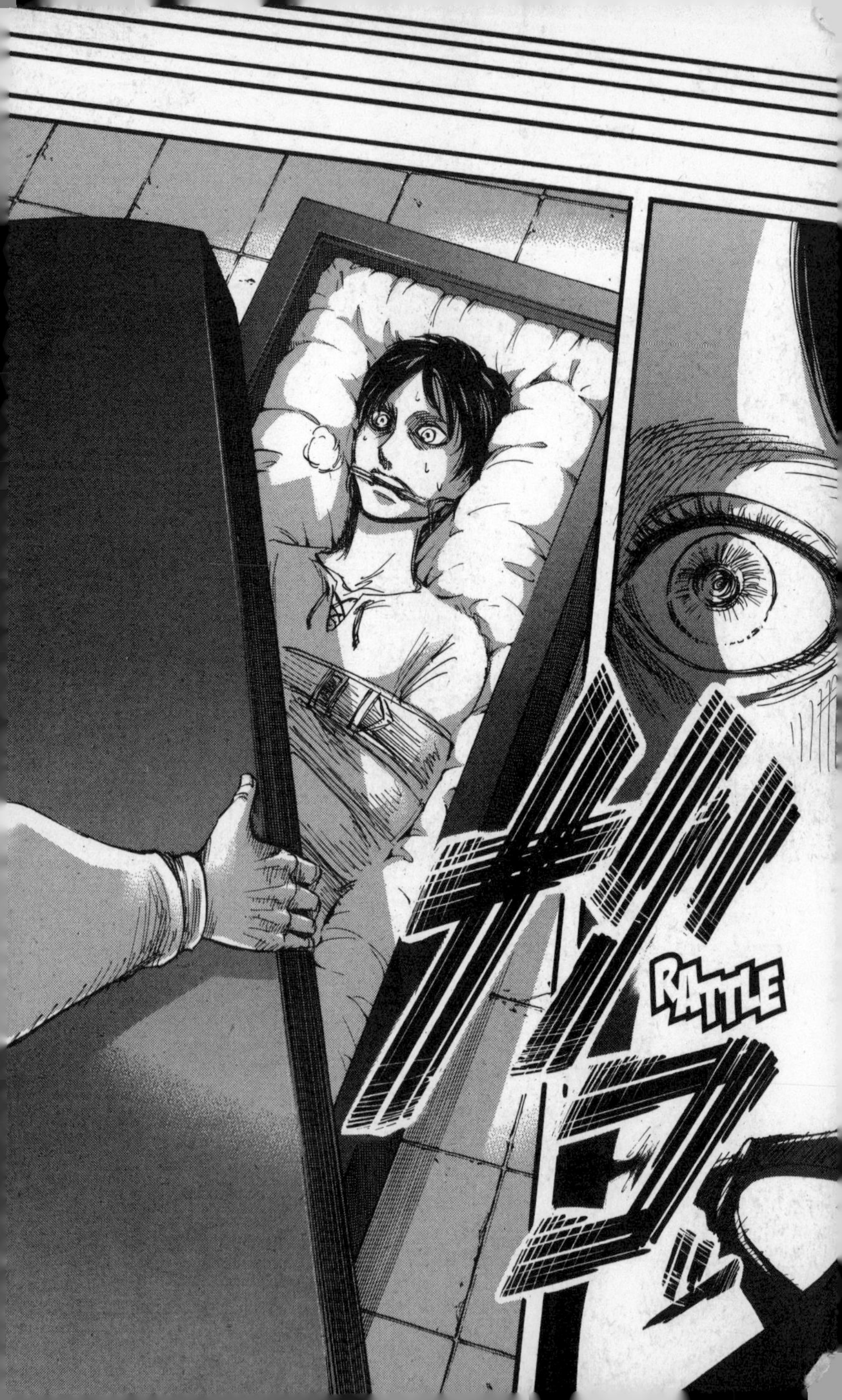
RATTLE

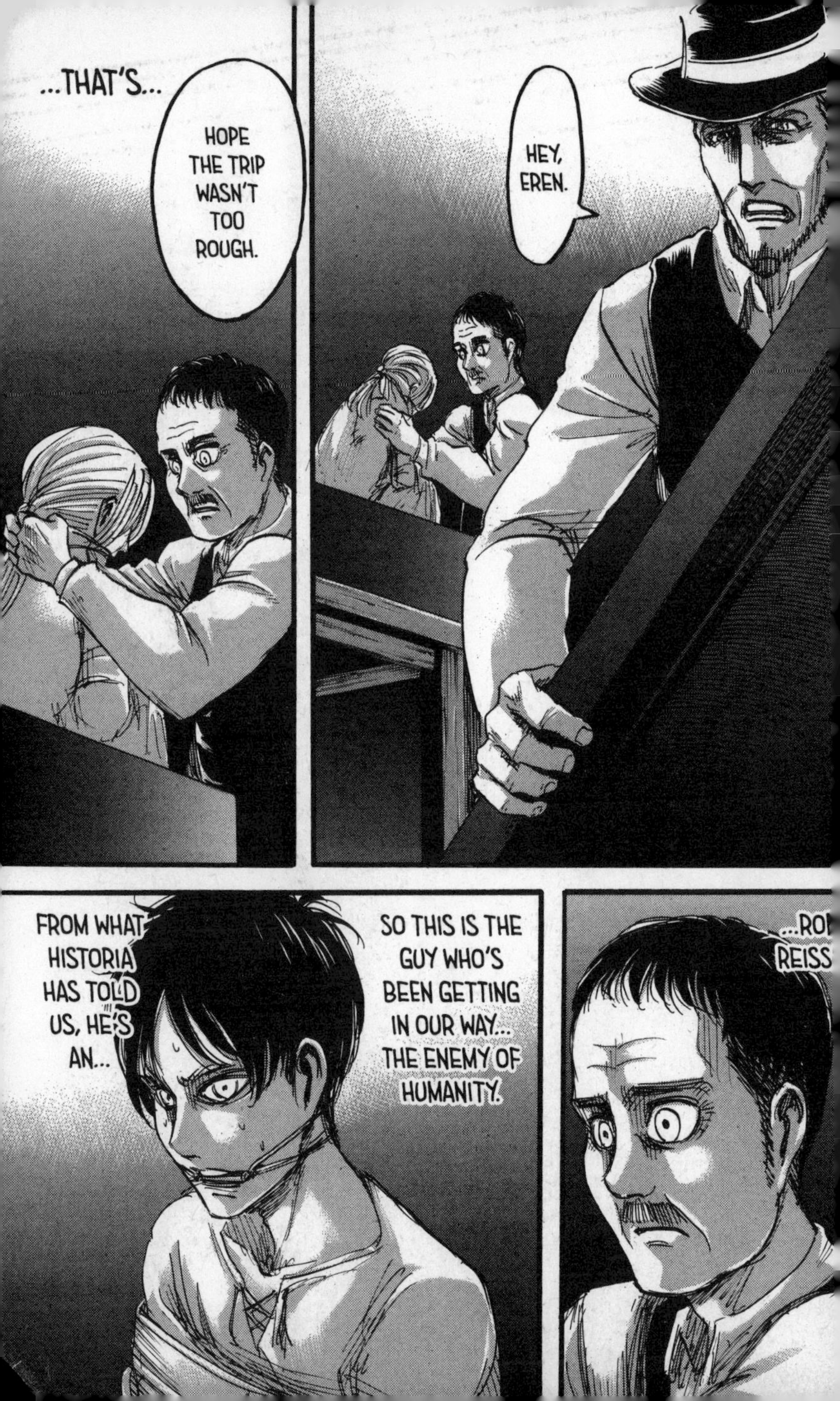
HEY, EREN.
HOPE THE TRIP WASN'T TOO ROUGH.
...THAT'S...
...RO
REISS
SO THIS IS THE GUY WHO'S BEEN GETTING IN OUR WAY... THE ENEMY OF HUMANITY.
FROM WHAT HISTORIA HAS TOLD US, HE'S AN...

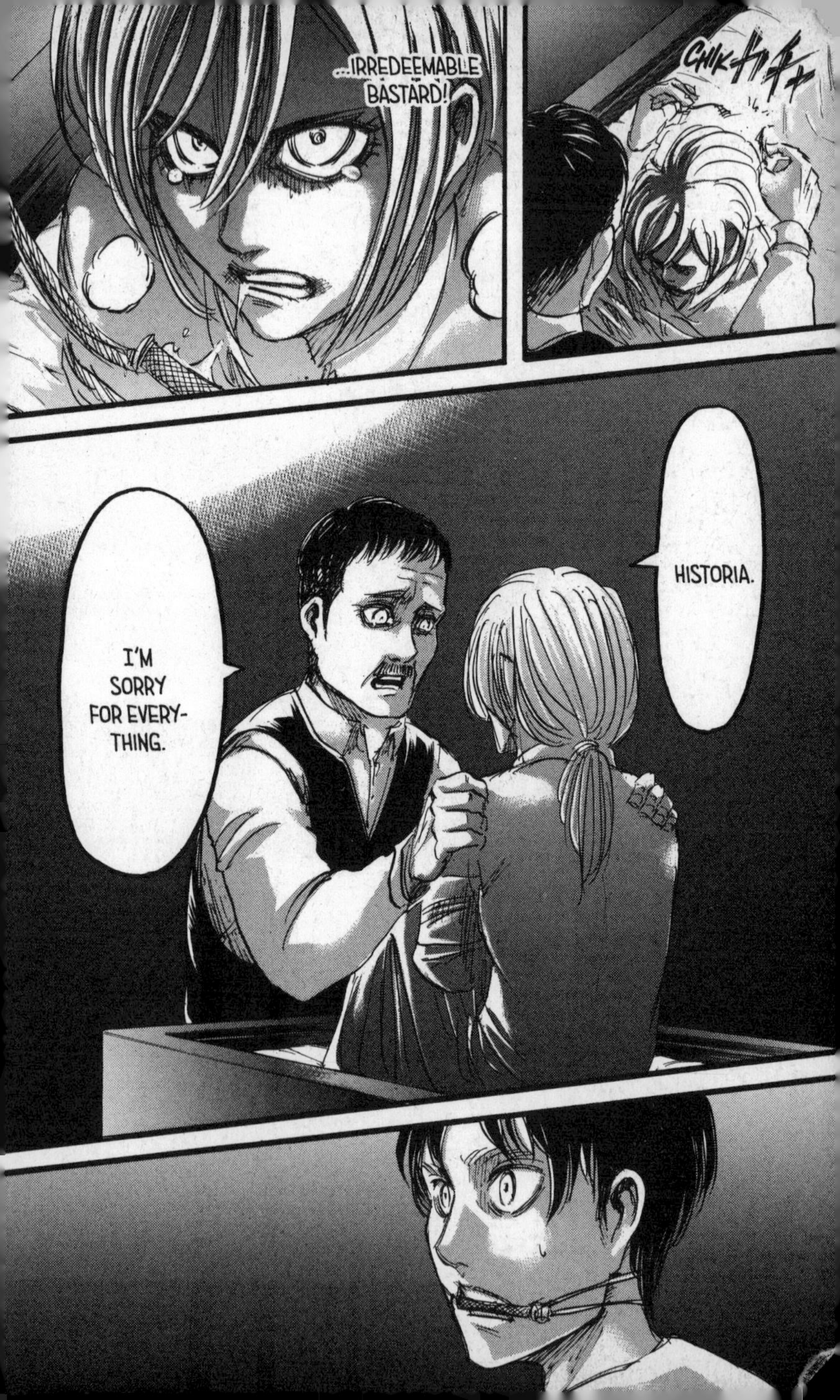
CHIK
...IRREDEEMABLE BASTARD!
HISTORIA.
I'M SORRY FOR EVERY-THING.

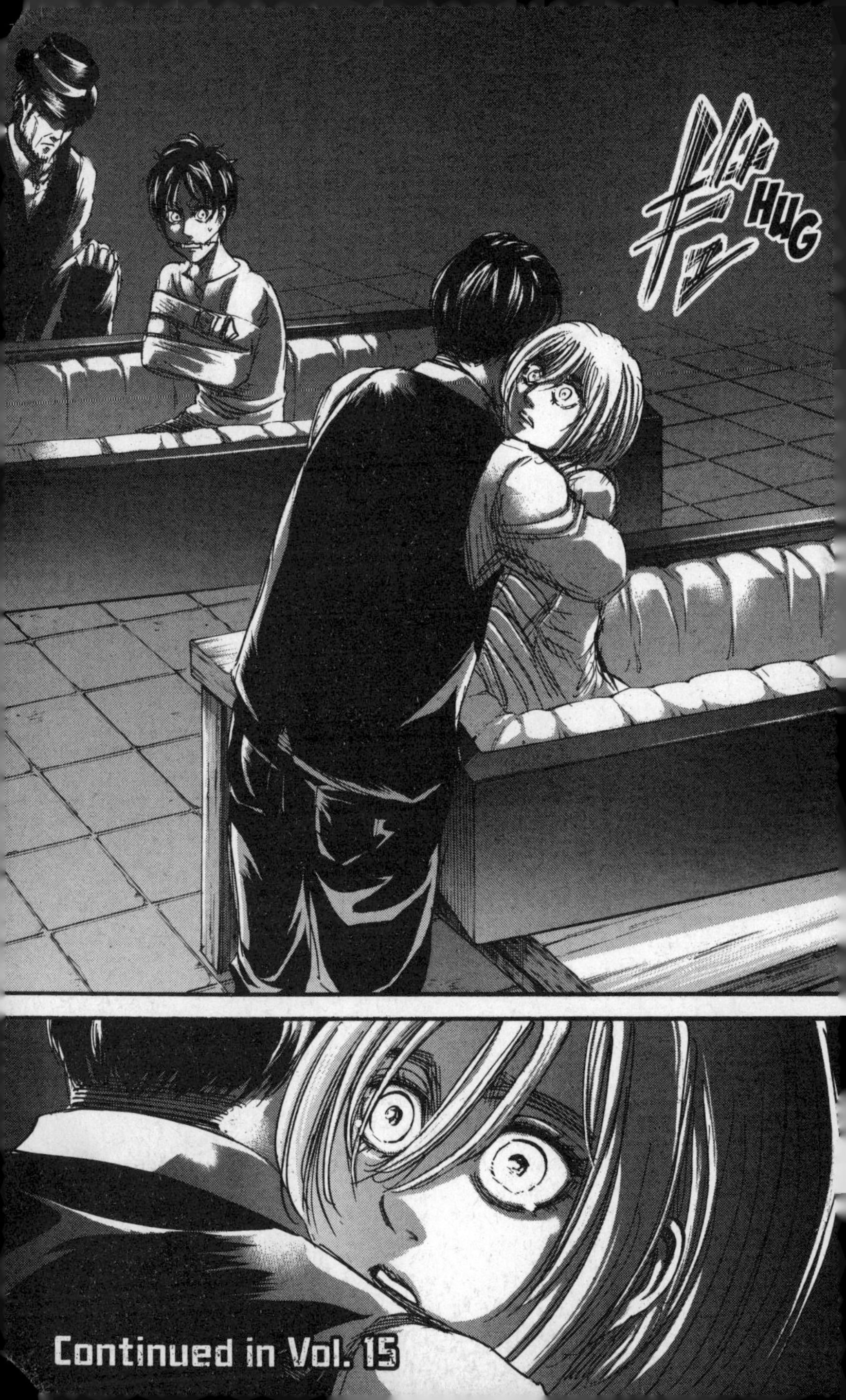
HUG

Continued in Vol. 15

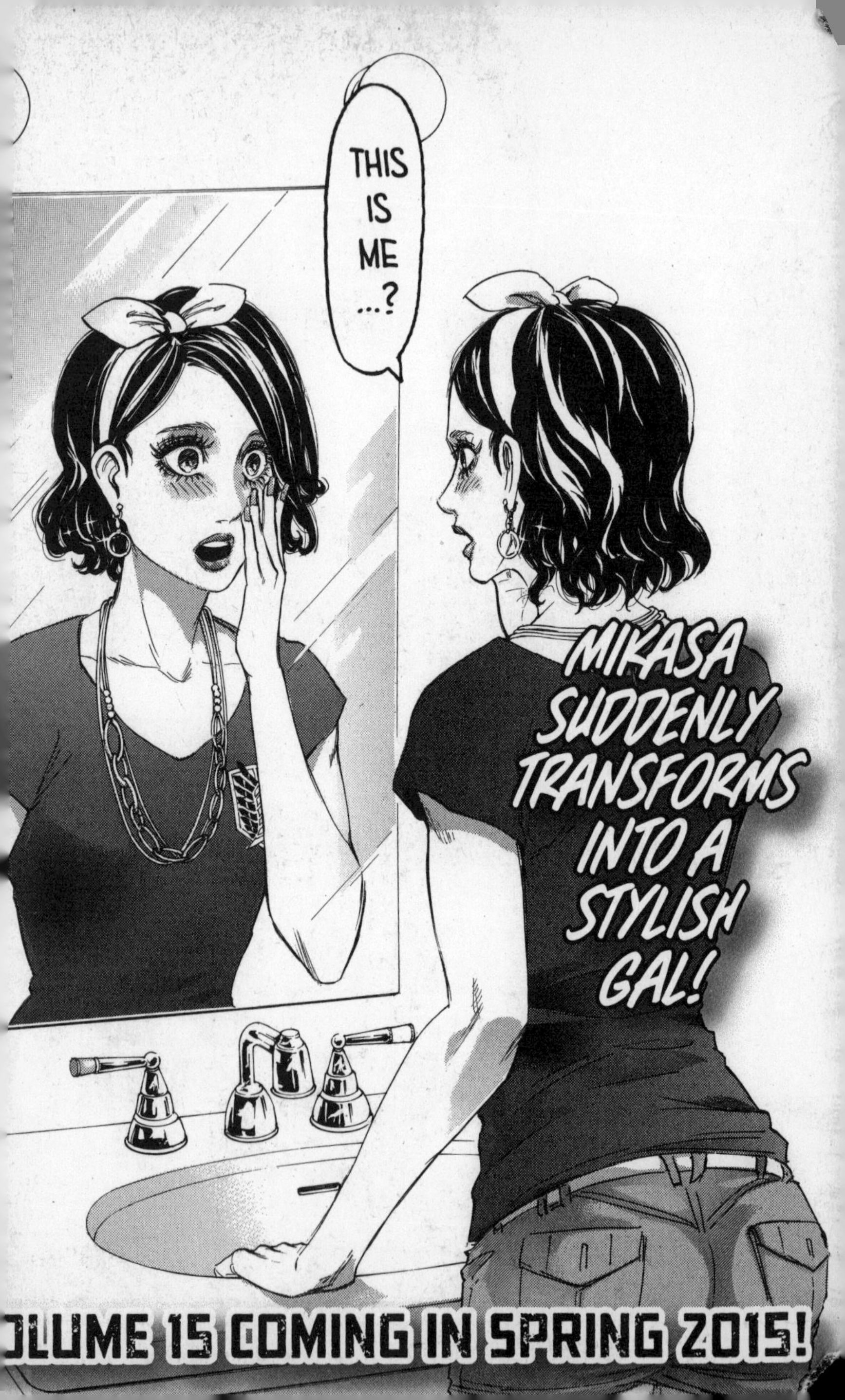
THIS IS ME ...?
MIKASA SUDDENLY TRANSFORMS INTO A STYLISH GAL!
OLUME 15 COMING IN SPRING 2015!

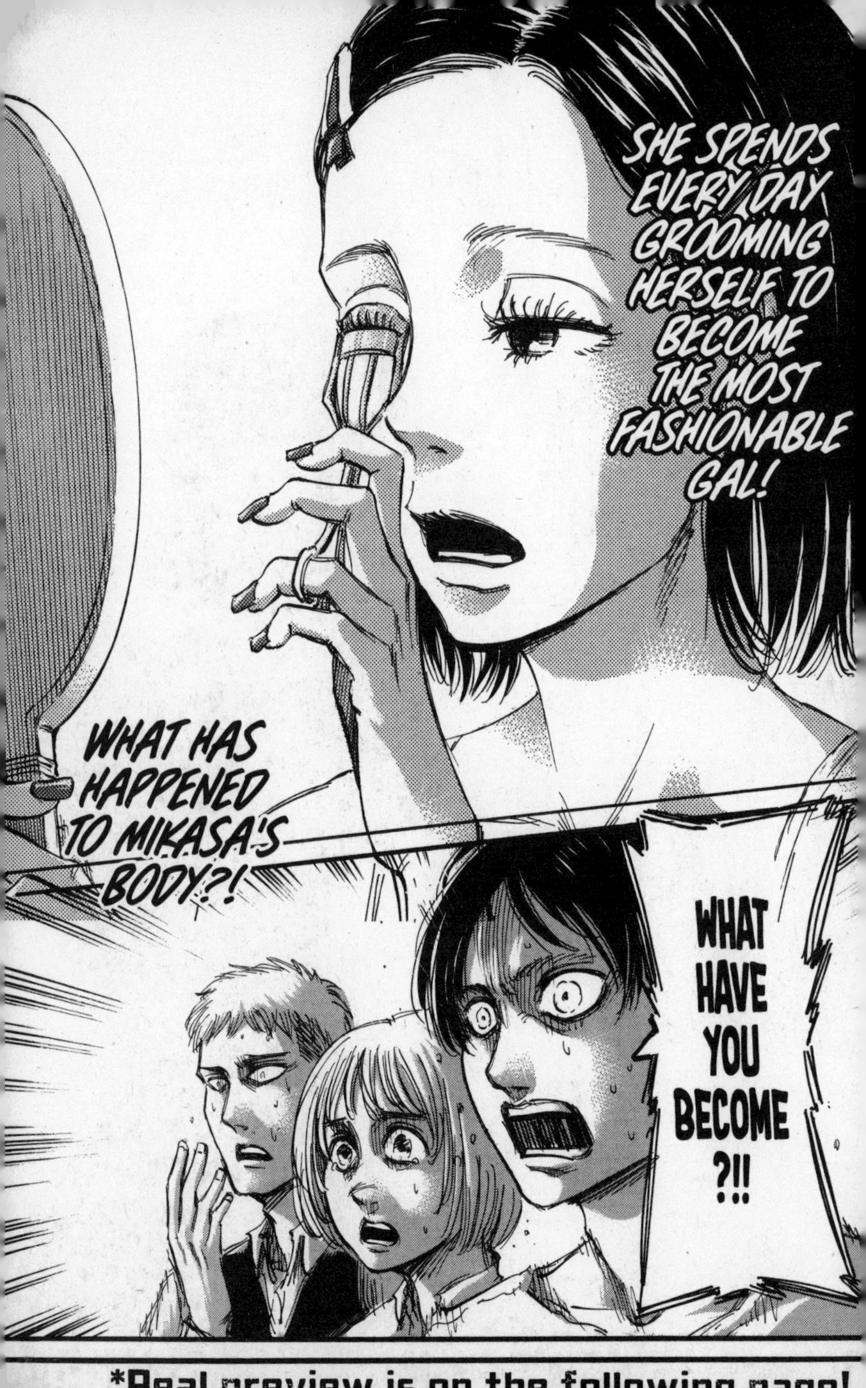
SHE SPENDS EVERY DAY GROOMING HERSELF TO BECOME THE MOST FASHIONABLE GAL!
WHAT HAS HAPPENED TO MIKASA'S BODY?!
WHAT HAVE YOU BECOME ?!!

*Real preview is on the following page!

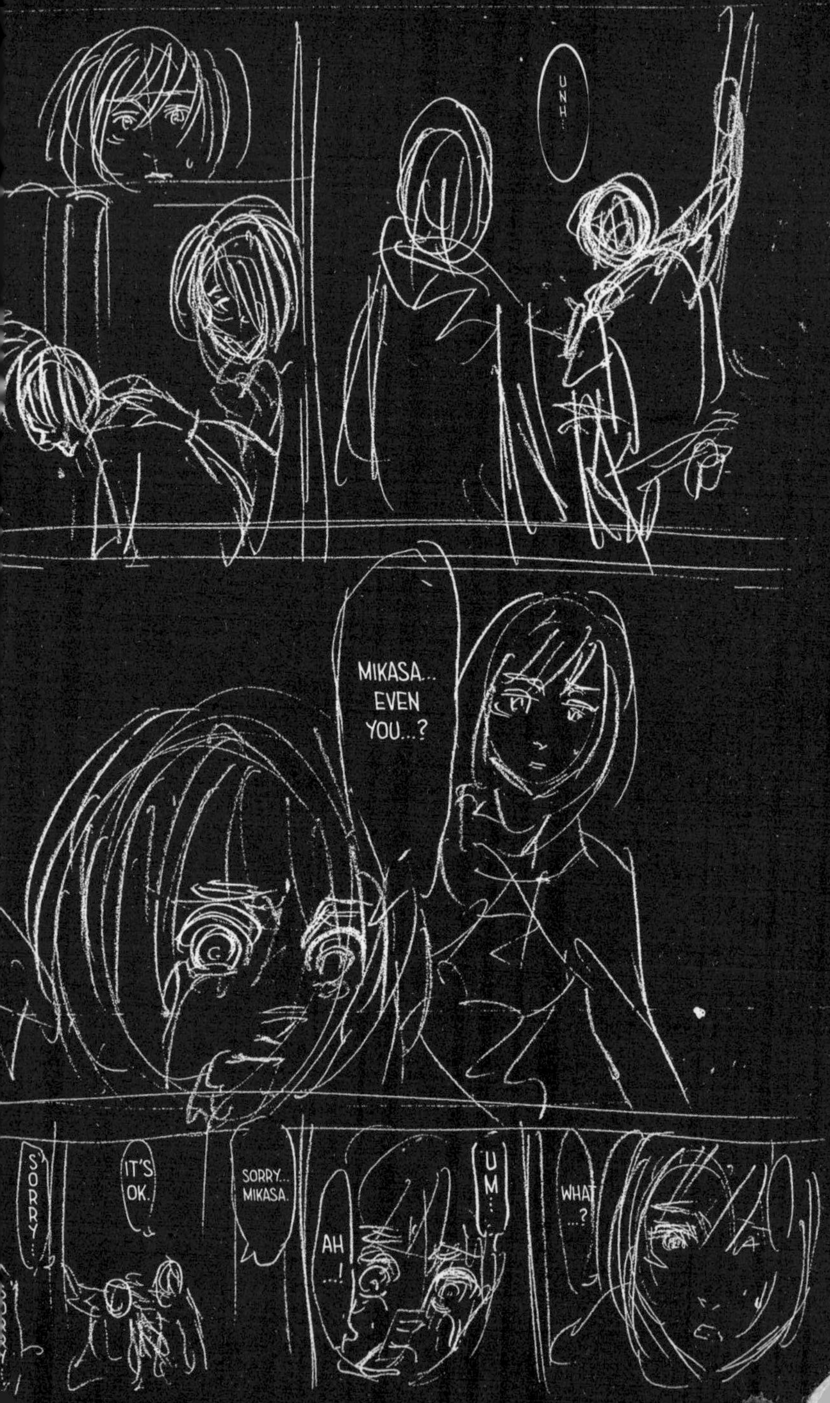
UNH...
MIKASA... EVEN YOU...?
WHAT ...?
UM...
AH ...!
SORRY... MIKASA.
IT'S OK.
SORRY...

THE SURVEY CORPS FACES THEIR BITTEREST STRUGGLE YET, WITH NO END IN SIGHT...

VOLUME 15 COMING SPRING 2015!

A Kodansha Comics Trade Paperback Original
Attack on Titan volume 14 copyright © 2014 Hajime Isayama
English translation copyright © 2014 Hajime Isayama

Published in the United States by Kodansha Comics, an imprint of Kodansha USA Publishing, LLC, New York.

Publication rights for this English edition arranged through Kodansha Ltd, Tokyo.

First published in Japan in 2014 by Kodansha Ltd., Tokyo as *Shingeki no Kyojin*, volume 14.

ISBN 978-1-61262-680-2

Original cover design by Takashi Shimoyama (Red Rooster)

Printed in the United States of America.

www.kodanshacomics.com

9 8 7 6 5 4 3 2 1
Translation: Ko Ransom
Lettering: Steve Wands
Editing: Ben Applegate
Kodansha Comics edition cover design by Phil Balsman